Connect

SECOND EDITION

Jack C. Richards
Carlos Barbisan
with Chuck Sandy

Teacher's Edition 2

CAMBRIDGE
UNIVERSITY PRESS

CAMBRIDGE UNIVERSITY PRESS
Cambridge, New York, Melbourne, Madrid, Cape Town, Singapore, São Paulo, Delhi, Dubai, Tokyo

Cambridge University Press
32 Avenue of the Americas, New York, NY 10013-2473, USA

www.cambridge.org
Information on this title: www.cambridge.org/9780521737098

First published 2004
Second Edition 2009
3rd printing 2010

Printed in Hong Kong, China, by Golden Cup Printing Company Limited

A catalog record for this publication is available from the British Library

ISBN 978-0-521-73703-6 Student's Book 2 (English)
ISBN 978-0-521-73704-3 Student's Book 2 (Portuguese)
ISBN 978-0-521-73707-4 Workbook 2 (English)
ISBN 978-0-521-73708-1 Workbook 2 (Portuguese)
ISBN 978-0-521-73709-8 Teacher's Edition 2 (English)
ISBN 978-0-521-73710-4 Teacher's Edition 2 (Portuguese)
ISBN 978-0-521-73706-7 Class Audio CDs

....

Art direction, photo research, and layout services: A+ comunicação
Audio production: Full House, NYC
Book design: Adventure House, NYC

Table of Contents

Connect Student's Book 2

Syllabus

Unit 1 — All About You and Me

Lesson	Function	Grammar	Vocabulary
Lesson 1 New friends	Asking about others	Negative statements / Questions with the verb *be*	Name, age, country of origin, likes
Lesson 2 Neighborhoods	Describing your neighborhood	*There is / There are… Is there a / Are there any…?*	Recreational, commercial, and public places
Lesson 3 Talents	Describing someone's talents	*be good at*	Talents
Lesson 4 Our pets	Talking about likes and dislikes	*like + a lot / very much / a little don't like + very much / at all*	Animals and adjectives to describe them
Get Connected	Reading · Listening · Writing		
Theme Project	Make a poster about things you like and things you're good at.		

Unit 2 — Our Lives and Routines

Lesson	Function	Grammar	Vocabulary
Lesson 5 School days	Describing daily routines	Simple present statements with *I*	Daily routines
Lesson 6 Free time	Asking about free-time activities	*Do you + (verb)…?*	Free-time activities
Lesson 7 People I admire	Talking about people's lives	Simple present statements with *I / he / she*	Activities
Lesson 8 The weekend	Talking about weekend activities	*doesn't*	Weekend activities
Get Connected	Reading · Listening · Writing		
Theme Project	Make a booklet about teachers in your school.		

Unit 3 — Sports and Activities

Lesson	Function	Grammar	Vocabulary
Lesson 9 Sports fun	Asking what sports someone does	*Does he / she…?*	Sports verbs
Lesson 10 Sports equipment	Talking about sports equipment	*They* + verb: statements *Do they* + verb: questions	Sports equipment
Lesson 11 Off to camp	Talking about rules	Imperatives	Camp supplies
Lesson 12 At camp	Talking about when activities happen	*What time / When…?*	Camp activities
Get Connected	Reading · Listening · Writing		
Theme Project	Make a sports card.		

Unit 4 — My Interests

Lesson	Function	Grammar	Vocabulary
Lesson 13 I like music.	Talking about music preferences	*her / him / it / them*	Types of music
Lesson 14 Let's look online.	Asking about prices	*How much is / are…?*	Items in a natural science catalog
Lesson 15 Our interests	Talking about free-time activities	*like / don't like + to* (verb)	Free-time activities and interests
Lesson 16 In and out of school	Talking about habits and routines	Adverbs of frequency	Habits and daily activities
Get Connected	Reading · Listening · Writing		
Theme Project	Make a booklet of advertisements.		

Unit 5 Favorite Activities	Lesson	Function	Grammar	Vocabulary
	Lesson 17 In San Francisco	Describing vacation activities	Present continuous affirmative statements	Vacation activities
	Lesson 18 At the park	Describing how someone is not following rules	Present continuous negative statements	Rules at a park
	Lesson 19 At the beach	Asking what someone is doing	Present continuous *Yes / No* questions	Beach activities
	Lesson 20 At the store	Asking what someone is doing	Present continuous *What* questions	Store items
	Get Connected	Reading · Listening · Writing		
	Theme Project	Make a city guide for tourists.		

Unit 6 Entertainment	Lesson	Function	Grammar	Vocabulary
	Lesson 21 Where are you going?	Asking where someone is going	*Where + (be) . . . going?*	Entertainment events and adjectives to describe them
	Lesson 22 Birthday parties	Talking about special events	Simple present vs. present continuous	Favorite birthday activities
	Lesson 23 Let's see a movie.	Talking about types of movies to see	*want / don't want + to* (verb)	Types of movies
	Lesson 24 In line at the movies	Asking what someone looks like	*What* questions about people	Adjectives to describe appearance
	Get Connected	Reading · Listening · Writing		
	Theme Project	Make a weekend activity poster.		

Unit 7 What We Eat	Lesson	Function	Grammar	Vocabulary
	Lesson 25 I'm hungry!	Talking about food	Countable and uncountable nouns	Food
	Lesson 26 Picnic plans	Asking about quantities	*How much / How many . . . ?*	Picnic foods and utensils
	Lesson 27 A snack	Planning menus	*some / any*	Condiments
	Lesson 28 On the menu	Ordering from a menu	*would like*	Menu items
	Get Connected	Reading · Listening · Writing		
	Theme Project	Make a group menu.		

Unit 8 The Natural World	Lesson	Function	Grammar	Vocabulary
	Lesson 29 World weather	Talking about the weather	*What's the weather like?*	Adjectives to describe the weather
	Lesson 30 Natural wonders	Talking about outdoor activities	*can* (for possibility)	Water and land forms
	Lesson 31 World of friends	Asking who does different activities	*Who + (verb) . . . ?*	Languages and countries
	Lesson 32 International Day	Asking about personal information	*What + (noun) . . . ?*	Numbers 101 +
	Get Connected	Reading · Listening · Writing		
	Theme Project	Make an informational poster about a country.		

Course description

Connect, Second Edition is an updated and revised edition of the popular *Connect, First Edition*. It is a fun, multi-skill course, written and designed especially for adolescents who are studying English for the first time. It develops speaking, listening, reading, and writing skills while simultaneously connecting students with one another, their community, and the world outside the classroom. Theme Projects provide a local perspective, encouraging students to find out more about the world in which we live. High-interest topics provide a global perspective and present relevant, up-to-date information, motivating students to learn.

Course principles

Connect, Second Edition is based on the notion that generating and maintaining motivation is essential for successful learning. This is incorporated into the series in the following ways:

Motivational strategies	Features
Generate and maintain interest	• Units are built around contemporary, high-interest topics. • Students can relate all tasks to their own interests and experience.
Promote success	• Students are provided with adequate preparation and support for tasks throughout the learning process. • Tests and quizzes assess only language that students know and do not assume that students know more.
Promote fun in learning	• The tasks are varied. • A multitude of games and game-like activities make learning fun.
Provide opportunities for students to speak about themselves	• The personalization activities provide opportunities for students to use target language to speak about themselves.

Components

Each level of *Connect, Second Edition* consists of a Student's Book with Self-study Audio CD, Class Audio CDs, a Workbook, and a Teacher's Edition. Web-based material includes *Connect* Arcade (online activities for students) and the Teacher Support Site.

Student's Book with Self-study Audio CD

Each Student's Book contains eight units divided into two-page lessons. Two lessons of each unit are review lessons. All lesson themes and content are pertinent to adolescent learners. At the back of each Student's Book, there is a Game and a Theme Project section. The Games provide enjoyable practice of the grammar and / or vocabulary of each unit. The Theme Projects foster cooperation and strong relationships within the classroom. Additionally, they help students connect their English to the world outside the classroom.

The Student's Book Self-study Audio CD is intended for student use and includes recordings for specific sections of each lesson. The recordings are in natural, conversational American English. Students can use the CD for practice at home or in a language lab.

Class Audio CDs

The Class Audio CDs are intended for class use. They are in natural, conversational American English.

A unique feature of the audio program is the recordings for the "Listen and check your answers" tasks in many of the Language Focus practice activities. This feature reduces teacher-talking time and encourages greater student autonomy in the process of checking answers. Track numbers appear in the Teacher's Edition and make it easy to locate specific recordings on the CDs.

Workbook

The Workbook is a natural extension of the Student's Book. Each Workbook provides reading and writing reinforcement of the vocabulary and grammar in the Student's Book lesson. No new language is presented in the Workbook. The wide variety of exercise types keeps students motivated, and photographs and illustrations provide context and support for many of the activities. There is one Workbook page for each Student's Book lesson.

A unique feature of the Workbook is the Check Yourself section at the end of each unit. These pages provide students with the opportunity to assess their performance and ascertain where they need further practice. This section prepares students to do the worksheet activities and quizzes that are provided in the Teacher's Edition.

The Workbook activities can be done at home or in class. They can be assigned individually after each lesson is completed or all at once at the end of each unit. The Answer key for the Workbook is provided in the Teacher's Edition.

Teacher's Edition

The comprehensive, interleaved Teacher's Edition provides step-by-step instructions to present, practice, and review the language in each lesson of the Student's Book. The Teacher's Edition offers a wide variety of communicative, interactive classroom activities. It also features suggestions for optional activities and linguistic, methodological, and cultural notes where appropriate. The Answer key to the Student's Book is printed in red on the reproduced Student's Book pages for ease of use.

There is a rich source of support materials in the back of each Teacher's Edition. These materials include audio scripts for all recorded material, photocopiable worksheets for each unit, one quiz per unit, and answer keys for all photocopiable materials as well as for the Workbook. There is also a special Games and Activities section for practicing vocabulary, grammar, listening, pronunciation, and speaking skills.

Teacher Support Site

The Teacher Support Site contains a wealth of downloadable support material, including Extra Grammar worksheets, Extra Reading worksheets, Placement Tests, Unit Tests, Oral Quizzes, and Learning Logs.

All Extra Grammar and Extra Reading worksheets are provided in two forms (Form A and Form B) to offer variety for both teachers and students. They can be assigned to all students or to individual students who need additional practice.

Unit Tests are also provided in Form A and Form B for greater flexibility in giving tests to different classes.

All answer keys are available upon request. Many of the materials are password-protected to prevent student access, and it is easy for teachers to create their own passwords once on the Teacher Support Site. See **www.cambridge.org/connect2e/teacher**

The following material is found on the Teacher Support Site:

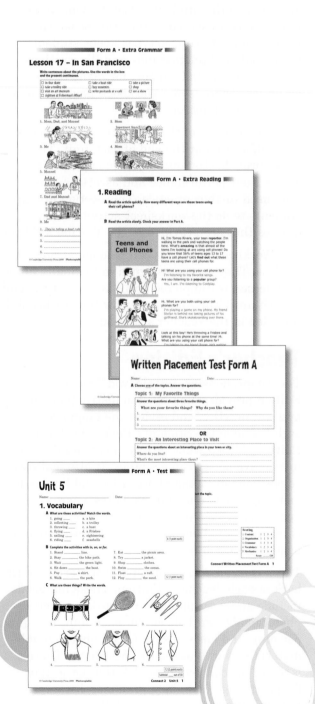

Extra Grammar worksheets

The Extra Grammar worksheets provide students with additional grammar practice and are similar in style to the activities in the Student's Book and Workbook.

Extra Reading worksheets

The Extra Reading worksheets provide students with additional reading and writing practice and are similar in style to the Get Connected lessons in the Student's Book. The Extra Reading worksheets can be assigned after the Get Connected lessons.

Placement Tests

The Placement Tests are to be done by students before they begin *Connect* to help determine the level of *Connect* best suited to them. They are extremely comprehensive and test all four skills (listening, speaking, reading, and writing). They include Objective Tests with an audio program, Written Tests, an Oral Test, Answer keys, and student answer sheets.

Unit Tests

Each Unit Test is designed to assess students' progress in Vocabulary, Language Focus (grammar), Reading, and Writing. The Unit Tests can be given after each unit.

Oral Quizzes

There is one Oral Quiz for each unit. Each Oral Quiz consists of questions and sample answers that teachers can use, along with a rating guide to evaluate students' speaking ability. The Oral Quizzes can be given after the Unit Test or at the teacher's discretion.

Learning Logs

The Learning Logs provide students with the opportunity to reflect on their progress as they complete each unit of the Student's Book. They can also help teachers determine which students might need extra practice. There is one Learning Log for each unit. They can be assigned after each unit and can be done at home or in class.

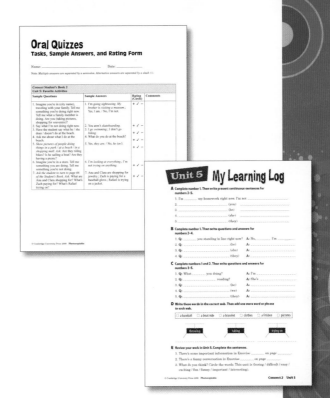

Web-Based Student Arcade Activities

The Arcade is a free student support Web site with a wealth of interactive, self-study activities for each unit of the Student's Book. These activities provide engaging vocabulary, grammar, and pronunciation practice. They feature animation, audio, and illustrations that make English practice come to life. Students can do these activities at home or in a language lab.

The following task types are included in each level of Arcade: Choose the right word, Crossword, Drag and drop, Fill in the blank, Guess the word, Matching, Multiple choice, Put the sentences in order, What do you hear?, and What do you see?

See **www.cambridge.org/connectarcade**

Student's Book Unit Structure

- **Two language lessons** —

- **Followed by a mini-review** —

- **Two more language lessons** —
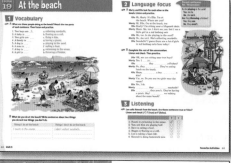

- **Followed by Get Connected and a unit review** —
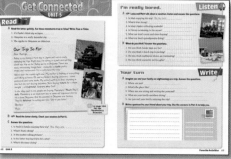
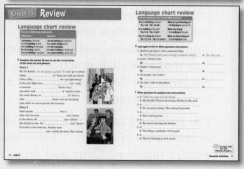

At the back of the book

- **Game**
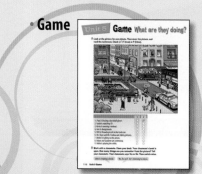

- **Get Connected Vocabulary Practice**

- **Theme Project**
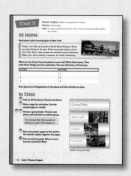

Student's Book Unit Features

Language lessons

Vocabulary Presents and practices the words students need to talk about the topic of the unit. Part A introduces the new words and illustrates their meanings. Part B provides additional practice of the new words.

Language focus Presents and practices the target grammar. Part A includes either a conversation or a mini-text to help students understand how the new grammar is used. The language chart highlights the form of the new structures. Part B provides controlled practice of the new grammar.

Listening Helps to develop receptive skills such as identifying the purpose of conversations and listening for specific information.

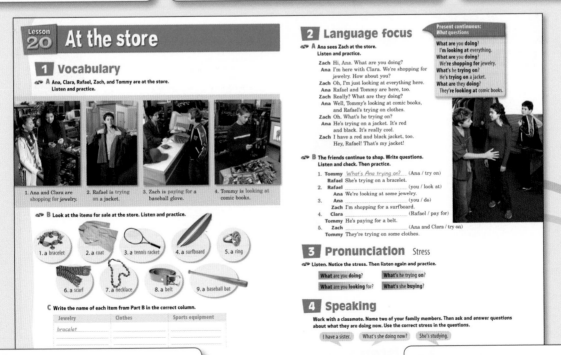

Pronunciation Highlights a pronunciation point that students often find challenging. The exercise allows students to listen to and practice the pronunciation point.

Speaking Provides an opportunity for students to practice the new grammar in a natural context. Most of the tasks are interactive and allow students to personalize the grammar.

Mini-review

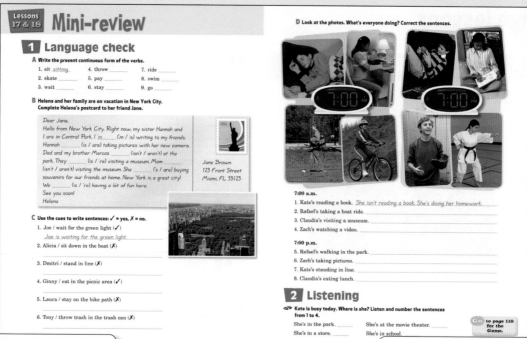

Language check Provides further review and practice of the grammar and vocabulary presented in the first two lessons of each unit.

Listening Offers further listening practice to reinforce grammar and vocabulary presented in the first two lessons of each unit.

Get Connected

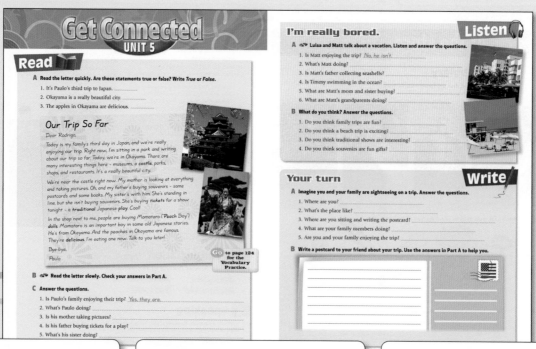

Read Provides tasks to develop reading skills such as skimming and scanning, and answering comprehension questions. A recorded version of the reading is provided.

Listen Part A helps students to improve receptive skills such as listening for specific information.
Part B encourages students to think critically about the theme of the Get Connected lesson.

Write Provides writing tasks that are natural extensions of the readings. Part A helps students organize their ideas for the writing task in Part B.

Review

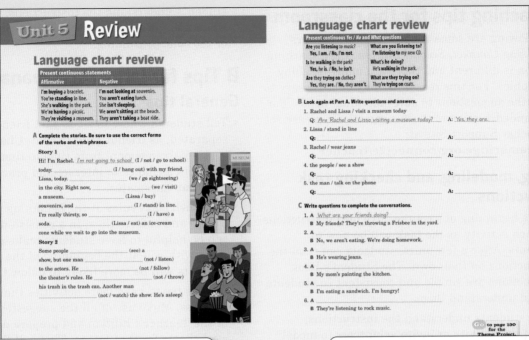

Language chart review Summarizes and provides further review and practice of the grammar introduced in the unit.

Review tasks Provides additional practice of the unit grammar and vocabulary.

At the back of the book

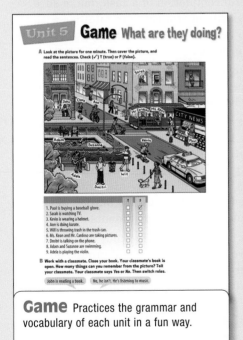

Game Practices the grammar and vocabulary of each unit in a fun way.

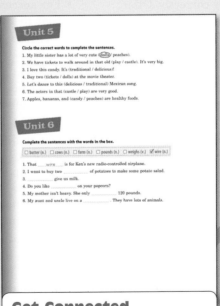

Get Connected Vocabulary Practice

Provides additional practice for new words (in bold) in the Get Connected readings.

Theme project Connects students' English to the world outside the classroom. The At Home section helps students organize their ideas for the In Class activity.

Teaching Tips

A Teaching tips for the classroom

The following are some suggestions for teachers when using *Connect, Second Edition*. Each teaching situation is different and there are many teaching philosophies. For this reason, it may be necessary to modify the suggestions to suit individual needs. For an expanded version of these suggestions, please see the Teacher Support Site at:
www.cambridge.org/connect2e/teacher

Giving, modeling, and checking task instructions

- At the beginning of a course, give oral instructions for each activity as the task will be new to students. After a few units, students can read the instructions on their own. The Student's Book instructions are simple and consistent so students should understand them.

- After students understand the instructions, model the activity or invite volunteers to model it. Students need to understand how to do the activity in order to complete it successfully.

- To be sure they understand, follow up instructions and / or modeling by asking students *Yes / No* questions.

- Once students begin an activity, monitor their progress. Walk around the class and check that students are doing the activity correctly. Offer help and correct students when necessary.

Error correction

- Correction is an integral and crucial part of the learning process. Once students become aware of mistakes they are making, they are able to focus their attention on further study of the language item in question.

- For vocabulary, grammar, and pronunciation activities, it is important to correct mistakes since these types of activities are accuracy focused. It is advisable to correct mistakes as they occur. Speaking activities are fluency focused, so it is better to correct mistakes after students finish the activity, so as not to interrupt "real" communication.

Use of native language

- In a monolingual class, judicious use of the students' native language can be beneficial. Use of the native language can not only convey the meaning of target or incidental vocabulary and grammar but also can help students understand information in listening and reading texts.

- In a monolingual class, it may be beneficial to use the students' native language to check that students understand the instructions. Do this only when using English would be too difficult or too time consuming.

B Tips for large class management
General tips

- Tell students where to sit so that friends are separated, as friends tend to chat. Change the seating arrangement from time to time to give students a chance to interact and practice with different classmates.

- Establish class rules at the beginning of the course and enforce them in a consistent way. It can be helpful to have students make a list of rules with you at the beginning of the year as students will be more likely to follow them.

- Always try to have more activities than necessary for class. Make use of all the suggested activities in the Teacher's Edition and prepare any extra worksheets for that lesson. This will fill time if and when the lesson runs short.

- Vary the way activities are done to avoid being predictable. Vary between whole class work, individual work, group work, and pair work to allow for a more interesting class.

Tips for pair and group work

- For successful completion of a task, make sure that the majority of students are familiar with the language to be practiced before having them work in pairs or groups.

- Confirm that pairs know exactly what to do in order to complete an activity. Model the activity first before having pairs or groups do it.

- Match pairs and groups according to ability and personality. In many cases, pairing stronger students with weaker ones can be beneficial. Pair or group shy students with more extroverted students, as well as disruptive students with well-behaved ones. This way the burden of class management is shared with students.

- If pair work is not possible for your entire class, you can have a few pairs or small groups do the activity in front of the class. The rest of the class listens and offers help as necessary.

C Tips for multilevel class management

Every class is a multilevel class to some degree. Try to understand what the differences are among students in a class. These can be differences in learning styles and speed, ability to focus, and students' experiences and attitudes toward learning.

- Identify the *who*, *what*, and *why* of a difficult situation so that you can then decide how best to proceed. One way to do this is to observe students when they are working in pairs or groups, and keep a list of names of students who need help.

- Determine why some students are sufficiently challenged and others are over- or under-challenged. Take steps to remedy the situation in the following ways:

  - If a student has not had much exposure to English, it may be necessary to provide extra help or supplementary materials at the student's level.

  - If a student finds the materials too easy, group him or her with other students at a similar level to increase the challenge.

  - For under-challenged students, increase the quantity and / or difficulty of the work given. The photocopiable worksheets are useful for this.

  - Call on the more-advanced students in the class to participate first. This will allow the advanced students to be challenged, and at the same time, give the less-advanced students a chance to absorb the new material before they have to participate.

- Include many interesting and varied activities in lessons. The more-advanced students will have a good time just joining in and using what they know, and the less-advanced students will be motivated to improve because the activities are interesting and fun. The more varied the class, the more students will be inspired to participate.

- Avoid having rigid expectations for students, as this will only lead to frustration on your part and theirs.

- Remember to encourage the less-advanced students frequently, but do not forget to encourage the more-advanced students. Encouragement is a great motivator.

- Alert parents to any difficulties that students are experiencing and ask for their support in making sure students study and complete homework.

D Tips for establishing and maintaining discipline

Teacher's role

- Communicate your expectations for students' behavior, tell students what consequences they can expect for breaking the rules, and be consistent in carrying them out.

- Plan lessons carefully and always have more material than necessary, in order to keep students engaged at all times. This will increase students' motivation and decrease opportunities for misbehavior.

- Give clear instructions when explaining how to do an activity to ensure that all students understand what they are to do.

- Establish a method to get students to stop what they are doing and focus their attention on you when needed – for example, by turning off the lights or ringing a bell.

Tips for resolving discipline problems

- To stop disruptive talking, you can simply ask the student to stop in a friendly, yet authoritative, way. If this does not work, have the student sit in the back of the room away from his or her friends for a few minutes. If the talking persists, meet with the student after class and try to find out why he or she is not paying attention.

- Students who come late to class disrupt the flow of a lesson. Keep vacant desks near the door so late students can sit there and not interrupt the class. Discourage lateness and absenteeism by establishing a policy at the beginning of the year whereby points are deducted from the student's final grade if he or she is often late or disruptive.

- If students consistently do not do their homework, meet with them one-on-one to find out why. Encourage completion of homework by correcting the assignments in class the next day and giving points for completed homework.

- To deter cheating on tests, place students' desks with enough space between them to make it impossible to look at another student's work without being noticed. If a particular student has been known to cheat in the past, move his or her desk away from other classmates.

- If a student is unwilling to speak English in class, meet with that student to find out why. Low self-esteem and a fear of appearing foolish are two common reasons for not speaking in class.

- Remember not to take any students' misbehavior personally. Deal with problems quietly and individually after class. Be sure to treat all students with dignity, even when reprimanding them.

New friends

1 Vocabulary review

A Read about the new students at Kent International School. Then listen and practice.

New Students at Kent International School

I'm Zach. I'm from the U.S., and I'm 12. I like baseball and volleyball.

Hello. I'm from Puerto Rico. My name is Ana, and I'm 13. I like movies and concerts.

My name is Tommy. I'm from Australia. I like music and comic books. I'm 13.

Hi. I'm Kate. I'm 13. I'm from Canada. I like computers and math.

Hello there! My name is Claudia. I'm 13. I'm from Colombia. My favorite sports are Ping-Pong and tennis.

My name is Rafael. I'm from Brazil. I like soccer and video games. I'm 13.

B Complete the chart with information from Part A.

Name	Age	Place	Likes
1. _Claudia_	_13_	_Colombia_	_Ping-Pong and tennis_
2. _Rafael_	_13_	_Brazil_	_soccer and video games_
3. _Zach_	_12_	_the U.S._	_baseball and volleyball_
4. _Kate_	_13_	_Canada_	_computers and math_
5. _Ana_	_13_	_Puerto Rico_	_movies and concerts_
6. _Tommy_	_13_	_Australia_	_music and comic books_

Lesson 1 New friends

This lesson reviews and practices vocabulary and expressions for introducing oneself, and asking and answering questions with the verb be.

1 Vocabulary review

This exercise reviews and practices vocabulary and expressions for introducing oneself.

A 💿 CD1, Track 2

- Have students quickly look through their Student's Book. Explain that, as in Student's Book 1, there are 8 units and that each unit contains 4 lessons. There is a mini-review in the middle of each unit, a "Get Connected" lesson (reading, listening, and writing practice), and a review at the end. Tell them that there are six new characters in this level. Encourage students to ask any questions they may have about *Connect*.

- Have students read the directions and the title and then look at the photos. Ask: *Who are the people in the photos?* (New students at Kent International School.)

- Have students read the captions. Then have them close their books. Say the characters' names, one by one, and ask students what they remember about each character.

- Play the recording. Students listen and read along.

> **Audio script**
> Same as the captions in the Student's Book.

- Play the recording again, or model the captions. Students listen and repeat.

- **Optional** Ask volunteers to stand and introduce themselves to the class. Ask them to limit their introductions to name, country of origin, age, and interests. Students may also do the introductions in pairs.

> **Teaching Tip** Conduct as much of your lesson in English as possible. Start using classroom commands on the first day of class. Tell students not to worry if they do not understand completely. Encourage them to guess by paying attention to the context of the language.

B

- Have students read the directions. Ask: *Where is the information for the blanks in the chart?* (In the captions in Part A.) Students work individually to complete the exercise. While they are doing this, copy the chart onto the board. Then circulate, monitoring and helping students fill in the chart.

- Check answers with the class. Invite volunteers to fill in one blank each in the chart on the board.

- **Optional** Invite a volunteer to stand and make an introductory statement – for example, *I'm from Japan.* Ask another student to stand. Tell the second student to convert the first student's sentence into the third person singular – for example, *He's from Japan.* Invite pairs of volunteers to continue the activity.

This unit reviews and introduces vocabulary and expressions for introducing oneself, asking about others, and sharing information about personal likes and abilities.

2 Language focus review

This exercise reviews and practices negative statements and questions with the verb *be*.

A

- **Language Chart** Have students study the examples in the language chart. Focus students' attention on the negative statements and the use of *not*.

- Focus students' attention on the question-and-answer patterns. Ask: *Where is the verb be in the question?* (At the beginning of the question in *Yes / No* questions, and after the question word in information questions.) *Where is it in the answer?* (After the pronoun.) Then focus their attention on the contractions. Call out the contractions, one by one: *she's, who's, they're, name's, what's, it's, when's, where's, I'm, he's.* Students respond with the full form.

- Focus students' attention on the words in bold. Write *Who, What, When, Where,* and *How old* on the board. Point to each question word and ask what kind of information it calls for. (*Who:* people; *What:* names, objects, colors, animals, etc.; *When:* time; *Where:* places; *How old:* ages.)

- Model the examples, pausing for students to repeat.

- **Optional** Invite three volunteers to come to the front of the room. Give each student a piece of chalk or a whiteboard marker. Tell the students to listen and write *Who, What, When, Where,* or *How old.* Say: *She's my mother.* The first student to write *Who* becomes the "teacher." Ask that student to invite three new students to the front to continue the activity.

B   CD1, Track 3

- Focus students' attention on the conversation. Have them read the first two lines. Ask: *Are Zach and Ana meeting for the first time?* (Yes.)

- Remind students that in this type of exercise, they should pick the correct answer from the choices in parentheses.

- Explain *actually.*

- Have students read the conversation. Students work individually to complete the exercise.

- Have students check their answers in pairs.

- Play the recording. Students listen and verify their answers.

> ### Audio script
> Same as the conversation in the Student's Book.

- Check answers with the class. Invite volunteers to read aloud one sentence each.

- Play the recording again, or model the conversation. Students listen and repeat.

- **Optional** Have students practice in pairs.

....

3 Speaking

This exercise reviews Student's Book 1 vocabulary, and questions and answers with the verb *be.*

- Have students read the directions and the example conversation. Demonstrate the task with two volunteers.

- Invite three other volunteers to demonstrate the task for the class with a version of their own (other than the Student's Book example).

- Have students work in groups of three. Students do the task three times so that each student has a chance to ask and answer questions.

- Invite volunteers to tell the class the things they were thinking about.

> ### Workbook
> *Note:* Explain that the Workbook provides extra practice of the language studied in the Student's Book. All Workbook exercises can be done either in class or for homework.
>
> - Assign the exercises on Workbook page 2. (Workbook answers begin on page T-190.)

> ### Extra Grammar
> *Note:* The Extra Grammar activities can be downloaded from the Teacher Support Site at: www.cambridge.org/connect2e/teacher The activities are intended to be done as homework. The site also has information about how teachers can obtain an answer key.
>
> - Assign the exercises for the Extra Grammar, Lesson 1.

2 Language focus review

A Review the language in the chart.

Negative statements / Questions with the verb *be*		
She**'s not** my art teacher.	They**'re not** my classmates.	My name**'s not** Anita.
Who's she? She**'s** my math teacher.	**Who are they?** They**'re** my friends.	**What's your name?** My name**'s** Ana.
It**'s not** in July.	It**'s not** in Brazil.	I**'m not** from São Paulo.
When's your birthday? It**'s** in November.	**Where's San Juan?** It**'s** in Puerto Rico.	**Where are you from?** I**'m** from San Juan.
He**'s not** fourteen. **How old is he?** He**'s** thirteen.	**Is he nice?** Yes, he **is**. No, he**'s not**.	**Are you in her class?** Yes, I **am**. No, I**'m not**.

B Complete the conversation. Listen and check. Then practice.

Zach Hi. __What's__ (What's / Where's) your name?

Ana My name's Ana. ___I'm___ (I'm / He's) from San Juan.

Zach Hi, Ana. My name's Zach.
So, __where's__ (who's / where's) San Juan? ___Is___ (Is / Are) it in Brazil?

Ana No, __it's not__ (it's / it's not). It's in Puerto Rico.

Zach Oh, right. How old ___are___ (is / are) you, Ana?

Ana I'm 13. My birthday is in May.
__When's__ (Where's / When's) your birthday?

Zach It's in June. Hey, __who's__ (who's / what's) she?

Ana __She's__ (They're / She's) my math teacher, Mrs. Archer.

Zach __Are__ (Are / Is) you in Ms. Kelley's science class?

Ana No, __I'm not__ (she's not / I'm not). I'm in Mr. Perez's class.

Zach __Is__ (Is / Are) he nice?

Ana Yes, he is. Actually, __he's__ (I'm / he's) my father.

3 Speaking

Think of a country, a hobby, or a school subject. Give clues. Your classmates guess.

You It's a country. It's not the U.S.

Classmate 1 Is it Peru?

You No, it's not.

Classmate 2 Is it Canada?

You Yes, it is!

1 Language focus review

What are Carson's and Johnny's neighborhoods like? Look at the pictures, and complete the sentences. Then listen and check.

There is / There are . . .

There's a park. / **There's no** park.
There are basketball courts. / **There are no** basketball courts.

Is there a / Are there any . . . ?

Is there a mall?
  Yes, **there is.** / No, **there isn't.**
Are there any stores?
  Yes, **there are.** / No, **there aren't.**

Carson's neighborhood

Johnny's neighborhood

Carson's neighborhood		Johnny's neighborhood	
1. _There's a_ beautiful park.		4. _There's no_ gym.	
2. _There are two_ tennis courts.		5. _There are_ many stores.	
3. _There are no_ basketball courts.		6. _There's a_ big mall.	

Neighborhoods

This lesson presents and practices the names of common recreational, commercial, and public places found in most American neighborhoods. It reviews There is / There are . . . and Is there a / Are there any . . . ?

Review of Lesson 1

- Write four statements on the board: *I'm thirteen. It's in May. I'm from Puerto Rico. I like soccer.* Invite volunteers to make *Wh*- questions for the statements. Write them on the board. (How old are you? When's your birthday? Where are you from? What do you like?)

- Ask a volunteer, Classmate 1, to come to the front and face the board. Ask another volunteer, Classmate 2, to stand up at his or her desk. Classmate 1 guesses the identity of Classmate 2 by asking questions like the ones on the board. Classmate 2 may use a disguised voice when answering. Classmate 1 asks up to five questions and then guesses Classmate 2's identity. Play once more with two new volunteers.

- Invite a volunteer to introduce himself or herself to the class using four or five statements about name, age, country of origin, month of birth, and favorite activities. Make corrections by modeling the statement correctly.

1 Language focus review

This exercise practices and reviews *There is / There are . . .* and *Is there a / Are there any . . . ?* in combination with places in the neighborhood.

CD1, Track 4

- Focus students' attention on the pictures. Explain that many students in the U.S. live in either urban or suburban neighborhoods. Have students identify the places and facilities familiar to them in the two neighborhoods. Write the singular nouns in one column and the plural nouns in a second column on the board.

- Ask: *Is there a mall in Carson's neighborhood?* (No.) *Are there stores in Johnny's neighborhood?* (Yes.)

- **Language Chart** Have students study the examples in the language chart. Focus students' attention on the statements. Ask: *Why do some of the statements use* is *and some* are? (Singular nouns use the verb *is* and plural nouns use *are*.) Point out that the negative statements use *no* instead of *not* before the place or facility.

- Continue on to the question-and-answer pattern. Ask: *Where are* is *and* are *in questions?* (At the beginning, before *there*.) *Where are* is *and* are *in statements?* (They follow *There*.)

- Focus students' attention on the contractions in the negative responses. Ask: *What is the full form* of isn't? (Is not.) *How about* aren't? (Are not.)

- Model the examples, pausing for students to repeat.

- Focus students' attention on the activity at the bottom of the page. Copy the incomplete sentences on the board. Above the sentences on the board, write *There is* and *There are*. Explain to students that these are the words they should use to begin their answers.

- Have students work individually to fill in the blanks.

- Have students check their answers in pairs.

- Play the recording. Students listen and verify their answers.

Audio script
See page T-201.

- Check answers with the class. Invite volunteers to come to the board to write their answers.

- Ask: *Is your neighborhood like Carson's or Johnny's?* Invite one or two volunteers to make both a positive and a negative statement about their own neighborhoods using *There is / There are.*

2 Listening

In this exercise, students listen for the places and facilities in a neighborhood.

💿 CD1, Track 5

- Have students read the directions. Ask students to say what you can buy or do at each of the eight places listed.
- Tell students that they will listen to a conversation between Carson and Johnny about other things found in Johnny's neighborhood. They should check the places that they hear.

Note: Remind students that in the Listening section of a lesson you will usually play the recording three times: first for them to listen only, a second time for them to do the task, and a third time for them to verify their answers.

- Play the recording once. Students only listen.

> **Audio script**
> See page T-201.

- Play the recording again. Students listen and check the places they hear.
- Play the recording once again. Students listen and verify their answers.
- Check answers with the class.

----

3 Speaking

This exercise practices *Is there a / Are there any . . . ?*

A

- Focus students' attention on the chart in Part B. Write *Is there a . . . ?* and *Are there any . . . ?* on the board. Drill students by calling out a series of plural and singular nouns. Students respond with *Is there a* or *Are there any*.
- Have students work individually to complete questions 1 to 6. Invite volunteers to give ideas for questions 7 and 8.
- Check answers with the class. Invite volunteers to come to the board to write one question each.

B

- Have students answer the questions about themselves in the *You* column.
- Have students work in pairs to complete the survey about a classmate.

C

- Have students tell the class about their own neighborhoods using at least one singular and one plural statement. They may use either the positive or negative form. Encourage students to elaborate, making use of the adjectives provided.
- **Optional** Play "Gossip." Divide the class into four or five groups with an equal number of students in each. Whisper a lengthy statement to Classmate 1 in each group – for example, *There are T-shirts on the bed, socks in the drawer, and a lamp on the desk.* (Have the statements written down so that you can check them later.) Tell students that they are not allowed to write down the sentence. Classmate 1 whispers the statement to Classmate 2, Classmate 2 to Classmate 3, and so on. The last student in each group comes to the board and writes what he or she heard. Write the original statement on the board.

> **Workbook**
> Assign the exercises on Workbook page 3.
> (Workbook answers begin on page T-190.)

> **Extra Grammar**
> Assign the exercises for the Extra Grammar, Lesson 2.

2 Listening

What other places are in Johnny's neighborhood?
Listen and check (✓) the correct places.

✓ music store

✓ video arcade

☐ park

☐ basketball court

☐ swimming pool

✓ library

☐ school

☐ bookstore

3 Speaking

A Complete survey questions 1–6 with *Is there a* or *Are there any*.
Write questions 7 and 8 with your classmates.

B Complete the survey for yourself.
Then ask a classmate the questions. *(Answers to the questions will vary.)*

Neighborhood Survey	You		Your classmate	
	Yes	No	Yes	No
1. _Is there a_ school?	☐	☐	☐	☐
2. _Are there any_ movie theaters?	☐	☐	☐	☐
3. _Is there a_ swimming pool?	☐	☐	☐	☐
4. _Is there a_ mall?	☐	☐	☐	☐
5. _Are there any_ restaurants?	☐	☐	☐	☐
6. _Is there a_ library?	☐	☐	☐	☐
7. _(Answers will vary.)_	☐	☐	☐	☐
8. _(Answers will vary.)_	☐	☐	☐	☐

Is there a school in your neighborhood?

Yes, there is.

C Tell your classmates about your neighborhood.
Use the words below or your own ideas.

big exciting **nice** **great**
boring
fun *interesting* small

There's a big music store in my neighborhood. There are . . .

Mini-review

1 Language check

A Read Kate's and Rafael's bulletin boards. Then write questions and answers.

1. **Q:** _Where's Kate from?_

   A: She's from Canada.

2. **Q:** Is Rafael from Brazil?

   A: _Yes, he is._

3. **Q:** _Where's Vancouver?_

   A: It's in Canada.

4. **Q:** How old is Kate?

   A: _She's 13._

5. **Q:** _How old is Rafael?_

   A: He's 13.

6. **Q:** Where's São Paulo?

   A: _It's in Brazil._

7. **Q:** Is Kate from Canada?

   A: _Yes, she is._

8. **Q:** Are Rafael and Kate in the same French class?

   A: _Yes, they are._

B Now ask and answer questions about Kate and Rafael.

Is Kate 13?

Yes, she is.

This lesson reviews the language presented and practiced in Lessons 1 and 2.

1 Language check

This exercise reviews the structures presented so far in this unit.

A

- Have students read the directions. Explain *bulletin board*.

- Have students study the items on Kate's and Rafael's bulletin boards. Ask: *Where's Kate from?* (Canada.) *What language do both Kate and Rafael study?* (French.)

- Say the following: *Lesson 1, Vancouver, Canada, pages 5 and 6, Happy 13th Birthday, Student of the Month.* As you say them, students point to them in their books.

- Read the statements below. Ask students to say *Yes* if the statement is true, *No* if the statement is false, and *I don't know* if the information is not provided.

  Rafael is from Vancouver. (No.)

  Kate is 13 years old. (Yes.)

  Rafael is in seventh grade. (Yes.)

  Kate and Rafael are in the same math class. (No.)

  Kate likes soccer. (I don't know.)

- Have students review the Language chart on page 3 of their book. Remind them to use short answers for *Yes / No* questions. Students work individually to complete the exercise by filling in the appropriate questions and answers.

- Check answers with the class. Invite volunteers to come to the board to write one answer each.

- Have students ask and answer the questions in pairs.

B

- Invite two volunteers to demonstrate the task.

- Have students work in pairs to ask and answer questions. Encourage them to ask questions that vary from those in the activity above.

C

- Have students review the Language chart on page 4. Write two sentences on the board, and ask students to fill in the blanks: *There ___ a pencil on the desk.* (is) and *There ___ desks in the classroom* (are). Elicit that we use *is* with singular nouns and *are* with plural ones.

- Focus students' attention on the picture on page 7. Ask: *What's the name of the street?* (Main Street.) *Is there a bookstore on Main Street?* (Yes, there is.)

- Elicit vocabulary for the kinds of stores in the picture (sports store, music store, computer store, bookstore).

- Invite a volunteer to read the directions and the example aloud.

- Have students work individually to complete the questions and answers.

- Have students check answers in pairs by reading the questions and answers aloud.

- Check answers with the class. Invite several pairs to read the questions and answers aloud.

- **Optional** Have students ask and answer questions about a street in their town or city.

2 Listening

In this exercise students listen for information about a school.

CD1, Track 6

- Tell students that they are going to listen to Monica talking about her new school.

- Have students read the directions and the statements in the chart. Explain that they should check *Yes* if a statement is true or *No* if it is false.

- Play the recording. Students only listen.

Audio script

See page T-201.

- Play the recording again. Students listen and check Yes or No for each statement.

- Play the recording once again. Students listen and verify their answers.

- Check answers with the class.

Workbook

Assign the exercises on Workbook page 4. (Workbook answers begin on page T-190.)

Game

Assign the game on Student's Book page 114.

C What's in the stores on Main Street? Complete the questions and answers with *there is, there isn't, there are, there aren't, are there,* or *is there.*

1. _Is there_ a bookstore on Main Street?

   Yes, _there is_ . Read More! is a bookstore.

2. _Are there_ any comic books in the bookstore?

   No, _there aren't_ . _There are_ no comic books at the bookstore.

3. _Is there_ a bicycle at Town Sports?

   Yes, _there is_ . _There are_ soccer balls at the store, too.

4. _Is there_ a music store on Main Street?

   Yes, _there is_ . Notes is next to the bookstore.

5. _Are there_ any video games in the computer store?

   No, _there aren't_ . But, look, _there are_ some new laptops.

2 Listening

Monica describes her new school. Listen and check (✓) Yes or No.

	Yes	No
1. Is there a big library?	✓	
2. Is there a swimming pool?	✓	
3. Are there any basketball courts?	✓	
4. Are there any tennis courts?		✓
5. Is there a music room?	✓	

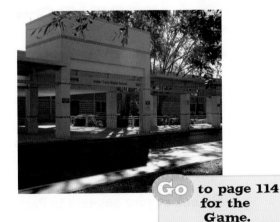

Go to page 114 for the Game.

1 Vocabulary

What are these students' talents? Write the sentences below the correct people. Then listen and practice.

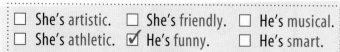

☐ She's artistic.   ☐ She's friendly.   ☐ He's musical.
☐ She's athletic.   ☑ He's funny.   ☐ He's smart.

1. He can tell jokes.

He's funny.

2. She can make friends easily.

She's friendly.

3. He can speak three languages.

He's smart.

4. She can play a lot of sports.

She's athletic.

5. He can play a lot of instruments.

He's musical.

6. She can draw great pictures.

She's artistic.

2 Listening

A What do you think these students can do? Listen and check (✓) the correct activities.

1. Silvio: ☑ He can play basketball.   ☐ He can play video games.
2. Beth: ☑ She can play the guitar.   ☐ She can play volleyball.
3. Tony: ☑ He can speak a lot of languages. ☐ He can dance.
4. Lina: ☐ She can play soccer.   ☑ She can draw.

B Look at your answers to Part A. Write the word that describes each student.

1. *athletic*   2. *musical*   3. *smart*   4. *artistic*

Lesson 3 Talents

This lesson presents and practices adjectives for describing people, verbs for special abilities with can, and be good at.

Review of Lesson 2

Say: *There are books on the desk.* Classmate 1 repeats the sentence and adds a noun – for example, *There are books and a pen on the desk.* Classmate 2 repeats Classmate 1's sentence and adds a third noun, and so on. Tell students that they are not allowed to take notes. Continue until one student is unable to remember the complete sentence. That student is "out." Continue play until only one student is left. Some suggested starter sentences are: *There are basketball courts in my neighborhood. There are students in the classroom. There are apples in the supermarket.*

Note: For large classes, divide the class into four or five groups. Each group plays as above.

1 Vocabulary

This exercise presents and practices adjectives for describing people, and verbs for special abilities with *can*.

CD1, Track 7

- Have students read the directions. Ask them to suggest an equivalent for the word *talents*. (Things you are good at.)
- On the board, write the six vocabulary words in the box. Say: *Look at photo number 1. He's funny.* Say the name of a famous comedian. Ask: *Is he funny?* (Yes, he is.) Continue in this way until you have taught the meanings of all the vocabulary words.
- Mime the actions of someone who has one of the six talents. The first student to guess the talent correctly comes to the front and continues the activity.

- Have students work individually to write the sentences under the correct photos.
- Play the recording. Students listen and verify their answers.

Audio script
Same as the sentences in the Student's Book.

- Check answers with the class.
- Play the recording again, or model the sentences. Students listen and repeat.

2 Listening

In this exercise, students listen for people's abilities.

A CD1, Track 8

- Have students read the directions and the sentences next to each name.
- Tell students that they will listen to four short conversations about what people are good at. They should decide which of the abilities fits each person.
- Play the recording. Students only listen.

Audio script
See page T-201.

- Play the recording again. Students listen and check the correct sentences.
- Play the recording once again. Students listen and verify their answers.
- Check answers with the class.

B

- Have students read the directions.
- Have students look back at Part A and write the adjectives in the blanks.
- Check answers with the class.

3 Language focus

This exercise presents and practices *be good at.*

A 💿 CD1, Track 9

- Focus students' attention on the photo. Explain that the boys in the background are Tommy and Zach. The girls in the foreground are Claudia and Kate.
- Play the recording. Students listen and read along.

> **Audio script**
> Same as the conversation in the Student's Book.

- Ask: *Who's good at soccer?* (Claudia.) *Is Tommy good at soccer?* (No.) *How about Zach?* (He's pretty good at soccer.) Explain that *pretty good at* is not as good as *good at,* but it still has a positive meaning.
- Play the recording again, or model the conversation. Students listen and repeat.
- **Optional** Have students practice in pairs.
- Language Chart Have students study the top part of the language chart. Focus students' attention on the words in bold.
- Have students study the middle part of the chart.
- Model the examples, pausing for students to repeat.
- Have students study the bottom part of the chart.
- Ask: *What's the full form of* Tommy's? (Tommy is.)

B

- Have students read the directions and look at the words in the categories of *Subjects* and *Sports.* With the class, brainstorm other words that could be used with the phrases *good at, pretty good at,* and *not good at.* Write them on the board.
- Have students work individually to complete the task.
- Have students read their sentences in pairs.

C

- Have students read the directions and the example in the speech balloon.
- Give students several minutes to think about their classmates and some positive things they can say about their abilities.
- Invite volunteers to talk about what different students are good at.

4 Pronunciation Stress

In this exercise, students practice the pronunciation of stressed words.

💿 CD1, Track 10

- Tell students that just as syllables within a word have different stress, the words within a sentence have different stress.
- Say: *I'm **good** at teaching English. I'm an **English** teacher. I'm **not** good at science. I'm **not** a science teacher.* Ask: *Where's the stress in each sentence?* (Good, English, not, not.)
- Focus students' attention on the sentences in the chart. Play the recording. Students listen, paying special attention to the stressed words.

> **Audio script**
> Same as the sentences in the Student's Book.

- Play the recording again. Students listen and repeat.

> **Workbook**
> Assign the exercises on Workbook page 5. (Workbook answers begin on page T-190.)

> **Extra Grammar**
> Assign the exercises for the Extra Grammar, Lesson 3.

3 Language focus

A Who's good at soccer? Listen and practice.

Kate Hey, Claudia! You're good at soccer!
You're really athletic!

Claudia Thanks.

Kate Who's that?

Claudia That's Zach.

Kate He's pretty good at soccer.

Claudia Yeah.

Kate Oh, no! Who's that?

Claudia Uh, that's Tommy. He's not good
at soccer.

Kate No. But he can play a lot of
instruments. He's very musical.

be good at

You**'re good at** soccer.
He**'s pretty good at** soccer.
Tommy**'s not good at** soccer.

👍👍 good at
👍 pretty good at
👎 not good at

Tommy's = Tommy is

B What are you good at? Write sentences.
Use the words below or your own ideas.
(Answers will vary.)

> **Subjects:** English history
> math science art
>
> **Sports:** volleyball soccer
> tennis basketball

(good at) *I'm good at English.*

1. (good at) _____

2. (pretty good at) _____

3. (not good at) _____

C What are different students in your class
good at? Tell your classmates.

> Heather's good at volleyball.

4 Pronunciation Stress

Listen. Notice the stress in the sentences. Then listen again and practice.

I'm **good** at drawing. I'm **artistic**.	I'm **not** good at drawing. I'm **not** artistic.
I'm **good** at sports. I'm **athletic**.	I'm **not** good at sports. I'm **not** athletic.
He's **good** at the guitar. He's **musical**.	He's **not** good at the guitar. He's **not** musical.

Our pets

1 Vocabulary

A Students describe their pets at the school pet show. Match the students to the correct texts. Then listen and practice.

6 | Binky and Cleo are boring. They're my brother's rabbits.

3 | Daisy is my cat. She's my favorite pet. She's really cute.

5 | Max is my dog. He's very active. I love dogs.

2 | Hans and Terry are my two spiders. They're very interesting.

1 | Polly is my parrot. She can speak English. She's messy.

4 | I like my snake. His name is Ollie. He's not dangerous.

B Which pets in Part A do you think are great? Which pets are not so great? Complete the chart. Then tell your classmates. *(Answers will vary.)*

Great	Why		Not so great	Why
dogs	cute			

Dogs are great pets. They're cute.

Snakes are not so great. They're boring.

This lesson presents and practices the names of common and unusual pets, adjectives to describe them, like + a lot / very much / a little, *and* don't like + very much / at all.

Review of Lesson 3

- Ask two students to come to the front. Give each a piece of chalk or a whiteboard marker. Ask another student to stand and make a sentence using the *I'm good at . . .* pattern – for example, *I'm good at (science).* Students at the board listen to the statement and write the appropriate adjective. (Smart.) The first student to do so correctly continues the activity with another student at the front.

- Have students work in pairs. Tell them to ask their partner several *Are you good at . . . ?* questions. Have two or three volunteers report their findings to the class. Encourage them to describe things their partners are *good at, pretty good at,* and *not good at.*

1 Vocabulary

This exercise presents and practices the names of common and unusual pets and adjectives to describe them.

Culture Note More than 50 percent of U.S. households own a pet. Dogs, cats, birds, and horses are the most popular pets. The Labrador retriever is the most popular dog. Persians are the most popular cat. Sometimes owners give their pets silly names, like Fluffy and Spot, and sometimes they give them people's names, like Max and Samantha.

A CD1, Track 11

- Focus students' attention on the picture. Explain that the students have brought their pets to school to show and talk about. Elicit any names students know for the animals shown.

- Ask students to raise their hand if they have a pet. Ask some of the students who own pets to tell the class the names of their pets.

- Have students read the text below each picture. On the board, draw simple illustrations of the six different animals. Elicit the names of the animals from students. Supply any names that they do not know. Ask students to suggest equivalents for the adjectives in the texts.

- Have students work individually to write the number of each student next to the corresponding text.

- Play the recording. Students listen and verify their answers.

Audio script

Same as the sentences in the Student's Book.

- Check answers with the class.
- Play the recording again, or model the sentences. Students listen and repeat.

B

- Write *Good* and *Bad* on the board. Have students look at the texts again and tell you the adjectives from Part A that describe good qualities in pets. Write them under the word *Good* on the board. (Cute, active, interesting, not dangerous.) Encourage students to think of other positive adjectives from previous lessons. Follow the same procedure for *Bad.* (Boring, messy, dangerous.)

- Ask students to read the directions and the example. Ask: *Do you agree with the example?* Explain that there are no correct or incorrect answers. Tell them that they may add the names of other animals, such as *fish, hamsters, lizards,* etc. Supply any additional vocabulary students may need.

- Have students work individually to complete the exercise.

- Write on the board: *Dogs are great pets. They're cute.* Tell students that when generalizing in English, we use the plural form of the noun.

- Ask volunteers to tell the class their "pet opinions" using the model on the board.

2 Language focus

This exercise presents and practices *like + a lot / very much / a little*, and *don't like + very much / at all*.

A 🔊 CD1, Track 12

- Have students look at the picture. Ask: *Does Ned like cats?* (No.) *Does Dora like them?* (Yes.)
- Play the recording. Students listen and read along.

> **Audio script**
> Same as the conversation in the Student's Book.

- Write across the board: *like a lot, like very much, like a little, don't like very much, don't like at all.* Explain that these phrases express varying degrees of like and dislike. Draw faces below each phrase to show the expressions on a continuum from very positive to very negative. Have students copy the phrases and faces into their notebooks.
- Using appropriate facial expressions, tell the class some of your personal likes and dislikes. Use the above patterns. Say: *I like (pizza) a lot. I like (hamburgers) very much. I like (hot dogs) a little. I don't like (fish) very much. I don't like (candy) at all.*
- Invite volunteers to make several sentences using these patterns.
- Play the recording again, or model the conversation. Students listen and repeat.
- **Optional** Have students practice in pairs.
- **Language Chart** Have students study the examples in the language chart. Focus students' attention on the words in bold.
- Model the examples, pausing for students to repeat.

B 🔊 CD1, Track 13

- Check students' understanding that *a lot* and *a little* are used in the positive form of the pattern, *at all* is used in the negative, and *very much* is used in both. Call them out one by one. Students respond with *like, don't like,* or *both like and don't like.*
- Have students read the directions and the example.
- Have students work individually to complete the exercise.
- Play the recording. Students listen and verify their answers.

> **Audio script**
> Same as the sentences in the Student's Book.

- Check answers with the class. Invite volunteers to come to the front to write the answers on the board.

....

3 Speaking

This exercise practices talking about pet preferences.

- Tell students that they are going to talk about the kinds of pets they like and do not like. Use the sample conversation to model a conversation with a student. Then give another example using your own idea. Say: *I like _____ very much. How about you?* The student answers with his or her own opinion.
- Put students in groups of four. One student begins by saying to the group: *I like (spiders) very much. How about you?* Then each student responds with his or her own opinion. Students repeat this four times so that each student has a chance to start the conversation.
- **Optional** To conclude the activity, invite students to name the pets they like and do not like. Write the names of the pets on the board. Next to each pet, write the number of students who like it or do not like it. What's the class's favorite pet?

> **Workbook**
> Assign the exercises on Workbook page 6. (Workbook answers begin on page T-190.)

> **Extra Grammar**
> Assign the exercises for the Extra Grammar, Lesson 4.

2 Language focus

A Dora shows Ned the animals at the pet show. Listen and practice.

**like + a lot / very much / a little
don't like + very much / at all**

I **like** cats **a lot.**
I **like** rabbits **very much.**
I **like** dogs **a little.**
I **don't like** spiders **very much.**
I **don't like** snakes **at all.**

Dora Hey, Ned. Look at the cute cat. I like cats a lot.

Ned You do? I don't like cats very much. They're boring.

Dora But you like dogs, right?

Ned Yeah, they're really friendly.

Dora Well, I like dogs a little.

Ned Wow! Look at that snake over there.

Dora Ugh! I don't like snakes at all. They're dangerous.

B Complete these sentences with the correct words. Then listen and check.

1. Rabbits are boring. I don't like rabbits __*at all*__ (a little / at all).
2. Parrots are OK. I like parrots __*a little*__ (at all / a little).
3. Cats aren't very nice. I don't like cats *very much* (a little / very much).
4. Dogs are cute. I like dogs __*a lot*__ (a lot / at all).
5. Snakes are very bad pets. I don't like snakes __*at all*__ (a little / at all).
6. Spiders are interesting. I like spiders *very much* (at all / very much).

3 Speaking

Learn what animals four of your classmates like and don't like.

You I like dogs a lot. How about you?

Classmate 1 I don't like dogs at all. I like cats very much.

Classmate 2 Well, I don't like cats at all. I like snakes a lot.

Classmate 3 Really? I don't like snakes at all. I like spiders a little.

Classmate 4 Hmm. I don't like . . .

Read

A Read the article quickly. Check (✓) the statements that are true.

☑ 1. The Jonas Brothers play in a band.

☐ 2. Jessica is a friend of the Jonas Brothers.

☑ 3. Kevin, Joe, and Nick all write songs.

The Jonas Brothers

Hi, I'm Jessica and this is my Jonas Brothers' fan Web site. The Jonas Brothers are a cool band. They're famous and I like their music a lot. They're not only a band, they're also brothers. They're from New Jersey, but they live in Hollywood now.

There are three brothers in the band: Kevin, Joe, and Nick. Kevin is the oldest brother. He's 21. Joe is 19, and Nick – the youngest in the band – is 16. Nick and Joe are both **lead** singers. Kevin sings **backup** and plays the guitar. All three brothers write songs. Their first song – "Mandy" – is about a **special** girl they know. Their other songs are about **typical** teenage things like friends.

All three brothers are good at acting, too. Sometimes, they're on TV or in a **Broadway musical**. They're amazing.

There's one more Jonas brother – Frankie. He plays the **drums**, but he's not in the band. He's only 8!

Go to page 122 for the **Vocabulary Practice.**

B 👓 Read the article slowly. Check your answers in Part A.

C Answer the questions.

1. What's the name of the band? _The name of the band is The Jonas Brothers._

2. Where are they from? _They're from New Jersey._

3. Are there four brothers in the band? _No, there aren't._

4. Are the brothers good at acting? _Yes, they are._

5. How old is Frankie? _He's 8._

This lesson practices reading, listening, and writing skills.

Review of Lesson 4

- Play several rounds of "Charades." Divide the class into two or three teams. Ask one member from each team to come to the front. Hand each one a small slip of paper with the same sentence written on each slip – for example, *I like spiders a lot* or *I don't like snakes at all.* Students in the front act out the sentence for their group. The first group to guess the sentence wins a point for its team.
- Ask students to write down a sentence about an animal that they like or dislike. Tell them to walk around the classroom repeating their sentence until they find a classmate with the same sentence.

Read

This exercise practices reading for information about a famous band.

Note: Tell students that there is a "Get Connected" lesson in each unit. This lesson provides additional practice in reading, listening, and writing. It uses vocabulary and grammar from previous lessons in the unit, and it presents new vocabulary.

A

- Have students look at the title of the article and the photos. Ask: *What's the name of this band?* (The Jonas Brothers.) *Where are they from?* (The United States.) Invite students to tell the class about their favorite bands.
- Invite a volunteer to read the directions and the statements aloud. Tell students *read quickly* means they read quickly to find the true statements, and they should not read every word carefully.
- Have students work individually to read the article quickly and check the true statements. Do not check answers at this point.

B 💿 CD1, Track 14

- Invite a volunteer to read the directions aloud. Tell students *read slowly* means they read slowly and carefully, and concentrate on getting the meaning of the entire text.
- List the new vocabulary words on the board: *lead, backup, special, typical, Broadway musical, drums.* Explain their meaning. (Lead: the person or thing in front [here, *lead singer* is the singer who stands in front of the band on stage and sings most of the songs]; backup: the person or thing that helps [here, *backup singer* sings with the lead singer, sometimes standing behind or next to him or her]; special: someone or something that is important; typical: average or ordinary – not different from other people or things; Broadway musical: a show with singing and dancing to tell a story. [Broadway is a street with theaters that show musicals and plays in New York City – for example, *West Side Story* and *The Lion King* are famous Broadway musicals.]; drum: a round musical instrument that someone plays by beating on it.) As an alternative, have students use their dictionaries to find the meanings of the new vocabulary words.

- Have students read the article again.
- Have students check their answers in Part A in pairs. Elicit the answers from one pair.
- **Optional** Play the recording. Students listen and read along.

Audio script
Same as the article in the Student's Book.

Get Connected Vocabulary

Note: The Get Connected Vocabulary provides extra practice of new vocabulary words (the words in bold) in the Get Connected readings.

- Have students do the exercise on Student's Book page 122 in class or for homework. (Get Connected Vocabulary answers begin on page T-122.)

C

- Invite a volunteer to read the directions and the first question aloud.
- Ask: *What's the name of the band?* Elicit the answer. (The Jonas Brothers.)
- Have students work individually to answer the questions.
- Have students check their answers in pairs.
- Check answers with the class. Invite volunteers to read aloud one answer each.
- **Optional** Have students work in pairs to write two more questions about the article. As students do this, walk around and check their work. Invite a few students to write their questions on the board for everyone to answer.

Listen

In this exercise, students listen for information about singers and bands.

A 🎵 CD1, Track 15

- Focus students' attention on the photo. Explain that this is a poster of the band, the Plain White T's.
- Tell students that they will listen to Alex and Ana talk about a band, the Plain White T's.
- Have students read the first question and the example answer.
- Explain that students should listen to the conversation and answer the questions.
- Play the recording. Students only listen.

> **Audio script**
> See page T-201.

- Play the recording again. Students listen and answer the questions.
- Play the recording once again. Students listen and verify their answers.
- Check answers with the class. Invite volunteers to read their answers aloud.

> **Teaching Tip** Tell students that the first time you play a recording, they should just listen but not write anything. Trying to write and listen at the same time often makes it difficult to concentrate. You might want to pause after the first listening to give students time to write answers lightly in pencil. Then they can write these answers when they listen the second time. They can then check their answers when they listen the third time.

B

- Have students read the directions and all the statements.
- Explain that *I agree* means you think something is right, *I disagree* means you think something is not right, and *I'm not sure* means you cannot say if you think it is right or not. Tell students that there are no right or wrong answers for this exercise – they are giving their opinions.
- Have students work individually to write whether they agree, disagree, or are not sure.
- Have students work in pairs to compare answers, or elicit opinions from volunteers.
- **Optional** Take a class poll. Read each statement and ask for a show of hands. Say: *Raise your hand if you agree. Now raise your hand if you disagree. Now raise your hand if you're not sure.* Record the results in a chart on the board.

Write

In this exercise, students answer questions and write an article about their favorite band.

A

- Invite a volunteer to read the directions and the questions aloud. Elicit the names of some of the bands students mentioned in Part A of the Reading activity and write them on the board. Add more band names, if possible.
- Have students work individually to answer the questions.
- **Optional** Have students ask and answer the questions in pairs.

B

- Invite a volunteer to read the directions aloud. Tell students that they will use their answers in Part A to help them write about their favorite band.
- Have students work individually to write an article for their fan Web site.
- **Optional** Have students work in groups of four and read each other's articles. Students should ask questions about anything they do not understand. They can also ask questions for more information about the bands.

> **Workbook**
> Assign the exercises on Workbook page 7. (Workbook answers begin on page T-190.)

That's not very important!

A 💿 **Alex and Anna talk about a band. Listen and answer the questions.**

1. Is Anna on a science Web site? _No, she isn't._
2. Are the Plain White T's Anna's favorite band? _Yes, they are._
3. Are they from New York? _No, they aren't._
4. What's the lead singer's first name? _It's Tom._
5. Are Alex and Anna classmates? _No, they aren't._

B **What do you think? Write *I agree*, *I disagree*, or *I'm not sure*.**
(Answers will vary.)
1. Fan Web sites are great. _____
2. The Plain White T's are a cool band. _____
3. Mariah Carey is a great singer. _____
4. Music Web sites are interesting. _____
5. Homework is fun. _____

Write

Your turn

A **Answer the questions about your favorite band.** *(Answers will vary.)*

1. What's the name of the band? _____
2. Where are they from? _____
3. Who are the members in the band? _____
4. How old are the band members? _____
5. What's your favorite song? _____

B **Write an article for your fan Web site. Use the answers in Part A to help you.** *(Answers will vary.)*

Hi, I'm _____ and this is my fan Web site for _____

_____

_____

_____

Language chart review

The verb *be*

Statements	Wh- and How questions	Yes / No questions	Short answers
I**'m** from Brazil. I**'m not** from Peru.	Where are you from?	Are you in my class?	Yes, I **am**. No, I**'m not**.
She**'s** 12. She**'s not** 13.	How old is she?	Is he from Australia?	Yes, he **is**. No, he**'s not**.
We**'re** at the mall. We**'re not** at the park.	Where are you?	Are you brothers?	Yes, we **are**. No, we**'re not**.
They**'re** my friends. They**'re not** my sisters.	Who are they?	Are they fun?	Yes, they **are**. No, they**'re not**.

is not = isn't / 's not   *are not = aren't / 're not*

be good at

You**'re good at** sports.   Jason**'s pretty good at** music.   We**'re not good at** science.

Jason's = Jason is

A **Tom, Alex, and Eliza are in a new TV show. Complete the sentences.**

Meet the kids from City Middle School

My ___name's___ (name / name's) Tom Pond.
___I'm___ (I'm / He's) on a cool, new television show
on Teen TV. The show is called *City Middle School*. My friends and I
___are___ (am / are) students at City Middle School. City Middle
School ___is___ (is / are) in Lake City.

___These are___ (This is / These are) my friends. This is Alex. Alex is
___good at___ (good is / good at) art. ___He's___ (He's / She's)
not good at math. ___We're___ (They're / We're) in the same math class.
Our teacher ___isn't___ (isn't / aren't) happy with Alex.

Say hello to Eliza. ___She's___ (He's / She's) not from
Lake City. ___She's___ (She's / We're) Alex's cousin from
Brazil. ___She's___ (She / She's) pretty and very smart.
Eliza's ___pretty good___ (pretty good / is pretty) at sports, too.

Unit 1 Review

This lesson reviews the grammar and vocabulary introduced in Unit 1.

Language chart review

These charts summarize the main grammar presented and practiced in Unit 1.

Note: Explain that there is a "Review" lesson at the end of every unit, which reviews the language of the whole unit. Review lessons start with a Language chart review that summarizes the unit grammar. The chart is followed by a series of exercises. Some Review lessons contain two Language chart reviews.

- Books closed. Write on the board:

    I'm from <u>Brazil</u>. _____ ?

    She's <u>12</u>. _____ ?

    We're at the <u>mall</u>. _____ ?

    They're my <u>friends</u>. _____ ?

    ____ _____ in my class? Yes, I am.

    ____ _____ from Australia? No, he's not.

    ____ _____ brothers? Yes, we are.

    ____ _____ fun? No, they're not.

- Focus students' attention on the material on the board. For the first group, have them write appropriate questions for the answers, paying attention to the underlined words. Then have them fill in the blanks to complete the questions in the second group.

- Invite volunteers to come to the front to write their answers on the board.

- Books open. Have students check their answers against the examples in the top chart. Then ask them to check the answers on the board.

- Focus students' attention on the contractions at the bottom of the top chart. Invite volunteers to tell you the full forms of the contracted words.

- Focus students' attention on the bottom chart. Invite volunteers to make sentences with *good at, pretty good at,* and *not good at.*

- Answer any questions students may have.

....

Exercises A through D (pages T-14 to T-15)

Note: Students can do these exercises for homework or in class. They should do these exercises with minimal teacher input or help. If you choose to do these exercises as homework, briefly review the exercise directions in class. Make sure that students understand what they should do. Check the answers with the class during the next class meeting. If you choose to do the exercises in class, follow the directions below.

Exercise A

- Have a volunteer read the directions aloud.

- Tell students to complete the sentences with the words in parentheses.

- Have students work individually to complete the sentences.

- Check answers with the class. Invite volunteers to read the completed sentences aloud.

Exercise B

- Have students read the directions. Explain that there are two parts to the task. First, students write questions with the correct forms of *be*. Then, they write answers to the questions.
- Have students work individually to write questions using the words given.
- Have students work individually to answer the questions.
- Check answers with the class.
- Have students ask and answer the questions in pairs.

Language chart review

These charts summarize further grammar presented and practiced in Unit 1.

- Have students study the examples in the charts.
- Remind students to use *There is* with singular nouns and *There are* with plural nouns.
- Remind students also that *a lot* and *a little* are used in the positive form of the pattern, *at all* in the negative, and *very much* in both.
- Answer any questions students may have.

Exercise C

- Have students read the directions and look at the picture.
- Have students work individually to complete the conversation.
- Have students check their answers in pairs.
- Check answers with the class. Invite pairs of volunteers to read the completed conversation aloud.

Exercise D

- Invite a volunteer to read the directions aloud.
- Tell students they should look at Part C to help them with Part D.
- Have students work individually to complete the exercise.
- Check answers with the class.

Optional Unit Wrap-Up

- If students did the Review exercises for homework, check answers with the class.
- Have students work in groups of three to role-play the TV show in Exercise A. One student reads the part of Tom from City Middle School.
- Have students in each group create and present a similar TV show with their own information.
- Write two column headings (*Subjects* and *Sports*) on the board with two words under each one: *Subjects: English, history; Sports: volleyball, soccer.* Elicit the names of more subjects and sports and add them.
- Elicit opinions from a few volunteers. Ask: *What do you think about volleyball?* Students answer with sentences such as *I like volleyball a lot,* or *I don't like volleyball at all.*

Theme Project

Note: Explain that the Theme Projects reinforce the unit vocabulary and language structures in a creative way. They also help students connect their English to the world outside the classroom.

- Assign the *At Home* section of the Unit 1 Theme Project on Student's Book page 126.

Workbook

- Assign the Unit 1 Check Yourself on Workbook page 8. (Workbook answers begin on page T-190.)

Extra Practice Worksheets

Note: Explain that these provide extra vocabulary and grammar practice. These worksheets can be done for homework or in class.

- Assign the Unit 1 Extra Practice worksheets starting on page T-139.

Extra Speaking Practice Worksheet

Note: Explain that this provides extra speaking practice. This worksheet can be done for homework or in class.

- Assign the Unit 1 Extra Speaking Practice worksheet on page T-165.

Arcade Activities

Note: Explain that the Arcade provides fun, interactive activities that review and practice vocabulary and grammar.

- Assign the Unit 1 Arcade activities found at: www.cambridge.org/connectarcade

Learning Log

Note: Explain that these provide a way for students to assess their progress for the unit. The Learning Log can be done for homework or in class.

- Assign the Unit 1 Learning Log. These can be downloaded from the Teacher Support Site at: www.cambridge.org/connect2e/teacher

Quiz

- Give the Unit 1 Quiz on page T-176.

Test

- Give the Unit 1 Test (Form A and / or Form B). These can be downloaded from the Teacher Support Site at: www.cambridge.org/connect2e/teacher

B Write questions with the correct forms of *be*. Then look again at Part A, and answer the questions.

1. Tom's last name / Pond
   Q: _Is Tom's last name Pond?_   A: _Yes, it is._

2. where / City Middle School
   Q: _Where's City Middle School?_   A: _It's in Lake City._

3. who / Alex and Eliza
   Q: _Who are Alex and Eliza?_   A: _They're Tom's friends._

4. Eliza / good at sports
   Q: _Is Eliza good at sports?_   A: _Yes, she is._

Language chart review

There is / There are . . .	
There's a tennis court.	**There are** restaurants.
There's no basketball court.	**There are no** movie theaters.
Is there a mall?	**Are there any** music stores?
Yes, **there is.** / No, **there isn't.**	Yes, **there are.** / No, **there aren't.**

a lot / very much
a little / not at all

I **like** science **a lot**.
I **like** geography **a little**.
I **don't like** math **very much**.
I **don't like** P.E. **at all**.

C Sam and Ann are at a pet store. Complete the conversation with *are*, *is*, *there's*, and *they're*.

Sam There ___are___ a lot of animals here!

Ann I know. ___Is___ there a parrot?

Sam Yes, there ___is___ . Look!

Ann Oh, it's beautiful! And ___there's___ a very cute cat.
Sam Cats aren't friendly.

Ann Oh, cats aren't bad. Look! ___There's___ a black spider.

Sam Ugh! I don't like spiders at all. ___Are___ there any dogs?

Ann Yes, there ___are___ . ___They're___ in front of you.

D What do you think Sam and Ann say? Look again at Part C. Then write sentences with *like* or *don't like*.

1. (parrots / a lot)   **Ann** _I like parrots a lot._

2. (cats / a little)   **Ann** _I like cats a little._

3. (cats / at all)   **Sam** _I don't like cats at all._

4. (dogs / a lot)   **Sam** _I like dogs a lot._

Go to page 126 for the Theme Project.

School days

1 Vocabulary

A Read about Marcia's day. Then listen and practice.

Every day, I get up at 6:00 in the morning.

I eat breakfast at home.

Then I go to school with my brother.

I eat lunch with my friends in the cafeteria.

At 4:00, I go home.

Then I do my homework.

At 7:30, I eat dinner with my family.

Then I watch TV.

I go to bed at 10:00.

B Imagine you are Marcia. Complete her sentences with the correct words from Part A.

1. I _____get up_____ at 6:00 a.m.
2. I _____watch TV_____ at 8:00 p.m.
3. I ___eat breakfast___ at 6:35 a.m.
4. I _do my homework_ at 4:30 p.m.

5. I _____eat lunch_____ at 12:30 p.m.
6. I _____go to bed_____ at 10:00 p.m.
7. I _____go home_____ at 4:00 p.m.
8. I _____eat dinner_____ at 7:30 p.m.

Lesson 5 School days

This lesson presents and practices the names of daily activities, time phrases, and simple present statements with I.

1 Vocabulary

This exercise presents and practices daily activities.

A ⊙ CD1, Track 16

- Have students look at the pictures. Explain that this is a day in the life of a typical American student, Marcia. Ask students how their daily routines vary from Marcia's.

- Have students read the captions. Explain *every day* and *then*. Ask: *How many specific times are mentioned?* (4.) *What are they?* (At 6:00 in the morning, at 4:00, at 7:30, at 10:00.) *What word is used before specific times?* (At.)

- Play the recording. Students listen and read along.

> **Audio script**
> Same as the sentences in the Student's Book.

- Play the recording again, or model the captions. Students listen and repeat.

- Take the part of Marcia. Say: *I do my homework. What time is it?* (It's 4:30.) Ask the student who responds first to continue the activity. Continue until you have done all nine activities.

B

- Have students read the directions and the sentences. Ask: *Which words from Part A will go in the blanks?* (The words in red.)

- Have students work individually to complete the exercise.

- Check answers with the class. Invite volunteers to read aloud one sentence each.

- **Optional** Assign verb phrases to random students. Ask students to use the phrases in sentences describing their own daily routines.

> **Teaching Tip** Plan your lessons with extra activities and review practices so that you will have enough to do with the class. Have all of your materials ready beforehand: bingo grids, scrap paper, chalk or whiteboard markers, photocopiable activities, etc. Any unoccupied time for students during the lesson may lead to disruptive behavior on their part.

This unit introduces vocabulary and expressions for talking about schedules, routines, and free-time activities.

T-16

2 Language focus

This exercise presents and practices simple present statements with I.

A 💿 CD1, Track 17

- Focus students' attention on the photos of Roberto and Cindy. Explain that Roberto and Cindy have daily routines that are different from Marcia's.

- Play the recording. Students listen and read along.

> **Audio script**
> Same as the texts in the Student's Book.

- Say the following statements. Ask students to say *Yes* if a statement is true or *No* if it is false. *Cindy goes to school with her friends.* (Yes.) *Roberto goes home after school.* (No.) *Roberto watches TV after dinner.* (No.) *Cindy eats dinner at 6:00.* (Yes.) *Roberto does his homework after dinner.* (Yes.) *Cindy goes to school with her brother.* (No.)

- Play the recording again, or model the sentences. Students listen and repeat.

- **Language Chart** Have students study the examples in the language chart. Focus students' attention on the words in bold and the contracted form of *do not*. Ask: *Where is* don't *in negative sentences?* (Before the verb.)

- Model the examples, pausing for students to repeat.

B

- Have students read the directions and the example.

- Have students work individually to complete the exercise.

- Check answers with the class. Write *Same* and *Different* on the board. To the left and slightly below the words, write the numbers 1 to 4 in a column. Say: *Number 1. Same as Marcia, raise your hand.* Count the number of students raising their hands and write that number under the word *Same* in line with the number 1. Then ask one of those students to read his or her sentence. Then say: *Number 1. Different from Marcia, raise your hand.* Write the number of students raising their hands under the word *Different* in line with number 1. Ask a student to read his or her negative sentence. Follow the same procedure for numbers 2, 3, and 4. When you have finished the activity, tally up the *Same* and *Different* amounts to see how the students' activities compare and contrast with Marcia's.

C

- Invite volunteers to tell the class about their day, following the example.

3 Listening

In this exercise, students listen for details of daily activities.

💿 CD1, Track 18

- Have students read the directions. Tell students that they will listen to Claudia describe her day and should check the information they hear. Be sure students understand that each item has two choices.

- Play the recording. Students only listen.

> **Audio script**
> See page T-202.

- Play the recording again. Students listen and check the correct information.

- Play the recording once again. Students listen and verify their answers.

- Check answers with the class.

> **Workbook**
> Assign the exercises on Workbook page 9. (Workbook answers begin on page T-190.)

> **Extra Grammar**
> Assign the exercises for the Extra Grammar, Lesson 5.

2 Language focus

A How are Roberto's and Cindy's days
different from Marcia's? Listen and practice.

> **I go** home after my guitar lesson.
> **I don't go** home after school.
> ....
> *don't = do not*

> I don't go home after school.
> I go home after my guitar lesson.
> I don't watch TV after dinner.
> I do my homework.

Roberto – Brazil

> I don't go to school with my brother.
> I go to school with my friends.
> I don't eat dinner at 7:30.
> I eat dinner at 6:00.

Cindy – Australia

B How about you? Is your day like Marcia's day? Write sentences. *(Answers will vary.)*

    (get up at 6:00) *I get up at 6:00, too.* OR *I don't get up at 6:00. I get up at 7:00.*

1. (eat lunch with my friends) _____

2. (eat in the cafeteria) _____

3. (go home at 4:00) _____

4. (go to bed at 10:00) _____

C Now tell your classmates how your day is different from Marcia's day.

> I don't get up at 6:00. I get up at 7:00.

3 Listening

Claudia talks about her day. What does she say?
Listen and check (✓) the correct information.

1. I get up at   ☑ 7:00 a.m.   ☐ 8:00 a.m.
2. I go to school at   ☐ 8:30 a.m.   ☑ 9:00 a.m.
3. I eat lunch at   ☑ school.   ☐ home.
4. I go home at   ☐ 2:30.   ☑ 3:45.
5. I watch TV with   ☑ my brother.   ☐ my sister.

Free time

1 Vocabulary

A Who does these free-time activities? Write **K** (Kate), **R** (Rafael), or **A** (Ana). Then listen and practice.

I collect stamps. _R_	I listen to music. _A_	I take dance lessons. _A_
I hang out at the mall. _K_	I play video games. _R_	I use the Internet. _R_
I in-line skate. _K_	I talk on the phone. _K_	I watch videos and DVDs. _A_

Kate

Rafael

Ana

B What do you do in your free time? Write two things you do and two things you don't do. (Answer will vary

Things I do	Things I don't do
I...	I don't ...

Free time

*This lesson presents and practices the names of free-time activities popular
with teens and* Do you + (verb) . . . ?

Review of Lesson 5

- Write on the board: *do, eat, get, go,* and *watch.* Point to the verbs. Ask students to complete with verb phrases.

- Play a round of "Tic-Tac-Toe." Draw a grid on the board. Fill in each of the nine squares with the following verb phrases: *do my homework, eat breakfast, eat dinner, eat lunch, get up, go home, go to bed, go to school, watch TV.* Divide the class into two teams, X and O. Students earn squares for their team by using the verb phrases in sentences. The first team with three squares in a row wins.

- Ask several students to make a sentence about a part of their daily routine.

1   Vocabulary

**This exercise presents and practices the names of free-time activities popular
with teens.**

A 💿 CD1, Track 19

- Explain the title of the lesson, "Free time." (Time that is not spent working or studying.)

- Have students look at the photos of Kate, Rafael, and Ana. Ask students if they have similar free-time activities.

- Elicit as much language about the photos as possible.

- Have students read the sentences in the box above the photos. Students work individually to label the activities with the letters *K, R,* or *A.* Tell them to label *only* the sentences they are sure of.

- Play the recording. Students listen and verify their answers. They label any remaining sentences.

Audio script
See page T-202.

- Check answers with the class. Invite volunteers to read the sentences aloud. Tell the class to call out the appropriate letter, *K, R,* or *A.*

- Play the recording again, or model the sentences. Students listen and repeat.

B

- Have students read the directions and the sentence openers. Tell students they may choose from the activities in Part A or think of their own ideas.

- Have students work individually to complete the exercise.

- Check answers with the class. Invite volunteers to read aloud one positive and one negative sentence each. Write the activities on the board as students say them.

- Go through each activity and ask students to raise their hands if they do the activity. Tally the most and least popular free-time activities.

Culture Note   The most popular free-time activities for teens in 26 different countries are as follows: watching TV, being with friends, listening to music, listening to the radio, watching movies at home, going to the movies, going to parties, talking on the phone, and playing sports.

2 Language focus

This exercise presents and practices Do you + (verb) . . . ?

💿 CD1, Track 20

- Focus students' attention on the photo. Explain *survey*. Explain that Kate and Rafael take a survey about leisure activities. Ask students if they have ever completed a survey. Tell them that U.S. businesses use surveys to find out more about their customers.

- Have students read the conversation through once.

- **Language Chart** Have students study the examples in the language chart. Focus students' attention on the words in bold.

- Explain to students that *do* is a "helping" verb. It "helps" when we form a question and can take the place of the main verb in a short answer. Ask: *Where is* do *in the question?* (At the beginning of the sentence.) *What is the main verb in this question?* (Collect.) *Where is it?* (After the pronoun *you*.) Tell students that in the question form, the helping verb comes before the pronoun and the main verb comes after. Focus students' attention on the short answers. Ask: *Where is* do *in these two sentences?* (After the pronoun *I*.)

- Model the examples, pausing for students to repeat.

- Have students read the conversation again. Ask: *What words will go in the blanks?* (*Do*, the simple form of verbs, and short answers.) Tell students that some blanks will have two words in them – for example, *I do*.

- Have students work individually to complete the exercise.

- Play the recording. Students listen and verify their answers.

> ### Audio script
> Same as the conversation in the Student's Book.

- Check answers with the class. Invite volunteers to read aloud one sentence they completed.

- Have students practice the conversation in pairs.

- **Optional** Divide the class into two teams. Ask one student from each team to stand. Ask the first student to make a positive or negative statement about a free-time activity. Ask the other students to change that statement into a question. If the question is correct, give that student's team a point. Alternate turns. Give teams an equal number of turns.

3 Speaking

This exercise practices talking about free-time activities.

A

- Have students read the directions for Parts A and B and the survey in Part B. Invite volunteers to give ideas for questions 8 and 9. Have students write questions in the blanks.

B

- Have students complete the survey about themselves in the *You* column.

- Invite a volunteer to demonstrate the *Your classmate* portion of the task with you. Students then work in pairs to complete the exercise.

- **Optional** Play a guessing game. Invite a volunteer to come to the front. Tell the student to think of one of the free-time activities from the survey. Students take turns asking *Do you . . . ?* to guess the activity. The student who guesses correctly replaces the volunteer and continues the activity.

> ### Workbook
> Assign the exercises on Workbook page 10.
> (Workbook answers begin on page T-190.)

> ### Extra Grammar
> Assign the exercises for the Extra Grammar, Lesson 6.

2 Language focus

Kate and Rafael take a survey. Complete the conversation. Listen and check. Then practice.

Do you + (verb) . . . ?

Do you collect trading cards?
Yes, I do.
No, I don't.

Kate Oh, look! A survey!

Rafael Cool. Let's take it.

Kate Um, do you collect trading cards?

Rafael Yes, I do.

Kate OK . . . Do you take piano lessons?

Rafael No, I don't.

Kate _Do_ you _use_ the Internet?

Rafael Yes, _I do_ .

Kate _Do_ you _watch_ TV?

Rafael No, _I don't_ . But I watch videos.

Kate _Do_ you _listen_ to music?

Rafael _Yes_ , I do. My favorite singer is Jennifer Lopez.

Kate _Do_ you _play_ video games?

Rafael _Yes_ , _I do_ . I play video games every weekend.

3 Speaking

A Read the survey. Write questions 8 and 9 with your classmates. *(Answers will vary.)*

B Complete the survey for yourself. Then ask a classmate the questions. *(Answers will vary.)*

What do you do in your free time?	You		Your classmate	
	Yes	No	Yes	No
1. Do you use the Internet?	☐	☐	☐	☐
2. Do you collect stamps?	☐	☐	☐	☐
3. Do you listen to music?	☐	☐	☐	☐
4. Do you play video games?	☐	☐	☐	☐
5. Do you talk on the phone?	☐	☐	☐	☐
6. Do you hang out at the mall?	☐	☐	☐	☐
7. Do you collect trading cards?	☐	☐	☐	☐
8. _____	☐	☐	☐	☐
9. _____	☐	☐	☐	☐

Do you use the Internet?   No, I don't.

Our Lives and Routines 19

Mini-review

1 Language check

A Ricky writes about his day. What does he say? Write sentences.

6:30 a.m.
I get up at 6:30 a.m.

7:00 a.m.
I use the Internet at 7:00 a.m.

8:30 a.m.
I go to school at 8:30 a.m.

12:00 p.m.
I eat lunch at 12:00 p.m.

3:00 p.m.
I play basketball at 3:00 p.m.

5:30 p.m.
I go home at 5:30 p.m.

7:00 p.m.
I do my homework at 7:00 p.m.

9:00 p.m.
I read comic books at 9:00 p.m.

10:00 p.m.
I go to bed at 10:00 p.m.

B You are going to interview Ricky. Look at Part A, and write four questions you can ask. Then act out the interview with a classmate. *(Answers will vary.)*

1.	
2.	
3.	
4.	

You	Do you get up at 6:30 a.m.?
Classmate	Yes, I do.
You	Do you play basketball at 7:00 p.m.?
Classmate	No, I don't. I play basketball at 3:00 p.m.

This lesson reviews the language presented and practiced in Lessons 5 and 6.

1 Language check

This exercise reviews the structures presented so far in this unit.

A

- Have students look at the pictures. Elicit just the verb phrase to describe Ricky's activity in each picture.

- Say the times. Students respond with the corresponding verb phrases.

- Call out the verb phrases. Students respond with the corresponding times. (If further practice is necessary, drills may be continued with individual students. Conduct the drills first as a group so that students are confident and know what is expected.)

- Have students work individually to write what Ricky would say about each picture.

- Check answers with the class. Write the nine times on the board. Invite nine volunteers to come to the board to write one sentence each.

- **Optional** Draw two large faces on the board – one happy, one sad. Call two students to the front. Say: *I'm Ricky. I get up at 6:30 a.m.* If the statement is correct, the students touch the happy face. If it is not, they touch the sad face. The first student to touch the correct face gets a point. Do five sentences and then ask two other students to come up.

B

- Say: *I eat lunch at school. Ask me a* Yes / No *question.* (Do you eat lunch at school?) Continue with several more examples. Then ask random students to make statements for the class to convert into questions.

- Have students read the directions. Students work individually to write the questions.

- Check answers with the class. Invite volunteers to read their questions aloud.

- Have students ask and answer their questions in pairs, following the example.

- **Optional** Play a guessing game. Ask a volunteer to come to the front. The volunteer tells the class one aspect of his or her daily routine. Students try to guess the time of the activity, asking: *Do you _____ at _____ ?* The student who guesses correctly replaces the volunteer and continues the activity.

C

- Have students review the Language chart on page 19.
- Check that they understand the use of *do* in questions and short answers. Write these questions and answers on the board: *(Are / Do) you eat lunch at school? Yes, I (am / do). (Are / Do) you good at math? No, we (aren't / don't).* Invite two volunteers to come to the board and circle the correct words for each question and answer. Remind them that sentences with *be* as the main verb do not use *do* in the question or short answer.
- Have students read the conversation silently. Tell them not to write their answers at this time. Ask one or two comprehension questions: *Is Sally in the eighth grade?* (Yes.) *Does she play video games?* (No.)

- Have students work individually to complete the exercise.
- Check answers with the class. Invite two volunteers to read the conversation aloud.
- **Optional** Have students work in pairs to read the conversation.

Teaching Tip
When doing exercises based on texts such as conversations or paragraphs, it is a good idea to have students read the whole text before doing the exercise. This helps them focus on the meaning of the text as well as on the grammar.

2 Listening

In this exercise students listen for information about what teens do in their free time.

CD1, Track 21

- Tell students that they are going to listen to four teens talking about what they do in their free time.
- Have students read the directions and the items in the chart. Explain that they should listen and check the *Yes* or the *No* box for each person and activity.
- Play the recording. Students only listen.

Audio script
See page T-202.

- Play the recording again. Pause the recording after Sylvia says *In my free time, I read comic books.* Point out the check mark in the *Yes* box under Sylvia's name next to *Read comic books.*

- Continue playing the recording. Students listen and complete the exercise.
- Play the recording once again. Students listen and verify their answers.
- Check answers with the class. Invite volunteers to read their answers aloud.

Workbook
Assign the exercises on Workbook page 11. (Workbook answers begin on page T-190.)

Game
Assign the game on Student's Book page 115.

C Circle the correct words to complete the conversation.

Carlos Hi, I'm Carlos.

Sally Hi, Carlos. My name's Sally.

Carlos Can I ask you questions for a survey?

Sally Uh, yeah.

Carlos (**Are** / Do) you in the 8th grade?

Sally Yes, I (**am** / do).

Carlos (Are / **Do**) you collect things?

Sally Yes, I (**do** / am). I collect stamps.

Carlos (Are / **Do**) you play video games after school?

Sally No, (I'm not / **I don't**). I listen to music.

Carlos Oh, who's your favorite singer?

Sally Well, I like Kylie Minogue, but (I'm not / **I don't**) like Clay Aiken.

2 Listening

Sylvia, Kenji, Adam, and Cindy talk about their free time. Listen and check (✓) Yes or No.

1.	Sylvia	
	Yes	**No**
Read comic books	✓	
In-line skate	✓	
Hang out at the mall		✓
Take dance lessons		✓

2.	Kenji	
	Yes	**No**
Play video games	✓	
Collect stamps	✓	
Collect trading cards	✓	
Talk on the phone		✓

3.	Adam	
	Yes	**No**
Take piano lessons	✓	
Play soccer	✓	
Hang out at the mall		✓
Read books	✓	

4.	Cindy	
	Yes	**No**
Use the Internet	✓	
Watch DVDs		✓
Play tennis	✓	
Talk on the phone		✓

Go to page 115 for the Game.

People I admire

1 Vocabulary

Tommy admires his brother, Jordan. What does Jordan say about his life? Match the photos to the correct sentences. Then listen and practice.

5 I go to concerts every Saturday.

6 I have a piano, a bass, and an electric keyboard.

1 I live in an apartment.

3 I play in a jazz band.

4 I practice the piano every day.

2 I work at Bradley Music School.
I teach music to high school students.

2 Language focus

A Read what Tommy says. Study the language chart. Then listen and practice.

My brother, Jordan, is great. He works at Bradley Music School. He teaches the piano to students from all over the world. Jordan has a piano in his apartment, and he practices every day. At night, he plays in jazz clubs. He really loves music!

Simple present statements with *I / he / she*					
With *he* and *she*, add -s or -es to most verbs.					Exception:
I live	I work	I teach	I do	I go	I have
he lives	he works	he teaches	he does	he goes	he has
she lives	she works	she teaches	she does	she goes	she has

Lesson 7 — People I admire

This lesson presents and practices some verbs commonly used in the simple present, and simple present statements with I / he / she.

> **Review of Lesson 6**
> - Write these sentence stems on the board in a column: *I play ___. I watch ___. I listen to ___. I take ___ lessons. I hang out at ___. I collect ___.*
> - Have students work in pairs to write as many endings as they can for each stem, for example: *I play the guitar. I play soccer.* Encourage them to think of original ideas that are not in the book but that use vocabulary they know, such as *I take French lessons* or *I hang out at my friend's house.*
> - For each stem, invite volunteers to read their endings aloud. Write them on the board.

1 Vocabulary

This exercise presents and practices some verbs commonly used in the simple present.

💿 **CD1, Track 22**

- Explain the title of the lesson, "People I admire." Ask volunteers to tell the class whom they admire and why.
- Have students read the directions and look at the photos. Ask: *What subject does Jordan like a lot?* (Music.)
- Ask students to read the statements below the photos. Explain the meaning of any words that students are unsure of.
- Have students work individually to match the photos and the statements.
- Play the recording. Students listen and verify their answers.

Audio script
See page T-202.

- Check answers with the class.
- Play the recording again, or model the sentences. Students listen and repeat.

2 Language focus

This exercise presents and practices simple present statements with I / he / she.

A 💿 **CD1, Track 23**

- Have students read through the text once. Ask: *Who is Tommy talking about?* (His brother, Jordan.) *Does Tommy like his brother?* (Yes.) *What do you notice about the endings of the verbs?* (The verbs have *-s* or *-es* at the end.)
- Play the recording. Students listen and read along.

Audio script
Same as the text in the Student's Book.

- Play the recording again, or model the sentences. Students listen and repeat.

- **Language Chart** Have students study the examples in the language chart. Explain that with *he* and *she*, we add *-s* or *-es* to the simple form of most verbs. (If a verb ends in *s, x, z, sh,* or *ch, -es* is added to the verb.) However, an exception is *have*, which becomes *has* with *he* and *she*.
- Model the examples, pausing for students to repeat.
- Say *work*. Students respond with *works*. Continue until you have practiced each verb at least once. Continue the drill with individual students if extra practice is needed.

Our Lives and Routines T-22

B 🎧 CD1, Track 24

- Have students read the directions and the text. Remind students that they will have to change the verbs in parentheses to go with *he*. Tell them that they may refer back to the language chart on page 22 to check spelling.
- Have students work individually to do the exercise.
- Play the recording. Students listen and verify their answers.

- Check answers with the class. Ask two or three students to stand and read the passage aloud, alternating sentences.
- **Optional** Play "Fill in the Blanks." Write *goes, has, lives, teaches,* and *works* on the board. Say these sentences, pausing or saying *Blank* where students fill in the appropriate verb: *Ms. Mills _____ math.* (Teaches.) *His father _____ in a bank.* (Works.) *Maria _____ in a big apartment.* (Lives.) *Paul _____ a dog and a cat.* (Has.) *The student _____ to school very early.* (Goes.)
- For large classes, play this as a competition, dividing the class into teams and keeping score of correct answers.

3 Listening

In this exercise, students listen for information to determine whether statements are true or false.

🎧 CD1, Track 25

- Have students look at the photo. Ask: *Who is this?* (Caroline Zhang, a figure skater.)
- Elicit any facts students know about Caroline Zhang.
- Invite a volunteer to read the directions aloud.
- Play the recording. Students only listen.

- Play the recording again. Students listen and complete the exercise.
- Play the recording once again. Students listen and verify their answers.

- Check answers with the class. Invite volunteers to read the sentences and say whether they are true or false.

Teaching Tip

A common classroom problem is that students don't listen to each other. When you are correcting an exercise by calling on individual students, don't correct their answers immediately. First, ask another student. Say, for example: *Alex, do you agree with Maria's answer?* If the student says he or she did not hear the answer, do not repeat it yourself. Instead, say: *Maria, would you please repeat that?* Doing this will encourage your students to pay attention to each other as well as to you.

4 Pronunciation -*s* endings

In this exercise, students practice the pronunciation of -*s* endings.

A 🎧 CD1, Track 26

- Focus students' attention on the words in the chart.
- Explain that an -*s* ending is pronounced differently depending on the ending sound of the word:
  – If the word ends in a *voiceless* consonant, the ending is pronounced /s/.
  – If it ends in a *voiced* consonant or a vowel, the ending is pronounced /z/. (Tell students that they will feel a buzzing feeling if they touch the front of their throats when saying *voiced* consonants or vowels. When saying voiceless consonants, there is no buzzing feeling.)
  – If a verb ends in *s, x, z, sh,* or *ch, -es* is added to the verb. The -*es* ending is pronounced /ɪz/.
- Play the recording. Have students listen, paying close attention to the pronunciation of the -*s* endings.

- Play the recording again. Students listen and repeat.

B 🎧 CD1, Track 27

- Tell students that they will hear six verbs. They should write the verbs in the chart according to the pronunciation of the -*s* ending. Play the recording. Students only listen.

- Play the recording again. Students listen and write the words in the chart.
- Play the recording once again. Students listen and verify their answers.
- Check answers with the class.

Workbook

Assign the exercises on Workbook page 12. (Workbook answers begin on page T-190.)

Extra Grammar

Assign the exercises for the Extra Grammar, Lesson 7.

B Tommy also admires Esteban Cortazar. Complete Tommy's text with the correct forms of the verbs. Then listen and check.

I admire Esteban Cortazar. He's from Colombia, but he ___lives___ (live) in Miami. Esteban is a fashion designer. He's talented, and he ___works___ (work) hard. He ___makes___ (make) clothes for department stores. He ___goes___ (go) to fashion shows, and he sees his own clothing!

3 Listening

Caroline Zhang is a famous skating star. Are these sentences true or false about her? Listen and write *T* (true) or *F* (false).

1. Caroline Zhang is American. ___T___
2. She has a sister. ___T___
3. She lives with her family in New York. ___F___
4. She practices four days a week. ___F___
5. She plays the piano and the violin. ___T___
6. Her favorite singer is Jennifer Lopez. ___F___

4 Pronunciation -s endings

A Listen. Notice the -s endings. Then listen again and practice.

s = /s/	s = /z/	s = /ɪz/
takes	plays	practices
collects	goes	guesses

B Listen. Write these verbs in the correct columns: *lives, works, teaches, eats, watches,* and *has.* (*The order of the answers may vary.*)

s = /s/	s = /z/	s = /ɪz/
works	lives	teaches
eats	has	watches

The weekend

1 Vocabulary

A What do you do on the weekend? Check (✓) the correct boxes. Then listen and practice. *(Answers will vary.)*

1. ☐ I sleep late.
   ☐ I don't sleep late.

2. ☐ I eat out with my family.
   ☐ I don't eat out with my family.

3. ☐ I stay up late.
   ☐ I don't stay up late.

4. ☐ I go out on Friday night.
   ☐ I don't go out on Friday night.

5. ☐ I go to the movies.
   ☐ I don't go to the movies.

6. ☐ I stay home on Sunday.
   ☐ I don't stay home on Sunday.

B Tell your classmates about your weekend. Use sentences from Part A.

> I sleep late. I eat out with my family. I don't . . .

2 Language focus

A Ana and her sister, Clara, do different things on the weekend. Listen and practice.

My sister and I are very different. On the weekend, I go out with my friends. I go to the movies, or I go to a concert. Clara doesn't go out at all. She stays home and watches videos. On Sunday, I don't sleep late. I get up at 7:30 a.m. Clara sleeps late. She gets up at 10:30 a.m.

doesn't

She doesn't go out on Friday night.
Clara doesn't go out at all.

doesn't = does not

Lesson 8 The weekend

This lesson presents and practices the names of common weekend activities and *doesn't*.

Review of Lesson 7

- Write on the board: *go / goes, live / lives, have / has, play / plays, watch / watches, talk / talks*. Ask students for other examples. Write them on the board.
- Ask a random student (Classmate 1) to stand and choose Classmate 2. Classmate 1 makes a sentence about a daily or favorite activity using *I*: *I play soccer every Saturday*. Classmate 2 converts the statement into a sentence about Classmate 1: *(Ricardo) plays soccer every Saturday*. Repeat several times with different students.
- Erase the verbs from the board. Call two or three volunteers to the board. Give each student chalk or a whiteboard marker. Say one of the verbs with its -*s* ending. The first student to write the verb correctly gets a point. Say ten verbs. The student with the most points wins.

1 Vocabulary

This exercise presents and practices the names of common weekend activities.

A CD1, Track 28

- Ask: *Which days are considered the weekend?* (Friday night, Saturday, and Sunday.) Tell students that the other days, Monday morning to Friday afternoon, are called *weekdays*. Ask: *How are your routines different on the weekdays and the weekends?*
- Have students study the pictures and read the sentences.
- Ask students to check each sentence that describes *their own* weekend routine. Students work individually to complete the exercise.
- Have students compare their answers in pairs.
- Play the recording. Students listen and read along.

Audio script

Same as the sentences in the Student's Book.

- Play the recording again, or model the sentences. Students listen and repeat.
- **Optional** Read the sentences one by one. After each sentence, ask how many students checked it. Do a quick tally to find out which routines are the most popular in the class.

B

- Have students read the directions and the example. Invite volunteers to stand and tell the class about their weekends, using sentences from Part A and following the example.

2 Language focus

This exercise presents and practices *doesn't*.

A CD1, Track 29

- Ask students to raise their hands if they have brothers or sisters. Ask several students if they enjoy the same weekend activities as their siblings.
- Focus students' attention on the photo. Explain that it shows Ana and her sister, Clara. Tell students they will listen to Ana describing their weekend routines.
- Play the recording. Students listen and read along.

Audio script

Same as the text in the Student's Book.

- Ask: *Are Ana and her sister the same?* (No. They're different.) Say the following sentences. Students call out *Yes* if the sentence is correct and *No* if it is not.

Clara goes out every weekend. (No.)
Ana doesn't stay home. (Yes.)
Ana and Clara watch videos together. (No.)
Clara sleeps late, but Ana doesn't. (Yes.)

- Play the recording again, or model the sentences. Students listen and repeat.
- **Language Chart** Have students study the examples in the language chart. Focus students' attention on the contraction *doesn't*. Ask: *What is the full form of* doesn't? (Does not.) Point out that the verb after *does* and *doesn't* is the simple form (it has no -*s* ending). Also point out that we only use *does / doesn't* for the pronouns *he, she,* and *it*. Ask: *What do we use for* I, you, we, *and* they? (Do / don't.)
- Model the examples, pausing for students to repeat.

B

- Focus students' attention on the photos. Tell them that Rafael and Luis are brothers. Ask: *Do Rafael and Luis like the same activities?* (No.)

- Have students read the sentences. Answer any questions about the vocabulary.

- Have students work individually to decide if the sentences are true or false and to complete the exercise.

- Check answers with the class.

C CD1, Track 30

- Have students read the directions and the example.

- Have students work individually to correct the false sentences in Part B.

- Play the recording. Students listen and verify their answers.

Audio script

Same as the sentences in the Student's Book.

- Check answers with the class. Ask volunteers to come to the board to write one answer each.

- Play the recording again, or model the sentences. Students listen and repeat.

3 Speaking

This exercise practices *Do you . . . ?* and *doesn't*.

A

- Have students read the directions for Parts A and B and the survey in Part B. Invite volunteers to give ideas for questions 7 and 8. Have students write questions in the two blanks.

B

- Tell students that they will do the survey with a partner. Ask: *What are the two possible responses to each question?* (Yes, I do or No, I don't.) Students work in pairs asking each other the questions and checking either a *Yes* or a *No* box for each question, according to their partner's response.

C

- Invite volunteers to report their survey findings to the class, following the example.

- **Optional** Play verb-phrase "Bingo." Have students draw a bingo grid on a piece of paper. Write these 12 verb phrases on the board: *goes out, sleeps late, stays up late, stays home, teaches math, practices the piano, does homework, has a guitar, works at a bank, lives in the U.S., talks on the phone, plays video games.* Students choose nine phrases and write them in the nine spaces on their grids. Call out any nine of the verb phrases in random order. (Keep track of which phrases you have called. You will need to check answers later.) The first student with three in a row calls out *Bingo!* To check the student's answers, have the student read the three phrases that were in a row.

Workbook

Assign the exercises on Workbook page 13. (Workbook answers begin on page T-190.)

Extra Grammar

Assign the exercises for the Extra Grammar, Lesson 8.

B Rafael and his brother, Luis, are different, too. Look at the photos. Are these sentences true or false? Write *T* (true) or *F* (false).

1. Luis goes out with his parents. __F__
2. Luis goes to concerts. __F__
3. Rafael stays home. __T__
4. Rafael goes to bed early. __F__
5. Rafael watches videos in the living room. __F__
6. Luis likes popcorn. __T__

C Correct the false sentences in Part B. Then listen and check.

1. _Luis doesn't go out with his parents._
   He goes out with his friends.
2. _Luis doesn't go to concerts._
   He goes to the movies.
3. _Rafael doesn't go to bed early._
   He goes to bed late.
4. _Rafael doesn't watch videos in the living_
   room. He watches videos in his bedroom.

11:30 p.m.

Rafael

Luis

3 Speaking

A Read the survey. Write questions 7 and 8 with your classmates. *(Answers will vary.)*

B Ask a classmate the questions. *(Answers to the questions will vary.)*

What do you do on the weekend?	Your classmate	
	Yes	No
1. Do you sleep late?	☐	☐
2. Do you stay home?	☐	☐
3. Do you go to the movies?	☐	☐
4. Do you do your homework?	☐	☐
5. Do you go out with friends?	☐	☐
6. Do you play video games?	☐	☐
7. _____	☐	☐
8. _____	☐	☐

C Tell the class about your classmate's weekend activities.

Carla eats out. She doesn't sleep late. She . . .

Get Connected

UNIT 2

Read

A Read the article quickly. Check (✓) the words you find.

☑ answers ☐ eats ☑ has ☑ helps ☐ lives ☐ lunch ☑ makes ☑ takes ☐ works

Quizlet

Do you have quizzes in school? Are they fun? If not, **check out** the quizzes on *Quizlet* – a cool Web site with lots of quizzes. *Quizlet* makes learning vocabulary words fun and exciting. And it's free!

The quizzes on *Quizlet* help students **review** languages (like Japanese, Spanish, and Korean) and school subjects (like history, biology, and math). The quizzes are like games, so they're fun to do. Many students use *Quizlet* – over 130,000 students in 14 months!

Andrew Sutherland is the **creator** of *Quizlet*. *Quizlet* is so popular now, Andrew has a **company**, too. Its name is Brainflare. It helps him with important things, like **marketing** and computer **software** questions about *Quizlet*. Andrew is really great – he answers all the Web site **messages** from hundreds of people every week. It takes a lot of time, but it's important to him.

Go to page 122 for the **Vocabulary Practice.**

B 💿 Read the article slowly. Check your answers in Part A.

C Are these statements true or false? Write *True* or *False*. Then correct the false statements.

1. *Quizlet* makes learning fun and exciting. *True.* _____

2. The quizzes on *Quizlet* are for languages only. *False.* *They're for school subjects, too.*

3. Many teachers use *Quizlet*. *False.* *Many students use Quizlet.*

4. Andrew has a company, too. *True.* _____

5. He answers 50 messages every week. *False.* *He answers hundreds of messages each week.*

This lesson practices reading, listening, and writing skills.

Review of Lesson 8

- Call out: *he, sleep late, Sunday morning.* Students respond with the complete negative statement: *He doesn't sleep late on Sunday morning.* Continue the activity several times using the verb phrases from Lesson 8. For extra practice, continue the activity on an individual basis.
- Say the following sentences: *He stays home on Sunday. She eats out with her family. My sister sleeps late. Her brother goes to the movies. The teacher goes out on Friday night.* Students convert each sentence into a negative statement.
- Ask random students to stand. Ask the students to tell the class something that they do not do on the weekend: *I don't ____ .* The class converts the negative statement into the third person singular: *He / She / doesn't ____ .* For extra practice, continue the activity on an individual basis.

Read

This exercise practices reading for information about a Web site or quizzes.

A

- Have students look at the photo. Explain that this young man created a Web site with a lot of quizzes to make learning fun for students and to help kids do homework.

Culture Note Computers have become an important educational tool in and out of the classroom. In 2007, 87 percent of U.S. teens between the ages of 12 and 17 used the Internet. Of these, 51 percent went online every day. As a result, there are now many Web sites that offer students help with homework and research. Some of these sites just provide links to Web sites that have the information students need. Many, like the Web site in this article, provide practice exercises and tests in different subjects. Others actually provide live tutors to help students with homework in real time.

- Write the word *quiz* on the board and ask: *What is a quiz?* (It's a short test.) Then write *quizlet* on the board and say that a *quizlet* is a made-up word for a short quiz. Tell students that they are going to read an article about an unusual Web site with a lot of quizzes on it.

- Invite a volunteer to read aloud the directions and the words in the box. Remind students that they should read quickly to find the answers and that they should not read every word carefully.

- Have students work individually to read the article quickly and check the words. Do not check answers at this point.

B 🔊 CD1, Track 31

- Invite a volunteer to read the directions aloud. Remind students that they should read slowly and carefully, and concentrate on getting the meaning of the entire text.

- List the new vocabulary words on the board: *check out, review (v.), creator, company, marketing, software, message.* Explain their meaning. (Check out: to find out about; review [v.]: to study, read, or look at again; creator: the first person to think of and make something new – for example, Walt Disney was the creator of Mickey Mouse; company: a business, usually with a boss and workers; marketing: part of a company or group that makes advertisements and thinks about how to sell things; software: the programs for a computer; message: a note – for example, a note sent over the Internet is an e-mail message.) As an alternative, have students use their dictionaries to find the meanings of the new vocabulary words.

- Have students read the article again.

- Have students check their answers in Part A in pairs. Elicit the answers from one pair.

- **Optional** Play the recording. Students listen and read along.

Audio script
Same as the article in the Student's Book.

Get Connected Vocabulary
Have students do the exercise on Student's Book page 122 in class or for homework. (Get Connected Vocabulary answers are on page T-122.)

C

- Invite a volunteer to read the directions, the first statement, and the example answer aloud.

- Have students work individually to write *True* or *False* and then correct the false statements.

- Check answers with the class. Invite volunteers to read aloud one answer each.

Listen

In this exercise, students listen for information about schedules.

A 💿 CD1, Track 32

- Focus students' attention on the photo. Ask: *Where are these teens?* (In the library.)
- Tell students that they will listen to two friends, Ben and Julia, talk about their schedules.
- Have students read the first statement and the checked answer.
- Explain that students should listen to the conversation and check the correct words.
- Play the recording. Students only listen.

> ### Audio script
> See page T-203.

- Play the recording again. Students listen and check the correct words.
- Play the recording once again. Students listen and verify their answers.
- Check answers with the class. Read the first part of each statement and invite a volunteer to say the correct answer.

B

- Have students read the directions and all the statements.
- Explain that *I agree* means you think something is right, *I disagree* means you think something is not right, and *I'm not sure* means you cannot say if you think it is right or not. Tell students that there are no right or wrong answers for this exercise – they are giving their opinions.
- Have students work individually to write whether they agree, disagree, or are not sure.
- Have students work in pairs to compare answers, or elicit opinions from volunteers.
- **Optional** Take a class poll. Read each statement and ask for a show of hands. Say: *Raise your hand if you agree. Now raise your hand if you disagree. Now raise your hand if you're not sure*. Record the results in a chart on the board.

Write

In this exercise students complete an organizational web and write about an interesting person.

A

- Focus students' attention on the words in the box. Review the words.
- Copy the web onto the board. Complete it for your own interesting person.
- Have students work individually to complete the word web.
- **Optional** Have students share their webs in pairs before they write their paragraphs.

B

- Invite a volunteer to read the directions aloud. Tell students that they will use the ideas in their web in Part A to help them write about an interesting person.
- Have students work individually to write their paragraph.
- Invite several volunteers to read their paragraphs to the class.
- **Optional** Have students work in pairs to exchange paragraphs. Tell them to help their partners think of two more sentences to add about their person.

> ### Workbook
> Assign the exercises on Workbook page 14.
> (Workbook answers begin on page T-190.)

We can study together.

A 💿 **Julia and Ben talk about their schedules. Listen and check (✓) the correct words.**

1. Ben has a lot of   ☐ homework.   ☑ quizzes.
2. Ben doesn't have   ☑ a Spanish   ☐ an English quiz on Wednesday.
3. On Monday Julia has   ☐ dance class.   ☑ soccer practice.
4. On Tuesday Julia doesn't have any   ☐ homework.   ☑ extra classes.
5. Julia doesn't like   ☑ math.   ☐ English.

B **What do you think? Write *I agree, I disagree,* or *I'm not sure.*** *(Answers will vary.)*

1. Quizzes are fun. _____

2. It's good to use computers in class. _____

3. It's good to study with classmates. _____

4. Math is important. _____

Your turn

Write

A **Think of a person who does interesting things. Use the words in the box or your own ideas to complete the web about one person.** *(Answers will vary.)*

| collect eat go hang out have play read take use watch work write |

uses cool software

plays the piano

Julia

Ben

takes extra classes

studies English and Spanish

_____ (name)

B **Write a paragraph about an interesting person. Use your ideas in Part A to help you.** *(Answers will vary.)*

_____ does a lot of interesting things. He _____

_____

_____

_____

Language chart review

Simple present		
Statements: *I / He / She*	**Yes / No questions:** *Do you . . . ?*	**Short answers**
I take piano lessons. **I don't take** violin lessons. **He lives** in an apartment. **He doesn't live** in a house. **She gets up** late. **She doesn't get up** early.	**Do you take** piano lessons?	**Yes, I do.** **No, I don't.**
doesn't = does not		

A **Carly writes a fan letter to Enrique Iglesias. Complete Carly's letter and Enrique's reply. Use the verbs in the box.**

do	don't live	have	live
doesn't have	has		listens to	sing

Dear Enrique,

How are you? This letter is from my grandmother and me. I ___have___ all your CDs. My grandmother ___doesn't have___ your CDs, but she ___has___ all of your father's music. Your father, Julio, is her favorite singer. She ___listens to___ his music every day. Can you please answer some questions?

___Do___ you ___live___ in Spain? ___Do___ you ___have___ any brothers and sisters? ___Do___ you ___sing___ in English and in Spanish?

You're the best!

Love,
Carly

Dear Carly,

Hi! Here are pictures of my dad and me. No, I ___don't live___ in Spain. I ___live___ in the U.S. – in Miami, Florida. Yes, I ___have___ a big family. I have two brothers and three sisters! Yes, I ___sing___ in English and in Spanish.

Thanks for your letter! And thanks to your grandmother, too!

Enrique

Unit 2 Review

This lesson reviews the grammar and vocabulary introduced in Unit 2.

Language chart review

This chart summarizes the main grammar presented and practiced in Unit 2.

- Books closed. Write on the board:

	get up early	not get up late
I		
She		
He		
Do you get up early? __	Do you get up late? __	

- Focus students' attention on the chart on the board. Have students make an affirmative and a negative sentence for each pronoun using the verb phrases at the top of the chart. Then have students answer the questions at the bottom of the chart with short answers.
- Invite volunteers to come to the board to write their sentences and short answers.
- Books open. Have students check their sentences against the sentences in the language chart review.
- Invite volunteers to make simple present statements about their daily routines or habits.
- Answer any questions students may have.

Exercises A through C (pages T-28 to T-29)

Note: Students can do these exercises for homework or in class. They should do these exercises with minimal teacher input or help. If you choose to do these exercises as homework, briefly review the exercise directions in class. Make sure that students understand what they should do. Check the answers with the class during the next class meeting. If you choose to do the exercises in class, follow the directions below.

Exercise A

- Have students read the directions and look at the photos.
- Focus students' attention on the words in the box.
- Have students work individually to complete their letters.
- Check answers with the class. Invite volunteers to read their letters aloud.

Exercise B

- Have students read the directions. Explain that there are two parts to the task. First, students write *Do you* questions using the words in parentheses. Then, they write short answers to the questions.
- Have students work individually to write sentences using the words in parentheses.
- Have students work individually to write short answers to the questions using their own information.
- Check answers with the class.
- Have students ask and answer the questions in pairs.

Exercise C

- Have students read the directions.
- Tell students to read the paragraph and then correct the sentences.
- Have students work individually to complete the exercise.
- Have students check their answers in pairs.
- Check answers with the class. Invite volunteers to read aloud one corrected sentence each.

Optional Unit Wrap-Up

- If students did the Review exercises for homework, check answers with the class.
- Have students work in pairs. Classmate 1 thinks of a famous person to pretend to be. Classmate 2 asks the questions in Exercise B to Classmate 1 and tries to guess who Classmate 1 is, based on his / her answers.
- Have students work individually to write five sentences about themselves similar to those in the paragraph about Antonio Burgos in Exercise C. Three sentences should be false and two sentences should be true. Students should write the sentences on a single piece of paper and put their name at the top of the paper.
- Collect the papers and then redistribute them around the class. Students mark the sentences on their papers as *T* (true) or *F* (false) and correct the false sentences. (If they are not sure, they should guess.)
- Have students return the papers to the original writers. Those students then tell them if their guesses are right or wrong.

Theme Project

- Assign the *At Home* section of the Unit 2 Theme Project on Student's Book page 127.

Workbook

- Assign the Unit 2 Check Yourself on Workbook page 15. (Workbook answers begin on page T-190.)

Extra Practice Worksheets

- Assign the Unit 2 Extra Practice worksheets starting on page T-140.

Extra Speaking Practice Worksheet

- Assign the Unit 2 Extra Speaking Practice worksheet on page T-166.

Arcade Activities

- Assign the Unit 2 Arcade activities found at: www.cambridge.org/connectarcade

Learning Log

- Assign the Unit 2 Learning Log. These can be downloaded from the Teacher Support Site at: www.cambridge.org/connect2e/teacher

Quiz

- Give the Unit 2 Quiz on page T-177.

Test

- Give the Unit 2 Test (Form A and / or Form B). These can be downloaded from the Teacher Support Site at: www.cambridge.org/connect2e/teacher

B **Write *Do you* questions. Use Part A to help you. Then write short answers using your own information.**

1. (live / Spain)

   Q: _Do you live in Spain?_   **A:** _Yes, I do._ OR _No, I don't._

2. (listen / CDs)

   Q: _Do you listen to CDs?_   **A:** _(Answers will vary.)_

3. (have / brothers and sisters)

   Q: _Do you have any brothers and sisters?_   **A:** _(Answers will vary.)_

4. (sing / songs in English)

   Q: _Do you sing songs in English?_   **A:** _(Answers will vary.)_

C **Read about Antonio. Then correct the sentences.**

I'm Antonio Burgos. I live in Buenos Aires, Argentina, with my parents and my little sister, Monica. I go to a small school in the city. My first language is Spanish, but I speak English, too. In my free time, I play video games and listen to music. I don't like rap music very much, but I love rock. On weekends, I hang out at the park with my friends, but I eat dinner with my family.

1. Antonio lives in the United States.

   Antonio doesn't live in the United States. He lives in Argentina.

2. He has a little brother.

   He doesn't have a little brother. He has a little sister.

3. He speaks French and Portuguese.

   He doesn't speak French and Portuguese. He speaks Spanish and English.

4. Antonio plays soccer and watches TV.

   Antonio doesn't play soccer and watch TV. He plays video games and listens to music.

5. He likes rap music.

   He doesn't like rap music very much. He loves rock music.

6. He hangs out at the mall on weekends.

   He doesn't hang out at the mall on weekends. He hangs out at the park with his friends.

Go to page 127 for the Theme Project.

Sports fun

1 Vocabulary

A Who does these sports, Claudia or Zach? Listen and write C (Claudia) or Z (Zach).

I surf. __Z__

I do karate. __C__

I skateboard. __Z__

I go biking. __C__

I water-ski. __Z__

I play baseball. __Z__

I swim. __C__

I ski. __Z__

B Listen and practice.

C What sports do you do? What sports don't you do? Write sentences.
(Answers will vary.)

Sports I do	Sports I don't do
I skateboard.	I don't ski.

Lesson 9 Sports fun

This lesson presents and practices the names of sports popular with teens and Does he / she . . . ?

1 Vocabulary

This exercise presents and practices the names of sports popular with teens.

A 💿 CD1, Track 33

- Focus students' attention on the photos. Explain that these are some of the sports American teens like to do. Ask students to raise their hands if they do any of these sports.

- Write *surf, karate, skateboard, biking, water-ski, baseball, swim,* and *ski* on the board. Model the new words. Students listen and repeat.

- Number the words on the board from 1 to 8. Call out the words. Students respond with the corresponding numbers.

- Tell students that Claudia and Zach are athletic and both enjoy sports. Explain that they will listen to a conversation between Claudia and Zach about the sports they like. Students should listen and decide who likes each sport.

- Play the recording. Students only listen.

Audio script
See page T-203.

- Play the recording again. Students listen and write the appropriate initial (*C* for Claudia or *Z* for Zach) in the spaces provided.

- Play the recording once again. Students listen and verify their answers.

- Check answers with the class. Invite volunteers to read their answers aloud. Write their answers next to the corresponding sport on the board.

B 💿 CD1, Track 34

- Play the recording. Students listen and repeat.

Audio script
See page T-203.

C

- Have students read the directions and the examples. Students write three sentences about sports they do and three sentences about sports they do not do. Remind students that *karate, biking,* and *baseball* are not verbs and will need the verbs *do, go,* and *play* to precede them.

- Have students compare their answers in pairs.

- Invite several students to share their sentences with the class.

Culture Note In the U.S., the most popular sports for teenagers between the ages of 12 and 17 are bicycle riding, swimming, basketball, camping, football, bowling, fishing, volleyball, baseball, and softball.

This unit introduces vocabulary and expressions for talking about sports, camping, and sporting goods.

2 Language focus

This exercise presents and practices *Does he / she . . . ?*

A 💿 CD1, Track 35

- Focus students' attention on the top photo. Explain that Claudia and Zach are talking about a new student in school.
- Play the recording. Students listen and read along.

> **Audio script**
> Same as the conversation in the Student's Book.

- Ask: *What's the new student's name?* (Chris.) *Does Chris like sports?* (No.) *Can he use a computer?* (Yes.)
- Play the recording again, or model the conversation. Students listen and repeat.
- **Optional** Have students practice in pairs.
- **Language Chart** Have students study the examples in the language chart. Focus students' attention on the words in bold. Explain to students that *do* is a "helping" verb. *Do* has no meaning when it is used as a helping verb without a main verb. We cannot make a question with the helping verb alone. Ask: *Where is* does *in the question?* (At the beginning of the question, before the pronoun *he*.) *How about in the short answer form?* (After the pronoun.) *Do we repeat the main verb in a short answer?* (No, we don't.)
- Model the examples, pausing for students to repeat.

B 💿 CD1, Track 36

- Focus students' attention on the bottom photo. Ask: *Who is in the picture?* (Chris, Zach, and Claudia.) *What sport is Claudia playing?* (Basketball.) *Is she good at basketball?* (Yes.)
- Have students work individually to complete the conversation.
- Play the recording. Students listen and verify their answers.

> **Audio script**
> Same as the conversation in the Student's Book.

- Check answers with the class. Invite volunteers to read one of the completed sentences they wrote.
- Have students practice the conversation in pairs.

3 Pronunciation Intonation

In this exercise, students practice the rising intonation of *Yes / No* questions.

💿 CD1, Track 37

- Explain the concept of rising intonation. Explain that in English, *Yes / No* questions have rising intonation but *Wh-* questions do not. Focus students' attention on the questions and the arrows.
- Play the recording. Students listen. Tell them to pay special attention to the rising intonation at the end of each question.

> **Audio script**
> Same as the questions in the Student's Book.

- Play the recording again. Students listen and repeat.
- Ask volunteers to give more examples of *Yes / No* questions with rising intonation.

4 Speaking

This exercise practices *Yes / No* questions and short answers.

- Have students read the directions and the example questions and answers.
- Model the activity by telling students that you are thinking of a sports star. Students ask you questions as in the examples and try to guess the star.
- Continue by inviting a volunteer to think of a sports star. Students ask *Yes / No* questions until someone guesses the star. Continue until students have guessed three or four sports stars.
- **Optional** Set a limit of ten questions (or fewer) for each star. If classmates do not guess in ten questions, the student tells them the name. This will keep the activity moving more quickly.

Note: For large classes, divide the class into small groups.

> **Teaching Tip** When playing games in class, keep the activity short and make sure it moves quickly. This keeps interest high.

> **Workbook**
> Assign the exercises on Workbook page 16. (Workbook answers begin on page T-190.)

> **Extra Grammar**
> Assign the exercises for the Extra Grammar, Lesson 9.

2 Language focus

A Claudia and Zach talk about a new student. Listen and practice.

> **Does he / she . . . ?**
>
> **Does he do** karate?
> **Yes, he does.**
> **No, he doesn't.**

Claudia Hey, that guy's new. Who is he?
Zach That's Chris.
Claudia Does he like sports?
Zach Well, . . .
Claudia Does he do karate?
Zach No, he doesn't.
Claudia Does he play baseball?
Zach No, he doesn't.
Claudia Does he surf?
Zach Uh . . . yes, he does. He surfs the Internet!

B Chris and Zach talk about Claudia. Complete the conversation. Listen and check. Then practice.

Chris Wow! Your friend Claudia is good at basketball. ___Does___ she play other sports?
Zach ___Yes___ , she does. She's very athletic.
Chris ___Does___ she play soccer?
Zach Yes, she ___does___ . She likes it very much.
Chris ___Does___ she have a gym partner?
Zach No, she ___doesn't___ .
Chris Hey, maybe she can be my partner! She can help me!

3 Pronunciation Intonation

Listen. Notice the rising intonation in *Yes / No* questions. Then listen again and practice.

Does he swim?   Does he surf?   Does she do karate?   Does she play soccer?

4 Speaking

Think of a sports star. Give clues. Your classmates guess. Use the correct intonation.

Classmate 1 Does he ski?   **You** No, he doesn't.
Classmate 2 Does he skateboard?   **You** Yes, he does.
Classmate 3 Is he American?   **You** Yes, he is.
Classmate 4 Is he Ryan Scheckler?   **You** Yes, he is!

Sports and Activities 31

Sports equipment

1 Vocabulary

A Where does Claudia wear this sports equipment? Write the correct word next to each body part. Then listen and practice.

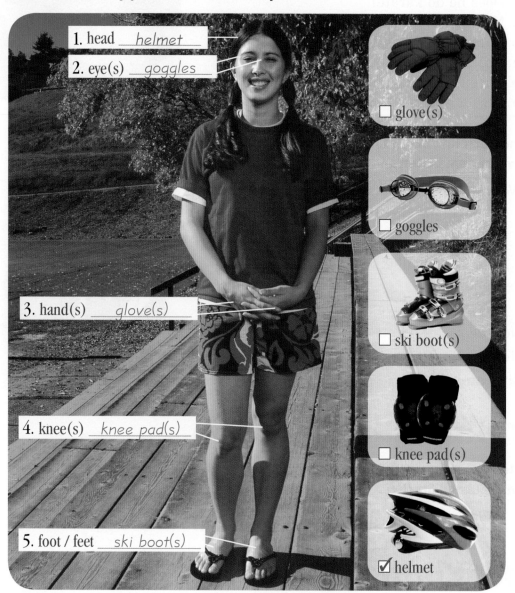

1. head __helmet__
2. eye(s) __goggles__

☐ glove(s)

☐ goggles

3. hand(s) __glove(s)__

☐ ski boot(s)

4. knee(s) __knee pad(s)__

☐ knee pad(s)

5. foot / feet __ski boot(s)__

☑ helmet

B What sports equipment do these athletes wear? Make guesses and complete the chart. *(Answers may vary.)*

A skateboarder	A skier	A cyclist
helmet	ski boots	helmet
knee pads	goggles	
	gloves	

This lesson presents and practices the names of parts of the body, sports equipment, and
They + *verb statements and* Do they + *verb questions.*

Review of Lesson 9

Play a guessing game. Write the eight sports verbs and verb phrases from Lesson 9 on the board. Include additional sports that students play, such as soccer, basketball, etc. Ask students to raise their hands if they play any of the sports listed on the board. Ask two of these students to come to the front. Tell Classmate 1 to whisper to Classmate 2 one of the sports he or she does. Students try to guess the sport by asking: *Does he / she (play soccer)?* Classmate 2 answers *Yes, he / she does* or *No, he / she doesn't.* The student who guesses correctly replaces Classmate 2 and chooses a classmate to replace Classmate 1.

1 Vocabulary

This exercise presents and practices the names of parts of the body and sports equipment.

A 💿 CD1, Track 38

- Explain the title of the lesson, "Sports equipment." Ask: *Which sports require you to use special equipment?*

- Focus students' attention on the photo. Go over the words for body parts with students.

- Point to your head, knees, feet, and eyes, and hold up your hands. Students respond with the correct word. Supply any words they do not know.

- Focus students' attention on the words and pictures at the right. Mime the actions of putting on each piece of sports equipment. Model the words. Students listen and repeat.

- Have students work individually to write the correct sports equipment next to each body part.

- Play the recording. Students listen and verify their answers.

Audio script
See page T-203.

- Check answers with the class. Ask volunteers to read their answers aloud.

- Play the recording again, or model the sentences. Students listen and repeat.

B

- Have students read the directions. Focus students' attention on the chart. Explain that when you add *-er* or *-ist* to some sports, the word then describes the person who does the sport.

- Tell students that they will write three pieces of equipment under each heading. Students work individually to complete the exercise. While students are working, copy the chart onto the board.

- Check answers with the class. Have volunteers come to the board to write their answers.

2 Language focus

This exercise presents and practices *They* + verb statements and *Do they* + verb questions.

A 🔊 CD1, Track 39

- Focus students' attention on the photo of Claudia and her little brother, Oscar. Explain that Oscar is trying to help Claudia with some sports equipment. *Does Claudia look happy?* (No.) Ask students to guess why.

- Play the recording. Students listen and read along.

> ### Audio script
> Same as the conversation in the Student's Book.

- Say the sentences below one by one. Students respond *Yes* or *No*.
  Swimmers wear knee pads. (No.)
  Swimmers wear goggles. (Yes.)
  Swimmers don't wear gloves. (Yes.)
  Swimmers don't wear helmets. (Yes.)

- Play the recording again, or model the conversation. Students listen and repeat.

- **Optional** Have students practice in pairs.

- **Language Chart** Have students study the examples in the language chart. Focus students' attention on the words in bold.

- Tell students that after the pronoun *They*, the verb does not take an *-s* ending. Ask: *Where is* don't *in negative statements?* (Before the verb.) *In the short answer?* (At the end.)

- Model the examples, pausing for students to repeat.

B 🔊 CD1, Track 40

- Have volunteers read aloud the directions and the example question and answer.

- Have students work individually to complete the exercise.

- Play the recording. Students listen and verify their answers.

> ### Audio script
> Same as the questions and answers in the Student's Book.

- Check answers with the class.

- Have students practice the questions and answers in pairs.

3 Listening

In this exercise, students listen and match athletes with the equipment they use.

🔊 CD1, Track 41

- Have students read the directions and look at the photos.

- Tell students they will hear Claudia playing a guessing game with Oscar about different athletes. Students should listen and number the photos.

- Play the recording. Students only listen.

> ### Audio script
> See page T-203.

- Play the recording again. Students listen and number the photos.

- Play the recording once again. Students listen and verify their answers.

- Check answers with the class. Say each number. Students respond with the correct athlete.

> ### Workbook
> Assign the exercises on Workbook page 17. (Workbook answers begin on page T-190.)

> ### Extra Grammar
> Assign the exercises for the Extra Grammar, Lesson 10.

They + (verb): statements

They wear goggles.
They don't wear helmets.

Do they + (verb): questions

Do they wear gloves?
    Yes, they do.
    No, they don't.

A Claudia's little brother, Oscar, helps get the sports equipment. Listen and practice.

Claudia Oscar, can you help me, please? I need the sports equipment for the swim team.

Oscar Sure! Here is the helmet . . .

Claudia Huh? Swimmers don't wear helmets.

Oscar Um, do they wear gloves?

Claudia No, they don't. They wear goggles.

Oscar Oh! Um, do swimmers wear knee pads?

Claudia No, they don't. They don't wear knee pads!

Oscar Sorry. I don't know a lot about sports.

Claudia No kidding!

B How much do you know about sports? Answer the questions. Listen and check. Then practice.

1. **Q:** Do skiers wear sneakers?

    A: *No, they don't. They wear ski boots.*

2. **Q:** Do soccer players have uniforms?

    A: *Yes, they do.*

3. **Q:** Do baseball players play on a court?

    A: *No, they don't. They play on a baseball field.*

4. **Q:** Do cyclists wear hats?

    A: *No, they don't. They wear helmets.*

5. **Q:** Do skateboarders use knee pads?

    A: *Yes, they do.*

6. **Q:** Do basketball players play on a field?

    A: *No, they don't. They play on a basketball court.*

3 **Listening**

Claudia plays a game with Oscar. What athletes do they talk about? Listen and number the pictures.

2

3

4

1

Mini-review

1 Language check

A Look at the pictures. Write sentences with *wear* or *don't wear*.

1. _They wear baseball gloves._ (glove)
   They don't wear boots. (boots)

2. _They don't wear knee pads._ (knee pads)
   They wear goggles. (goggles)

3. _They don't wear hats._ (hats)
   They wear uniforms. (uniforms)

4. _They wear helmets._ (helmets)
   They don't wear goggles. (goggles)

B Complete the sentences with the words in the box.

☐ eyes   ☐ feet   ☑ hands   ☐ head   ☐ knees

1. Cyclists wear gloves on their ___hands___ .
2. Swimmers wear goggles over their ___eyes___ .
3. Skateboarders wear pads on their ___knees___ .
4. Skiers wear boots on their ___feet___ .
5. You wear a helmet on your ___head___ .

Lessons 9 & 10 Mini-review

This lesson reviews the language presented and practiced in Lessons 9 and 10.

1 Language check

This exercise reviews the structures presented so far in this unit.

A

- Have students look at the pictures. Ask: *What sports are the people doing?* (Baseball, swimming, soccer, cycling.)
- Invite a volunteer to read the directions and the examples aloud.
- Have students work individually to complete the exercise.
- Have students compare answers in pairs.
- Check answers with the class. Invite volunteers to write their answers on the board.

B

- Invite a volunteer to read the directions and the example aloud.
- Have students work individually to complete the exercise.
- Check answers with the class. Invite volunteers to read aloud one sentence each.

C

- Have students read the directions and look at the photo and the caption. Explain *champion*. (Winner of a competition or contest.) Ask: *What sport does Angela do?* (She skateboards.)

- Review the usage of *do* and *does*. Write *do / don't* at the top left side of the board and *does / doesn't* at the top right side. Ask students which pronouns should be written under *do / don't (I, you, we, they)* and which pronouns should be written under *does / doesn't (he, she, it)*.

- Call out a variety of nouns and pronouns: *Claudia, you, Claudia and Zach, the student, the teachers, they, my sister*, etc. Students respond with *do* or *does*. Repeat this for *don't* and *doesn't*.

- Explain that the text is an interview with Angela for a magazine. Students work individually to complete the interview.

- Check answers with the class.

- Have students practice the conversation in pairs.

---

2 Listening

In this exercise, students listen to questions and decide on the correct responses.

A 💿 CD1, Track 42

- Tell students that they will listen to more of the interviewer's questions. They should choose the correct response for each question.

- Play the recording. Students only listen.

> **Audio script**
> See page T-204.

- Play the recording again. Students listen and check the correct responses.

B 💿 CD1, Track 43

- Play the complete interview. Students listen and verify their answers.

> **Audio script**
> See page T-204.

- Check answers with the class.

> **Workbook**
> Assign the exercises on Workbook page 18. (Workbook answers begin on page T-190.)

> **Game**
> Assign the game on Student's Book page 116.

C Complete the interview with Angela Moya, a champion skateboarder.
Use *do*, *does*, *don't*, and *doesn't*.

SPORTS FOR KIDS

Interviewer Hi, Angela. Nice to meet you.

Angela Hi!

Interviewer Angela, we know you love sports. Do your parents like sports, too?

Angela Yes, they ___do___ . My dad likes outdoor sports.

Interviewer ___Does___ he go biking?

Angela Yes, he ___does___ . He goes biking every day, actually.

Interviewer And your mother? ___Does___ she go biking, too?

Angela No, she ___doesn't___ . She swims and water-skis.

Interviewer And your sisters? ___Do___ they skateboard?

Angela No, they ___don't___ . They like team sports, like soccer and basketball.

Interviewer What about you? ___Do___ you play team sports?

Angela No, I ___don't___ . I skateboard, of course. And I run every day, too.

**Champion Skateboarder
Angela Moya, 13 – Denver, Colorado**

2 Listening

A Listen to more of the interviewer's questions from Exercise 1C.
Check (✓) the correct responses.

1. ☑ No, they don't. They don't like water sports.
   ☐ Yes, they do. They play every weekend.

2. ☐ Yes, I do. It's fun.
   ☑ Yes, they do. They love the mountains.

3. ☐ No, it isn't.
   ☑ Yes, she does. She's a great player.

4. ☐ Yes, she does. She's on the team.
   ☑ Yes, she does. She likes it very much.

5. ☐ Yes, we do. Every summer.
   ☑ No, he doesn't. He doesn't like the water.

B Now listen to the complete interview in Part A. Check your answers.

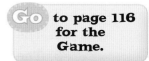

Go to page 116 for the Game.

Off to camp

1 Vocabulary

A Megan packs to go to camp. Match the items in Megan's room to the correct items on the checklist. Then listen and practice.

Camp Coby Camper Checklist

Bring:
blanket _4_
bug repellent _1_
flashlight _5_
hiking boots _9_
pillow _10_
raincoat _3_
sleeping bag _7_
soap _6_
sunscreen _8_
towel _2_

Remember:
No cell phones
No computers
No radios
No video games

B Complete the sentences with the words in Part A.

1. The _bug repellent_ is on the desk.
2. The _soap_ is under the desk.
3. The _raincoat_ is on the desk.
4. The _towel_ is on top of the blanket.
5. The _blanket_ is next to the bed.
6. The _sleeping bag_ is on the bed.
7. The _pillow_ is under the bed.
8. The _sunscreen_ is under the chair.
9. The _flashlight_ is on the chair.
10. The _hiking boots_ are next to the desk.

Lesson 11 Off to camp

This lesson presents and practices the names of common items taken to summer camp and imperatives.

Review of Lesson 10

- Write on the board:

  gloves, goggles, ski boots, knee pads, helmets

  Do people wear _____ ?

- Play a guessing game. Tell students that you are thinking of a particular sport. Students ask about the equipment used in order to guess the sport. The student who guesses correctly replaces you and continues the activity.

- Divide the class into groups of four or five students. Ask groups to try to think of the sport that requires the most equipment. Have the group spokesperson report to the class: *_____s wear the most equipment. They wear _____ , _____ , _____ , and _____ .*

1 Vocabulary

This exercise presents and practices the names of common items for campers.

A 💿 CD1, Track 44

- Explain the title, "Off to camp." (Going away to summer camp.)

- Focus students' attention on the picture. Tell them that Megan is getting ready for camp. Ask students to raise their hands if they have ever gone to camp. Ask them what items are appropriate for camp and what items are not. Ask them what type of clothing should be worn.

- Explain to students that the list shows the items that Megan is supposed to take with her to camp. Tell them the name of the camp is "Camp Coby." Explain *checklist*. (A list of items that you check off.)

- Ask volunteers to come to the board to draw simple illustrations of any of the vocabulary words in the checklist that they are familiar with. Ask them to point to the illustration and identify the object. Draw any remaining objects and ask students to look at the checklist and guess what the objects are.

- Have students work individually to match the number of the items in the picture to the correct items in the checklist.

- Play the recording. Students listen and verify their answers.

Audio script
Same as the items in the Student's Book.

- Check answers with the class. Write the items in the checklist on the board. Leave a space next to each item for students to write the number of the item in the picture. Invite volunteers to come to the board to write one answer each.

- Play the recording again, or model the words. Students listen and repeat.

B

- Have a volunteer read the directions and the example aloud. Explain that they will use the words on the checklist in Part A to fill in the blanks.

- Have students work individually to complete the exercise.

- Check answers with the class.

- **Optional** Ask two students to stand (three or four for large classes). Call out *Under the desk*. Students respond with *The soap*. The first one with the correct answer gets a point. Continue for three items and then change students.

Culture Note Every summer, many children and teenagers in the U.S. go to summer camp. Some camps are *day camps*, where the children spend the day but return home in the late afternoon. Other camps are *sleepaway camps*, where children can stay for a number of weeks or even the entire summer. Camps emphasize different activities. Some focus on sports in general or on one sport in particular – for example, tennis or gymnastics. There are acting camps, art camps, and computer camps. There are also camps for children with special needs and physical challenges.

2 Language focus

This exercise presents and practices imperatives.

A 🔊 CD1, Track 45

- Ask students to look at the picture of Megan and her mother. Ask: *Are Megan's clothes good for camp?* (No.) *Is Megan's mother happy?* (No.)
- Ask students to read the directions. Tell them they will listen to a conversation between Megan and her mother.
- Play the recording. Students listen and read along.

> **Audio script**
> Same as the conversation in the Student's Book.

- Ask: *Can Megan bring her computer?* (No, she can't.) *What does her mother say?* (Leave your computer at home, please.) *Does Megan's mother want her to wear a dress?* (No.) *What does she say?* (Don't wear a dress. Wear something comfortable.)
- Say: *Megan's mother asks her to do three things. What are they?* (Wear something comfortable. Read the checklist again. Leave your computer at home.)
- Say: *Megan's mother asks her NOT to do two things. What are they?* (Don't wear a dress. Don't stay up late.) Ask: *Does Megan tell her mother to do anything?* (Hurry up. Please stop.)
- Play the recording again, or model the conversation. Students listen and repeat.
- **Optional** Have students practice in pairs.

- **Language Chart** Have students study the examples in the language chart. Focus students' attention on the words in bold. Explain that in these types of statements the simple form of the verb is used. Ask: *What word is added if the statement is a negative one?* (Don't.) *Where is it in the statement?* (At the beginning.)
- Model the examples, pausing for students to repeat.
- Ask students to find the other imperative statements in the conversation and underline them. (Hurry up; Don't wear a dress; Wear something comfortable; Read the checklist again; Leave your computer at home, please; Don't stay up late; please stop.)

B 🔊 CD1, Track 46

- Explain *rules*. Have students read the directions.
- Have students work individually to complete the Camp Coby rules with imperatives.
- Play the recording. Students listen and verify their answers.

> **Audio script**
> Same as the rules in the Student's Book.

- Check answers with the class. Invite volunteers to read aloud one answer each.
- **Optional** Have students work in small groups. They should write down five or six rules at home and at school. Invite volunteers to share their rules with the class.

---

3 Speaking

This exercise practices imperatives.

- Ask students to read the directions. Make sure that students understand that their rules should be funny.
- Have students work individually to complete the exercise.
- Ask students to share their rules with the class. Vote on the craziest rules.

Note: For large classes, divide the class into groups of five or six students and have them vote on the two craziest rules in their group. Ask them to share the results with the class. Vote as a class on the two craziest rules.

> **Workbook**
> Assign the exercises on Workbook page 19. (Workbook answers begin on page T-190.)

> **Extra Grammar**
> Assign the exercises for the Extra Grammar, Lesson 11.

2 Language focus

Imperatives

Hurry up.
Don't stay up late.

A Megan's mother helps Megan pack for camp. Listen and practice.

Megan Let's go. Hurry up, Mom.

Mom Just a minute, Megan. Don't wear a dress. Wear something comfortable.

Megan But this *is* comfortable, Mom.

Mom Fine, Megan, but read the checklist again. It says "No computers." Leave your computer at home, please.

Megan But I use my computer at night, Mom.

Mom I know, but there are camp activities at night.

Megan Oh, good! I can stay up until midnight.

Mom No, Megan! It's camp. Don't stay up late.

Megan Mom, please stop. Camp is supposed to be fun!

B Look at the checklist in Exercise 1A. Can you guess the Camp Coby rules? Complete the rules. Then listen and check.

Camp Coby Rules

1. *Don't play*   video games. (play / don't play)
2. *Wear*   hiking boots. (wear / don't wear)
3. *Don't listen*   to the radio. (listen / don't listen)
4. *Don't bring*   cell phones. (bring / don't bring)
5. *Don't use*   computers. (use / don't use)
6. *Bring*   a flashlight. (bring / don't bring)
7. *Use*   sunscreen. (use / don't use)

3 Speaking

Write four crazy rules for Camp Coby. Close your book and tell your rules to your classmates. Who has the craziest rules? *(Answers will vary.)*

Get up at 11:00 every day.

Lesson 12 At camp

1 Vocabulary

A Look at the Camp Coby Web site. Match the photos to the correct activities. Then listen and practice.

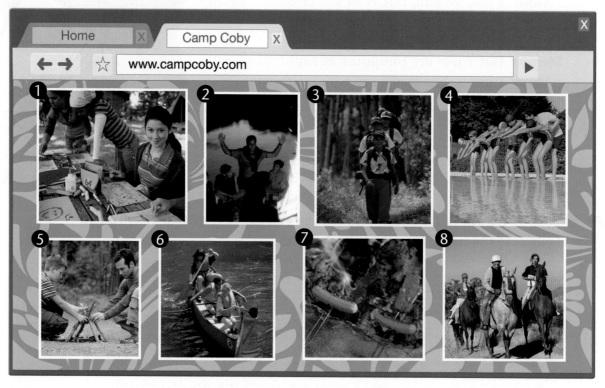

Campers . . .

☐ 7 cook hot dogs. ☐ 6 go canoeing. ☐ 3 go hiking. ☐ 4 take swimming lessons.

☐ 1 do arts and crafts. ☐ 8 go horseback riding. ☐ 5 make a campfire. ☐ 2 tell stories.

B What do campers do at Camp Coby? Listen and write an activity for each time.

Time	Activity
8:00 a.m.	_They go horseback riding._
10:00 a.m.	_They take swimming lessons._
1:15 p.m.	_They go canoeing._
3:30 p.m.	_They go hiking._
4:45 p.m.	_They do arts and crafts._
8:15 p.m.	_They make a campfire._
8:30 p.m.	_They cook hot dogs._
9:00 p.m.	_They tell stories._

Lesson 12 At camp

This lesson presents and practices the names of camping activities and What time / When . . . ?

Review of Lesson 11

- Have students tell you some of the imperative statements (both positive and negative) they learned in Lesson 11. Write them on the board.
- Play "Toss the Ball." Throw a ball to one of the students. Say: *Listen to the radio.* The student responds with *Don't listen to the radio* and then throws the ball to another student, saying a new command.

Note: For large classes, divide the class into two or three teams. Toss the ball to one of the teams. Say: *Listen to the radio.* Any of the students on that team can respond with *Don't listen to the radio.* If the student does so correctly, the team gets a point. That student then tosses the ball to the next team and continues the activity.

1 Vocabulary

This exercise presents the names of common camping activities.

A ☞ CD1, Track 47

- Have students look at the photos. Explain that these pictures are a part of Camp Coby's Web site. Ask students if they have ever visited a camping or travel Web site.
- Focus students' attention on the verb phrases below the photos. Model the phrases, one by one. As you do so, invite volunteers to mime any of the activities that they are familiar with. Mime any of the activities that students are not familiar with.
- Tell students that they should write the number of the photo next to the correct verb phrase.
- Have students work individually to complete the exercise.
- Play the recording. Students listen and verify their answers.

Audio script
Same as the sentences in the Student's Book.

- Check answers with the class. Write the activities on the board. Leave a space for students to write the numbers of the corresponding photos. Invite volunteers to come to the board to write their answers.
- Play the recording again, or model the sentences. Students listen and repeat.

B ☞ CD1, Track 48

- Explain that this is a Camp Coby daily schedule with missing information. Tell students they will listen to the schedule and will write the correct activity for each time.
- Play the recording. Students only listen.

Audio script
See page T-204.

- Play the recording again. Students listen and complete the schedule.
- Play the recording once again. Students listen and verify their answers.
- Check answers with the class. Write the times on the board. Invite volunteers to come to the board to write an activity for each time.

2 Language focus

This exercise presents *What time / When...?*

A 🔊 **CD1, Track 49**

- Focus students' attention on the picture. Ask: *What are Megan's parents reading?* (A letter from Megan.)
- Tell students that they will listen to a conversation between Megan's mom and dad.
- Play the recording. Students listen and read along.

> **Audio script**
>
> Same as the conversation in the Student's Book.

- Ask: *What time does Megan get up?* (At 6:30.) *When do the campers go hiking?* (In the afternoon.)
- Play the recording again, or model the conversation. Students listen and repeat.
- **Optional** Have students practice in pairs.
- **Language Chart** Have students study the top part of the language chart. Focus students' attention on the words in bold. Point out that there is more than one answer to each question. Ask: *How many answers are there for the first question?* (Two.) *How are they different?* (The first answer is a complete answer and the second is a short answer.) *How about the second question?* (Three answers.) Explain that *What time* is answered with specific times whereas *When* can be answered with either a specific time or any type of time phrase.

- Focus students' attention on the time equivalents in the bottom part of the chart.
- Model the examples, pausing for students to repeat.
- **Optional** Call out random times. Students respond with the appropriate time of day.

B 🔊 **CD1, Track 50**

- Have students read the directions and look at the schedule in Exercise 1B on page 38.
- Have students work individually to write questions with *When* or *What time.*
- Play the recording. Students listen and verify their answers.

> **Audio script**
>
> Same as the questions and answers in the Student's Book.

- Check answers with the class. Have volunteers write one answer each on the board.
- Have students practice the questions and answers in pairs.
- **Optional** Invite volunteers to ask classmates questions with *What time* and *When* about Megan's camp routine.

.....

3 Listening

In this exercise, students listen for the times of activities at another camp.

🔊 **CD1, Track 51**

- Ask students to read the directions and the chart. Tell students they will listen to people talking about activities at another camp and will check the correct times of the day when campers do these activities.
- Play the recording. Students only listen.

> **Audio script**
>
> See page T-204.

- Play the recording again. Students listen and complete the exercise.
- Play the recording once again. Students listen and verify their answers.
- Check answers with the class. Ask volunteers to read their answers in complete sentences – for example, *Campers go hiking in the morning.*

> **Workbook**
>
> Assign the exercises on Workbook page 20. (Workbook answers begin on page T-190.)

> **Extra Grammar**
>
> Assign the exercises for the Extra Grammar, Lesson 12.

2 Language focus

What time / When . . . ?

What time does Megan get up?
She gets up **at 6:30**.
At 6:30.
When do they go hiking?
They go hiking **in the afternoon**.
They go hiking **at 2:00**.
At 2:00.

- -

in the morning = about 5 a.m. to 12 p.m.
in the afternoon = about 12 p.m. to 6 p.m.
in the evening = about 6 p.m. to 10 p.m.
at night = about 10 p.m. to 5 a.m.

A Megan's parents read her letter.
Listen and practice.

Mom Wow! Megan is very busy at
Camp Coby!

Dad Great! What time does she get up?

Mom She gets up at 6:30.

Dad Wow. Campers get up early.
What do they do every day?

Mom Let's see. They do arts and crafts,
they go canoeing, they go hiking . . .

Dad When do they go hiking?

Mom They go hiking in the afternoon.

Dad It sounds like fun! Can parents go to camp, too?

B Look at the schedule in Exercise 1B. Write questions about
Megan. Use *When* or *What time*. Listen and check.
Then practice.

1. **Q:** _When does Megan take swimming lessons?_ OR

   What time does Megan take swimming lessons?

   A: She takes swimming lessons at 10:00.

2. **Q:** _When does Megan go canoeing?_

   A: She goes canoeing in the afternoon.

3. **Q:** _When does Megan do arts and crafts? /_
   What time does Megan do arts and crafts?

   A: At 4:45.

4. **Q:** _When does Megan make a campfire? /_
   What time does Megan make a campfire?

   A: At 8:15.

5. **Q:** _When does Megan tell stories?_

   A: She tells stories in the evening.

3 Listening

Listen to the activities at another camp – Camp Oakley. When do campers do
these activities? Check (✓) the correct times of the day.

	In the morning	In the afternoon	In the evening	At night
1. go hiking	✓	☐	☐	☐
2. go horseback riding	☐	✓	☐	☐
3. do arts and crafts	✓	☐	☐	☐
4. take swimming lessons	☐	☐	✓	☐
5. tell stories	☐	☐	☐	✓

Read

A **Read the article quickly. Check (✓) the main idea.**

☐ 1. Apolo Anton Ohno is a famous speed skater.

☐ 2. Apolo Anton Ohno doesn't have a big family.

☑ 3. Apolo Anton Ohno is a talented speed skater and a dancer, too.

Apolo Anton Ohno

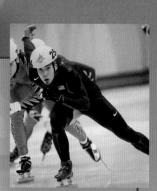

Meet the very talented Apolo Anton Ohno! Apolo is a **world champion speed skater**. He has five Olympic **medals**. Apolo is from Seattle, Washington, but now he lives in Colorado. His father is Japanese. He has an older **half brother**, but he doesn't have any sisters.

Apolo loves speed skating, and he practices two or three hours every day. Speed skating is a dangerous sport, so he always wears a helmet. But Apolo doesn't only like skating. He likes other things, too.

Apolo likes dancing. He's an awesome dancer. He's the May 2007 champion of the American TV show, *Dancing with the Stars*. People love him – he's handsome and friendly.

Apolo is really famous. He's a TV star, a sports star, and an **author**. His book, *A Journey*, is about his life. He's a cool guy! So, what do you think? Do you like him?

Go to page 12? for the **Vocabulary Practice.**

B 👁️‍🗨️ **Read the article slowly. Check your answer in Part A.**

C **Answer the questions.**

1. Does Apolo like speed skating? _Yes, he does._

2. Does he have a sister? _No, he doesn't._

3. Does he practice speed skating every day? _Yes, he does._

4. Does he wear any special sports equipment? _Yes, he does._

5. Does he sing? _No, he doesn't._

This lesson practices reading, listening, and writing skills.

Review of Lesson 12

- Review the question-and-answer patterns *What time / When do / does . . . ?* with the class. Ask Classmate 1: *What time do you get up?* Classmate 1 replies: *I get up at _____ .* Then ask the class: *What time does (Classmate 1) get up?* The class replies: *He / she gets up at _____ .* Repeat several times with both *What time . . . ?* and *When . . . ?*

- Write these questions and answers on four slips of paper (one question and answer per slip): *What time does Joe hike? He hikes at 8:30. When does Susan cook hot dogs? She cooks hot dogs in the evening. What time does Ellen do arts and crafts? She does arts and crafts at 3:15. When does Tim take swimming lessons? He takes swimming lessons in the morning.* Write the following times on the board: *7:15, 8:30, 11:00, 2:45, 3:15, 4:10, 5:00, morning, afternoon, evening, night.* Call a volunteer to the front. Give the volunteer one of the slips of paper. Ask the student to read the question on it to the class. Students guess the answer, choosing from the times on the board. The student who guesses correctly replaces the volunteer and continues the activity.

- Divide the class into three or four groups. Students take turns asking their group *What time / When . . . ?* questions about daily routines. Have each group report its most unusual finding.

Read

This exercise practices reading for information about a person.

A

- Have students look at the photos. Ask: *Who is the man in the pictures?* (Apolo Anton Ohno.)

- Invite a volunteer to read the directions and the statements aloud. Remind students that they should read quickly to find the answer and that they should not read every word carefully.

- Have students work individually to read the article quickly and check the main idea. Do not check answers at this point.

B 🔊 CD1, Track 52

- Invite a volunteer to read the directions aloud. Remind students that they should read slowly and carefully, and concentrate on getting the meaning of the entire text.

- List the new vocabulary words on the board: *world champion, speed skater, medal, half brother, author.* Explain their meaning. (World champion: the winner of a contest in which people from all over the world compete [ask students for examples of world champion men's and women's tennis players, etc.]; speed skater: someone who competes in timed skating on an ice track – for example, speed skaters compete in the Olympic Games; medal: usually, a round piece of metal, often of gold, silver, or bronze, that the winner of a competition receives; half brother: your brother related to you through your mother or your father only, not through both of your parents; author: the writer of a book, story, etc. [ask students for examples of authors of books they have read].) As an alternative, have students use their dictionaries to find the meanings of the new vocabulary words.

- Have students read the article again.

- Have students check their answer in Part A in pairs. Elicit the answer from one pair.

- **Optional** Play the recording. Students listen and read along.

Audio script
Same as the article in the Student's Book.

Get Connected Vocabulary
Have students do the exercise on Student's Book page 123 in class or for homework. (Get Connected Vocabulary answers are on page T-123.)

C

- Invite a volunteer to read the directions and the first question aloud.

- Ask: *Does Apolo like speed skating?* Elicit the answer. (Yes, he does.)

- Have students work individually to answer the questions.

- Have students check their answers in pairs.

- Check answers with the class. Invite volunteers to read one answer each.

- **Optional** Have students work in pairs to take turns reading the first two paragraphs of the article to each other. As one student reads, the other listens with book closed. If that student does not understand something, he or she can say: *I don't understand. Please, repeat that.*

Listen

In this exercise, students listen for information about a sports star who is good at two different things.

A 💿 CD1, Track 53

- Focus student's attention on the photos. Ask: *Who is the person in the photos?* (Serena Williams.) Ask students what she is doing in the top photo. (She's playing tennis.)

- Tell students that they will listen to two friends, Sam and Amy, talk about Serena Williams's talents.

- Have students read the first question and the example answer.

- Play the recording. Students only listen.

> **Audio script**
> See page T-205.

- Play the recording again. Students listen and answer the questions.

- Play the recording once again. Students listen and verify their answers.

- Check answers with the class. Invite volunteers to read aloud one answer each.

B

- Have students read the directions and the questions.

- Read the first question with the class and elicit answers from several students. Tell students there are no right or wrong answers for this exercise – they are giving their opinions.

- Have students work individually to answer the questions.

- Have students work in pairs to compare answers, or elicit opinions from volunteers.

Write

In this exercise, students answer questions and write a paragraph about a person who is good at two things.

A

- Invite a volunteer to read the directions and the questions aloud.

- Answer the questions for a person you know who is good at two things.

- Have students work individually to answer the questions.

- **Optional** Have students ask and answer the questions in pairs.

B

- Invite a volunteer to read the directions aloud. Tell students that they will use their answers in Part A to help them write about their person who is good at two things.

- Have students work individually to write their paragraph.

- Invite several volunteers to read their paragraphs to the class.

- **Optional** Have students work in groups of four and read each other's paragraphs. Students can vote for the person they think is the best at doing two things, and the writer can read the paragraph to the class.

> **Teaching Tip** When students work in groups, try to give students different roles in the group, as appropriate for the activity. For example, one student could be the leader, another the secretary, and others reporters. The reporters give information about the group's activity to the rest of the class. This ensures that all students participate in the activity.

> **Workbook**
> Assign the exercises on Workbook page 21. (Workbook answers begin on page T-190.)

She's good at two different things.

A 💿 **Sam and Amy talk about Serena Williams. Listen and answer the questions.**

1. Does Serena have a sister? _Yes, she does._

2. Does Venus design clothes? _No, she doesn't._

3. Does Serena have a company? _Yes, she does._

4. Does her company have offices in Paris? _No, it doesn't._

5. Is Amy at Sam's house? _No, she isn't._

B **What do you think? Answer the questions.** *(Answers will vary.)*

1. Do you think tennis matches on TV are interesting? _____

2. Do you think it's easy to be athletic? _____

3. Do you think fashion design is a cool subject? _____

4. Do you think it's important to be good at two things? _____

Your turn

A **Think about a person who is good at two things. Answer the questions.** *(Answers will vary.)*

1. What's his / her name? _____

2. Who is he / she? A friend? A family member? A classmate? A teacher? _____

3. What does he / she do? _____

4. What other special thing can he / she do? _____

5. What's he / she like? _____

B **Write a paragraph about a person who's good at two things. Use the answers in Part A to help you.** *(Answers will vary.)*

_____ is good at two things. She's good at _____

_____

_____

_____

Language chart review

Simple present		
They + (verb): statements	*Yes / No* questions: *he / she / they*	Short answers
Skateboarders wear helmets. **They don't wear** goggles.	**Does he swim?**	**Yes, he does.** **No, he doesn't.**
	Does she do karate?	**Yes, she does.** **No, she doesn't.**
	Do they like sports?	**Yes, they do.** **No, they don't.**

A The basketball team at Ryder School is very unusual. Look at the picture. Write *Do* or *Does* questions about the team. Use the correct forms of the verbs. Then answer the questions.

1. the players / play in the gym

   Q: *Do the players play in the gym?*   **A:** *No, they don't. They play in the cafeteria.*

2. the players / wear sneakers

   Q: *Do the players wear sneakers?*   **A:** *No, they don't. They wear hiking boots.*

3. the coach / wear goggles

   Q: *Does the coach wear goggles?*   **A:** *Yes, she does.*

4. player 2 / have a basketball

   Q: *Does player 2 have a basketball?*   **A:** *No, he doesn't. He has a parrot.*

5. players 4 and 5 / listen to music

   Q: *Do players 4 and 5 listen to music?*   **A:** *Yes, they do.*

Unit 3 Review

This lesson reviews the grammar and vocabulary introduced in Unit 3.

Language chart review

This chart summarizes the main grammar presented and practiced in Unit 3.

- Books closed. Write on the board:

  1. Do   2. Does

- Focus students' attention on the words on the board. Read aloud the statements below. Have students turn the statements into questions. They should first respond collectively with the appropriate heading. Then invite a volunteer to tell you the complete question.

  He does karate after school. (Does: Does he do karate after school?)

  I have a basketball. (Do: Do you have a basketball?)

  She wears sneakers in the gym. (Does: Does she wear sneakers in the gym?)

  They like sports very much. (Do: Do they like sports?)

- Read the statements one more time. This time, ask students to turn the affirmative statements into negative ones. (He doesn't do karate after school. I don't have a basketball. She doesn't wear sneakers in the gym. They don't like sports very much.)

- Books open. Focus students' attention on the Language chart review and on the contractions *don't* and *doesn't*. Ask volunteers to give you the full form of these two contractions. (Do not, does not.)

- Answer any questions students may have.

....

Exercises A through C (pages T-42 to T-43)

Note: Students can do these exercises for homework or in class. They should do these exercises with minimal teacher input or help. If you choose to do these exercises as homework, briefly review the exercise directions in class. Make sure that students understand what they should do. Check the answers with the class during the next class meeting. If you choose to do the exercises in class, follow the directions below.

Exercise A

- Have students read the directions and look at the picture.

- Explain that there are two parts to the task. First, students write *Do* or *Does* questions about the team. Then, they write answers to the questions.

- Have students work individually to write questions using the words given.

- Have students work individually to write answers to the questions.

- Check answers with the class.

- Have students ask and answer the questions in pairs.

Language chart review

This chart summarizes further grammar presented and practiced in Unit 3.

- Have students study the examples in the chart.
- Remind students to use the simple present form of the verb in imperative statements.
- Remind students also that *What time* is answered with specific times whereas *When* can be answered with either a specific time or any type of time phrase.
- Answer any questions students may have.

Exercise B

- Have students read the directions and look at the pictures. Focus students' attention on the verb phrases in the box.
- Tell students to write an imperative sentence under each picture using one of the verb phrases in the box.
- Have students work individually to write the imperative sentences.
- Check answers with the class. Invite volunteers to read aloud one sentence each.

Exercise C

- Have a volunteer read the directions aloud.
- Tell students to complete the conversations by writing the letters of the questions in the box.
- Have students work individually to complete the exercise.
- Check answers with the class.

Optional Unit Wrap-Up

- If students did the Review exercises for homework, check answers with the class.
- Write the name of a sport on the board. Invite a volunteer to ask a *Yes/No* question, as in Exercise A, about basketball – for example, *Do basketball players wear goggles?* Another student answers with a short answer and the correct information. (No, they don't. They wear sneakers.) Continue the activity with other sports. Do this activity as a whole class or put students into groups of three or four.
- Have students look at the pictures in Exercise B. Ask: *Where are these people?* (On the school bus, at the zoo, at the swimming pool, at home.) Elicit rules for each place, using imperatives.
- Ask students: *What do you do every day?* Make a list of activities on the board. Have students ask and answer questions with *When* and *What time,* as in Exercise C.

Theme Project

- Assign the *At Home* section of the Unit 3 Theme Project on Student's Book page 128.

Workbook

- Assign the Unit 3 Check Yourself on Workbook page 22. (Workbook answers begin on page T-190.)

Extra Practice Worksheets

- Assign the Unit 3 Extra Practice worksheets starting on page T-144.

Extra Speaking Practice Worksheet

- Assign the Unit 3 Extra Speaking Practice worksheet on page T-167.

Arcade Activities

- Assign the Unit 3 Arcade activities found at: www.cambridge.org/connectarcade

Learning Log

- Assign the Unit 3 Learning Log. These can be downloaded from the Teacher Support Site at: www.cambridge.org/connect2e/teacher

Quiz

- Give the Unit 3 Quiz on page T-178.

Test

- Give the Unit 3 Test (Form A and / or Form B). These can be downloaded from the Teacher Support Site at: www.cambridge.org/connect2e/teacher

Language chart review

Imperatives	What time . . . ?	When . . . ?
Read a book. **Don't play** video games.	**What time** does he go hiking? He goes hiking **at 5:00**. **At 5:00**.	**When** do they use their computers? They use their computers **at night**. They use their computers **at 7:30**. **At 7:30**.

B Write imperatives with the verb phrases in the box.

☐ go to bed early ☐ swim there ☑ talk on your cell phone ☐ use sunscreen

1. <u>Don't talk on your cell phone.</u>

2. <u>Don't swim there.</u>

3. <u>Use sunscreen.</u>

4. <u>Go to bed early.</u>

C Two swimming coaches are talking about their teams. Complete the conversation with the sentences in the box.

☐ a. What time do they eat breakfast?   ☑ d. Does Maggie Ferre swim on your team?
☐ b. So, when do your swimmers practice?   ☐ e. What about her brother, Joe? Does he swim, too?
☐ c. What time do they swim?

Coach Sala <u>d</u>	
Coach Hanes Yes, she does.	
Coach Sala <u>e</u>	
Coach Hanes No, he doesn't. He's on the baseball team.	
Coach Sala <u>b</u>	

Coach Hanes They practice in the morning.
Coach Sala   <u>c</u>
Coach Hanes Very early. At 6:30.
Coach Sala   <u>a</u>
Coach Hanes After they practice. At 8:00.

Go to page 128 for the Theme Project.

I like music

1 Vocabulary

A Listen to these kinds of music and practice.

classical country hip-hop jazz pop reggae rock

B Work with your classmates. Look at the photos, and complete the labels with words from Part A. Then listen and practice.

Music Magazine
Top Musicians of the Year

Pink

Joshua Bell

Kanye West

Sean Paul

4. __pop__ singer

2. _classical_ musician

1. _hip-hop_ singer

3. _reggae_ singer

Jon Bon Jovi

The Dixie Chicks

Wynton Marsalis

5. __rock__ singer

6. _country_ group

7. __jazz__ musician

C Learn what kinds of music four of your classmates like and don't like.

You	Yumi, what's your favorite kind of music?
Classmate 1	My favorite kind of music is jazz.
You	What's your favorite kind of music, Leah?
Classmate 2	My favorite kind of music is . . .

Lesson 13 · I like music.

This lesson presents and practices the names of different types of music and the object pronouns *her / him / it / them*.

1 Vocabulary

This exercise presents and practices the names of different types of music.

A 💿 CD1, Track 54

- Have students read the words in the banner. Ask: *Which of these types of music are familiar to you?*
- Play the recording. Students listen.

> **Audio script**
> Same as the words in the Student's Book.

- Play the recording again, or model the words. Students listen and repeat.

B 💿 CD1, Track 55

- Focus students' attention on the photos. Ask students to raise their hands if they recognize any of the musicians. Ask them to say the musicians' names.
- Model the names of the musicians. Students listen and repeat.
- Have students read the directions. Students work in pairs or small groups to complete the labels under the photos.
- Play the recording again. Students listen and verify their answers.

> **Audio script**
> See page T-205.

- Check answers with the class. Have volunteers come to the board to write one answer each.
- Play the recording again, or model the sentences. Students listen and repeat.

C

- Have volunteers read the directions and the example conversations aloud.
- Have students walk around the room and ask four different classmates the question, *What's your favorite kind of music?* They should make notes with the names of the students and their answers.
- Invite volunteers to report some of the answers to the class.
- **Optional** On the board, write the words for the different kinds of music. Have students vote on their favorite. Write the number of votes next to each one. (Tell students they can vote only once.) What kind of music is the class favorite?

> **Teaching Tip** When doing activities like this with the whole class, your students will enjoy it more if you participate as well. Walk around, ask a few students the question, and allow them to ask you. This also allows you to listen more closely to what your students are saying.

This unit introduces vocabulary and expressions for talking about music, shopping, other free-time activities, and study habits.

2 Language focus

This exercise presents and practices *her / him / it / them.*

A 🔊 CD1, Track 56

- Focus students' attention on the photo. Explain that Ana is being interviewed for *Music Magazine*. Ask students to raise their hands if they read magazine interviews of their favorite stars.
- Tell students they will listen to Ana being asked about her favorite kinds of music.
- Play the recording. Students listen and read along.

> ### Audio script
> Same as the conversation in the Student's Book.

- Ask: *Does Ana like jazz?* (No.) *Does she like Pink?* (Yes, she does.)
- Say the sentences below. Ask students to substitute the last word in each sentence with *her, him, it,* or *them.*

  Ana likes the Dixie Chicks. (Ana likes them.)

  Ana doesn't like jazz. (Ana doesn't like it.)

  Ana likes Wynton Marsalis. (Ana likes him.)

  Ana loves Pink. (Ana loves her.)

- Play the recording again, or model the conversation. Students listen and repeat.
- **Optional** Have students practice in pairs.

- **Language Chart** Have students study the examples in the language chart. Focus students' attention on the pronouns in bold. Explain that these pronouns are called *object pronouns.* Object pronouns come after the verb. *She, he, it,* and *they* are *subject pronouns.* Subject pronouns come before the verb. Point out that *it* is both a subject and an object pronoun.
- Model the examples, pausing for students to repeat.

B 🔊 CD1, Track 57

- Ask students to read the directions and the example. Ask: *In the example, why is* it *the correct answer?* (Because *it* takes the place of *pop music.*) Have students circle *pop music.* Then ask them to circle the words in items 2 through 6 that determine which pronoun to write. (The Dixie Chicks, Kanye West, classical music, Pink, Sean Paul.)
- Have students work individually to complete the exercise.
- Play the recording. Students listen and verify their answers.

> ### Audio script
> Same as the sentences in the Student's Book.

- Check answers with the class. Write the sentences on the board, leaving blanks for the object pronouns. Ask volunteers to come to the board to write their answers. They should also circle the word(s) to which each object pronoun refers.

3 Speaking

This exercise practices *Do you like . . . ?*

- Have students read the directions and look at the chart.
- Have students complete items 6, 7, and 8. Explain that they should think of specific examples of the words in parentheses to write in the blanks.
- Demonstrate the task with a volunteer, following the example in the speech balloons. Have students work in pairs to complete the exercise.
- Students ask each other the *Do you like . . . ?* questions and check the *A lot, A little,* or the *Not at all* box for each question, according to their partner's response.
- Invite volunteers to share their results with the class.
- **Optional** Ask: *Do you and your partner like the same music?* Ask pairs to tally the number of same and different answers and report their findings to the class.

> ### Workbook
> Assign the exercises on Workbook page 23. (Workbook answers begin on page T-190.)

> ### Extra Grammar
> Assign the exercises for the Extra Grammar, Lesson 13.

2 Language focus

She's great. I like **her** a lot.
He's my favorite. I like **him** a lot.

Hip-hop is cool. I like **it**.
They're boring. I don't like **them** at all.

A Daisy Fines of *Music Magazine* interviews Ana.
Listen and practice.

Daisy So, Ana, what's your favorite kind of music?

Ana Well, I think country is cool. The Dixie Chicks are great. I really like them.

Daisy I do, too! They're a *great* country group! How about other kinds of music? Do you like jazz?

Ana No, I don't like it at all.

Daisy Really? What about Wynton Marsalis? A lot of people like him.

Ana Well, yeah, I guess he's OK. But I don't listen to much jazz. I like country, pop, and rock.

Daisy Do you listen to Pink?

Ana Yes! I love her! She's my favorite pop singer.

B What do other teens tell Daisy? Complete their sentences with *her*, *him*, *it*, or *them*. Then listen and check.

1. Pop music isn't interesting. I don't like ____*it*____ .

2. The Dixie Chicks are cool. I like ____*them*____ a lot.

3. Kanye West is my favorite hip-hop singer. I love ____*him*____ .

4. Classical music is boring. I don't like ____*it*____ at all.

5. Pink is an interesting singer. I like ____*her*____ .

6. Sean Paul is great. I love ____*him*____ .

3 Speaking

Complete questions 6, 7, and 8. Then ask a classmate the questions. *(Answers will vary.)*

Do you like . . . ?	A lot	A little	Not at all
1. jazz	☐	☐	☐
2. country	☐	☐	☐
3. rock	☐	☐	☐
4. hip-hop	☐	☐	☐
5. reggae	☐	☐	☐
6. _____ (male singer)	☐	☐	☐
7. _____ (female singer)	☐	☐	☐
8. _____ (group)	☐	☐	☐

Peter, do you like jazz?

No, I don't like it at all.

Let's look online.

1 Vocabulary

A Look at some items in the *Discover Your World* online catalog.
Then listen and practice.

ONLINE STORE

SEARCH

keyword GO

Discover Your World

1 star map — $17.50

2 telescope — $49.95

3 radio-controlled airplane — $96.99

4 travel vest — $52.06

5 nature puzzles — $9.89 each

6 adventure DVDs — $34.79 each

7 science kit — $60.00

8 wall calendars — $16.00 each

B Look at the items and prices in Part A. Then listen and practice.

C Practice saying the items and prices with a classmate.

> The travel vest.

> It's fifty-two-oh-six. OR It's fifty-two dollars and six cents.

> The nature puzzles.

> They're nine eighty-nine each. OR They're nine dollars and eighty-nine cents.

> The wall calendars.

> They're sixteen dollars each.

Let's look online.

This lesson presents and practices the names of items found in a natural science catalog and the language for asking about prices with How much is / are . . . ?

Review of Lesson 13

- Write on the board:
  A: Do you like (Christina Aguilera)?
  B: Yes, I do. I like (her). OR No, I don't. I don't like (her).

- Divide the class into two groups. Ask the students in Group 1 to write the name of a singer, musician, or group on a small piece of paper. Tell them that they have to find someone in Group 2 who likes the same singer, musician, or group. Tell students they should talk about the singer, musician, or group using the conversation on the board.

1 Vocabulary

This exercise presents and practices the names of items commonly found in a natural science catalog.

A CD1, Track 58

- Focus students' attention on the photos and the labels. Explain the names of any items you think students may not be familiar with.
- Play the recording. Students listen.

Audio script
See page T-205.

- Play the recording again, or model the sentences. Students listen and repeat.

B CD1, Track 59

- Ask students to look at the price tags in Part A.
- Play the recording. Students listen.

Audio script
See page T-205.

- Play the recording again, or model the sentences. Students listen and repeat.

Culture Note In the U.S., the most commonly used bills come in amounts of 1, 5, 10, 20, 50, and 100 dollars. The most commonly used coins are the penny (one cent), the nickel (five cents), the dime (ten cents), and the quarter (twenty-five cents).

C

- Have students read the directions and the sentences.
- Tell students that the prices of two of the items can be said in two ways.
- Have students work in pairs to practice saying the items and prices.

2 Language focus

This exercise presents and practices *How much is / are . . . ?*

A 🔊 CD1, Track 60

- Ask students to look at the photo. Ask: *What's Ben looking at?* (An online science catalog.) *And Tina?* (A science catalog in printed form.)
- Play the recording. Students listen and read along.

> **Audio script**
> Same as the conversation in the Student's Book.

- Ask: *How much is the radio-controlled airplane?* (It's $96.99.) *Who likes the nature puzzles?* (Ben does.) *How much are the nature puzzles?* (They're $9.89 each.)
- Play the recording again, or model the conversation. Students listen and repeat.
- **Optional** Have students practice in pairs.
- **Language Chart** Have students study the examples in the language chart. Focus students' attention on the words in bold. Ask: *Why is* is *used in the first example and* are *in the second?* (Because *it* is singular and the word *puzzles* is plural.) Ask: *What else is different in the examples because of* it *and* puzzles? (The answers to the questions. The first answer uses *It's* and the second uses *They're*.)
- Model the examples, pausing for students to repeat.

B 🔊 CD1, Track 61

- Have students read the conversation and then work individually to complete it.
- Play the recording. Students listen and verify their answers.

> **Audio script**
> Same as the conversation in the Student's Book.

- Check answers with the class. Invite volunteers to read one of the sentences they completed.
- Have students practice the conversation in pairs.

3 Listening

In this exercise, students listen for the prices of items.

🔊 CD1, Track 62

- Focus students' attention on the chart. Copy it onto the board.
- Explain that students will listen to a conversation between Ben and Tina as they compare prices for five different items. Students should listen and write the prices in the chart.
- Play the recording. Students only listen.

> **Audio script**
> See page T-205.

- Play the recording again. Students listen and complete the chart.
- Play the recording once again. Students listen and verify their answers.

- Check answers with the class. Have volunteers come to the board to write the prices in the chart.
- **Optional** Ask a volunteer to come to the front and bring a personal item. The volunteer asks the class: *How much is this (notebook)?* The student who guesses the price within 25 cents replaces the volunteer and continues the activity.

> **Workbook**
> Assign the exercises on Workbook page 24. (Workbook answers begin on page T-190.)

> **Extra Grammar**
> Assign the exercises for the Extra Grammar, Lesson 14.

2 | Language focus

How much is / are ...?

How much is it?
It's **$96.99**.
How much are the puzzles?
They're **$9.89** each.

A Ben talks to Tina about things in the online catalog.
Listen and practice.

Ben Hey! This is a great Web site!
All these things are cool.
There's a great radio-controlled airplane.

Tina Really? Radio controlled? How much is it?

Ben It's $96.99.

Tina That's almost a hundred dollars!

Ben I know. I like these nature puzzles, too.

Tina How much are they?

Ben They're $9.89 each.

Tina Hmm. That's not very expensive.

B Complete the rest of the conversation.
Listen and check. Then practice.

Ben Wow. I like this telescope.

Tina _____How much is_____ it?

Ben _____It's_____ $49.95. And there's an
interesting star map, too. I can
study the stars!

Tina _____How much is_____ the star map?

Ben _____It's_____ $17.50. And these
adventure DVDs are exciting.

Tina And _____how much are_____ the
adventure DVDs, Ben?

Ben Well, _____they're_____ $34.79 each.

Tina You like a lot of things, Ben.
Too bad you don't have a lot of money!

3 | Listening

Ben and Tina compare prices in their catalogs. Listen and write
the prices in the chart.

	Watch	T-shirts	Camera	Hiking boots	Backpack
Ben's online catalog	$39.99	$19.89	$89.99	$68.00	$10.00
Tina's catalog	$29.99	$10.50	$99.99	$68.00	$40.00

Mini-review

1 Language check

A Bryan and Ashley shop for a birthday present for their friend, Matt. Complete the conversation with the correct words. Then practice.

Bryan It's Matt's birthday on Sunday. What can we get __him__ (her / him)?

Ashley How about a CD? Does he like reggae?

Bryan No, he doesn't like __it__ (it / them) at all.

Ashley Well, what about pop? Does he like pop?

Bryan Yes. Actually, he loves __it__ (it / them). His favorite singer is Pink.

Ashley Really? I like __her__ (him / her), too.

Bryan Oh, look. Here's a CD by the Dixie Chicks.

Ashley Does Matt like the Dixie Chicks?

Bryan Yes, he loves __them__ (it / them).

Ashley Great. How much __is__ (is / are) the CD?

Bryan __It's__ (It's / They're) $13.95.

Ashley OK. Let's buy __it__ (it / them).

B Bryan asks Ashley about the prices of other things in the music store. Write their questions and answers.

| electric guitar $98.99 | DVDs $32.99 | T-shirt $8.99 | posters $10.99 each |

1. **Bryan** _How much is the electric guitar?_

   Ashley _It's ninety-eight ninety-nine._ **OR** _It's ninety-eight dollars and ninety-nine cents._

2. **Bryan** _How much are the DVDs?_

   Ashley _They're thirty-two ninety-nine. / They're thirty-two dollars and ninety-nine cents._

3. **Bryan** _How much is the T-shirt?_

   Ashley _It's eight ninety-nine. / It's eight dollars and ninety-nine cents._

4. **Bryan** _How much are the posters?_

   Ashley _They're ten ninety-nine each. / They're ten dollars and ninety-nine cents each._

Lessons 13 & 14 Mini-review

This lesson reviews the language presented and practiced in Lessons 13 and 14.

1 Language check

This exercise reviews the structures presented so far in this unit.

A

- Have students look at the photo and read the conversation quickly.
- Ask: *What are Bryan and Ashley shopping for?* (A birthday present for Matt.) *Does Matt like reggae?* (No.) *Does he like pop music?* (Yes.) *What do they buy for Matt?* (A CD by the Dixie Chicks.)
- Have students work individually to complete the conversation.
- Check answers with the class.
- Have students practice the conversation in pairs.
- **Optional** Divide the class into four groups. Assign each group one of the four object pronouns – *her, him, it,* and *them*. Tell groups that they will substitute pronouns for nouns. Say: *I like Ashley. Students in the* her *group should stand.* Continue until each group has had a turn.

B

- Focus students' attention on the items in the photos. Elicit the names of the items. (A guitar, DVDs, a T-shirt, and posters.) Ask: *Why is the word* each *written next to one item and not the others?* (The posters have the word *each* written next to the price so that we know that the price is a per-item price.)
- Ask students to read the directions and the example. Make sure that students understand they will be writing both the questions and the answers. Tell them to write the questions and answers in the same order as the items appear in the photos.
- Have students work individually to complete the exercise.
- Check answers with the class. Have volunteers come to the board to write a question and an answer each.
- **Optional** Have students practice the questions and answers in pairs.

C

- Have volunteers read the directions and the example aloud.
- Have students read the sentences. Point out that Numbers 2 and 5 have two blanks each.

- Have students work individually to complete the exercise.
- Check answers with the class. Invite volunteers to read their answers aloud.

2 Listening

CD1, Track 63

- Tell students that they are going to listen to Rick and Beverly talk about music.
- Have students read the directions and the statements with the choices.
- Play the recording. Students only listen.

Audio script
See page T-206.

- Play the recording again. Students listen and check the correct answers.
- Play the recording once again. Students listen and verify their answers.
- Check answers with the class. Invite volunteers to read their completed sentences aloud.

Culture Note

Different cultures have different customs about gift-giving. In the U.S., when you receive a present (or gift), you are usually expected to open it immediately in the presence of the giver. Then, of course, you should say both "Thank you" and something nice about the gift. This is true even if the gift is something you do not really like or want. Nowadays, people sometimes "re-gift" presents they do not want. But this can cause problems if the original giver asks about the gift later – for example, "Let's listen to the CD I gave you." Or sometimes people have accidentally "re-gifted" a present to the person who gave it to them!

Workbook
Assign the exercises on Workbook page 25. (Workbook answers begin on page T-190.)

Game
Assign the game on Student's Book page 117.

C **Complete the sentences with the words in the box.**

☐ are ☐ him ☐ is ☐ it's ☐ them
☐ her ☐ how ☑ it ☐ much ☐ they're

1. Country music is boring. I don't like _____it_____ at all.

2. __How__ much __are__ the wall calendars?

3. Rihanna's my favorite singer. I like _____her_____ a lot.

4. The science kits are very expensive. __They're__ $89.99 each!

5. How __much__ __is__ the star map?

6. The Jonas Brothers are great. I really like _____them_____ !

7. Rob Thomas is my favorite singer. I like _____him_____ a lot.

8. This puzzle is cool. And _____it's_____ only $12.99.

2 Listening

Rick and Beverly talk about music at Beverly's birthday party.
Listen and check (✓) the correct answers.

1. Beverly's favorite kind of music
   is _____ .
   ☐ hip-hop   ☑ pop

2. Rick thinks Carrie Underwood _____ .
   ☐ isn't interesting   ☑ is great

3. Beverly _____ country music.
   ☑ likes   ☐ doesn't like

4. Yo-Yo Ma is a _____ musician.
   ☐ jazz   ☑ classical

5. Rick and Beverly buy a lot of music
   _____ .
   ☐ at the mall   ☑ online

6. On the Internet, one song is _____ .
   ☑ $0.99   ☐ $99.00

Go to page 117 for the Game.

1 Vocabulary

A These students sign up for a summer exchange program. Read about their free-time activities. Then listen and practice.

Lucas

I go camping.

Dana

I write poetry.

Karen

I go dancing a lot.

Fred

I spend time at the beach.

Colleen

I go shopping with my friends.

Kim

I do crossword puzzles.

B Match two students in Part A to the host student below with similar interests. Then write their names. *(The order of the answers may vary.)*

I love the outdoors. I'm a very active person.

Celso, Brazil

_____Lucas_____

_____Fred_____

I stay home a lot. I like quiet activities.

Kelly, Canada

_____Dana_____

_____Kim_____

I go out, and I do a lot of things with my friends.

Marta, Puerto Rico

_____Karen_____

_____Colleen_____

C You want to be a host student. How do you describe yourself? Tell your classmates. Use words from Part A or your own ideas.

> I like sports. I play tennis a lot. I spend time with my friends. I . . .

Lesson 15 Our interests

This lesson presents and practices the names of free-time activities and like / don't like + to *(verb).*

Review of Lesson 14

- Play a round of price "Bingo." Ask students to draw bingo grids on a piece of paper. Write eleven prices with dollar-and-cent amounts on the board – for example, $16.95 and $9.79. Students choose nine of these prices and write them on their grids. Randomly read nine of the prices and keep track of which ones you have read. The first three students to get bingo are the winners.

- Choose one of your personal belongings and place it somewhere where the class can see it. Write the price of the object on the board, along with three or four similar prices. Ask: *How much is this (ruler)?* The first student who guesses correctly comes to the front and continues the activity.

1 Vocabulary

This exercise presents and practices the names of free-time activities.

A CD1, Track 64

- Explain the title of the lesson, "Our interests." (What students are interested in or like to do.)

- Have students read the directions. Focus students' attention on the pictures and have them raise their hands if they do any of these activities.

- Have students focus on the captions.

- Play the recording. Students listen and read along.

> **Audio script**
> Same as the captions in the Student's Book.

- Play the recording again, or model the sentences. Students listen and repeat.

B

- Have students read the directions. Explain *host student.* (A student at whose home an exchange student lives.)

- Have students look at the pictures and read the text in the speech balloons. Explain *outdoors* and *active.* (Outdoors: out under the sky; active: having a lot of energy, and doing many things.)

- Explain that Celso, Kelly, and Marta want to invite students to their homes for the summer. Students have to pick which of the students from Part A have similar interests. They should write two names under each picture.

- Have students work individually to complete the exercise.

- While students are completing the exercise, write *Celso, Kelly,* and *Marta* on the board. Draw two blanks under each name.

- Check answers with the class. Invite volunteers to come to the board to write their answers.

C

- Have students read the directions. Give students a few minutes to think about how they describe themselves – the things they like and how they spend their time.

- Ask students to tell their classmates three or four of their free-time activities, following the example. Encourage students to use vocabulary from previous lessons.

- **Optional** Play "Toss the Ball." Throw the ball to one of the students. Say: *I go shopping.* That student responds with *(She) goes shopping, and I go dancing* and then tosses the ball to another student, who adds another part.

Note: For large classes, have the students play in groups of six to eight.

> **Culture Note**   Many students participate in exchange programs all over the world. American Field Service, or AFS, has been one of the largest organizations of this type in the U.S. since 1947. Their offices can be found in 52 countries. Students who participate in AFS exchange programs are 15 to 18 years old. They live abroad with a host family in a foreign community for a year, a semester, or a summer.

2 Language focus

This exercise presents and practices *like / don't like* + *to* (verb).

A 💿 CD1, Track 65

- Ask students to read the directions and the application form. Explain *application form*.
- Play the recording. Students listen and read along.

> **Audio script**
> Same as the form in the Student's Book.

- Ask: *How old is Daniela?* (Sixteen.) *Where's she from?* (Brazil.) *Can she swim?* (Yes, she can.)
- Play the recording again, or model the statements in number 4 on the application form. Students listen and repeat.
- **Language Chart** Have students study the examples in the language chart. Focus students' attention on the words in bold. Explain that if a verb follows the word *like*, the word *to* goes between *like* and the verb. Write on the board: *I like soccer. I like to play soccer.* Ask: *How are these two sentences different?* (The sentence with *play* has *to* after the word *like*.) Do the same for a negative statement. Write: *I don't like baseball. I don't like to play baseball.* Ask students to compare the sentences once again.
- Model the examples, pausing for students to repeat.

B

- Have students work individually to complete the form with their own information. While students are working, write the form on the board.
- Check answers with the class. Ask a student to come to the board to fill in his or her information.

C

- Ask students to share their information with the class, following the example.
- **Optional** Play a round of "Gossip." Whisper a long sentence with *like to* or *don't like to* to the first student in each group. Include at least three verb phrases. Demonstrate the Gossip game in the usual way (see Exercise 3C on page T-5).

----

3 Listening

In this exercise, students listen to what two people like to do in their free time.

💿 CD1, Track 66

- Copy the chart onto the board.
- Tell students that they will listen to Marta tell her friend Eve about Karen, the new exchange student. Students should check the correct name(s) for each activity.
- Play the recording. Students only listen.

> **Audio script**
> See page T-206.

- Ask: *What free-time activities did you hear?* (Go dancing, go to the mall, go shopping, play tennis, go to the movies, and watch DVDs.)
- Play the recording again. Students listen and check the correct boxes.

- Play the recording once again. Students listen and verify their answers.
- Check answers with the class. Invite volunteers to come to the board to complete the chart.

> **Workbook**
> Assign the exercises on Workbook page 26. (Workbook answers begin on page T-190.)

> **Extra Grammar**
> Assign the exercises for the Extra Grammar, Lesson 15.

2 Language focus

like / don't like + to (verb)

I **like to go** shopping.
I **like to play** video games.
I **don't like to practice** the piano.

A Daniela applies to an exchange program. Read her application form. Then listen and practice.

1. Name: _Daniela da Costa_   2. Age: __16__
3. Country: _Brazil_
4. Activities you like to do / don't like to do:
   I like to go swimming. I also like to go
   shopping. I don't like to watch TV.
5. Do you like to go camping? _No, I don't._
6. Do you like to spend time at home?
   Yes, I do.

B Complete the form with your own information.
(_Answers will vary._)

1. Name: _____   2. Age: _____
3. Country: _____
4. Activities you like to do / don't like to do:

   _____

   _____

5. Do you like to go camping? _____
6. Do you like to spend time at home?

   _____

C Tell your classmates things you like and don't like to do. Use Exercise 1A or your own information.

I like to listen to music. I don't like to go camping. I . . .

3 Listening

An exchange student, Karen, is staying with Marta's family. Marta is talking to her friend Eve about the experience. Who likes to do these activities? Listen and check (✓) the correct boxes.

	Karen	Marta	Karen and Marta
1. go dancing	☐	☐	✓
2. go shopping	✓	☐	☐
3. play tennis	✓	☐	☐
4. go to the movies	☐	✓	☐

In and out of school

1 Language focus

A Take the survey. Circle a letter to complete each sentence. *(Answers will vary.)*

Adverbs of frequency	
100%	I **always** do my homework.
	I **usually** come to class on time.
	{ **Sometimes** I talk in class.
	{ I **sometimes** talk in class.
	I **hardly ever** sleep in class.
0%	I **never** throw paper airplanes.

SURVEY
What Kind of Student Are You?

1. I ___usually___ do my homework.
   a. always
   b. usually
   c. sometimes
   d. hardly ever
   e. never

2. I ___always___ come to class on time.
   a. always
   b. usually
   c. sometimes
   d. hardly ever
   e. never

3. I ___usually___ listen to the teacher.
   a. always
   b. usually
   c. sometimes
   d. hardly ever
   e. never

4. I ___sometimes___ answer a lot of the teacher's questions.
   a. always
   b. usually
   c. sometimes
   d. hardly ever
   e. never

5. I ___never___ listen to music on my headphones in class.
   a. always
   b. usually
   c. sometimes
   d. hardly ever
   e. never

6. I ___sometimes___ get good grades.
   a. always
   b. usually
   c. sometimes
   d. hardly ever
   e. never

7. I ___hardly ever___ sleep in class.
   a. always
   b. usually
   c. sometimes
   d. hardly ever
   e. never

8. I ___hardly ever___ throw paper airplanes in class.
   a. always
   b. usually
   c. sometimes
   d. hardly ever
   e. never

B Zach completes the survey in Part A. Listen and write his answers on the lines. Then practice.

C Talk to four of your classmates. Find out their responses to the survey items.

You	I always do my homework. How about you, Mario?
Classmate 1	I usually do my homework.
You	I hardly ever sleep in class. How about you, Jen?
Classmate 2	I always answer a lot of the teacher's questions. How about you, . . . ?

In and out of school

This lesson presents and practices adverbs of frequency.

Review of Lesson 15

- Play a round of "Tic-Tac-Toe." Fill in the grid with nine free-time activities. Students make sentences using *like / don't like to . . .* in conjunction with the verb phrases to earn squares for their teams.

- Play "Something in Common." In pairs, students make *like / don't like to . . .* sentences to find one activity they both like and one activity they both dislike. Invite volunteers to share their findings with the class. Ask students to say *We like / don't like to . . . .*

1   Language focus

This exercise presents and practices adverbs of frequency.

A

- Focus students' attention on the pictures. Ask random students to identify in English as many of the activities in the illustrations as they can.

- **Language Chart** Have students study the examples in the language chart. Explain to students that when we use these adverbs we are usually describing our habits or those of others. Explain the adverbs of frequency in terms of percentage (always = 100%, usually = about 80%, sometimes = 50%, hardly ever = 20%, never = 0%). Point out that *sometimes* can come before or after the subject. The other adverbs come between the subject and the verb.

- Assign a frequency adverb to five students. Ask them to tell the class something about their routines using the assigned word. Write the sentence on the board with the appropriate percentage for added reinforcement.

- Model the examples, pausing for students to repeat.

- Focus students' attention on the survey. Explain *survey*. Ask students to read the directions. Make sure students understand that they should complete the survey with their own personal information by circling the appropriate letter for each item. They should *not* fill in the blanks.

- Have students work individually to complete the survey.

- Have students compare their answers in pairs.

B   CD1, Track 67

- Ask students to read the directions. Tell them that they will listen to Zach talk about his school habits. They should complete the sentences in Part A with the adverbs they hear.

- Play the recording. Students only listen.

> **Audio script**
> See page T-206.

- Play the recording again. Students listen and complete the sentences.

- Play the recording once again. Students listen and verify their answers.

- Check answers with the class. Invite volunteers to read the completed sentences.

C

- Have students read the directions and the example.

- Put students in groups of five. Students take turns saying sentences and asking *How about you?* until all the survey items have been answered.

- Have one student in the group act as the secretary and record the group's responses.

- Invite each group's secretary to share some of the group's responses with the class. For example, *Alberto sometimes sleeps in class. The students in our group never throw paper airplanes.*

2 Listening

In this exercise, students listen for the frequency of Ana's and Charlie's weekend activities.

A CD1, Track 68

- Tell students that they will listen to a conversation between Ana and her friend, Charlie, about their weekend activities.
- Copy the chart on the board while students read the directions.
- Elicit how to do the activity. (Students should write *A* for Ana in the chart under the correct frequency adverb for each activity.)
- Play the recording. Students only listen.

> **Audio script**
> See page T-206.

- Play the recording again. Students listen and write *A* under the correct adverbs in the chart.
- Play the recording once again. Students listen and verify their answers.
- Check answers with the class. Invite volunteers to come to the board to complete the chart. When you are finished, do not erase the chart from the board.

B CD1, Track 69

- Tell students that they will listen to the conversation again and should write *C* for Charlie in the chart under the correct frequency adverb for each activity.
- Play the recording from Part A again. Students listen and complete the exercise.

> **Audio script**
> Same as the script for Part A above.

- Play the recording once again. Students listen and verify their answers.
- Check answers with the class. Have volunteers come to the board to complete the chart for Charlie.

....

3 Speaking

This exercise practices using frequency adverbs to describe everyday activities.

A

- Have students read the directions and the activities in the box. Tell students that they can also use activities from previous lessons.
- Have students work individually to write sentences using the frequency adverbs in parentheses.

B

- Have students read their sentences in pairs.
- Ask students to tell the class two of their partner's activities, following the example.

- **Optional** On the board, write the five frequency adverbs side by side. Divide the class into two or three teams. Ask one student from each team to come to the front. Say an activity *(go dancing)*. The first student to say an adverb must use that adverb and activity in a sentence. *(I always go dancing on Saturday.)* If the sentence is correct, the student's team earns a point. The first team to earn ten points wins.

> **Workbook**
> Assign the exercises on Workbook page 27. (Workbook answers begin on page T-190.)

> **Extra Grammar**
> Assign the exercises for the Extra Grammar, Lesson 16.

2 Listening

A Ana talks about her weekend activities. How often does she do these things? Listen and write A (Ana) in the correct columns.

Weekend activities	Always	Usually	Sometimes	Hardly ever	Never
1. go dancing			A		C
2. go shopping	A			C	
3. sleep late		C		A	
4. read books	C				A
5. go bowling			A C		

B How often does Charlie do the things in Part A? Listen again and write C (Charlie) in the correct columns in Part A.

3 Speaking

A What do you do after school? Write sentences.
Use the activities in the box or your own ideas. *(Answers will vary.)*

☐ do my homework   ☐ go shopping   ☐ play the guitar   ☐ use the Internet   ☐ watch TV

(always) *I always watch TV after school.*

1. (always) _____

2. (usually) _____

3. (sometimes) _____

4. (hardly ever) _____

5. (never) _____

B Work with a classmate. Read your sentences from Part A to each other.
Then tell the class two things about your classmate.

Nadia always goes to soccer practice after school. She hardly ever goes shopping.

Read

A Read the article quickly. Check (✓) the words you find.

☐ 1. boring   ☐ 3. exciting   ☐ 5. interesting
☐ 2. cool   ☑ 4. fun   ☑ 6. popular

Check Out the iTunes Store!

American teens like to listen to music. They usually listen to music on their MP3 players and spend 30 minutes a day **downloading** songs. Where do they download songs from? From the iTunes Store. This store is the number one music store in the U.S., and it's all on the Internet. And it's not only popular in the U.S. People from many countries now buy and download songs from this store.

The iTunes Store is amazing. It has more than six **million** songs – from rock to classical to rap to country. And it also **sells** TV shows, movies, iPod games, and **audio books**. How much are songs? One song is usually $0.99 and an **album** is about $9.99. TV shows are around $1.99, and you can **rent** a new movie for $3.99.

You don't need to go to a music store or a bookstore. Check out the iTunes Store. It's really **convenient** . . . and it's fun.

Go to page 123 for the **Vocabulary Practice.**

B 💿 Read the article slowly. Check your answers in Part A.

C Answer the questions.

1. Do American teens like to listen to music? *Yes, they do.*

2. Do American teens usually spend 30 minutes a day downloading songs?
   Yes, they do.

3. How many songs does iTunes have? *It has more than six million songs.*

4. How much is one song? *One song is usually $0.99.*

5. How much are new movies? *New movies are $3.99.*

This lesson practices reading, listening, and writing skills.

Review of Lesson 16

- Write the five adverbs *always, usually, sometimes, hardly ever,* and *never* on five separate index cards. Place them face down on a desk in front of the room. Say: *I _____ go shopping on Saturday.* Pick up the card with the adverb that describes how often you do that particular activity, but keep it hidden from view. Students guess the adverb you have chosen by saying *You (usually) go shopping on Saturday,* filling in the adverb of their choice. The first student who guesses correctly comes to the front and continues the activity.

Note: For large classes, you can do this activity with one row of students at a time.

- Students work in pairs to find something that both of them *always, sometimes,* and *never* do. Ask volunteers to share their results with the class.

Read

This exercise practices reading for information about a music Web site.

A

- Have students look at the photos. Ask: *What do you see in the pictures?* (Students downloading and listening to music.)

Culture Note
The current trend of getting music online has led to a lot of changes in the music industry. When it started, people were downloading music online for free. This was illegal, because it meant that musicians and producers were not getting paid for their work. Now, with the arrival of online music stores like iTunes, people can buy music online legally. When people buy music online, they can load it directly onto an MP3 player. There is no need for a CD. Because of this, the sales of traditional CDs are declining and many "real world" music stores are closing. Some people are not happy about this situation. For one thing, they say that the quality of the downloaded music files is not as good as a CD.

- Invite a volunteer to read the directions and the six words aloud. Remind students that they should read quickly to find the words and that they should not read every word carefully.

- Have students work individually to read the article quickly and check the words they find. Do not check answers at this point.

B CD1, Track 70

- Invite a volunteer to read the directions aloud. Remind students that they should read slowly and carefully, and concentrate on getting the meaning of the entire text.

- List the new vocabulary words on the board: *downloading, million, sell, audio book, album, rent (v.), convenient.* Explain their meaning. (Downloading [songs]: taking songs from the Internet or an online music store and listening to them on CDs, your

computer, or an MP3 player; million: 1,000,000 – for example, a million dollars is a lot of money; sell: to give something to someone and get money in return for it [demonstrate by pretending to sell something to a student]; audio book: a book that you can listen to; album: one or more CDs that come in the same case and usually have songs by the same singer, musician, or group; rent [v.]: to pay money to borrow something – for example, you can rent a DVD for a few dollars and keep it for a few days before you have to return it; convenient: easy to use or get to – for example, if your school is easy for you to get to, then it is convenient for you.) As an alternative, have students use their dictionaries to find the meanings of the new vocabulary words.

- Have students read the article again.

- Have students check their answers in Part A in pairs. Elicit the answers from one pair.

- **Optional** Play the recording. Students listen and read along.

Audio script
Same as the article in the Student's Book.

Get Connected Vocabulary
Have students do the exercise on Student's Book page 123 in class or for homework. (Get Connected Vocabulary answers are on page T-123.)

C

- Invite a volunteer to read the directions and the first question aloud.

- Ask: *Do American teens like to listen to music?* Elicit the answer. (Yes, they do.)

- Have students work individually to answer the questions.

- Check answers with the class. Invite volunteers to read aloud one answer each.

Listen

In this exercise, students listen for information about two people.

A 🔊 CD1, Track 71

- Focus students' attention on the album cover. Ask: *What's the name of this band?* (The Dixie Chicks.) Ask for a show of hands of students who listen to the Dixie Chicks.

- Tell students they will listen to two friends, Yuki and Carlos, talk about music.

- Have students read the first question and the example answer.

- Explain that students should listen to the conversation and answer the questions.

- Play the recording. Students only listen.

> ### Audio script
> See page T-207.

- Play the recording again. Students listen and answer the questions.

- Play the recording once again. Students listen and verify their answers.

- Check answers with the class. Invite volunteers to read one answer each. When the answer to a question is *No*, have the student give the correct information.

B

- Have students read the directions and all the statements.

- Explain that *I agree* means you think something is right, *I disagree* means you think something is not right, and *I'm not sure* means you cannot say if you think it is right or not. Tell students that there are no right or wrong answers for this exercise – they are giving their opinions.

- Have students work individually to write whether they agree, disagree, or are not sure.

- Have students work in pairs to compare answers, or elicit opinions from volunteers.

Write

In this exercise, students answer questions and write about their musical habits.

A

- Invite a volunteer to read the directions aloud. Explain that a *habit* is something you do regularly. Elicit examples of good and bad habits. (Good habit: cleaning your room; bad habit: biting your nails.)

- Have students work individually to answer the questions.

- **Optional** Have students ask and answer the questions in pairs.

B

- Invite a volunteer to read the directions aloud.

- Tell students that they will use their answers in Part A to help them write about their musical habits.

- Have students work individually to write their paragraphs.

- Invite several volunteers to read their paragraphs to the class.

- **Optional** Have students work in groups to read each other's paragraphs. Students can ask about anything that was not clear or about which they would like to have more details. Write these questions on the board for students to discuss in their groups: *How are your musical habits the same? How are they different?*

> **Teaching Tip**
> When students work in groups, circulate and listen to their conversations but do not correct mistakes at this time. Take some notes and discuss common problems as a follow-up to the activity.

> ### Workbook
> Assign the exercises on Workbook page 28. (Workbook answers begin on page T-190.)

I always listen to country.

Listen

A 🔊 **Yuki and Carlos talk about music. Listen and answer the questions.**

1. Does Carlos often go to music stores? _No, he doesn't._

2. Does Yuki have an MP3 player? _No, she doesn't._

3. Does Carlos like to listen to country music? _Yes, he does._

4. Does Yuki like to listen to country music? _No, she doesn't._

5. Does Yuki often go to music stores on Mondays? _No, she doesn't._

B **What do you think? Write *I agree*, *I disagree*, or *I'm not sure*.**
(Answers will vary.)

1. It's fun to listen to music on MP3 players. _____

2. Downloading music online is easy. _____

3. Music stores (not online) are convenient. _____

4. Country music is cool. _____

5. Rock music is exciting. _____

Your turn

Write

A **Think about your musical habits. Answer the questions.** *(Answers will vary.)*

1. What kind of music do you like? _____

2. Do you usually listen to CDs? _____

3. Do you listen to music online? _____

4. Do you have an MP3 player? _____

5. How much time do you usually spend downloading songs?

   _____

B **Write about your musical habits. Use the answers in Part A to help you.** *(Answers will vary.)*

○○○

I like _____ music a lot, and I like _____ music, too.

_____

_____

_____

◄ ►

Language chart review

her / him / it / them	like / don't like + to (verb)
She's cool. I like **her**.	I **like to hang out** with friends.
He's a pop singer. I like **him** a lot.	I **don't like to stay** home.
Jazz is boring. I don't like **it**.	
These CDs are great. I like **them**.	

A Read these sentences. Then write sentences with *like* or *don't like*.

1. My new neighbors are great!
   I like them.

2. That book is boring.
   I don't like it.

3. She's my best friend.
   I like her.

4. My baby brother is really cute.
   I like him.

5. Snakes are dangerous.
   I don't like them.

6. I think rock is cool.
   I like it.

B Josh writes an e-mail message to you. Read Josh's message. Then complete your message to him. Tell him about your free-time activities. *(Answers will vary.)*

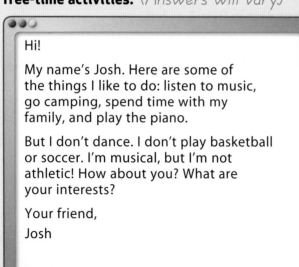

Hi!

My name's Josh. Here are some of the things I like to do: listen to music, go camping, spend time with my family, and play the piano.

But I don't dance. I don't play basketball or soccer. I'm musical, but I'm not athletic! How about you? What are your interests?

Your friend,

Josh

Dear Josh,

Hi! My name's _____ .

Here are some of the things I like to do:

_____

_____ .

Here are some of the things I don't like to do:

_____

_____ .

Please write again soon.

Your friend, _____

Unit 4 Review

This lesson reviews the grammar and vocabulary introduced in Unit 4.

Language chart review

This chart summarizes the main grammar presented and practiced in Unit 4.

- Books closed. Write on the board:

  She's nice. I like _____ .

  He's a jazz musician. I like _____ a lot.

  Classical music is boring. I don't like _____ .

  These shoes are great. I like _____ .

like	*like to*
I like poetry.	_____ *(write)*
I don't like basketball.	_____ *(play)*

- Focus students' attention on the information on the board. Have them complete the top sentences with the correct object pronouns. Then have them rewrite the bottom sentences using *like to* and the verbs in parentheses.
- Invite volunteers to write the answers on the board.
- Books open. Have students check their answers and those on the board against the examples in the Language chart review.
- Invite volunteers either to make sentences with an object pronoun or to share with the class something they like to do.
- Answer any questions students may have.

··

Exercises A through D (pages T-56 to T-57)

Note: Students can do these exercises for homework or in class. They should do these exercises with minimal teacher input or help. If you choose to do these exercises as homework, briefly review the exercise directions in class. Make sure that students understand what they should do. Check the answers with the class during the next class meeting. If you choose to do the exercises in class, follow the directions below.

Exercise A

- Have a volunteer read the directions and the example aloud.
- Tell students to write sentences with *like* or *don't like* and the correct object pronoun.
- Have students work individually to write the sentences.
- Check answers with the class.

Exercise B

- Have students read the directions and Josh's e-mail message.
- Ask: *What does Josh do in his free time?* (Listen to music; go camping; spend time with his family; play the piano.)
- Have students work individually to complete their e-mail message to Josh.
- Invite three or four students to read their e-mail messages to the class.

Language chart review

This chart summarizes further grammar presented and practiced in Unit 4.

- Have students study the examples in the chart.
- Remind students to use *How much is . . . ?* with singular nouns and *How much are . . . ?* with plural nouns. Remind students also that for answers, the singular will use *It's,* and the plural will use *They're.*
- Remind students also that they can use adverbs of frequency to describe their routines.
- Answer any questions students may have.

Exercise C

- Have students read the directions and the example.
- Focus students' attention on the pictures and the prices.
- Have students work individually to complete the questions and answers.
- Have students check their answers in pairs.
- Check answers with the class. Invite several pairs of volunteers to read the completed questions and answers aloud.

Exercise D

- Have a volunteer read the directions and the example aloud.
- Focus students' attention on Sam's schedule and the example. Ask: *Does Sam do homework every night?* (Yes, he does.) Explain that this is why the example sentence uses the word *always.*
- Have students work individually to complete the exercise.
- Have students compare answers in pairs.
- Check answers with the class. Invite volunteers to read aloud one sentence each.

Optional Unit Wrap-Up

- If students did the Review exercises for homework, check answers with the class.
- Review the use of object pronouns, as in Exercise A. With students, make a list on the board of singers, musical groups, kinds of music, popular CDs, etc. Have students ask and answer questions about the items on the list. One student asks, *Do you like . . . ?* Another student answers with the correct object pronoun. For example, Classmate 1: *Do you like the Jonas Brothers?* Classmate 2: *Yes, I like them a lot.*
- Have students form pairs. Have students write an e-mail message to their partner about things they like to do in their free time, as in Exercise B. Have partners read each other's messages.
- Ask students to think about some popular stores in their community. Ask what they can usually buy in these stores. Have students ask and answer questions, as in Exercise C, about the prices of common items using *How much is / are . . . ?*

Theme Project

- Assign the *At Home* section of the Unit 4 Theme Project on Student's Book page 129.

Workbook

- Assign the Unit 4 Check Yourself on Workbook page 29. (Workbook answers begin on page T-190.)

Extra Practice Worksheets

- Assign the Unit 4 Extra Practice worksheets starting on page T-145.

Extra Speaking Practice Worksheet

- Assign the Unit 4 Extra Speaking Practice worksheet on page T-168.

Arcade Activities

- Assign the Unit 4 Arcade activities found at: www.cambridge.org/connectarcade

Learning Log

- Assign the Unit 4 Learning Log. These can be downloaded from the Teacher Support Site at: www.cambridge.org/connect2e/teacher

Quiz

- Give the Unit 4 Quiz on page T-179.

Test

- Give the Unit 4 Test (Form A and / or Form B). These can be downloaded from the Teacher Support Site at: www.cambridge.org/connect2e/teacher

Language chart review

How much is / are . . . ?	Adverbs of frequency
How much is this DVD? It's **$29.99**. **How much are** those boots? They're **$60.00**.	100% **I always** get good grades. **I usually** get up early. **Sometimes** I / I **sometimes** hang out with friends. **I hardly ever** go to bed early. 0% **I never** stay home on Friday night.

C Complete the questions with *How much is* or *How much are*.
Then look at the photos, and answer the questions.

 **$6.95 each**  **$9.79 each**  **$89.00**  **$49.95**

1. **Q:** _How much are_ those puzzles?   **A:** _They're six ninety-five each._
2. **Q:** _How much is_ the skateboard?   **A:** _It's eighty-nine dollars._
3. **Q:** _How much is_ that science kit?   **A:** _It's forty-nine ninety-five._
4. **Q:** _How much are_ those cameras?   **A:** _They're nine seventy-nine each._

D How often does Sam do these things? Look at his schedule. Then write sentences with
always, usually, sometimes, hardly ever, or *never*.

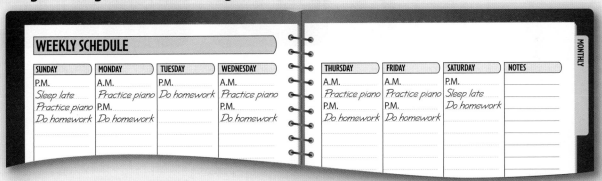

1. (do homework at night)

   I always do my homework at night.

2. (sleep late)

   I sometimes sleep late.

3. (practice the piano in the morning)

   I usually practice the piano in the morning.

4. (practice the piano in the afternoon)

   I hardly ever practice the piano in the afternoon.

5. (go bowling)

   I never go bowling.

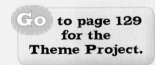

Go to page 129
for the
Theme Project.

1 Vocabulary

A Claudia and her family are on vacation in San Francisco. What do they do there? Match the photos to the correct activities. Then listen and practice.

Visit San Francisco

In San Francisco, they . . .

[5] buy souvenirs.	[8] ride a trolley.
[7] go sightseeing.	[4] see a show.

[2] take a boat ride.	[1] visit a museum.
[6] take pictures.	[3] walk in the park.

B What can people do in your town or city? Write the activities. Use Part A or your own ideas. *(Answers will vary.)*

1. *Take a boat ride.*
2. _____
3. _____

4. _____
5. _____
6. _____

This lesson presents and practices the names of vacation activities and present continuous affirmative statements.

1 Vocabulary

This exercise presents and practices the names of common vacation activities.

Culture Note

San Francisco is a city located in the state of California. It was originally called *Yerba Buena* and was renamed San Francisco in 1847. Today about 750,000 people live there, but almost 16 million people visit each year! Some popular tourist attractions include: Chinatown, the Golden Gate Bridge, Fisherman's Wharf – the famous historic waterfront that offers tourists shopping, food, and incredible views of San Francisco Bay – and Alcatraz, the "escape-proof" prison.

A CD2, Track 2

- Have students look at the photos. Elicit as much information as possible about what the people in the photos are doing.

- Write the eight verb phrases on the board and elicit the meaning of any words students know.

- Have students write the number of each photo in the box of the corresponding verb phrase.

- Play the recording. Students listen and verify their answers.

Audio script

Same as the activities in the Student's Book.

- Check answers with the class. Say the number of each photo, and have volunteers respond with the correct verb phrase.

- Play the recording again, or model the verb phrases. Students listen and repeat.

- **Optional** Ask: *What do you like to do on vacation?* Students respond with *I like to _____* , completing the sentence with the verb phrase of their choice.

B

- Ask students to read the directions and the example. Make sure they understand that the sentences should be about where they live. Tell them they can refer to the phrases in Part A or use verb phrases from previous lessons.

- Have students work individually to complete the exercise.

- Have students work in pairs to compare their sentences.

- Check answers with the class. Invite several volunteers to share their sentences with the class.

- **Optional** Have students work in groups of four or five to decide on the four best activities. Invite two students from each group to come to the board to write the activities.

UNIT 5 Favorite Activities

This unit introduces vocabulary and expressions for talking about common recreational and vacation activities and places.

2 Language focus

This exercise presents and practices present continuous affirmative statements.

A 🔊 CD2, Track 3

- Focus students' attention on the photos. Explain that they all show Claudia and her family on a trip to San Francisco.
- Elicit as much information as possible about what the people in the photos are doing.
- Play the recording. Students listen and read along.

> ### Audio script
> Same as the text in the Student's Book.

- Ask: *Who is in San Francisco with Claudia?* (Her parents; her cousin Ruben; and her brother, Oscar.) *Where are they now?* (At Fisherman's Wharf.) Write the following on the board:

  Claudia is ___ the trip. They are ___ Fisherman's Wharf. Her mom and dad are ___ souvenirs. Ruben is ___ lunch. Oscar is ___ pictures.

- Play the recording again. Students listen and fill in the blanks.
- Invite volunteers to read the sentences aloud, filling in the correct *-ing* verbs.
- Model the sentences on the board. Students listen and repeat.
- **Language Chart** Have students study the examples in the language chart. Focus students' attention on the words in bold. Elicit the full forms of *I'm, She's, We're, You're,* and *They're.* Then focus students' attention on the *-ing* endings. Ask: *Which verb is different after adding -ing? How is it different?* (*Take.* The final *-e* is dropped when *-ing* is added.) Explain that adding *-ing* to a verb means that the action is currently taking place.

Note: Tell students that if a verb ends in a short vowel sound and a single consonant, the consonant is doubled before adding *-ing.* Write the following verbs as examples on the board:

put – putting	*stop – stopping*
run – running	*swim – swimming*
shop – shopping	

- Model the examples, pausing for students to repeat. *Note:* A little extra drilling may be necessary for students to feel comfortable pronouncing the verbs in this form.
- **Optional** Elicit previously learned verbs from students. Ask the class to say the verb using an *-ing* ending.

B 🔊 CD2, Track 4

- Ask students to read the directions and the example.
- Have students work individually to complete the exercise.
- Play the recording. Students listen and verify their answers.

> ### Audio script
> Same as the sentences in the Student's Book.

- Check answers with the class. Invite volunteers to come to the board to write their sentences.
- **Optional** Ask students to point to any picture or photo in their Student's Book and use the present continuous to describe what the people are doing.

....

3 Speaking

This exercise practices present continuous affirmative statements.

A

- Have students read the directions and the example.
- Explain that students are taking imaginary vacations, and give your own example: *I'm in (Madrid. I'm visiting a museum.)* Invite two or three volunteers to say where they are for their imaginary vacation.
- Have students work in groups of three. Students tell one another where they are and what they are doing. They can give more than one activity.

B

- Have volunteers read the directions and the example aloud.
- Invite volunteers to tell the class about one of the students in their group.

> ### Workbook
> Assign the exercises on Workbook page 30. (Workbook answers begin on page T-190.)

> ### Extra Grammar
> Assign the exercises for the Extra Grammar, Lesson 17.

2 Language focus

A Claudia is videotaping her trip to San Francisco. Listen and practice.

Today is our first day in San Francisco. I'm videotaping our trip. Right now, we're visiting Fisherman's Wharf. Let's see . . . There are Mom and Dad. They're buying souvenirs. My cousin, Ruben, is eating lunch over there. My brother, Oscar, is taking pictures with his new camera. And now you see me. You can do so much in San Francisco. It's a great city!

> I**'m videotaping** our trip.
> She**'s taking** pictures.
> We**'re visiting** Fisherman's Wharf.
> You**'re skateboarding**.
> They**'re buying** souvenirs.
> ....
> *buying = buy + ing*
> *taking = take + ing*

B Everybody's doing different things now. Write the sentences with the correct forms of the verbs. Then listen and check.

1. (Ruben / go sightseeing) _He's going sightseeing._

2. (Mom and Dad / see a show) _They're seeing a show._

3. (Oscar / take pictures) _He's taking pictures._

4. (Oscar and I / take a boat ride) _We're taking a boat ride._

3 Speaking

A Work with two classmates. Imagine you are on vacation right now. Where are you? What are you doing?

You I'm in San Francisco. I'm visiting a museum.
Classmate 1 I'm at the beach. I'm swimming.
Classmate 2 I'm in Puerto Rico. I'm taking pictures.

B Tell the class about your classmates.

You Mario is at the beach. He's swimming.
Tori is in Puerto Rico. She's taking pictures.

At the park

1 Vocabulary

A Ms. Nolan and Mr. Brown take their students to the park. Match the rules in the box to the correct signs in the picture. Then listen and practice.

> **1** Eat in the picnic area.   **3** Stand in line.   **5** Throw trash in the trash can.
> **2** Sit down in the boat.   **4** Stay on the bike path.   **6** Wait for the green light.

B Look at Part A again. Read the sentences and check (✓) T (true) or F (false).

			T	F
1.		They're waiting for the green light.	✓	☐
2.		Molly and Peter are staying on the bike path.	☐	✓
3.		The girls are eating in the picnic area.	✓	☐
4.		Dan is standing in line.	☐	✓
5.		He's throwing trash in the trash can.	✓	☐

This lesson presents and practices common rules and regulations at recreational facilities and present continuous negative statements.

Review of Lesson 17
- Write on the board:

buying	souvenirs
riding a	our trip
taking	trolley
videotaping	in the park
visiting	pictures
walking	a museum

- Have the class match the verbs on the left to the nouns or phrases on the right.
- Ask the class to think of other nouns or phrases that could be used in combination with these verbs.
- Call out these nouns, one by one. Students respond with an appropriate present continuous verb. *TV* (watching), *lunch* (eating), *soccer* (playing), *milk* (drinking), *songs* (singing), *a book* (reading), *English* (speaking).

---

1 Vocabulary

This exercise presents and practices the words for common rules and regulations at recreational facilities.

A CD2, Track 5

- Focus students' attention on the picture. Ask: *What is this?* (A park.) Ask students to describe what they see in the picture.
- Have students read the directions. Explain *rules* and *correct signs*.
- Ask students to look at the rules in the box and identify the words they know. Remind students that the rules are imperatives.
- Have students work individually to number the signs correctly.
- Play the recording. Students listen and verify their answers.

> **Audio script**
> Same as the rules in the Student's Book.

- Check answers with the class.
- Play the recording again, or model the rules. Students listen and repeat.

B

- Ask students to read the directions. Explain to students that they are to look at the picture in Part A to decide whether the statements are true or false. Students check T (true) or F (false) in the boxes.
- Have students work individually to complete the exercise.
- Check answers with the class.
- **Optional** Have students form groups of five or six. Ask a volunteer in each group to point to a picture in the Student's Book of a character doing an activity. The student then makes a positive present continuous statement about the picture, which may be either true or false. The rest of the group members call out *True* or *False*.

2 Language focus

This exercise presents and practices present continuous negative statements.

A 🔘 CD2, Track 6

- Focus students' attention on the picture. Ask: *Where are they?* (In the park.) *Are Ms. Nolan and Mr. Brown happy?* (No, they aren't.) Explain *following the rules.* (Obeying the laws or regulations.)
- Play the recording. Students listen and read along.

> **Audio script**
> Same as the conversation in the Student's Book.

- Ask: *Are Peter and Molly on the bike path?* (No, they aren't.) *What color is the light?* (It's red.) Say the following incomplete sentences. Students respond by completing them.
  Ms. Nolan isn't ___ (paying attention). Dan isn't ___ (standing in line). Ms. Nolan and Mr. Brown ___ (aren't following the rules). Peter and Molly ___ (aren't staying on the bike path).
- Play the recording again, or model the conversation. Students listen and repeat.
- **Optional** Have students practice in pairs.
- **Language Chart** Have students study the examples in the language chart. Focus students' attention on the words in bold. Point out that *not* comes between the verb *be* and the main verb + *-ing*.

- Focus students' attention on the negative contractions. Drill for pronunciation. Write *aren't* and *isn't* on the board. Call out the following words: *You, you and I, the teacher, the students, the book, Peter and Molly, Mr. Brown.* Students respond with *aren't* or *isn't*.
- Model the examples, pausing for students to repeat.

B 🔘 CD2, Track 7

- Have students read the directions.
- Have students work individually to complete the sentences.
- Play the recording. Students listen and verify their answers.

> **Audio script**
> Same as the sentences in the Student's Book.

- Check answers with the class. Invite volunteers to come to the board to write their answers.

....

3 Listening

In this exercise, students listen for what people are doing wrong.

🔘 CD2, Track 8

- Tell students that they will listen to Ms. Nolan and Mr. Brown telling the students how they are breaking the rules. Students should write the letters in the blanks to match the two parts of the sentences.
- Play the recording. Students only listen.

> **Audio script**
> See page T-207.

- Play the recording again. Students listen and complete the exercise.
- Play the recording once again. Students listen and verify their answers.
- Check answers with the class.

> **Workbook**
> Assign the exercises on Workbook page 31. (Workbook answers begin on page T-190.)

> **Extra Grammar**
> Assign the exercises for the Extra Grammar, Lesson 18.

2. Language focus

A The students aren't following the rules. Listen and practice.

> **Present continuous: negative statements**
>
> I'm **not paying** attention.
> You **aren't standing** in line.
> He **isn't standing** in line.
> We **aren't following** the rules.
> They **aren't staying** on the bike path.
> ....
> *aren't = are not   isn't = is not*

Ms. Nolan Oh, no. The students aren't following the rules! Look at Dan. He isn't standing in line.

Mr. Brown Hey, Dan! You aren't standing in line!

Ms. Nolan And look at Molly and Peter. They aren't staying on the bike path.

Mr. Brown Molly! Peter! Please stay on the bike path.

Ms. Nolan Oh, no, wait! It's a red light. I'm not paying attention.

Mr. Brown You're right. Now *we* aren't following the rules!

B Look at the picture in Exercise 1A again. What are the students doing wrong? Complete the sentences. Then listen and check.

 1. Dan _isn't standing in line_ .

2. Molly and Peter _aren't staying on the bike path_ .

 3. Fred _isn't waiting for the green light_ .

4. Brad and Jeff _aren't eating in the picnic area_ .

 5. Lisa _isn't sitting down in the boat_ .

6. Nan _isn't throwing trash in the trash can_ .

3. Listening

Now what are the students doing wrong? Listen and match the two parts of each sentence.

1. Nan and Lisa aren't _b_   a. sitting down in the boat.
2. Jeff isn't _d_   b. eating in the picnic area.
3. Dan and Fred aren't _e_   c. standing in line.
4. Brad isn't _a_   d. staying on the bike path.
5. Molly isn't _c_   e. throwing trash in the trash can.

Mini-review

1 Language check

A Write the present continuous form of the verbs.

1. sit _sitting_
2. skate _skating_
3. wait _waiting_
4. throw _throwing_
5. pay _paying_
6. stay _staying_
7. ride _riding_
8. swim _swimming_
9. go _going_

B Helena and her family are on vacation in New York City.
Complete Helena's postcard to her friend Jane.

Dear Jane,

Hello from New York City. Right now, my sister Hannah and
I are in Central Park. I _'m_ ('m / is) writing to my friends.
Hannah _is_ (is / are) taking pictures with her new camera.
Dad and my brother Marcos _aren't_ (isn't / aren't) at the
park. They _'re_ (is / 're) visiting a museum. Mom _isn't_
(isn't / aren't) visiting the museum. She _'s_ ('s / are) buying
souvenirs for our friends at home. New York is a great city!
We _'re_ (is / 're) having a lot of fun here.
See you soon!
Helena

Jane Brown
123 Front Street
Miami, FL 33123

C Use the cues to write sentences: ✓ = yes, ✗ = no.

1. Joe / wait for the green light (✓)

   Joe is waiting for the green light.

2. Alicia / sit down in the boat (✗)

   Alicia isn't sitting down in the boat.

3. Dmitri / stand in line (✗)

   Dmitri isn't standing in line.

4. Ginny / eat in the picnic area (✓)

   Ginny is eating in the picnic area.

5. Laura / stay on the bike path (✗)

   Laura isn't staying on the bike path.

6. Tony / throw trash in the trash can (✗)

   Tony isn't throwing trash in the trash can.

This lesson reviews the language presented and practiced in Lessons 17 and 18.

1 Language check

This exercise reviews the structures presented so far in this unit.

A

- Have students read the directions and the example.
- Focus students' attention on the spelling of *sitting*. Remind them to double the final consonant in words with a single short vowel sound followed by a single consonant.
- Have students work individually to complete the exercise.
- Have students check answers in pairs. Ask: *Is there another word like* sit → sitting *on the list?* (Swim → swimming.)
- Check answers with the class. Write the base form of the verbs on the board, and invite volunteers to come to the board to write the *-ing* form.

Note: Students may ask: *Why don't we double the final* w *or* y *in* throw *and* stay? Explain that the letters *w* and *y* do not follow the rule.

B

- Invite a volunteer to read the directions aloud.
- Have students read the postcard. Tell them not to write the answers yet.
- Ask: *Who is Jane?* (Helena's friend.) *Where are Helena and Hannah?* (In Central Park in New York City.)
- Have students work individually to complete the postcard.
- Check answers with the class. Invite volunteers to read aloud one sentence each.

C

- Invite a volunteer to read the directions and the example aloud.
- Focus students' attention on the cues (✓) = *yes* and (✗) = *no* in the directions and at the end of each line.
- Use the example to explain that students will use the words given to write a present continuous affirmative sentence when (✓) is at the end of the line. Ask: *What kind of sentence will you write when an (✗) is at the end of the line?* (A present continuous negative sentence.)
- Have students work individually to complete the exercise.
- Check answers with the class. Invite volunteers to read aloud one sentence each.

D

- Ask students to look at the photos. Ask: *When is 7 a.m. – in the morning or the evening?* (In the morning.) *When is 7 p.m.?* (In the evening.)

- Invite volunteers to make present continuous affirmative and negative statements about Rafael, Claudia, Kate, and Zach. Write them on the board.

- Explain to students that they will look at the photos and correct the statements. Have students read the example.

- Write *Is Kate reading a book?* on the board. Elicit the answer from students. (No.) Write *No* on the board. Then ask: *Do we use* he *or* she? (She.) Write *she* on the board next to *No*. Ask: *Do we use* is *or* isn't? (Isn't.) Write *isn't* and then the complete sentence – *No, she isn't reading a book* – on the board.

- Then ask: *What is Kate doing?* Elicit the answer from students. (She's doing her homework.) Ask: *Which pronoun would we use if the questions were asked about Rafael?* (He.)

- Have students work individually to complete the exercise.

- Check answers with the class.

- **Optional** Have students work in pairs to say and correct additional present continuous statements about the photos.

---

2 Listening

In this exercise, students listen and identify where someone is.

CD2, Track 9

- Tell students that they will listen to four separate conversations between Kate and various people. They should decide where Kate is in each one.

- Play the recording. Students only listen.

> **Audio script**
> See page T-208.

- Play the recording again. Students listen and number the sentences from 1 to 4.

- Play the recording once again. Students listen and verify their answers. While students are listening, write the sentences on the board.

- Check answers with the class. Invite volunteers to come to the board to write their answers.

> **Workbook**
> Assign the exercises on Workbook page 32. (Workbook answers begin on page T-190.)

> **Game**
> Assign the game on Student's Book page 118.

D Look at the photos. What's everyone doing? Correct the sentences.

7:00 a.m.

1. Kate's reading a book. _She isn't reading a book. She's doing her homework._

2. Rafael's taking a boat ride. _He isn't taking a boat ride. He's sleeping._

3. Claudia's visiting a museum. _She isn't visiting a museum. She's going biking._

4. Zach's watching a video. _He isn't watching a video. He's walking in the park._

7:00 p.m.

5. Rafael's walking in the park. _He isn't walking in the park. He's playing a video game._

6. Zach's taking pictures. _He isn't taking pictures. He's playing baseball._

7. Kate's standing in line. _She isn't standing in line. She's drawing._

8. Claudia's eating lunch. _She isn't eating lunch. She's doing karate._

2 Listening

Kate is busy today. Where is she? Listen and number the sentences
from 1 to 4.

She's in the park. ___3___   She's at the movie theater. ___1___

She's in a store. ___4___   She's in school. ___2___

Go to page 118 for the Game.

At the beach

1 Vocabulary

A What are these people doing at the beach? Match the two parts of each sentence. Then listen and practice.

1. Two boys are _h_   a. collecting seashells.
2. A baby is _e_   b. floating on a raft.
3. Two girls are _a_   c. flying a kite.
4. A family is _d_   d. having a picnic.
5. A dog is _g_   e. playing in the sand.
6. A man is _f_   f. sailing a boat.
7. A boy is _c_   g. swimming in the ocean.
8. A girl is _b_   h. throwing a Frisbee.

B What do you do at the beach? Write sentences about two things you do and two things you don't do. *(Answers will vary.)*

Things I do at the beach	Things I don't do at the beach
I swim in the ocean.	I don't collect seashells.

At the beach

This lesson presents and practices the names of common beach activities and present continuous Yes / No *questions.*

Review of Lesson 18

- Say a series of present continuous affirmative statements. Students convert them to the negative.
- Play a round of "Tic-Tac-Toe." Draw a grid on the board. Fill in each of the nine squares with nine verbs with -*ing* endings. Divide the class into two teams, X and O. Students earn squares for their team by using the verbs to make negative present continuous statements about their classmates – for example, *(John) isn't watching TV*. The first team with three squares in a row wins.

1 Vocabulary

This exercise presents and practices the names of common beach activities.

A CD2, Track 10

- Focus students' attention on the picture. Ask: *Where is this?* (At the beach.) Elicit as much information as possible about what the people in the picture are doing.
- Write the eight verb phrases on the board and elicit the meaning of any of the activities students know.
- Mime any of the activities that students were not able to identify. Ask students to guess which activity you are miming.
- Have students work individually to match the two parts of each sentence.
- Check answers with the class. Say each sentence number and invite volunteers to say the letter of the correct ending.

- Play the recording or model the sentences. Students listen and repeat.

Audio script

Same as the sentences in the Student's Book.

- **Optional** Call out the simple form of the verb – for example, *collect*. Students respond with the -*ing* form of the verb. (Collecting.) Continue until you have practiced all eight verbs. Then reverse the drill.

B

- Have volunteers read aloud the directions and the examples in the chart.
- Have students work individually to complete the exercise.
- Check answers with the class. Invite volunteers to share what they wrote with their classmates.

2 Language focus

This exercise presents and practices present continuous *Yes / No* questions.

A 💿 CD2, Track 11

- Focus students' attention on the picture of Marty and Ella at the beach. Ask: *What are Marty and Ella doing?* (Talking on cell phones.) Ask: *Can they see each other?* (No, they can't.)
- Explain *lifeguard*. (A person whose job it is to protect swimmers.)
- Play the recording. Students listen and read along.

> ### Audio script
> Same as the conversation in the Student's Book.

- Ask: *Are Ella and Marty talking on cell phones?* (Yes, they are.) *Is Ella sitting near a boat?* (No, she isn't.) *Is the little girl playing in the water?* (No, she isn't.) *Is she collecting seashells?* (Yes, she is.) *Are Marty and Ella looking at the same little girl?* (No, they aren't.)
- Play the recording again, or model the conversation. Students listen and repeat.
- **Optional** Have students practice in pairs.
- **Language Chart** Have students study the examples in the language chart. Focus students' attention on the first question and short answers.
- Ask: *Where is the verb* is *in the question?* (At the beginning of the sentence.) *Where is the verb* is *in the short answer?* (At the end, after *she*.) Elicit the full form of *isn't*. (Is not.) Ask: *Where is* isn't *in the short answer?* (After *she*.)
- Model the examples, pausing for students to repeat.

B 💿 CD2, Track 12

- Have students read the directions. Tell students that this is a continuation of the conversation in Part A.
- Have students work individually to complete the exercise.
- Play the recording. Students listen and verify their answers.

> ### Audio script
> Same as the conversation in the Student's Book.

- Check answers with the class. Have volunteers read aloud one sentence each.
- Have students practice the conversation in pairs.
- **Optional** Play "Toss the Ball." Say: *They are swimming in the ocean.* Toss the ball to Classmate 1. Classmate 1 stands and says: *Are they swimming in the ocean?* Classmate 1 then says another present continuous affirmative statement and tosses the ball to Classmate 2. Classmate 2 responds by converting the statement to a question, and so on.

....

3 Listening

In this exercise, students listen to a phone conversation and decide if statements are true or false.

💿 CD2, Track 13

- Tell students that they will listen to a phone conversation between Lee and Hannah. They should listen and decide whether the statements are true or false.
- Have students read the statements.
- Play the recording. Students only listen.

> ### Audio script
> See page T-208.

- Play the recording again. Students listen and check T (true) or F (false).

- Play the recording once again. Students listen and verify their answers.
- Check answers with the class.

> ### Workbook
> Assign the exercises on Workbook page 33. (Workbook answers begin on page T-190.)

> ### Extra Grammar
> Assign the exercises for the Extra Grammar, Lesson 19.

2 Language focus

Present continuous:
Yes / No questions

A Marty and Ella look for each other at the beach. Listen and practice.

Ella Hi, Marty. It's Ella. I'm at the beach. Where are you?

Marty Hi, Ella. I'm at the beach, too.

Ella Really? I'm sitting near a lifeguard chair.

Marty Hmm. Me, too. I don't see you, but I see a little girl in a red bathing suit.

Ella Me, too. Is she playing in the sand?

Marty No, she isn't. She's collecting seashells.

Ella Seashells? I guess there are a lot of girls in red bathing suits here today!

> **Is** she **playing** in the sand?
>   **Yes**, she **is**.
>   **No**, she **isn't**.
> **Are** they **throwing** a Frisbee?
>   **Yes**, they **are**.
>   **No**, they **aren't**.

B Complete the rest of the conversation. Listen and check. Then practice.

Ella OK, are you sitting near two boys?

Marty Yes, I ____am____ .

Ella ____Are____ they ___throwing___ a Frisbee?

Marty No, they ___aren't___ . They're eating lunch on the beach.

Ella Hmm. ____Is____ a boy ___flying___ a kite?

Marty Um, no. Do you see two girls near the ocean?

Ella Yes, I do.

Marty ____Are____ they ___collecting___ seashells?

Ella ____No____ , they aren't. They're having a picnic. Hey! ____Are____ we talking about the same beach?

3 Listening

Lee calls Hannah from the beach. Are these sentences true or false? Listen and check (✓) T (true) or F (false).

	T	F
1. Naomi is swimming in the ocean.	✓	☐
2. Tom and Ken are playing ball.	☐	✓
3. Dave is sailing a boat.	✓	☐
4. Megan is floating on a raft.	✓	☐
5. Lee is taking a boat ride.	☐	✓
6. Hannah is doing homework now.	✓	☐

At the store

1 Vocabulary

A Ana, Clara, Rafael, Zach, and Tommy are at the store.
Listen and practice.

1. Ana and Clara are shopping for jewelry.

2. Rafael is trying on a jacket.

3. Zach is paying for a baseball glove.

4. Tommy is looking at comic books.

B Look at the items for sale at the store. Listen and practice.

1. a bracelet
2. a coat
3. a tennis racket
4. a surfboard
5. a ring
6. a scarf
7. a necklace
8. a belt
9. a baseball bat

C Write the name of each item from Part B in the correct column. *(The order of the answers may vary.)*

Jewelry	Clothes	Sports equipment
bracelet	coat	tennis racket
ring	scarf	surfboard
necklace	belt	baseball bat

Lesson 20 At the store

This lesson presents and practices verb phrases connected with shopping; the names of clothing, jewelry, and sports equipment; and present continuous What . . . ? *questions.*

Review of Lesson 19

- Write the eight *-ing* verb phrases from Lesson 19 (and any verb phrases from Lessons 17 and 18) on the board in random order. Students read the phrases aloud as you point to them.
- Invite three or four students to the front. Say one of the verb phrases. The first student to mime the verb phrase appropriately becomes the "teacher" and continues the activity. Ask the student to continue miming the activity long enough for a volunteer to describe what that student is doing.

---

1 Vocabulary

This exercise presents and practices verb phrases connected with shopping and the names of clothing, jewelry, and sports equipment.

A 💿 CD2, Track 14

- Have students look at the photos. Elicit the names of as many of the items as possible.
- Say: *Look at number 1. Look at Ana and Clara. Are they swimming?* (No, they aren't.) *Are they sailing?* (No, they aren't.) *Are they shopping?* (Yes, they are.) If students do not understand *shopping*, answer the question yourself, nodding your head as you do so. Follow the same procedure for numbers 2, 3, and 4, using verbs familiar to the students at first.
- Focus students' attention on the sentence under each of the photos.
- Play the recording. Students listen and read along.

Audio script

Same as the sentences in the Student's Book.

- Play the recording again, or model the sentences. Students listen and repeat.
- Invite several volunteers to ask their classmates present continuous *Yes / No* questions about the photos.

B 💿 CD2, Track 15

- Focus students' attention on the items for sale at the store. Elicit the names of any items students know.
- Play the recording. Students listen and read along.

Audio script

Same as the items in the Student's Book.

- Play the recording again, or model the words. Students listen and repeat.
- **Optional** Play "Tic-Tac-Toe." Draw a grid with the nine vocabulary items from Part B in the spaces. Above the grid, write *shopping for, trying on, paying for,* and *looking at.* Divide the class into two teams. Teams take turns making sentences by combining the verb phrases with the items to earn squares for their teams. The first team with three squares in a row wins.

C

- Tell students that they are going to write the names of the items from Part B in the correct columns in Part C. Do one or two with the class as examples.
- Have students work individually to complete the exercise. While they are working, copy the chart onto the board.
- Check answers with the class. Invite volunteers to write their answers on the board.
- **Optional** Have students work in small groups to think of additional items to add to the chart.

2 Language focus

This exercise presents and practices present continuous *What . . . ?* questions.

A 💿 CD2, Track 16

- Focus students' attention on the photo. Elicit sentences in the present continuous from students about what they see. (Rafael's trying on a jacket.)
- Tell students that they will listen to Zach and Ana talk about what they are doing at the store.
- Play the recording. Students listen and read along.

> **Audio script**
> Same as the conversation in the Student's Book.

- Ask: *What are Ana and Clara doing?* (They're shopping.) *What are they shopping for?* (Jewelry.) *What's Tommy looking at?* (Comic books.) *What's Rafael trying on?* (A red-and-black jacket.)
- Play the recording again, or model the conversation. Students listen and repeat.
- **Optional** Have students practice in pairs.
- **Language Chart** Have students study the examples in the language chart. Write on the board: *What are you doing?* Underline *are you*. Ask: *What words do we change to ask this question about a girl?* (Change *are you* to *is she*.) *And about a boy?* (Change to *is he*.) *About a boy and a girl?* (Change to *are they*.)
- Focus students' attention on the first two examples. Ask: *Which word is the same but has a different meaning in the first two questions?* (You.) Ask: *How do you know?* (It's answered with *I* in the first question and *We* in the second.) Tell students that the only way to know if *you* is

referring to one or more than one person is from the context.

- Have students read the third question. Ask: *How is this question different from the others?* (In this question, the verb is the same as in the answer; in the other three questions, the answers use different verbs.)
- Model the examples, pausing for students to repeat.
- **Optional** Elicit additional questions of this type from students. If necessary, prompt with *-ing* verbs such as *eating, playing, reading, drawing, throwing*.

B 💿 CD2, Track 17

- Have students read the directions and the example. Ask: *What will be the first word in the questions you write?* (What.) Tell them that they should include the words in parentheses in the questions they write. Ask: *What ending will the verbs have?* (*-ing*.)
- Have students work individually to complete the exercise.
- Play the recording. Students listen and verify their answers.

> **Audio script**
> Same as the conversations in the Student's Book.

- Check answers with the class. Invite volunteers to come to the front and write the questions on the board.
- Have students practice the conversations in pairs.

---

3 Pronunciation Stress

This exercise introduces the concept of stressed words in present continuous *What . . . ?* questions.

💿 CD2, Track 18

- Explain the concept of stressed words in a sentence or a question. Say a sentence and ask students to tell you which word(s) are stressed.
- Focus students' attention on the questions.

- Tell students to listen for the stressed words in the questions. Play the recording. Students listen.

> **Audio script**
> Same as the questions in the Student's Book.

- Play the recording again. Students listen and repeat.

---

4 Speaking

This exercise practices talking about what people are doing right now.

- Have students read the directions and the sample conversation. Demonstrate the task with a volunteer.
- Invite two other volunteers to demonstrate the task, using different vocabulary.
- Have students practice in pairs.
- Ask several students to share their findings with the class.

> **Workbook**
> Assign the exercises on Workbook page 34. (Workbook answers begin on page T-190.)

> **Extra Grammar**
> Assign the exercises for the Extra Grammar, Lesson 20.

A Ana sees Zach at the store.
Listen and practice.

Zach Hi, Ana. What are you doing?

Ana I'm here with Clara. We're shopping for jewelry. How about you?

Zach Oh, I'm just looking at everything here.

Ana Rafael and Tommy are here, too.

Zach Really? What are they doing?

Ana Well, Tommy's looking at comic books, and Rafael's trying on clothes.

Zach Oh. What's he trying on?

Ana He's trying on a jacket. It's red and black. It's really cool.

Zach I have a red and black jacket, too. Hey, Rafael! That's my jacket!

What are you **doing**?
  I**'m looking at** everything.
What are you **doing**?
  We**'re shopping for** jewelry.
What's he **trying on**?
  He**'s trying on** a jacket.
What are they **doing**?
  They**'re looking at** comic books.

B The friends continue to shop. Write questions.
Listen and check. Then practice.

1. **Tommy** _What's Ana trying on?_ (Ana / try on)
   Rafael She's trying on a bracelet.

2. **Rafael** _What are you looking at?_ (you / look at)
   Ana We're looking at some jewelry.

3. **Ana** _What are you doing?_ (you / do)
   Zach I'm shopping for a surfboard.

4. **Clara** _What's Rafael paying for?_ (Rafael / pay for)
   Tommy He's paying for a belt.

5. **Zach** _What are Ana and Clara trying on?_ (Ana and Clara / try on)
   Tommy They're trying on some clothes.

3 **Pronunciation** Stress

Listen. Notice the stress. Then listen again and practice.

What are you **doing**?

What are you **looking** for?

What's he trying **on**?

What's she **buying**?

4 **Speaking**

Work with a classmate. Name two of your family members. Then ask and answer questions about what they are doing now. Use the correct stress in the questions.

I have a sister.

What's she doing now?

She's studying.

Get Connected

UNIT 5

Read

A **Read the letter quickly. Are these statements true or false? Write *True* or *False*.**

1. It's Paulo's third trip to Japan. _False_

2. Okayama is a really beautiful city. _True_

3. The apples in Okayama are delicious. _False_

Our Trip So Far

Dear Rodrigo,

Today is my family's third day in Japan, and we're really enjoying our trip. Right now, I'm sitting in a park and writing about our trip so far. Today, we're in Okayama. There are many interesting things here - museums, a **castle**, parks, shops, and restaurants. It's a really beautiful city.

We're near the castle right now. My mother is looking at everything and taking pictures. Oh, and my father's buying souvenirs - some postcards and some books. My sister's with him. She's standing in line, but she isn't buying souvenirs. She's buying **tickets** for a show tonight - a **traditional** Japanese **play**. Cool!

In the shop next to me, people are buying Momotaro ("**Peach** Boy") **dolls**. Momotaro is an important boy in some old Japanese stories. He's from Okayama. And the peaches in Okayama are famous. They're **delicious**. I'm eating one now. Talk to you later!

Bye-bye,

Paulo

Go to page 124 for the **Vocabulary Practice**.

B **Read the letter slowly. Check your answers in Part A.**

C **Answer the questions.**

1. Is Paulo's family enjoying their trip? _Yes, they are._

2. What's Paulo doing? _He's sitting in a park._

3. Is his mother taking pictures? _Yes, she is._

4. Is his father buying tickets for a play? _No, he isn't._

5. What's his sister doing? _She's buying tickets for a show tonight._

This lesson practices reading, listening, and writing skills.

Review of Lesson 20

• Write *Jewelry*, *Clothes*, and *Sports equipment* on the board. Call out an item – for example, *bracelet, coat, baseball bat*. Students respond with the appropriate category. This activity may be conducted as a competition between two or three students. The first student to respond correctly calls out the item for the next pair or group of students.

• Have students work in pairs to ask each other present continuous *What . . . ?* questions about any of the pictures in the Student's Book.

Read

This exercise practices reading for information about vacation activities.

A

• Have students look at the photo. Ask: *Where do you think this is?* Do not give the correct answer at this time. Focus students' attention on the building and ask: *What do you think this is?* If possible, elicit the word *castle*.

Culture Note **Okayama** is a city in southern Japan. Its population is about 700,000 people. It is famous for the Korakuen Garden, one of the three great gardens of Japan, and the black Okayama Castle, which is next to the garden. The castle was originally built between 1346 and 1369. It was destroyed during World War II, and a replica was built in 1966. It is unique because it is the only castle in Japan that is painted black on the outside. On the inside, there is now a museum about the history of the castle.

Momotaro is a character in Japanese folklore. *Momo* means "peach" in Japanese. For this reason, the name is translated as "Peach Boy." In the legend, a boy, Momotaro, comes to Earth from heaven in a giant peach. The peach is found by an old childless couple who have always wanted a son. When they go to eat the peach, Momotaro comes out and tells them that he was sent from heaven to be their son.

• Invite a volunteer to read the directions and the statements aloud. Remind students that they should read quickly to find the answers and that they should not read every word carefully.

• Have students work individually to read the letter quickly and write *True* or *False* next to each statement. Do not check answers at this point.

B 💿 CD2, Track 19

• Invite a volunteer to read the directions aloud. Remind students that they should read slowly and carefully, and concentrate on getting the meaning of the entire text.

• List the new vocabulary words on the board: *castle, ticket, traditional, play (n.), peach, doll, delicious.* Explain their meaning. (Castle: a large, strong building or group of buildings where kings, queens, and emperors

used to live to keep safe from enemies [point to the picture to clarify]; ticket: a slip of paper that you buy to see a movie or show; traditional: something, like beliefs or customs, that a culture or country has had for a long time [point to the kimono for an example of traditional Japanese clothing]; play [n.]: a work of literature that is acted out by actors on stage [ask students for examples of plays they have seen or read]; peach: a sweet, juicy, yellowish-pink fruit with fuzzy skin; doll: a toy that usually looks like a baby or child; delicious: tasting very good, like a delicious peach.) As an alternative, have students use their dictionaries to find the meanings of the new vocabulary words.

Note: Remind students that they have learned other meanings of the word *play* as a verb – *to play a sport* or *play a musical instrument*.

• Have students read the letter again.

• Have students check their answers in Part A in pairs. Elicit the answers from one pair.

• **Optional** Play the recording. Students listen and read along.

Audio script

Same as the letter in the Student's Book.

Get Connected Vocabulary

Have students do the exercise on Student's Book page 124 in class or for homework. (Get Connected Vocabulary answers are on page T-124.)

C

• Invite a volunteer to read the directions and the first question aloud.

• Ask: *Is Paulo's family enjoying their trip?* Elicit the answer. (Yes, they are.)

• Have students work individually to answer the questions.

• Have students check their answers in pairs.

• Check answers with the class. Invite several pairs to read aloud one question and answer each.

Listen

In this exercise, students listen for information about family members and their vacation activities.

A ⊙ CD2, Track 20

- Focus students' attention on the photos. Tell students that Matt is on vacation in Miami, Florida, with his family and that he is calling Luisa to chat.
- Tell students that they will listen to Matt and his friend Luisa talk about Matt's vacation.
- Have students read the first question and the example answer.
- Explain that students should listen to the conversation and answer the questions.
- Play the recording. Students only listen.

> **Audio script**
> See page T-208.

- Play the recording again. Students listen and answer the questions.
- Play the recording once again. Students listen and verify their answers.
- Check answers with the class. Invite volunteers to read aloud one answer each.

B

- Have students read the directions and the questions.
- Read the first question with the class and elicit answers from several students. Tell students that there are no right or wrong answers for this exercise – they are giving their opinions.
- Have students work individually to answer the questions.
- Have students work in pairs to compare answers, or elicit opinions from volunteers.

Write

In this exercise, students answer questions and write a postcard about a trip.

A

- Have a volunteer read the directions and the questions aloud. Invite two or three students to say where they might go on their imaginary trip.
- Have students work individually to answer the questions.
- **Optional** Have students ask and answer the questions in pairs.

B

- Invite a volunteer to read the directions aloud. Tell students that they will use their answers in Part A to help them write a postcard about their trip.
- Have students work individually to write their postcard.
- Invite several volunteers to read their postcards to the class.
- **Optional** Have students work in groups of four and read each other's postcards. Students should discuss the trips and decide which trip is the most interesting. Each group tells the class about the group's most interesting trip.

> **Workbook**
> Assign the exercises on Workbook page 35. (Workbook answers begin on page T-190.)

I'm really bored.

A 💿 **Luisa and Matt talk about a vacation. Listen and answer the questions.**

1. Is Matt enjoying the trip? _No, he isn't._
2. What's Matt doing? _He's sitting in the hotel._
3. Is Matt's father collecting seashells? _No, he isn't._
4. Is Timmy swimming in the ocean? _No, he isn't._
5. What are Matt's mom and sister buying? _They're buying souvenirs._
6. What are Matt's grandparents doing? _They're sightseeing._

B **What do you think? Answer the questions.** *(Answers will vary.)*

1. Do you think family trips are fun? _____
2. Do you think a beach trip is exciting? _____
3. Do you think traditional shows are interesting? _____
4. Do you think souvenirs are fun gifts? _____

Your turn

Write

A **Imagine you and your family are sightseeing on a trip. Answer the questions.**
(Answers will vary.)
1. Where are you? _____
2. What's the place like? _____
3. Where are you sitting and writing the postcard? _____
4. What are your family members doing? _____
5. Are you and your family enjoying the trip? _____

B **Write a postcard to your friend about your trip. Use the answers in Part A to help you.**

(Answers will vary.)
_____
_____
_____
_____
_____
_____

Language chart review

Present continuous statements	
Affirmative	**Negative**
I'**m buying** a bracelet.	I'**m not looking at** souvenirs.
You'**re standing** in line.	You **aren't eating** lunch.
She'**s walking** in the park.	She **isn't sleeping**.
We'**re having** a picnic.	We **aren't sitting** at the beach.
They'**re visiting** a museum.	They **aren't taking** a boat ride.

A Complete the stories. Be sure to use the correct forms of the verbs and verb phrases.

Story 1

Hi! I'm Rachel. _I'm not going to school_ (I / not / go to school) today. _I'm hanging out_ (I / hang out) with my friend, Lissa, today. _We're going sightseeing_ (we / go sightseeing) in the city. Right now, _we're visiting_ (we / visit) a museum. _Lissa's buying_ (Lissa / buy) souvenirs, and _I'm standing_ (I / stand) in line. I'm really thirsty, so _I'm having_ (I / have) a soda. _Lissa's eating_ (Lissa / eat) an ice-cream cone while we wait to go into the museum.

Story 2

Some people _are seeing_ (see) a show, but one man _isn't listening_ (not / listen) to the actors. He _isn't following_ (not / follow) the theater's rules. He _isn't throwing_ (not / throw) his trash in the trash can. Another man _isn't watching_ (not / watch) the show. He's asleep!

Unit 5 Review

This lesson reviews the grammar and vocabulary introduced in Unit 5.

Language chart review

This chart summarizes the main grammar presented and practiced in Unit 5.

- Books closed. Write on the board:

Simple form	*Present continuous*		*Simple form*	*Present continuous*
buy			eat	
have			look	
stand			sit	
visit			sleep	
walk			take	

Full form	*Contracted form*		*Full form*	*Contracted form*
I am			he is	
you are			she is	
they are			we are	
is not			are not	

- Elicit when to use the present continuous form of a verb. (When the action is currently taking place.)

- Have students copy the chart and work in pairs to complete the *Present continuous* and *Contracted form* portions of the chart.

- Books open. Have students study the Language chart review and compare it to their charts. Have them correct any errors. While they are doing so, ask random students to the front to fill in the chart on the board. Check answers with the class.

- Answer any questions students may have.

....

Exercises A through C (pages T-70 to T-71)

Note: Students can do these exercises for homework or in class. They should do these exercises with minimal teacher input or help. If you choose to do these exercises as homework, briefly review the exercise directions in class. Make sure that students understand what they should do. Check the answers with the class during the next class meeting. If you choose to do the exercises in class, follow the directions below.

Exercise A

- Have a volunteer read the directions.

- Tell students to complete the stories with the correct form of the verbs and verb phrases in parentheses. Focus students' attention on the example in Story 1.

- Have students work individually to complete the stories.

- Check answers with the class. Invite volunteers to read the completed stories aloud.

Language chart review

This chart summarizes further grammar presented and practiced in Unit 5.

- Have students study the examples in the chart.
- Remind students to use *Are* and *Is* at the beginning of present continuous *Yes / No* questions.
- Remind students also that in *What . . . ?* questions, the verb may or may not be the same as in the answer.
- Answer any questions students may have.

Exercise B

- Have students read the directions and the example.
- Have students work individually to write the questions and answers.
- Check answers with the class.
- Have students practice the questions and answers in pairs.

Exercise C

- Have students read the directions.
- Focus students' attention on the example.
- Have students work individually to complete the conversations.
- Have students check their answers in pairs.
- Check answers with the class. Invite volunteers to read the completed conversations aloud.

Optional Unit Wrap-Up

- If students did the Review exercises for homework, check answers with the class.
- Play "Charades" to practice present continuous statements, as in Exercise A. Write some short phrases with verbs in the present continuous on small slips of paper – for example: *standing in line, sitting in a boat, having a picnic,* etc. Invite a pair of students (one from each team) to come to the front of the classroom and act out the phrase. As the students are doing this, ask the question *What are they doing?* The first team to guess the phrase and say it correctly in a sentence gets a point. For example, students answer: *They're standing in line.* If the guess is wrong, the students who are acting it out say: *We aren't standing in line.*
- Play a question-and-answer game to practice questions, as in Exercises B and C. Have all the students think about a friend their classmates will know or someone in their family and write down what they think the person is doing at the moment. One student stands in front of the class and says: *I'm thinking about (name of person). What is he / she doing now?* Classmates guess by asking *Yes / No* questions. Set a limit of about ten questions for each turn. If students do not guess after the tenth question, the student tells them the answer.

Theme Project

- Assign the *At Home* section of the Unit 5 Theme Project on Student's Book page 130.

Workbook

- Assign the Unit 5 Check Yourself on Workbook page 36. (Workbook answers begin on page T-190.)

Extra Practice Worksheets

- Assign the Unit 5 Extra Practice worksheets starting on page T-149.

Extra Speaking Practice Worksheet

- Assign the Unit 5 Extra Speaking Practice worksheet on page T-169.

Arcade Activities

- Assign the Unit 5 Arcade activities found at: www.cambridge.org/connectarcade

Learning Log

- Assign the Unit 5 Learning Log. These can be downloaded from the Teacher Support Site at: www.cambridge.org/connect2e/teacher

Quiz

- Give the Unit 5 Quiz on page T-180.

Test

- Give the Unit 5 Test (Form A and / or Form B). These can be downloaded from the Teacher Support Site at: www.cambridge.org/connect2e/teacher

Language chart review

Are you **listening** to music? **Yes**, I **am**. / **No**, I'm **not**.	**What are** you **listening** to? I'm **listening to** my new CD.
Is he **walking** in the park? **Yes**, he **is**. / **No**, he **isn't**.	**What's** he **doing**? He's **walking in** the park.
Are they **trying on** clothes? **Yes**, they **are**. / **No**, they **aren't**.	**What are** they **trying on**? They're **trying on** coats.

B **Look again at Part A. Write questions and answers.**

1. Rachel and Lissa / visit a museum today

   Q: _Are Rachel and Lissa visiting a museum today?_   **A:** _Yes, they are._

2. Lissa / stand in line

   Q: _Is Lissa standing in line?_   **A:** _No, she isn't._

3. Rachel / wear jeans

   Q: _Is Rachel wearing jeans?_   **A:** _Yes, she is._

4. the people / see a show

   Q: _Are the people seeing a show?_   **A:** _Yes, they are._

5. the man / talk on the phone

   Q: _Is the man talking on the phone?_   **A:** _Yes, he is._

C **Write questions to complete the conversations.**

1. **A** _What are your friends doing?_

   B My friends? They're throwing a Frisbee in the yard.

2. **A** _Are you eating?_

   B No, we aren't eating. We're doing homework.

3. **A** _What's he wearing?_

   B He's wearing jeans.

4. **A** _What's your mom doing?_

   B My mom's painting the kitchen.

5. **A** _What are you doing?_

   B I'm eating a sandwich. I'm hungry!

6. **A** _What are they listening to?_

   B They're listening to rock music.

Go to page 130 for the Theme Project.

Where are you going?

1 Vocabulary

A Look at these events. Complete the sentences with the words in the box. Then listen and practice.

- ☑ amazing robots
- ☐ awesome musicians
- ☐ fascinating animals
- ☐ incredible teams
- ☐ popular movies
- ☐ thrilling shows

1. _Amazing robots_ walk and talk!

2. These _thrilling shows_ are fun for children and adults!

3. Learn about these _fascinating animals_ .

4. See six _popular movies_ for only $18.00.

5. Two _incredible teams_ play on Saturday.

6. _Awesome musicians_ play rock and country music!

B Complete the sentences with your opinions. Then tell a classmate.
(Answers will vary.)

1. _Roberto Carlos_ is an incredible athlete.

2. _____ is a thrilling movie.

3. _____ are amazing animals.

4. _____ is an awesome singer.

5. _____ is a fascinating class.

6. _____ is a popular song.

Roberto Carlos is an incredible athlete.

This lesson presents and practices the names of common entertainment events and Where + (be) . . . going?

1 Vocabulary

This exercise presents and practices the names of common entertainment events.

A 🔘 CD2, Track 21

- Focus students' attention on the pictures. Explain that they show things to do on the weekend.

- Elicit information from students about the events. Say: *Look at number 1. What things can you see at a science exhibit?* (Robots, computers, telescopes, etc.) *Number 2. What can you see at a circus?* (Tightrope walkers, acrobats, animal acts, clowns, etc.) *Number 3. This is a bat exhibit. What other kinds of exhibits are there?* (Insect, butterfly, bird, etc.) *Number 4. What are some current popular movies? Number 5. This is a basketball game. Name some popular sports teams. Number 6. This is a concert. What kinds of music can you hear at a concert?* (Rock, jazz, pop, reggae, classical, etc.) Ask students to look at the words in red in the word box. Model the words for students, one by one.

- Tell students that they should complete the sentences under the pictures with the words in the box. Have students work individually to complete the exercise.

- Play the recording. Students listen and verify their answers.

> **Audio script**
> Same as the sentences in the Student's Book.

- Check answers with the class. Invite volunteers to come to the board to write their answers.

- Play the recording again, or model the sentences. Students listen and repeat.

- **Optional** Write on the board: *I like the (Science Exhibit) the best.* Invite volunteers to tell the class which event they like the best. Remind students to add the word *game* if they choose basketball.

B

- Ask students to read the directions and the sentences. Explain that they should write their own opinions.

- Have students work individually to complete the exercise.

- Have students work in pairs to compare their opinions. Ask pairs to share with the class one opinion that was the same.

- **Optional** Ask students to complete the exercise once again, but this time they should write their opinions in the negative. As an example, write on the board: *1. (My little brother) is not an incredible athlete.* Have students write the negative statements on a separate sheet of paper and then work in pairs to compare their opinions.

This unit introduces vocabulary and expressions for weekend events and leisure activities.

2 Language focus

This exercise presents and practices *Where + (be) . . . going?*

A 💿 CD2, Track 22

- Focus students' attention on the photo.
- Ask students to read the directions. Tell students that they will hear a conversation among Rafael, Claudia, and Oscar.
- Play the recording. Students listen and read along.

> **Audio script**
> Same as the conversation in the Student's Book.

- Ask: *How many times was "Where are you going?" asked in the conversation?* (Two times.) Then ask: *Where's Rafael going?* (To the basketball game.) *Where are Claudia and Oscar going?* (To the Nature Center.)
- Explain *What a surprise!*, *you two, fascinating,* and *hate.* Ask: *What's the opposite of* hate? (Love.)
- Play the recording again, or model the conversation. Students listen and repeat.
- **Optional** Have students practice in groups of three.
- **Language Chart** Have students study the examples in the language chart. Remind students that questions with *you* as the subject can be answered in two different ways, with *I'm* or *We're*, depending on the context. Ask: *What's the question when the subject is* they? (Where are they going?)
- Model the examples, pausing for students to repeat.

B 💿 CD2, Track 23

- Have students read the directions and the example. Elicit the names of the places in the pictures.
- Have students work individually to complete the exercise.
- Play the recording. Students listen and verify their answers.

> **Audio script**
> Same as the questions and answers in the Student's Book.

- Check answers with the class. Invite volunteers to read one of the questions and answers they wrote.
- Have students practice the questions and answers in pairs.
- **Optional** Write *Where __ __ going?* on the board three times. Ask three students to come to the board. Give each a piece of chalk or a whiteboard marker. Say: *Claudia's going to the circus.* Students fill in the blanks of the question with *is she*. The first student to complete the question correctly continues the activity.

3 Listening

In this exercise, students listen for people's destinations.

💿 CD2, Track 24

- Have students read the directions. Explain to students that they will listen to four short conversations and should decide where the people are going.
- Play the recording. Students only listen.

> **Audio script**
> See page T-209.

- Play the recording again. Students listen and check the correct destinations in the boxes.
- Play the recording once again. Students listen and verify their answers.
- Check answers with the class. While students are listening to the recording, write *Joanne, Jerome, Cynthia,* and *Ruben* on the board. Ask four volunteers to come to the front to write their answers on the board.

> **Workbook**
> Assign the exercises on Workbook page 37. (Workbook pages begin on page T-190.)

> **Extra Grammar**
> Assign the exercises for the Extra Grammar, Lesson 21.

2 Language focus

Where + (be) . . . going?

Where are you **going?**
I'm going to the basketball game.
We're going to the Nature Center.

A Claudia and her little brother, Oscar, meet Rafael. They talk about where they're going. Listen and practice.

Rafael Claudia! Oscar!
Claudia Rafael? What a surprise! Where are you going?
Rafael I'm going to the basketball game. I want to see the Rockets. They're an incredible team!
Claudia Yeah, I know! They're awesome!
Rafael How about you two? Where are you going?
Claudia We're going to the Nature Center.
Oscar There's a bat exhibit today!
Rafael Really? Do you like bats?
Claudia I hate bats, but Oscar thinks they're fascinating.

B Where are these people going? Write questions and answers. Listen and check. Then practice.

1

1. **Q:** _Where's he going?_
   A: _He's going to the movies._

2. **Q:** _Where are they going?_
   A: _They're going to the mall._

2

3

3. **Q:** _Where are they going?_
   A: _They're going to the circus._

4. **Q:** _Where's she going?_
   A: _She's going to the park._

4

5

5. **Q:** _Where's she going?_
   A: _She's going to the gym._

6. **Q:** _Where's he going?_
   A: _He's going to the library._

6

3 Listening

Where are these people going? Listen and check (✓) the correct information.

1. Joanne ☑ to a concert ☐ to her piano lesson
2. Jerome ☐ home ☑ to soccer practice
3. Cynthia ☐ to the library ☑ to Sarah's house
4. Ruben ☑ to the circus ☐ to the beach

Birthday parties

1 Vocabulary

A What do these people like to do on their birthdays?
Complete the sentences with the verb phrases in the box.
Then listen and practice.

☐ celebrate at a restaurant	☐ have a barbecue	☐ play cards	☐ relax at home
☑ eat cake	☐ open presents	☐ play party games	☐ sing songs

1. Sarah likes to
   eat cake .

2. Tim likes to
   celebrate at a restaurant .

3. Diana likes to
   sing songs .

4. Greg likes to
   relax at home .

5. Paul likes to
   play party games .

6. Jack likes to
   open presents .

7. Rita likes to
   have a barbecue .

8. Hilary likes to
   play cards .

B Work with two classmates. Talk about what you like to do on your birthdays.

You What do you like to do on your birthday, Nellie?
Classmate 1 I like to open my presents! How about you?
Classmate 2 I like to . . .

 Birthday parties

This lesson presents and practices the names of activities people like to do on their birthdays and simple present vs. present continuous.

Review of Lesson 21

- Write the six weekend events from Lesson 21 on the board. Review the words with students. Elicit other recreational destinations from previous lessons. (Soccer game, picnic, park, etc.)

- Play a guessing game. Ask students to work in pairs. Tell them to write a recreational destination on a slip of paper. Ask one pair of students to come to the front. The spokesperson of the pair asks the class: *Where's he / she going?* while pointing to his or her partner. The class tries to guess the destination using *Is he / she going to____ ?* The student who guesses correctly comes to the front with his or her partner.

- Divide the class in half. Ask one half of the class to write a weekend event or destination on a slip of paper. Collect the papers and redistribute them to the other half of the class. The students holding the papers find their owners by walking around asking classmates: *Where are you going?* The first three students to find their owners are the winners.

1 Vocabulary

This exercise presents and practices birthday activities.

A ◎ CD2, Track 25

- Focus students' attention on the pictures of the teens celebrating their birthdays. Elicit as many words about the pictures as possible. Say: *Number 1. What's she eating?* (Cake.) *Number 2. Where are they?* (At a restaurant.) *Number 3. What's that?* (A guitar.) *What's she doing?* (Singing.) *Number 4. Where is he?* (At home.) *Number 5. Are they playing games?* (Yes, they are.) *Number 6. What's he opening?* (A present.) *Number 7. What are they barbecuing?* (Hot dogs.) *Number 8. Are they playing cards?* (Yes, they are.) Tell students to guess the answers if they are not sure. If they do not respond, answer the questions for them.

- Have students work individually to complete the sentences with the phrases from the box. Ask them to do only those sentences that they are sure of.

- Play the recording. Ask students to listen and verify their answers, finishing any incomplete sentences.

Audio script
Same as the sentences in the Student's Book.

- Check answers with the class. Invite volunteers to come to the board to write one answer each.

- Play the recording again, or model the sentences. Students listen and repeat.

- **Optional** Books closed. Ask students to close their eyes. Erase one of the verb phrases from the board. Ask students to open their eyes. Students call out the missing phrase.

B

- Tell students that they are going to talk about what they like to do on their birthdays.

- Have a student read the directions and the example.

- Have students work in groups of three and take turns asking and answering the question.

- Invite volunteers to tell the class about one of the students in their group.

2 Language focus

This exercise presents and practices simple present vs. present continuous.

A 💿 CD2, Track 26

- Focus students' attention on the picture. Tell them that they will listen to Rita talk about how she celebrates her birthday.
- Play the recording. Students listen and read along.

> **Audio script**
> Same as the text in the Student's Book.

- Write on the board: *Usually Today / Now.* Elicit the three simple present statements about what Rita's family *usually* does. Write them on the board under the word *Usually*. Do the same for the present continuous statements about what they are doing *today* and *now*. Ask: *Are they eating at 6:00 today?* (No.) *Do they usually eat at 7:30?* (No.) Check students' understanding of the two forms in this way for the other pairs of sentences.
- Model the sentences on the board. Students listen and repeat.
- **Language Chart** Have students study the examples in the language chart. Ask: *What form of the verb do you see in the first sentence?* (The simple form.) *What about the second sentence?* (The -ing form.) *What's the difference in the meaning of the two sentences?* (The first sentence describes a routine habit, while the second sentence describes an activity that is taking place now.)
- Model the examples, pausing for students to repeat.

B 💿 CD2, Track 27

- Have students read the directions and the example. Ask: *Which picture shows what the Cooksons are doing now?* (The picture on the left.) *Which picture shows what the Cooksons usually do?* (The picture on the right.) Elicit the verbs in their simple form (*read, talk, watch, do, play, eat, practice, sing*) and write them on the board. Tell students that they should write two statements for each family member, one in the present continuous and one in the simple present.
- Have students work individually to complete the exercise.
- Play the recording. Students listen and verify their answers.

> **Audio script**
> Same as the sentences in the Student's Book.

- Check answers with the class.

3 Listening

In this exercise, students listen for whether activities usually happen or are happening now.

💿 CD2, Track 28

- Tell students that they will be listening to a phone conversation between Tommy and his aunt about his family's activities. Students should write a check under *usually* if the activities are things Tommy's family usually does. They should write a check under *now* if the activities are taking place at the time Tommy is speaking to his aunt.
- To check understanding, say these sentences and ask students to respond with *usually* or *now*. *I'm teaching my students English.* (Now.) *I eat dinner at 6:30.* (Usually.)
- Play the recording. Students only listen.

> **Audio script**
> See page T-209.

- Play the recording again. Students listen and write checks in the correct column.
- Play the recording once again. Students listen and verify their answers.
- Check answers with the class.

> **Workbook**
> Assign the exercises on Workbook page 38. (Workbook pages begin on page T-190.)

> **Extra Grammar**
> Assign the exercises for the Extra Grammar, Lesson 22.

2 Language focus

Simple present vs. present continuous

My mom usually **cooks**.
My dad **is cooking** hot dogs now.

A It's Rita's birthday. How is her family celebrating? Listen and practice.

We usually eat in the kitchen, but not today. My mom usually cooks. But my dad is cooking hot dogs now. He always cooks on my birthday.

We usually eat at 6:00. But it's 7:30 now, and we're still waiting for our dinner. My dad is a good cook. But he's very slow!

B Rita's family is relaxing after the barbecue. What are they doing now? What do they usually do after dinner? Write sentences. Then listen and check.

NOW

8:00 p.m.

USUALLY

8:00 p.m.

1. Rita *is playing cards* . *She usually practices the violin.*
2. Mr. Cookson *is eating cake* . *He usually reads the newspaper.*
3. Mrs. Cookson *is playing the piano* . *She usually talks on the phone.*
4. Peter *is taking pictures* . *He usually watches TV.*
5. Lucy *is playing cards* . *She usually does homework.*

3 Listening

Tommy's aunt calls on his birthday. Does Tommy talk about what people in his family usually do or about what they are doing now? Listen and check (✓) the correct column.

	Usually	Now
1. Tommy's brother	✓	☐
2. Tommy's little sister	☐	✓
3. Tommy's mother	✓	☐
4. Tommy's father	☐	✓

Mini-review

1 Language check

A The sports announcers are at an ice-skating event. Complete their sentences with the correct forms of the verbs.

1. Look! Here's Terry. _He's skating_ (he / skate) across the rink.

2. _He_ always _skates_ (he / skate) so beautifully.

PRESS

3. And now _he's dancing_ (he / dance) on the ice.

4. Oh! Look! _He's jumping_ (he / jump)! Amazing!

5. Of course, _he practices_ (he / practice) every day.

6. OK. Now _he's waiting_ (he / wait) for his scores.

B The competition is finished. What are these people doing now? What do they usually do at night? Write sentences.

1. The announcers: _They're eating dinner at a restaurant._ _They usually stay home._
   (eat dinner at a restaurant)   (stay home)

2. Terry: _He's talking to fans._   _He usually watches TV._
   (talk to fans)   (watch TV)

3. Diana, the coach: _She's sleeping._   _She usually reads sports magazines._
   (sleep)   (read sports magazines)

76   Unit 6

This lesson reviews the language presented and practiced in Lessons 21 and 22.

1 Language check

These exercises review the structures presented so far in this unit.

A

- Ask students to read the directions. Explain *sports announcer*. (A person on radio or TV who talks about a sports event while it is happening.)

- Have students study the pictures. Ask: *What's the man doing?* (He's ice-skating.) Explain that the text in the speech balloons is what the announcers are saying about the skater's performance.

- Explain that students should complete the sentences with the correct form of the verbs in parentheses. They have to use either the present continuous or the simple present. Ask students to read the example in the first speech balloon. Ask: *Which words help us decide that the answer is* He's skating? (Look! Here's Terry.) Point out that when you tell someone to look at something, it is happening at that moment. Ask students which words are clues to indicate the present continuous. (Look, now.) Then ask which words indicate the simple present. (Always, usually, every day.)

- Have students work individually to complete the exercise.

- Check answers with the class.

- **Optional** Have students role-play the parts of the two announcers.

- **Optional** Ask students to work in groups of three. They choose a verb and make two statements, one in the simple present and one in the present continuous. Ask each group to choose a representative from the group to share the group's sentences with the class.

B

- Have students read the directions and the example.

- Have students work individually to write sentences in the present continuous on the left and in the simple present on the right.

- Check answers with the class. Invite volunteers to read aloud one answer each.

C

- Invite a volunteer to read the directions and the example aloud.
- Have students read the first conversation. Tell them not to write the answers yet.
- Have students work individually to complete the exercise.

- Check answers with the class. Invite two volunteers to read the conversation, aloud.
- Follow the same procedure for conversation 2.
- **Optional** Have students work in pairs to read both conversations.

---

2 Listening

In this exercise, students listen for whether activities usually happen or are happening now.

CD2, Track 29

- Explain that it is Mariah's birthday and she is having a party.
- Have students read the items in the chart. Focus their attention on the example answer.
- Tell students they will listen to Mariah talk about what she usually does at her birthday parties and what she is doing now. They should listen and check *usually* or *now*.
- Play the recording. Students only listen.

Audio script
See page T-209.

- Play the recording again. Students listen and write checkmarks in the correct columns.
- Play the recording once again. Students listen and verify their answers.

- Check answers with the class. Invite volunteers to answer with complete sentences using *usually* or *now*. (She is having a party at home now. She usually celebrates at a restaurant.)
- **Optional** Have students write complete sentences in their notebooks for each item. They can also write negative sentences. (She is not celebrating at a restaurant now. She is having a party at home.)

Workbook
Assign the exercises on Workbook page 39. (Workbook pages begin on page T-190.)

Game
Assign the game on Student's Book page 119.

C **Choose the correct words to complete the conversations.**

1. **Jack** Hi, Sarah. ___Where___ (What / Where) are you?
   Sarah ___I'm___ (I'm / She's) on the bus.
   Jack On the bus? Where ___are___ (is / are) you going?
   Sarah I'm with Joanna. ___We're___ (He's / We're) going to the mall.
   Jack But today's Monday. What about school?
   Sarah Well, we usually ___go___ (go / are going) to school on Monday, but today's a holiday.
   Jack Oh, yeah, that's right. Well, have fun!

2. **Greg** Hi, Paul. Where ___are___ (are / is) you going today?
   Paul ___I'm___ (I'm / She's) going to the park.
   Greg Really? You usually ___work___ (work / is working) on Saturday.
   Paul I know, but there's a concert today.
   Greg Cool! Well, have a good time.
   Paul Thanks. Oh . . . the concert ___is starting___ (starts / is starting) now. Talk to you later.

2 Listening

Mariah is talking about her birthday party. What does she usually do? What's she doing now? Listen and check (✓) Usually or Now.

	Usually	Now
1. have a party at home	☐	✓
2. celebrate at a restaurant	✓	☐
3. eat cake at a restaurant	✓	☐
4. relax at home	✓	☐
5. have a barbecue	☐	✓
6. sing songs	☐	✓

Go to page 119 for the Game.

Lesson 23 Let's see a movie.

1 Vocabulary

A Label the movies with the words in the box. Then listen and practice.

> ☐ an action movie ☑ a comedy ☐ a drama
> ☐ an animated movie ☐ a documentary ☐ a horror movie

1. This is _a comedy_ . 2. This is _an animated movie_ . 3. This is _an action movie_ .

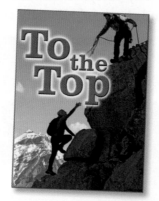

4. This is _a drama_ . 5. This is _a documentary_ . 6. This is _a horror movie_ .

B Write the plural form of each kind of movie. Then write your opinion using *like* or *don't like*.

Singular	Plural	Your opinion
1. a comedy	comedies	I like comedies.
2. a horror movie	horror movies	(Answers will vary.)
3. an action movie	action movies	(Answers will vary.)
4. a drama	dramas	(Answers will vary.)
5. a documentary	documentaries	(Answers will vary.)
6. an animated movie	animated movies	(Answers will vary.)

This lesson presents and practices types of movies and want / don't want + to *(verb).*

1 Vocabulary

This exercise presents and practices the names of different types of movies.

A 🔘 **CD2, Track 30**

• Have students look at the posters. Explain to them that the posters show different types of movies. Tell them that the words in the posters are the movie titles.

• Ask students to read the words for types of movies in the box at the top of the page. Think of some current movies and say: _____ *is an action movie,* filling in the blank with the title of a current action movie. Then ask: *What's another action movie?* Students respond with other current popular titles. Follow the same procedure for the other five types of movies.

• Have students work individually to complete the sentences with the words in the box.

• Play the recording. Students listen and verify their answers.

> **Audio script**
> Same as the sentences in the Student's Book.

• Check answers with the class.

• Play the recording again, or model the sentences. Students listen and repeat.

• **Optional** Call out one of the movie titles (or current movies, if you prefer). Students respond with the corresponding movie type.

B

• Ask students to read the directions and the example. Explain *singular, plural,* and *opinion*. Remind students that if a word ends in a consonant and a *y*, the *y* changes to *i* and *-es* is added – for example, *comedy* ➔ *comedies.*

• Have students work individually to complete the exercise.

• Check answers with the class. Invite volunteers to write the plural form on the board.

• Have students work in small groups to share their opinions. Have one student write how many students like each type of movie. Then have each group share with the class the most and least popular movie types in their group.

• **Optional** Write the six types of movies on six separate slips of paper. Tell students these are "movie tickets." Ask a volunteer to come to the front and choose one of the "tickets." Students try to guess which word is on the ticket by asking: *Is it a ticket to an (action movie)?* The student who guesses correctly replaces the volunteer and continues the activity.

2 Language focus

This exercise presents and practices *want / don't want + to* (verb).

A 💿 CD2, Track 31

- Tell students that they will listen to a conversation between Ana and Rafael.
- Play the recording. Students listen and read along.

> **Audio script**
> Same as the conversation in the Student's Book.

- Ask students to find the two questions in the conversation. (Do you want to come? Well, what do you want to see?)
- Play the recording again, or model the conversation. Students listen and repeat.
- **Optional** Have students practice in pairs.

  Language Chart Have students study the first two examples in the language chart. Then write on the board: *I want a sandwich. I want to eat a sandwich.* Ask: *What's different about these two sentences?* (When a verb follows *want*, *to* must be added.)

- Ask students to look at the first question. Ask: *Which word is at the beginning of the question?* (Do.)

- Then have students look at the second question. Ask: *Where is* do *in this question?* (After *What*.) *Can this question be answered with* yes *or* no? (No.)
- Model the examples, pausing for students to repeat.

B 💿 CD2, Track 32

- Ask a volunteer to read the directions and the example aloud.
- Have students work individually to complete the sentences in the conversation.
- Play the recording. Students listen and verify their answers.

> **Audio script**
> Same as the conversation in the Student's Book.

- Check answers with the class.
- Have students practice the conversation in pairs.

---

3 Pronunciation Reduction

This exercise introduces the reduction of *want to* in everyday conversation.

💿 CD2, Track 33

- Explain that in spoken English, some words are reduced. Write on the board: *want to = wanna.*
- Have students read the sentences.
- Play the recording. Students only listen.

> **Audio script**
> Same as the sentences in the Student's Book.

- Play the recording again. Students listen and repeat.

---

4 Listening

In this exercise, students listen for the type of movie each person wants to see.

💿 CD2, Track 34

- Tell students that they will listen to four people talking about movies. Students should check the type of movie that each person wants to see.
- Play the recording. Students only listen.

> **Audio script**
> See page T-209.

- Play the recording again. Students listen and check the correct columns in the chart.
- Play the recording once again. Students listen and verify their answers.
- Check answers with the class.

> **Workbook**
> Assign the exercises on Workbook page 40. (Workbook pages begin on page T-190.)

> **Extra Grammar**
> Assign the exercises for the Extra Grammar, Lesson 23.

2 Language focus

want / don't want + to (verb)

I **want to go** to the movies tonight.
I **don't want to see** a horror movie.
Do you **want to come**?
   Yes, I **do**. / No, I **don't**.
What **do** you **want to see**?
   I **want to see** a horror movie.

A Rafael invites Ana to a movie.
Listen and practice.

Rafael I want to go to the movies tonight.
Do you want to come?

Ana Well, what do you want to see?

Rafael I want to see a horror movie –
Late at Night. It's a new movie.
It's very popular. Julia James
is in it. She's awesome!

Ana Well, thanks, but I don't want to see a horror
movie. I want to stay home and watch TV.

B Now Rafael invites Kate. Complete the conversation.
Listen and check. Then practice.

Rafael *Do* you *want to* go to
the movies?

Kate No. I *don't want* to go to the movies.

Rafael Are you sure? I want to see *Late at Night*.

Kate Sorry. I really *don't want to* go.

Rafael OK. *Do* you *want to watch*
a drama on TV?

Kate No. I don't like dramas.

Rafael Well, what *do* you *want to* do?

Kate I *want to* stay home and sleep.

3 Pronunciation Reduction

Listen. Notice how *want to* is reduced in conversation. Then listen
again and practice.

I **wanna** see an action movie.	They **wanna** go to the concert.
We **wanna** have a picnic.	I **wanna** play video games.

4 Listening

What does each person want to see? Listen and check (✓)
the correct kind of movie.

	A comedy	A horror movie	An action movie	A drama	A documentary	An animated movie
1. Ted	✓					
2. Joe			✓			
3. Maggie					✓	
4. Connie				✓		

In line at the movies

1 Vocabulary

A Read the descriptions and look at the people waiting in line at the movies. Match the people to the correct sentences. Then listen and practice.

Carlos is tall and slim. He has wavy, black hair. __6__
Carolyn is short and heavy. She has short, straight, red hair. __3__
David is short and slim. He has curly, black hair and blue eyes. __4__
Kevin is average height. He has short, brown hair. __5__
Marci is average height. She has medium-length hair and brown eyes. __2__
Sandra is tall and slim. She has long, blond hair. __1__

B Complete the chart. Use the words from Part A. *(The order of the answers may vary.)*

Height	Body type	Hair length	Hairstyle	Hair color	Eye color
tall	slim	long	curly	blond	blue
short	heavy	short	wavy	black	brown
average		medium-length	straight	brown	
				red	

This lesson presents and practices words that describe physical characteristics and What *questions about people.*

Review of Lesson 23

- Write the six types of movies introduced in Lesson 23 on the board. Review with students. Call out the singular form. Students respond with the plural.

- Play a round of "Memory Game." Say: *I like (dramas)*. Ask a student to stand and say: *The teacher likes (dramas). I like (horror movies)*. Another student stands, repeats the first two statements, and adds another. Continue until all the words have been reviewed or a student is unable to remember what the other students have said.

- Ask students to write on a piece of scrap paper: *I want to see a (comedy). Do you want to come?* Ask students to walk around the room repeating their sentence to classmates until they find someone with the same sentence.

---

1 Vocabulary

This exercise presents and practices words that describe physical characteristics.

A 💿 CD2, Track 35

- Have students look at the picture. Ask them to look at the differences in the physical characteristics of the people standing in line.

- Ask students to look at the words in red and read the sentences.

- Show the meaning of the vocabulary by saying the name of famous people who have each characteristic. Draw illustrations on the board if you prefer.

- Have students work individually to match the names and the people.

- Play the recording. Students listen and verify their answers.

> **Audio script**
> Same as the sentences in the Student's Book.

- Check answers with the class.

- Play the recording again, or model the sentences. Students listen and repeat.

B

- Ask students to read the directions and the examples.

- Have students work individually to complete the chart. While students are working, copy the chart onto the board.

- Check answers with the class. Ask volunteers to fill in the words in the chart.

- **Optional** Play "Odd Man Out." Ask three students to stand. Say a group of three words like these: *short, heavy, slim*. The first student to call out the word that does not belong (here, *short*) becomes the teacher for the next round.

2 Language focus

This exercise presents and practices *What* questions about people.

A 💿 CD2, Track 36

- Explain that Marci and Sandra are waiting for Sandra's friend, John. Marci has never seen him, and Sandra is describing him to her.
- Play the recording. Students listen and read along.

> ### Audio script
> Same as the conversation in the Student's Book.

- Ask: *What does John look like?* (He's tall and slim.) *What color is his hair?* (It's blond.) *What does the girl look like?* (She has long, brown hair, and she's wearing a yellow blouse. She's cute.)
- Explain *end of the line, cute,* and *guess.* (End of the line: at the back of a line of people; cute: pretty or handsome; guess: think or suppose.)
- Play the recording again, or model the conversation. Students listen and repeat.
- **Optional** Have students practice in pairs.
- **Language Chart** Have students study the examples in the language chart. Tell students that there can be more than one answer to the first type of question, *What does John look like?*
- Ask: *How is the first question different from the other three?* (The first question uses *does* and the other questions use *is / are*.)
- Ask: *Why is it "What color is his hair" but "What color are his eyes?"* (*Hair* is singular, but the word *eyes* is plural.)
- Ask: *How would we change the last two questions if we were asking about a woman or a girl?* (What color is her hair? What color are her eyes?)
- Model the examples, pausing for students to repeat.

B 💿 CD2, Track 37

- Have students read the directions and the example. Explain that all four questions are about Carolyn.
- Have students work individually to write questions for the answers given.
- Play the recording. Students listen and verify their answers.

> ### Audio script
> Same as the questions and answers in the Student's Book.

- Check answers with the class.

C

- Explain to students that they are going to complete the questions about their classmates and then answer the questions. Tell them if *boy* is in parentheses, they should use a boy's name. If it is *girl*, they should use a girl's name.
- Have students work individually to complete the exercise.
- Check answers with the class. Invite volunteers to read their questions and answers aloud.
- **Optional** Have students practice their questions and answers in pairs.

3 Speaking

This exercise practices describing people.

- Play a guessing game. Ask students to read the directions and the example.
- Demonstrate the game, using the example. Ask four volunteers to stand. They play the parts of Classmates 1, 2, 3, and 4. You play the part of "You."
- Ask a volunteer to come to the front and take your place to continue the activity. Play several rounds.

  Note: The game can also be played in pairs.

> ### Workbook
> Assign the exercises on Workbook page 41. (Workbook answers begin on page T-190.)

> ### Extra Grammar
> Assign the exercises for the Extra Grammar, Lesson 24.

2 Language focus

What does John look like?
He's tall and slim.
He has short, curly hair.
He has brown eyes.
What's his hair like?
It's short and curly.
What color is his hair?
It's blond.
What color are his eyes?
They're blue.

A Marci and Sandra are still in line at the movies. They're waiting for Sandra's friend, John. Listen and practice.

Sandra Where's John? I don't see him. The movie starts at 2:20!

Marci What does John look like?

Sandra He's tall and slim.

Marci What color is his hair?

Sandra It's blond. He has short, curly hair.

Marci I think I see him. He's near the end of the line. He's talking to a girl.

Sandra What does the girl look like?

Marci She has long, brown hair, and she's wearing a yellow blouse. Do you see her? She's cute.

Sandra Yes, I see her. I see John, too! He's not looking for *us*. I guess he's too busy!

Admission

B Look at the picture of Carolyn in Exercise 1A. Write a question for each answer. Then listen and check.

1. _What does she look like?_   She's short and heavy.

2. _What's her hair like?_   It's short and straight.

3. _What color is her hair?_   It's red.

4. _What color are her eyes?_   They're brown.

C Complete the questions with names of your classmates. Then write answers. (*Answers will vary.*)

1. (boy) What does _____ look like? _____

2. (boy) What color is _____'s hair? _____

3. (girl) What's _____'s hair like? _____

4. (girl) What color are _____'s eyes? _____

3 Speaking

Play a game. Think of a teacher in your school. Your classmates ask questions and guess.

Classmate 1 Is it a man or a woman?   **Classmate 3** Is it curly?
      You It's a man.   **You** No. It's short and straight.

Classmate 2 What color is his hair?   **Classmate 4** Is it Mr. Santos?
      You It's blond.   **You** Yes, it is!

Get Connected

UNIT 6

Read

A Read the article quickly. Check (✓) the things you can do at the fair.

- ☑ eat great food
- ☐ have a barbecue
- ☑ listen to music
- ☐ play party games
- ☐ see a movie
- ☑ see thrilling talent shows

Come to the Fair!

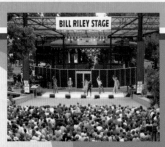

It's August in Des Moines, Iowa. What are people doing? They're going to the famous Iowa State Fair. Every year in August, people from around the world go to this fair. For 11 days, people eat great food, listen to incredible music, and see thrilling talent shows and fascinating **farm** animals. But there's one thing that *everyone* wants to see at the fair: the **butter cow**!

The butter cow is a very popular exhibit. Every year someone – these days, Sarah Pratt – makes the butter cow. She uses a lot of butter and **wire**. It usually takes about 24 hours to make it. The cow is tall and very big. It **weighs** 600 **pounds**. And, of course, it's yellow! Both young and old people love to watch Sarah make it. You can't eat the butter cow, but it's amazing to look at it!

Go to page 124 for the **Vocabulary Practice.**

B 👓 Read the article slowly. Check your answers in Part A.

C Answer the questions.

1. Where do people come from to go to the Iowa State Fair?

   They come from around the world.

2. What do people usually do at the fair? Write two things. (*Answers will vary.*)
   People usually eat great food / listen to incredible music /
   see thrilling talent shows / see fascinating farm animals.

3. What does everyone at the fair want to see?

   Everyone at the fair wants to see the butter cow.

4. Who makes the butter cow these days?

   Sarah Pratt makes the butter cow these days.

5. What's the butter cow like?

   The butter cow is tall and very big.

This lesson practices reading, listening, and writing skills.

Review of Lesson 24
- Write on the board: *average height, blond, brown, curly, heavy, long, medium-length, slim, short, straight, tall, thin, wavy*. Review with students.
- Invite volunteers to describe family members to their classmates using the vocabulary and patterns from Lesson 24.
- Say the sentences below. Invite volunteers to tell you appropriate questions for the statements.

She's short and heavy. (What does she look like?)

They're brown. (What color are his / her eyes?)

It's brown. (What color is his / her hair?)

His hair is brown, and his eyes are brown, too. (What does he look like?)

Read

This exercise practices reading for information about a famous state fair in the United States.

A

- Have students look at the photos. Tell students that the photos show a famous *fair* in the U.S. Write the word *fair* on the board. Explain that a fair is a big event with many different activities. Ask if students have similar events in their city or town.

Culture Note
Most states in the U.S. have a "state fair" once a year. The Iowa State Fair is one of the most famous. It started in 1854 and has been held almost every year since then. It is a traditional fair that celebrates the state's best achievements in industry, agriculture, and entertainment. There are exhibits and contests for the best farm animals and the best fruits and vegetables grown in the area. There is also a famous talent show, a lot of home-cooked food, free musical events, and amusement park rides.

- Invite a volunteer to read aloud the directions and the activities in the box. Remind students that they should read quickly to find the answers and that they should not read every word carefully.
- Have students work individually to read the article quickly and check the things they can do at the fair. Do not check answers at this point.

B 🖸 CD2, Track 38

- Invite a volunteer to read the directions aloud. Remind students that they should read slowly and carefully, and concentrate on getting the meaning of the entire text.
- List the new vocabulary words on the board: *farm, butter cow, wire (n.), weigh, pound (n.).* Explain their meaning. (Farm: land for raising fruits and vegetables and animals, like cows and chickens; butter cow: a sculpture of a cow made out of butter [point to the

picture to clarify]; wire [n.]: a thin piece of metal; weigh: to measure how many pounds [kilograms] something or someone is; pound [n.]: a unit of weight used in the U.S. that is equal to 2.2 kilograms.) As an alternative, have students use their dictionaries to find the meanings of the new vocabulary words.

- Have students read the article again.
- Have students check their answers in Part A in pairs. Elicit the answers from one pair.
- Check answers with the class. Invite volunteers to read the words they checked.
- **Optional** Play the recording. Students listen and read along.

Audio script
Same as the article in the Student's Book.

Get Connected Vocabulary
Have students do the exercise on Student's Book page 124 in class or for homework. (Get Connected Vocabulary answers are on page T-124.)

C

- Invite a volunteer to read the directions and the first question aloud.
- Ask: *Where do people come from to go to the Iowa State Fair?* Elicit the answer. (They come from around the world.)
- Have students work individually to answer the questions.
- Check answers with the class. Invite volunteers to read aloud one answer each.
- **Optional** Have students work in pairs to take turns reading the two paragraphs of the article. One student reads while the other listens with book closed.

Listen

In this exercise, students listen for information about a town fair.

A CD2, Track 39

- Focus students' attention on the photo. Ask: *What are the boy and girl doing?* (They're walking.) *Are they happy?* (Yes, they are.)
- Tell students they will listen to two friends, Chris and Jean, talk about the town fair.
- Have students read the first question and the example answer.
- Explain that students should listen to the conversation and answer the questions.
- Play the recording. Students only listen.

> **Audio script**
> See page T-210.

- Play the recording again. Students listen and answer the questions.
- Play the recording once again. Students listen and verify their answers.
- Check answers with the class. Invite volunteers to read aloud one answer each.

B

- Have students read the directions and all the statements.
- Remind students that *I agree* means you think something is right, *I disagree* means you think something is not right, and *I'm not sure* means you cannot say if you think it is right or not. Tell students that there are no right or wrong answers for this exercise – they are giving their opinions.
- Have students work individually to write whether they agree, disagree, or are not sure.
- Have students work in pairs to compare answers, or elicit opinions from volunteers.

Write

In this exercise, students answer questions and write a paragraph about an ideal fair or festival.

A

- Invite a volunteer to read the directions and the questions aloud. Tell students that they should make up their answers because this is an imaginary fair or festival. Invite two or three students to say an ideal fair or festival they might write about.
- Have students work individually to answer the questions.
- **Optional** Have students ask and answer the questions in pairs.

B

- Invite a volunteer to read the directions aloud. Tell students that they will use their answers in Part A to help them write about their ideal fair or festival.
- Have students work individually to write their paragraph.
- Invite several volunteers to read their paragraphs to the class.
- **Optional** Have students work in groups of four and read each other's paragraphs. Students in each group can vote on the group's most interesting fair or festival.

> **Workbook**
> Assign the exercises on Workbook page 42. (Workbook answers begin on page T-190.)

Forget the bookstore!

A 🔊 **Jean and Chris are talking about the town fair. Listen and answer the questions.**

1. Where's Chris going? *He's going to the bookstore.*

2. Where's Jean going? *She's going to the town fair.*

3. What's the fair like? *It's a lot of fun.*

4. Are the bands at the fair famous? *No, they aren't.*

5. Does Chris want to go to the fair? *Yes, he does.*

B **What do you think? Write *I agree, I disagree,* or *I'm not sure.***
(Answers will vary.)

1. Fairs are fun. _____

2. Free concerts are a good idea. _____

3. The music of every famous band is great. _____

4. It's good to do things with friends. _____

Your turn

A **Imagine your ideal fair or festival. Answer the questions.** *(Answers will vary.)*

1. What's the name of the fair or festival? _____

2. When is it? _____

3. Where is it? _____

4. What fun things are there to do? _____

5. What can you eat there? _____

6. Who do you want to go with? _____

B **Write about your ideal fair or festival. Use the answers in Part A to help you.** *(Answers will vary.)*

> I'm going to the _____ Fair. _____
>
> _____
>
> _____
>
> _____
>
> _____

Language chart review

Where + (be) ... going?	want / don't want + to (verb)
Where are you **going**? I**'m going** to the circus. We**'re going** home. **Where's** Sarah **going**? She**'s going** to the concert.	**Do** you **want to come** to my house? Yes, I **do**. / No, I **don't**. What **do** you **want to do**? I **want to stay** home tonight. I **don't want to go** out.

A Blake Winters from *Connect! TV News* talks to people for a report called "Where Are You Going?" Complete the conversations with the correct forms of the verbs.

1. **Blake** Hi! *Where are you going?*

   (where / you / go?)

   Hugo *I'm going to my karate class.*

   (I / go / to my karate class.)

   Blake *Where is your friend going?*

   (where / your friend / go?)

   Hugo *She's going to the mall.*

   (she / go / to the mall.)

   May Yeah, I want to find some new sneakers.

   Blake Awesome!

2. **Blake** And *where are you going?*

   (where / you / go?)

   Lori *We're going to the movies.*

   (we / go / to the movies.)

   Blake *What do you want to see?*

   (what / you / want / to see?)

   Lori We want to see the new James Bond movie.
   Hey, Blake! *Do you want to come with us?*

   (you / want / to come / with us?)

   Blake No, thanks. But have fun!

Unit 6 Review

This lesson reviews the grammar and vocabulary introduced in Unit 6.

Language chart review

This chart summarizes the main grammar presented and practiced in Unit 6.

- Books closed. Write on the board:

  1. Where + (be) _____ going?

  2. Do _____ want to . . . ?

  3. What _____ want to . . . ?

- Focus students' attention on the incomplete questions on the board. Tell them that you will give them prompts, along with the number of the type of question you want them to make. They should say the complete questions. The prompts are as follows:

You / stay home	2	(Do you want to stay home?)
She	1	(Where is she going?)
You / do	3	(What do you want to do?)
You	1	(Where are you going?)
You / see	3	(What do you want to see?)

- Books open. Have students study the Language chart review.
- Invite volunteers to ask a classmate one of the three types of questions.

Note: Students may want to use the Student's Book pictures as prompts for *Where + (be) _____ going?* questions.

- Answer any questions students may have.

....

Exercises A through C (pages T-84 to T-85)

Note: Students can do these exercises for homework or in class. They should do these exercises with minimal teacher input or help. If you choose to do these exercises as homework, briefly review the exercise directions in class. Make sure that students understand what they should do. Check the answers with the class during the next class meeting. If you choose to do the exercises in class, follow the directions below.

Exercise A

- Have a volunteer read the directions aloud.
- Tell students to complete the conversations with the correct form of the verbs.

- Have students work individually to complete the conversations.
- Check answers with the class.
- Have students practice the conversations in pairs.

Language chart review

This chart summarizes further grammar presented and practiced in Unit 6.

- Have students study the examples in the chart.
- Remind students to use the simple present for routine activities and the present continuous for activities that are currently taking place.
- Remind students also that there can be more than one answer to the first type of question, *What does (someone) look like?*
- Answer any questions students may have.

Exercise B

- Have students read the directions and the examples.
- Have students work individually to complete the sentences with the correct forms of the words in the box.
- Check answers with the class.

Exercise C

- Have students read the directions.
- Focus students' attention on the examples in the first conversation. Explain that students will be using different kinds of words to complete the conversations. Complete Joe's second line with the whole class to make sure students understand.
- Have students work individually to complete the conversations.
- Have students check their answers in pairs.
- Check answers with the class. Invite volunteers to read the completed conversations aloud.

Optional Unit Wrap-Up

- If students did the Review exercises for homework, check answers with the class.
- To practice the material in Exercise A, have students ask four different classmates the question: *Where are you going after class?* Students stand up and walk around the room asking the question. They should make notes of the answers. As a follow-up, invite volunteers to report some of the answers.
- Practice the simple present and the present continuous, as in Exercise B. Ask students *What do we usually do in class?* Make notes of their replies on the board. Then ask: *What are we doing today?* Focus students' attention on the things that are different. Have students write pairs of sentences in the simple present and present continuous – for example, *We usually learn new vocabulary in class. Today we're reviewing vocabulary.*
- To practice the language for descriptions in Exercise C, have students write three or four sentences describing themselves on a separate piece of paper. Tell them not to put their name on the paper. Collect the papers and pass them around the class. Students read the descriptions and try to guess who is being described.

Theme Project

- Assign the *At Home* section of the Unit 6 Theme Project on Student's Book page 131.

Workbook

- Assign the Unit 6 Check Yourself on Workbook page 43. (Workbook answers begin on page T-190.)

Extra Practice Worksheets

- Assign the Unit 6 Extra Practice worksheets starting on page T-150.

Extra Speaking Practice Worksheet

- Assign the Unit 6 Extra Speaking Practice worksheet on page T-170.

Arcade Activities

- Assign the Unit 6 Arcade activities found at: www.cambridge.org/connectarcade

Learning Log

- Assign the Unit 6 Learning Log. These can be downloaded from the Teacher Support Site at: www.cambridge.org/connect2e/teacher

Quiz

- Give the Unit 6 Quiz on page T-181.

Test

- Give the Unit 6 Test (Form A and / or Form B). These can be downloaded from the Teacher Support Site at: www.cambridge.org/connect2e/teacher

Language chart review

Simple present vs. present continuous	What questions about people	
I usually **practice** the piano after school.	**What does Claire look like?**	**What color is her hair?**
Today, I**'m reading** a book.	**She's** short and slim.	**It's** black.
We usually **sing** songs in music class.	**She has** long, brown hair.	
Today, we**'re listening** to CDs.	**What's her hair like?**	**What color are her eyes?**
	It's long and straight.	**They're** brown.

B Complete the sentences. Use the correct forms of the words in the box.

> eat play talk wear

1. My name's Eddie. I usually
   _____wear_____ jeans, but today I'm
   _____wearing_____ nice clothes. I always
   _____wear_____ nice clothes on my
   birthday.

2. Ramon is usually very shy. He
   hardly ever _____talks_____ in class,
   but today he's _____talking_____ a lot.

3. I'm Grace, and this is my family.
   We usually _____eat_____ dinner at
   home, but today is special. We're
   _____eating_____ in a restaurant. The cake
   at this restaurant is great!

4. Paula is _____playing_____ cards with Tony
   right now. They usually _____play_____
   cards on Sunday, but this week
   they're _____playing_____ on Saturday.

C Complete the conversations.

1. **Joe** My cousin wants to visit me. She wants to come in December.
   Lee Cool! What _____does_____ she _____look_____ like?
   Joe _____She's_____ pretty. _____She's_____ tall and slim. She _____has_____ short,
   red _____hair_____ .
   Lee _____What_____ color _____are_____ her eyes?
   Joe _____They're_____ blue.

2. **Cara** There's a new boy in my class.
   Dora Really? What _____does_____ he look _____like_____ ?
   Cara _____He's_____ cute. He's short _____and_____ heavy.
   Dora _____What's_____ his hair like?
   Cara He _____has_____ curly, brown hair. Oh, and _____his_____ eyes
   _____are_____ brown.

3. **Val** I think my brother is in your English class.
   Dina Really? What _____does_____ he _____look_____ like?
   Val _____He's_____ tall and slim.
   Dina A lot of boys in the class are tall and slim!
   Val He _____has_____ black hair, and _____his_____ eyes
   _____are_____ brown.
   Dina Oh, I know him!

Go to page 131
for the
Theme Project.

I'm hungry!

1 Vocabulary

A Match the items in the kitchen to the correct words.
Then listen and practice.

apples _3_	broccoli _8_	cheese _9_	meat _10_	rice _1_
bananas _2_	butter _6_	eggs _7_	potatoes _4_	water _5_

B How often do you eat or drink the items in Part A at lunchtime?
Write the items in the correct columns. Then tell your classmates.
(Answers will vary.)

Always	Sometimes	Never
	rice	

> I sometimes eat rice.

Lesson 25 I'm hungry!

This lesson presents and practices the names of common foods and countable and uncountable nouns.

1 Vocabulary

This exercise presents and practices the names of common foods.

A 💿 CD2, Track 40

- Focus students' attention on the picture. Elicit the names of any foods students know.
- On the board, write the ten food items from the box. Invite ten volunteers to come to the board and draw a picture of each food next to the word.
- Model the words. Students listen and repeat.
- Tell students that they will match the numbers of the items in the picture to the correct words in the box.
- Have students work individually to fill in the blanks in the box.
- Play the recording. Students listen and verify their answers.

> **Audio script**
> Same as the words in the Student's Book.

- Check answers with the class.
- Play the recording again, or model the words. Students listen and repeat.
- **Optional** Erase the words from the board but not the pictures. Ask students to close their eyes. Erase one of the pictures. Ask students to open their eyes. Students call out the missing food item. Play three or four times.

B

- Ask students to read the directions. Review the words in the chart by writing them on the board along with their percentages: *always - 100%, sometimes - 50%,* and *never - 0%.*
- Have students work individually to fill in the chart, writing the items in the correct columns.
- Invite several volunteers to report to the class, following the example.
- **Optional** Divide the class into groups of four or five students. Write on the board: *We sometimes eat rice.* Using the information in their charts, students report those habits that are the same for everyone in the group, following the example.

This unit introduces vocabulary and expressions for talking about foods, menus, and eating utensils.

2 Language focus

This exercise presents and practices countable and uncountable nouns.

A ⟳ CD2, Track 41

- Have students look at the photo. Ask: *Where are Zach and his mom?* (In the kitchen.)
- Tell students that they are going to listen to a conversation between Zach and his mom.
- Play the recording. Students listen and read along.

> **Audio script**
> Same as the conversation in the Student's Book.

- Explain *yuck, healthy food,* and *for a change.*
- Ask: *Which food items have an -s ending?* (Bananas, apples, eggs.) *Which items do not?* (Cheese, ice cream, egg sandwich, hot dog, cookie.)
- Play the recording again, or model the conversation. Students listen and repeat.
- **Language Chart** Explain *countable* and *uncountable.* Have students study the top half of the language chart. Ask: *Can countable nouns have singular and plural forms?* (Yes, they can.)
- Ask students to read the two examples next to the words *Specific* and *General.* Explain that in the first example, you are talking about a specific amount. In the second example, you are stating that you like eggs in general. Then focus students' attention on the singular and plural forms of the countable noun examples.
- Have students study the bottom half of the chart. Ask: *Can uncountable nouns have singular and plural forms?* (No, they can't.) *What form can they have?* (Singular only.) *Is it wrong to say* two bottles of water? (No, it isn't.) *Why not?* (Because you're counting the bottles, not the water.)

- Ask students to read the specific and general examples for uncountable nouns.
- Model the examples, pausing for students to repeat.

B ⟳ CD2, Track 42

- Ask students to read the directions. Tell them that they should use items from Exercise 1A on page 86.
- Have students work individually to write the items in the correct columns.
- Play the recording. Students listen and verify their answers.

> **Audio script**
> Same as the chart in the Student's Book.

- Check answers with the class. Write the headings *Countable* and *Uncountable* on the board. Invite volunteers to come to the board to write one word each under the correct heading.
- **Optional** Read the following list of words one by one. Ask students if the word is countable. Students call out *Yes* if the word is countable (C) and *No* if it is uncountable (U). *Juice* (U), *homework* (U), *key* (C), *notebook* (C), *paper* (C / U), *computer* (C), *money* (U).
- Play "Odd Man Out." Read four words at a time. Three words should be countable and one uncountable or vice versa. Students call out the word that does not belong.

---

3 Speaking

This exercise practices using countable and uncountable nouns in general statements.

- Tell students they are going to talk about foods they like and do not like. Have students read the directions and the example.
- Give another example with your own idea. Say: *I like (apples), but I don't like (bananas). How about you (student name)?* The student replies as in the example.

Note: Students' replies can be two separate sentences or two sentences joined by the conjunction *but.*

- Have students work in groups of five and continue talking about foods they like or do not like.
- Have volunteers report some of the answers to the class.
- **Optional** Write the words for the different kinds of foods on the board. Have students vote for their favorite food. Write the number of votes next to each kind of food. What kind of food is the class favorite?

> **Teaching Tip** Try the following techniques to control group noise without having to raise your voice. Before you begin a group activity, tell students that you will give a signal when there is too much noise. For example, raise your hand high in the air. As soon as any students see this signal, they should also raise their hands **and** stop talking. Another option is to turn the lights on and off as the "quiet" signal.

> **Workbook**
> Assign the exercises on Workbook page 44. (Workbook answers begin on page T-190.)

> **Extra Grammar**
> Assign the exercises for the Extra Grammar, Lesson 25.

2 Language focus

🔊 **A Zach is hungry. Listen and practice.**

Zach Hey, Mom! I'm hungry,
but there's nothing to eat.

Mom Nothing to eat? Look in the
refrigerator. There's cheese . . .

Zach Yuck! I don't like cheese.
Do we have ice cream?

Mom No, but we have bananas
and apples, and . . .

Zach Mom, you know I don't like bananas!

Mom What about eggs? There's an egg.
You can make an egg sandwich.

Zach No, thanks. I want a hot dog
or a cookie.

Mom Oh, Zach. How about some
healthy food for a change?

Countable and uncountable nouns

Countable nouns (things you can count)
Specific: There's **an egg** in the refrigerator.
General: I like egg**s**.

Uncountable nouns (things you cannot count)
Specific: There's **cheese** in the refrigerator.
General: I don't like **cheese**.

🔊 **B Look at the items in the kitchen in Exercise 1A.
Write the items in the correct columns.
Then listen and check.** *(The order of the answers may vary.)*

Countable nouns	Uncountable nouns
apples	rice
bananas	water
potatoes	butter
eggs	broccoli
	cheese
	meat

3 Speaking

Learn what foods four of your classmates like and don't like.

You	I like carrots. I don't like broccoli. How about you, Kim?
Classmate 1	Well, I like pizza. I don't like meat. How about you, Freddie?
Classmate 2	Hmm. I like apples. I don't like eggs.
Classmate 3	Well, I like rice. I don't like bananas. How about you, Luis?
Classmate 4	I like cheese. I don't like . . .

Picnic plans

1 Vocabulary

A Ana and Rafael plan a picnic. Listen and practice.

1. milk
2. cups
3. juice
4. bread
5. plates
6. fruit
7. pasta
8. spoons
9. forks
10. knives

B Where do the items in Part A belong? Write the items in the correct columns.
(The order of the answers may vary.)

Food	Drinks	Supplies
bread	milk	cups
fruit	juice	plates
pasta		spoons
		forks
		knives

Lesson 26 Picnic plans

This lesson presents and practices the names of some common picnic items and How much / How many . . . ?

Review of Lesson 25

- Write the ten food items from Lesson 25 on the board. Review with students.

- Erase the words from the board (or leave them if they are difficult for students). Scramble the letters of one of the words. Say *A-E-M-T*. Students say *Meat: M-E-A-T*, responding with the word and the spelling of the word. Play several times.

- Tell students that you are going to say a series of food items. If the item is countable, students should raise their right hand. If it is uncountable, students should raise their left hand.

- Ask random students to make two *I like . . .* statements, one with a countable noun and one with an uncountable noun.

1 Vocabulary

This exercise presents and practices the names of some common picnic items.

A CD2, Track 43

- Explain that Ana and Rafael are planning a picnic. Have students study the photo of the picnic table. Ask students if they use similar items when they have picnics.

- Have students read the ten picnic items.

- Play the recording. Students listen and read along.

Audio script
See page T-210.

- Play the recording again, or model the words. Students listen and repeat.

Note: Point out that the singular form of the word *knives* is *knife*. Tell students that most singular words that end in *-fe* end in *-ves* in the plural form.

- Write the words on the board. Pointing to each word, ask: *Is this a countable or an uncountable noun?*

- **Optional** Books closed. Divide the class into two teams. Tell students to try to remember the photo. Teams alternate making *There is / There are _____ on the table* statements to win points for their teams.

- **Optional** Play a few rounds of "Lip Reading." Say one of the vocabulary words without making a sound. Students look at the shape of your lips and call out the word.

B

- Ask students to read the directions. Explain the category headings.

- Tell students that they are going to write the items from Part A in the correct columns.

- Have students work individually to write the words in the correct columns. While students are writing, copy the chart onto the board.

- Check answers with the class. Invite volunteers to come to the board to write their answers.

- **Optional** Randomly call out one of the items from Part A. Students respond with the appropriate category: *Food, Drinks,* or *Supplies.* To increase the level of difficulty, ask students to close their books.

- **Optional** Ask the students in one half of the class to each write one of the categories (*Food, Drinks,* or *Supplies*) on a scrap of paper. Ask the students in the other half of the class to each choose one of the picnic items and write it on a piece of scrap paper. Students walk around the room, looking for an appropriate item or category, asking: *What do you have? I have _____ .*

2 Language focus

This exercise presents and practices *How much / How many . . . ?*

A 💿 CD2, Track 44

- Ask students to read the directions and look at the photo. Explain *decide*. (To choose or make a decision.)
- Explain to students that Ana and Rafael are making a list of things to buy for their picnic.
- Play the recording. Students listen and read along.

> **Audio script**
> Same as the conversation in the Student's Book.

- Ask: *How many cups do they have?* (About 20.) *How many plates do they have?* (Only three.) *How much pasta is there?* (A little.) *How much milk do they need?* (A lot.)
- Explain *What else?* (What other things do we need?)
- Ask: *Does Rafael know how much pasta there is?* (No, he doesn't.) *What does he ask?* (How much pasta is there?) *Does he know how many cups there are?* (No, he doesn't.) *What does he ask?* (Um, how many cups do we have?)
- Play the recording again, or model the conversation. Students listen and repeat.
- **Optional** Have students practice in pairs.
- **Language Chart** Have students study the top part of the language chart. Ask: *Do we use* how much *or* how many *with countable nouns?* (How many.)
- Explain to students that they may answer this type of question with a specific (20) or an unspecific (a lot of) amount.

- Ask students to look at the examples in the middle of the chart. Again, statements can use specific (3) or unspecific (a few) amounts.
- Have students study the bottom part of the chart. Ask: *What do we ask to find out the amount of uncountable nouns?* (How much . . . ?)
- Demonstrate the meanings of *a lot of* and *a little* with some paper. Holding up one or two sheets, say *a little paper*. Holding up a thick stack, say *a lot of paper*.
- Model the examples, pausing for students to repeat.

B 💿 CD2, Track 45

- Focus students' attention on the photos of food items and supplies.
- Have students read the directions and the sample question.
- Have students work individually to write questions for the answers given.
- Play the recording. Students listen and verify their answers.

> **Audio script**
> Same as the questions and answers in the Student's Book.

- Check answers with the class. Invite volunteers to read aloud one question each.
- Have students practice the questions and answers in pairs.

3 Listening

In this exercise, students listen for quantities of items.

💿 CD2, Track 46

- Tell students that they will listen to a boy and a girl making a shopping list of food to buy for a picnic. Students should listen for the amounts mentioned for each item.
- Play the recording. Students only listen.

> **Audio script**
> See page T-210.

- Play the recording again. Students listen and write a number or a check in the correct column.
- Play the recording once again. Students listen and verify their answers.
- Check answers with the class. Copy the chart onto the board. Invite volunteers to write their answers.

> **Workbook**
> Assign the exercises on Workbook page 45. (Workbook answers begin on page T-190.)

> **Extra Grammar**
> Assign the exercises for the Extra Grammar, Lesson 26.

2 Language focus

A The friends decide what they need for their picnic. Listen and practice.

Rafael OK, what do we need for the picnic? Um, how many cups do we have?

Ana Let's see. We have about 20 cups. But there are only 3 plates. We need plates.

Rafael OK. What about food? How much pasta is there?

Ana Um, there's a little pasta. We need pasta and a lot of milk. There's a little bread, but let's buy bread, too.

Rafael What else? How much juice do we have?

Ana I think we have a lot of juice.

Rafael Wait! Look at Zach! We need juice *now*!

How much / How many ... ?

Countable nouns

How many cups do we have?
We have **20** cup**s**.
We have **a lot of** cups.

There are **3** plate**s**.
There are **a few** plates.

Uncountable nouns

How much pasta is there?
There's **a lot of** pasta.
There's **a little** pasta.

B Look at the photos. Complete the questions and answers. Listen and check. Then practice.

1. **Q:** _How many spoons are there?_
   A: There are 4 spoons.

2. **Q:** _How much juice is there?_
   A: There's a little juice.

3. **Q:** _How many cups are there?_
   A: There are 3 cups.

4. **Q:** _How much fruit is there?_
   A: There's a lot of fruit.

5. **Q:** _How many knives are there?_
   A: There are 4 knives.

6. **Q:** _How much bread is there?_
   A: There's a lot of bread.

3 Listening

Another group plans a picnic. How much or how many of each thing do they need? Write the number or check (✓) the correct column.

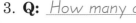

	Number	A few	A little	A lot
1. hot dogs	25	☐	☐	☐
2. fruit		☐	☐	✓
3. cheese		☐	✓	☐
4. pasta		☐	☐	✓
5. cups		✓	☐	☐
6. cookies	60	☐	☐	☐

Mini-review

1 Language check

A Choose the correct words to complete the conversation.

Doctor Do you eat healthy food?

Michiko Well, yeah. I eat _a lot of_ (a lot of / a few) fruit.

Doctor How _much_ (many / much) fruit do you eat in a week?

Michiko Well, I have a banana for breakfast every day, and I usually eat _a few_ (a few / a little) apples each week, too.

Doctor That's good. How _much_ (many / much) soda do you drink?

Michiko I only drink _a little_ (a few / a little) soda. I know it's not good for me.

Doctor Great. How _many_ (many / much) hot dogs do you eat in a week?

Michiko Oh, maybe about eight. I eat _a lot of_ (a lot of / a little) hot dogs.

Doctor Yes, you do! How about cookies?

Michiko Well, I don't like cookies, but I eat _a little_ (a few / a little) ice cream on Sundays.

B Check (✓) four things you eat or drink. Put an ✗ next to four things you don't eat or drink. Then write sentences. *(Answers will vary.)*

I eat eggs.

I don't eat meat.

1. _____
2. _____
3. _____
4. _____
5. _____
6. _____
7. _____
8. _____

☐ apples	☐ ice cream
☐ bananas	☐ juice
☐ bread	☒ meat
☐ broccoli	☐ milk
☐ butter	☐ pasta
✓ eggs	☐ potatoes
☐ hamburgers	☐ rice
☐ hot dogs	☐ water

This lesson reviews the language presented and practiced in Lessons 25 and 26.

1 Language check

This exercise reviews the structures presented so far in this unit.

A

- Invite a volunteer to read the directions. Focus students' attention on the example.
- Have students read the conversation. Tell them not to write the answers at this time.
- Have students work individually to complete the exercise.
- Check answers with the class. Invite volunteers to read aloud one answer each.

B

- Have students read the directions and the example sentences in the chart.
- Tell students that they will be making sentences about the foods they eat and do not eat and the beverages they drink and do not drink. Ask them to write the sentences under the correct heading in the chart.
- Have students work individually to write sentences.
- Invite volunteers to share their sentences with the class.
- **Optional** Have students share their sentences in small groups of four or five.

C

- Ask students to read the directions and the example.

- Tell them that they should answer the questions with their own information. Remind students that questions with countable nouns can be answered with either specific or unspecific amounts.

- Have students work individually to answer the questions.

- Check answers with the class. Invite volunteers to share their answers.

- **Optional** Have students ask and answer the questions in pairs.

- **Optional** Call out any of the food or drink items from Part A on page 90. Students respond with *How much . . . ?* or *How many . . . ?*

2 Listening

This exercise reviews the names of common foods.

🔊 **CD2, Track 47**

- Tell students that they will listen to two students, Minnie and Amanda, talking about a class party.

- Have students read the directions and the statements and choices.

- Play the recording. Students only listen.

Audio script
See page T-210.

- Play the recording again. Students listen and check the correct answer for each statement.

- Play the recording once again. Students listen and verify their answers.

- Check answers with the class. Invite volunteers to read aloud sentences with the correct answers.

Workbook
Assign the exercises on Workbook page 46. (Workbook answers begin on page T-190.)

Game
Assign the game on Student's Book page 120.

C **Answer these questions about yourself. Write a number or use** *a lot, a little, or a few.* (*Answers will vary.*)

1. How much rice do you eat in a week?

   I eat a lot of rice.

2. How many books do you have in your bag?

   _____

3. How much homework do you do every day?

   _____

4. How many T-shirts do you have?

   _____

5. How many magazines do you read in a month?

   _____

6. How much TV do you watch in a week?

   _____

7. How many DVDs do you have?

   _____

8. How much water do you drink every day?

   _____

2 Listening

Minnie and Amanda talk about what they need for a class party. Listen and check (✓) the correct answers.

1. There are _____ plates.

   ☑ a lot of   ☐ a few

2. Minnie and Amanda have _____ students in their class.

   ☐ 25   ☑ 20

3. There's _____ juice.

   ☐ a few   ☑ a little

4. Minnie and Amanda need some _____ .

   ☐ cookies   ☑ bananas and apples

5. _____ is Amanda's favorite food.

   ☐ Fruit   ☑ Ice cream

Go to page 120 for the Game.

A snack

1 Vocabulary

A Look at the messy kitchen. Match the two parts of
each sentence. Then listen and practice.

1. The chicken is __e__   a. next to the salt.
2. The jelly is __g__   b. next to the jelly.
3. The ketchup is __c__   c. behind the chicken.
4. The lettuce is __h__   d. in the cabinet.
5. The mayonnaise is __d__   e. in front of the ketchup.
6. The mustard is __b__   f. next to the pepper.
7. The pepper is __a__   g. next to the mustard.
8. The salt is __f__   h. on a plate.

B What do people put on the food items below? Write two things
for each item. Use words from Part A or your own ideas. *(Answers will vary.)*

1. sandwich: *mustard, lettuce* _____

2. eggs: _____

3. hamburger: _____

4. hot dog: _____

5. meat: _____

Lesson 27 A snack

This lesson presents and practices the names of common foods and condiments and statements with some / any.

1 Vocabulary

This exercise presents and practices the names of some common foods and condiments.

A CD2, Track 48

- Have students look at the picture. Ask: *Is this kitchen clean or messy?* (Messy.) Ask them to identify any foods or condiments that they know.
- Have students read the labels in the picture.
- Model the new words. Students listen and repeat.
- Explain that students should match the two parts of each sentence according to the location of the food item.
- Have students work individually to match the two parts of the sentences.
- Play the recording. Students listen and verify their answers.

- Check answers with the class. Have volunteers write the numbers and letters of the answers on the board.
- Play the recording again, or model the sentences. Students listen and repeat.

B

- Have students read the directions and the example.
- Have students write appropriate foods and condiments on the lines provided. Students should use the words from Part A or their own ideas.
- Check answers with the class.
- **Optional** Call out a condiment, such as mayonnaise. A volunteer responds with a food (appropriate or inappropriate) for the condiment. The class responds to the combination with *Yum!* or *Yuck!*

2 Language focus

This exercise presents and practices statements with *some / any*.

A 📀 CD2, Track 49

- Have students look at the picture. Ask: *What does Wendy want?* (She wants a sandwich.) *Does the sandwich look good?* (Yes, it does. / No, it doesn't.)
- Have students read the directions.
- Play the recording. Students listen and read along.

> ### Audio script
> Same as the conversation in the Student's Book.

- Tell students that there are four things that Wendy will put on her sandwich. Call out the following incomplete sentences. Students complete the sentences in the order they appear in the conversation:

  There's (some chicken).

  There's (some mustard).

  There's (some pepper).

  There are (some bananas).

- Then tell students that there are two things Wendy and Luke do not have. Again, ask students to complete the sentences you call out with the appropriate items in the order they appear in the conversation:

  There isn't (any mayonnaise).

  There aren't (any potatoes).

- Ask: *Does Luke want to eat the sandwich?* (No, he doesn't.) *Do you?* (Yes, I do. / No, I don't.)

- Play the recording again, or model the conversation. Students listen and repeat.
- **Optional** Have students practice in pairs.
- **Language Chart** Have students study the examples in the language chart. Ask: *Which word do we use with positive statements?* (Some.) *Which word do we use with negative statements?* (Any.)
- Ask: *When do we use* There is . . . ? (With uncountable or singular nouns.) *How about* There are . . . ? (With plural nouns.)
- Then ask: *Do we use* some *and* any *with countable or uncountable nouns?* (Both.)
- Model the examples, pausing for students to repeat.

B 📀 CD2, Track 50

- Have students read the directions and the example.
- Have students work individually to write seven more statements about the photos.
- Have students check their answers in pairs.
- Play the recording. Students listen and verify their answers.

> ### Audio script
> Same as the sentences in the Student's Book.

- Check answers with the class.

3 Speaking

This exercise practices talking about food items in the kitchen.

- Ask students to read the directions and the sample conversation. Then ask them to look at the words on the right. Explain that these words are suggestions and that students may use other food items from previous lessons.
- Have students work in pairs to complete the exercise.
- Check answers with the class. Write *There is / are some _____ in _____'s refrigerator. There isn't / aren't any _____ in _____'s refrigerator.* Ask students to report one finding about their partner's refrigerator, following this example.

> ### Workbook
> Assign the exercises on Workbook page 47. (Workbook answers begin on page T-190.)

> ### Extra Grammar
> Assign the exercises for the Extra Grammar, Lesson 27.

2 Language focus

A Wendy makes a sandwich. Listen and practice.

Wendy I'm hungry. Let's make a sandwich!
Luke Good idea. I'm hungry, too.
Wendy Um, there's some chicken here.
Luke Good! I like chicken sandwiches.
Wendy There's some mustard, but there isn't any mayonnaise.
Luke That's OK. Mustard is fine.
Wendy There's some pepper. Oh, no! There aren't any potatoes!
Luke What? Potatoes on a sandwich?
Wendy Sure! Oh, look! There are some bananas . . .
Luke What kind of sandwich is that?
Wendy It's my favorite! Do you want one?
Luke No, thanks. I'm not hungry now.

> **some / any**
>
> **Countable nouns**
>
> There **are some** banana**s**.
> There **aren't any** potatoe**s**.
>
> **Uncountable nouns**
>
> There**'s some** mustard.
> There **isn't any** mayonnaise.

B Look at the photos. Write sentences with *some* or *any*. Then listen and check.

1. *There isn't any salt.*
(salt)

2. *There's some mustard.*
(mustard)

3. *There aren't any eggs.*
(eggs)

4.  *There's some chicken.*
(chicken)

5. *There aren't any apples.*
(apples)

6.  *There are some cups.*
(cups)

7.  *There aren't any bananas.*
(bananas)

8.  *There isn't any ketchup.*
(ketchup)

3 Speaking

Think of your refrigerator. Tell a classmate what is and what isn't in it.
Use the words in the box or your own ideas.

> There's some juice. There isn't any water.

> There's some ice cream. There isn't any mustard.

juice   milk   ice cream
eggs   *ketchup*   mustard
meat   apples   chicken   water

On the menu

1 Vocabulary

A Look at the restaurant menu. Write the names of the items in the correct places on the menu. Then listen and practice.

Bob's DINER

Lunch Menu

Appetizers
salad $3.00
black bean soup $2.50
vegetable soup $2.50

Main Dishes
hamburger $4.50
cheeseburger $5.00
steak sandwich $5.00
chicken sandwich $6.00
today's fish $4.50
rice and beans with meat $6.50

Side Orders
French fries $2.00
baked potato $1.50

Desserts
ice cream $1.50
cookies $1.00
chocolate cake $2.00
carrot cake $2.00
pie $2.00

Drinks
soda $1.50
iced tea $2.00
milk $1.00
milk shake $2.00

☐ baked potato ☐ black bean soup ☐ cheeseburger

☐ steak sandwich ☐ vegetable soup

☐ carrot cake ☐ chocolate cake ☐ iced tea

☐ milk shake ☐ pie

B What are some of your favorite foods in a restaurant?
Complete the chart. Then compare with your classmates. *(Answers will vary.)*

Favorite appetizer : _____
Favorite main dish : _____
Favorite side order : _____
Favorite dessert : _____
Favorite drink : _____

What's your favorite appetizer?

My favorite appetizer is . . .

Lesson 28 · On the menu

This lesson presents and practices some common food items and categories and would like.

Review of Lesson 27

- Write the eight food items from Lesson 27 on the board. Write each word slowly, letter by letter. As you write, stop after each letter and ask students to guess which word it is.

- Divide the class into two teams. Erase the eight food items from the board. Start the game by saying: *There's some chicken on my sandwich.* A student on the first team repeats the sentence and adds an item. *There's some chicken with mustard on my sandwich.* A student on the second team repeats the sentence and adds another item. Teams alternate adding different items to the sentence until one team makes a mistake, or until all eight items have been used.

- Call out the following sentences: *I want some jelly. There is some mayonnaise. He has some lettuce. They're eating some chicken.* Students convert the sentences to the negative, using *any*.

1 Vocabulary

This exercise presents and practices some common food names and food categories.

A CD2, Track 51

- Have students look at the menu. Say: *This is a menu.* Ask students to repeat. Ask: *Where do we find menus?* (At restaurants.)

- Ask students to look at the food category headings on the menu. Model the headings. Students listen and repeat. Ask students to give examples of foods that fit the food categories.

- Ask: *Are potatoes a dessert?* (No.) *Is a sandwich an appetizer?* (No.) *Is it a main dish?* (Yes.) *Is juice a drink?* (Yes.)

- Have students look at the photos and read the labels.

- Model the new words. Students listen and repeat.

- Tell students they should write the food items in the blanks under the appropriate headings.

- Have students work individually to fill in the menu.

- Check answers with the class. Write the headings on the board. Invite volunteers to write the food items under the correct headings.

- Play the recording. Students listen and repeat.

Audio script
See page T-211.

- **Optional** Call out a food. Students respond with an appropriate heading.

B

- Have students read the directions. Explain that their answers should be based on their own personal preferences. They can write items from Part A or any food items from previous lessons.

- Have students work individually to complete the chart.

- Ask students to read the sample conversation.

- Have students ask and answer the questions (starting with the appetizer) in small groups of four or five.

- **Optional** Ask groups to report on one finding for each group member.

2 Language focus

This exercise presents and practices *would like*.

A 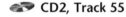 CD2, Track 52

- Have students read the directions and look at the photo. Explain *order* (v.) and *server*. (Order: to tell a worker in a restaurant what you want to eat; server: a worker in a restaurant who brings your food.)
- Play the recording. Students listen and read along.

> **Audio script**
>
> Same as the conversation in the Student's Book.

- Ask: *What words does the server use to ask Tommy what he wants?* (Would you like.) *What does Tommy say in his answers?* (I'd like.)
- Play the recording again, or model the conversation. Students listen and repeat.
- **Optional** Have students practice in pairs.
- **Language Chart** Have students study the examples in the language chart. Explain that *Would you like . . . ?* is a polite way to ask if someone wants something. Contrast this with: *Do you like soup?*

- Focus students' attention on the contracted form *I'd.*
- Model the examples, pausing for students to repeat.

B 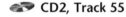 CD2, Track 53

- Ask students to read the directions and the example.
- Have students work individually to fill in the blanks.
- Play the recording. Students listen and verify their answers.

> **Audio script**
>
> Same as the conversation in the Student's Book.

- Check answers with the class. Have students practice the conversation in pairs.

---

3 Pronunciation Intonation

In this exercise, students practice the intonation of questions with *would like*.

CD2, Track 54

- Have students read the directions and the questions. Explain *intonation*. (When your voice rises or falls.)
- Play the recording. Students listen.

> **Audio script**
>
> Same as the questions in the Student's Book.

- Ask: *What kind of questions are these?* (Yes / No questions.) *Does the intonation rise or fall?* (It rises.)
- Play the recording again. Students listen and repeat.

---

4 Listening

In this exercise, students listen for the speakers' lunch orders.

CD2, Track 55

- Tell students that they will listen to Ana, Kate, Rafael, and Zach order lunch in a restaurant. Students should label the pictures with *A, K, R,* or *Z.*
- Play the recording. Students only listen.

> **Audio script**
>
> See page T-211.

- Play the recording again. Students listen and write the letters of the names in the boxes.
- Play the recording once again. Students listen and verify their answers.
- Check answers with the class.

> **Workbook**
>
> Assign the exercises on Workbook page 48. (Workbook answers begin on page T-190.)

> **Extra Grammar**
>
> Assign the exercises for the Extra Grammar, Lesson 28.

2 Language focus

A **Tommy orders lunch. Listen and practice.**

Server Hi. Are you ready to order?
Tommy Yes, I am.
Server OK. Would you like an appetizer?
Tommy Yes. I'd like vegetable soup, please.
Server OK. What else?
Tommy I'd like a chicken sandwich, please.
Server And would you like a side order?
Tommy No, thanks.
Server Would you like a drink?
Tommy Yes, please. I'd like a milk shake
and some water. I'm really thirsty!

would like

I**'d like** vegetable soup, please.
Would you **like** a drink?
Yes, please. I**'d like** some water.
No, thanks.

I'd = I would

B **Tommy orders dessert. Complete the
conversation. Listen and check. Then practice.**

Server _Would you like_ anything else?
Tommy Yes. _I'd like_ some cake.
Server What kind of cake _would_ you _like_ ?
Tommy _I'd like_ chocolate cake.
And _I'd like_ some ice cream,
too, please.
Server OK.
Tommy Oh! _I'd like_ some cookies, too.
Server Wow! That's a lot of dessert!

3 Pronunciation Intonation

Listen. Notice the intonation. Listen again and practice.

Would you like an appetizer?

Would you like a drink?

Would you like a side order?

Would you like anything else?

4 Listening

**What do Ana, Kate, Rafael, and Zach order? Listen and write A (Ana),
K (Kate), R (Rafael), or Z (Zach).**

Read

A Read the Web site quickly. Write the names of five foods in *Get Cooking*. (Answers will vary.)

1. _tomatoes_ 2. _cheese_ 3. _pasta_ 4. _vegetables/ meat_ 5. _potatoes/ chocolate_

Get Cooking with Sam Stern

Sam Stern is from Yorkshire, England. He's only 17, and he's already a cooking star. He has three **cookbooks** and a cool Web site. He also writes a **column** – "Sam's Super Kids" – for *First News*, a British **newspaper** for teens. Sam doesn't only like cooking, though. He also likes hanging out with his friends. So he put the two things (food and friends) together in his third cookbook, *Get Cooking*.

In *Get Cooking*, there aren't the usual **sections** in a cookbook – appetizers, main dishes, desserts. Instead, there are eight sections – one for each of his seven friends, and one for Sam. Each section has some special **recipes** using his friends' favorite foods – tomatoes (Jess), cheese (Henry), pasta (Ariyo), vegetables (Joe), meat (Andy), potatoes (Liv), and desserts (Vez). In the eighth section, there are some recipes for one of Sam's favorite foods – chocolate. There are also a lot of great cooking and **nutrition** tips in *Get Cooking*. Check it out the next time you cook.

Go to page 125 for the **Vocabulary Practice.**

B 💿 Read the Web site slowly. Check your answers in Part A.

C Are these statements true or false? Write *True* or *False*. Then correct the false statements.

1. Sam Stern has one cookbook and a Web site.

   False. _He has three cookbooks, a Web site, and a column._

2. There's one recipe for each of his seven friends' favorite foods.

   False. _There are some recipes for each of his seven friends' favorite foods._

3. Henry's favorite food is pasta.

   False. _Henry's favorite food is cheese._

4. There are chocolate recipes in the last section.

   True. _____

5. There aren't any cooking or nutrition tips.

   False. _There are a lot of cooking and nutrition tips._

This lesson practices reading, listening, and writing skills.

Review of Lesson 28

- Write on the board: *Appetizers, Main Dishes, Side Orders, Desserts,* and *Drinks*. Elicit several food items for each category and write them on the board under the appropriate category.

- Divide the class in half. Ask one half to be "servers" and the other half to be "customers." Write on the board: *Would you like a (dessert)?* and *What kind of (dessert) would you like?* Tell the servers to take orders from the customers, using the menu and the examples on the board. Tell them to write down the orders.

- After three minutes, ask students to return to their seats. Invite random servers to share what was ordered with the class. Do a quick tally of the most popular items.

Read

This exercise practices reading for information about food and cooking.

A

- Have students look at the photos. Ask: *What does Sam like to do?* (Cook.) *Do you and your friends like to cook?* If some students answer "yes," ask more questions.

> **Culture Note**
> A common perception is that American teenagers have bad eating habits and eat nothing but junk food. This may be true for some, but there is a growing interest in cooking and eating healthier food among young people. According to one source, TV cooking programs are now more popular with teenagers than with adults. All over the U.S., companies like Kids Cooking Company of Dallas, Texas, offer after-school cooking classes and other cooking programs for teens and children as young as three. Kids learn basic cooking skills and also learn to appreciate new kinds of food. For older teens, these classes often start them on their way to a career as a chef. There are also summer camp programs in cooking. These are often sponsored by culinary institutes and attract famous chefs, like Emeril Lagasse, as teachers.

- Invite a volunteer to read the directions aloud. Remind students that they should read quickly to find the answers and that they should not read every word carefully.

- Have students work individually to read the Web site quickly and write the names of the five foods they find. Do not check answers at this point.

B 🔊 CD2, Track 56

- Invite a volunteer to read the directions aloud. Remind students that they should read slowly and carefully, and concentrate on getting the meaning of the entire text.

- List the new vocabulary words on the board: *cookbook, column, newspaper, section, recipe, nutrition.* Explain their meaning. (Cookbook: a book that tells you how to make certain kinds of food; column: an article that appears regularly in a newspaper or magazine, usually written by the same person; newspaper: printed sheets of folded paper with news, columns, advertising, and so on that you may read every day; section: a part of a newspaper with articles about the same topic, like sports, entertainment, and international news; recipe: instructions for how to make a certain kind of food – for example, a cookbook has many recipes in it; nutrition: healthy eating.) As an alternative, have students use their dictionaries to find the meanings of the new vocabulary words.

- Have students read the Web site again.

- Have students check their answers in Part A in pairs. Elicit the answers from one pair.

- **Optional** Play the recording. Students listen and read along.

> **Audio script**
> Same as the Web site in the Student's Book.

> **Get Connected Vocabulary**
> Have students do the exercise on Student's Book page 125 in class or for homework. (Get Connected Vocabulary answers are on page T-125.)

C

- Invite a volunteer to read the directions aloud.

- Read the first statement: *Sam Stern has one cookbook and a Web site.* Ask: *So is the statement true or false?* Elicit the answer. (False.)

- Have students read the example corrected statement.

- Have students work individually to write *True* or *False,* and then correct the false statements.

- Check answers with the class. Invite volunteers to read aloud one answer each.

Listen

In this exercise, students listen to two teens talk about cooking.

A 💿 CD2, Track 57

- Focus students' attention on the photo. Ask: *Where is this teen?* (In the kitchen.) *What do you think she's doing?* (Looking for a snack, cooking something.)
- Tell students that they will listen to two friends, Nick and Rachel, talk about the food they want to cook and the things they need for cooking.
- Have students read the first question and the example answer.
- Explain that students should listen to the conversation and answer the questions.
- Play the recording. Students only listen.

> **Audio script**
> See page T-211.

- Play the recording again. Students listen and answer the questions.
- Play the recording once again. Students listen and verify their answers.
- Check answers with the class. Invite volunteers to read aloud one answer each.

B

- Have students read the directions and the questions.
- Read the first question with the class and elicit answers from several students. Remind students that there are no right or wrong answers for this exercise – they are giving their opinions.
- Have students work individually to answer the questions and give reasons for their answers.
- Have students work in pairs to compare answers, or elicit opinions from volunteers.

Write

In this exercise, students complete a chart and write a paragraph about a dish they like to make.

A

- Focus students' attention on the chart. Review the words in the first column.
- Copy the chart onto the board. Fill it in with your own information, not using complete sentences.
- Have students work individually to complete the chart about a dish they like to make.

B

- Invite a volunteer to read the directions aloud. Tell students that they will use the information that they wrote in the chart in Part A to help them write a paragraph about making a dish they like.
- Have students work individually to write their paragraph.
- Invite several volunteers to read their paragraphs to the class.
- **Optional** Have students work in groups of four and read each other's paragraphs. Write these questions on the board for students to discuss: *Are any of the paragraphs about the same dish? Are the recipes the same or different? Which dishes would you like to eat?*

> **Workbook**
> Assign the exercises on Workbook page 49. (Workbook answers begin on page T-190.)

It's only pasta!

A  Nick and Rachel talk about cooking. Listen and answer the questions.

1. What do Nick and Rachel want to make?

   They want to make some pasta.

2. How many tomatoes do they have? _They have four tomatoes._

3. How much cheese is there? _There's a lot of cheese._

4. How much pasta is there? _There isn't any pasta._

5. How many cans of soup are there? _There are a few cans of soup._

B What do you think? Answer the questions. Give reasons.
(Answers will vary.)

1. Do you think cooking with friends is fun? _____

2. Do you think cooking is easy or difficult? _____

3. Do you think it's a good idea to use a cookbook? _____

4. Would you like to be a good cook? _____

Your turn

A Think about a dish you like to make. Complete the chart.
(Answers will vary.)

Name of the dish	
Things you need to make it	
How much you need	

B Write about making a dish. Use the answers in Part A to help you.
(Answers will vary.)

I can make _____ . It's really delicious! You need

_____

_____

_____

Language chart review

Countable and uncountable nouns	
Countable	**Uncountable**
Specific: There are **two apples**.	There's **broccoli** on the table.
General: I love apple**s**.	I don't like **broccoli**.

How much / How many . . . ?	
With countable	**With uncountable**
How many apples do we need?	**How much** bread do we have?
We need **a few** apple**s**.	We have **a little** bread.
We need **three** apple**s**.	We have **a lot of** bread.

some / any
Countable nouns
There **are some** cups.
There **aren't any** plates.
Uncountable nouns
There**'s some** salt.
There **isn't any** rice.

A Betty and Jacob make breakfast for their family.
Complete the conversation.

Betty Let's make breakfast.

Jacob Good idea. How about eggs? We all like
_____eggs_____ (eggs / ten eggs).

Betty OK. _How many_ (How much / How many)
eggs do we need?

Jacob Well, I think we need eight eggs. And
we need __a little__ (a little / a few) cheese, too.

Betty We don't have ____any____ (some / any) cheese.

Jacob Oh. So let's put ___a few___ (a little / a few)
potatoes in the eggs.

Betty But Mom doesn't like __potatoes__ (potatoes / the potatoes)
in her eggs.

Jacob That's true. How about ___a little___ (a little / a lot)
chicken? There's ___some___ (some / any) chicken in
the refrigerator.

Betty Yes! And let's put ___some___ (some / any) milk
in the eggs, too. _How much_ (How much / How many)
milk do we need?

Jacob We just need __a little__ (a little / a few) milk.
Do we want bread, too?

Betty Yes, we do. And there's _a lot of_ (a lot / a lot of)
bread here.

Jacob OK! Let's cook!

Unit 7 Review

This lesson reviews the grammar and vocabulary introduced in Unit 7.

Language chart review

These charts summarize the main grammar presented and practiced in Unit 7.

- Books closed. Write on the board:

Countable	Uncountable
There are ___ .	*There is ___ .*
I love / don't like ___ .	*I love / don't like ___ .*
How many ___ ?	*How much ___ ?*
some / any	*some / any*
a few	*a little*
a lot of	*a lot of*

- Elicit examples of countable nouns (*eggs, sandwiches, forks,* etc.) and uncountable nouns (*milk, cheese, mustard,* etc.) and write them on the board in two columns.

- Focus students' attention on the headings on the board.

- Call out a countable noun (*plate*) and point to *There are ____* under the *Countable* heading. Invite a volunteer to use the countable noun in combination with *There are ____* to make a sentence. Continue, calling on different volunteers, until you have practiced all of the words under both headings.

- Books open. Have students study the Language chart review.

- Remind students once again that *some* is used in positive sentences and *any* is used in questions and negative statements. Also remind students that numbers can be used with countable nouns only.

- Answer any questions students may have.

....

Exercises A through C (pages T-98 to T-99)

Note: Students can do these exercises for homework or in class. They should do these exercises with minimal teacher input or help. If you choose to do these exercises as homework, briefly review the exercise directions in class. Make sure that students understand what they should do. Check the answers with the class during the next class meeting. If you choose to do the exercises in class, follow the directions below.

Exercise A

- Have a volunteer read the directions aloud.
- Tell students to complete the conversation with the correct word in parentheses.

- Have students work individually to complete the conversation.
- Check answers with the class.
- Have students practice the conversation in pairs.

Exercise B

- Have students read the directions and the examples.
- Explain that there are two parts to the task. First, students write questions with *How much* or *How many*, using the words given. Then, they write answers to the questions, using the picture in Part A on page 98.
- Have students work individually to complete the exercise.
- Check answers with the class.

Language chart review

This chart summarizes further grammar presented and practiced in Unit 7.

- Have students study the examples in the chart.
- Remind students that *would like* is a polite way to express *want*.
- Answer any questions students may have.

Exercise C

- Have students read the directions.
- Tell students to complete the conversation with the sentences in the box.
- Have students work individually to complete the conversation.
- Have students check their answers in pairs.
- Check answers with the class. Invite volunteers to read the completed conversation aloud.

> **Optional Unit Wrap-Up** ....
>
> - If students did the Review exercises for homework, check answers with the class.
> - Have students work in pairs and choose a dish from the Writing activity on page 97. Students create a conversation with information about their dish. They should use the conversation in Exercise A and the questions in Exercise B as models. Invite one or two pairs to act out their conversation for the class.
> - Have students work in groups of three or four. Each group creates a menu. Students then use the menu to create a conversation like the one in Exercise C. One student plays the role of the server. The others are customers and order foods from the menu.

Theme Project

- Assign the *At Home* section of the Unit 7 Theme Project on Student's Book page 132.

Workbook

- Assign the Unit 7 Check Yourself on Workbook page 50. (Workbook answers begin on page T-190.)

Extra Practice Worksheets

- Assign the Unit 7 Extra Practice worksheets starting on page T-154.

Extra Speaking Practice Worksheet

- Assign the Unit 7 Extra Speaking Practice worksheet on page T-171.

Arcade Activities

- Assign the Unit 7 Arcade activities found at: www.cambridge.org/connectarcade

Learning Log

- Assign the Unit 7 Learning Log. These can be downloaded from the Teacher Support Site at: www.cambridge.org/connect2e/teacher

Quiz

- Give the Unit 7 Quiz on page T-182.

Test

- Give the Unit 7 Test (Form A and / or Form B). These can be downloaded from the Teacher Support Site at: www.cambridge.org/connect2e/teacher

B Write questions about Betty and Jacob with *How much* or *How many*. Then look again at the picture in Part A, and answer the questions. Use *a few*, *a little*, or *a lot of*.

1. milk

   Q: _How much milk do they have?_
   A: _They have a little milk._

2. potatoes

   Q: _How many potatoes do they have?_
   A: _They have a few potatoes._

3. chicken

   Q: _How much chicken do they have?_
   A: _They have a lot of chicken._

4. fruit

   Q: _How much fruit do they have?_
   A: _They have a little fruit._

5. bread

   Q: _How much bread do they have?_
   A: _They have a lot of bread._

6. eggs

   Q: _How many eggs do they have?_
   A: _They have a lot of eggs._

Language chart review

would like

I'**d like** a sandwich.
 Would you **like** a side order?
   Yes, please. I'**d like** french fries.
   No, thanks.

C Molly orders lunch. Complete the questions. Then write answers. Use the sentences in the box.

☐ I'd like a chicken sandwich.	☑ Yes. I'd like a sandwich.
☐ I'd like chocolate ice cream.	☐ Yes. I'd like some ice cream.
☐ No, thanks.	☐ Yes, please. I'd like apple juice.

Server Hi. Are you ready to order?
Molly _Yes. I'd like a sandwich._
Server What kind of sandwich _would_
you _like_ ?
Molly _I'd like a chicken sandwich._
Server _Would you like_ a side dish?
Maybe some french fries?
Molly _No, thanks._
Server Would you like a drink?
Molly _Yes, please. I'd like apple juice._
Server _Would_ you _like_ dessert?
Molly _Yes. I'd like some ice cream._
Server What kind of ice cream _would you like_ ?
Molly _I'd like chocolate ice cream._

Go to page 132 for the Theme Project.

World weather

1 Vocabulary

A Match the symbols to the sentences describing weather and temperature. Then listen and practice.

Weather

1. _d_   a. It's cloudy.

2. _e_   b. It's rainy.

3. _c_   c. It's snowy.

4. _a_   d. It's sunny.

5. _b_   e. It's windy.

Temperature

6. _h_   f. It's cold.

7. _i_   g. It's cool.

8. _g_   h. It's hot.

9. _f_   i. It's warm.

B It's December. Look at the weather map, and complete the sentences with words from Part A. Then listen and practice.

1. It's __cold__ and __snowy__ in Moscow.

2. It's __cold__ and __windy__ in Chicago.

3. It's __cool__ and __rainy__ in Tokyo.

4. It's __hot__ and __sunny__ in Rio de Janeiro.

5. It's __warm__ and __cloudy__ in Cape Town.

C What kind of weather do you like?
What kind of weather don't you like?
Tell your classmates.

> I like hot, sunny weather. I don't like . . .

Lesson 29 World weather

This lesson presents and practices words that describe weather conditions and What's the weather like?

1 Vocabulary

This exercise presents and practices words that describe weather conditions.

A CD2, Track 58

- Focus students' attention on the weather terms in red. Model the terms. As you say the words, ask students to call out the number of the appropriate weather icon or symbol.
- Write the weather terms on the board. Invite volunteers to draw the simple weather symbols next to the appropriate terms.
- Ask students to read the directions, look at the exercise, and read the example. Students work individually to complete the matching exercise.
- Play the recording. Students listen and verify their answers.

Audio script
Same as the sentences in the Student's Book.

- Check answers with the class.
- Play the recording again, or model the sentences. Students listen and repeat.

B CD2, Track 59

- Have students read the directions, the example, and the incomplete sentences.
- Give students several minutes to study the map. Ask: *Where is Tokyo on the map? Where is Rio de Janeiro? Where is Cape Town?* Students point to the cities.
- Have students work individually to complete the sentences with the appropriate weather terms.
- Play the recording. Students listen and verify their answers.

Audio script
Same as the sentences in the Student's Book.

- Check answers with the class. Invite volunteers to read their completed sentences aloud.
- Play the recording again, or model the sentences. Students listen and repeat.

C

- Ask students to read the directions and the example sentences.
- Write on the board: *What kind of weather do / don't you like?* Model the two sentences for students. Have each student ask four classmates these questions and take notes on their responses.
- Invite volunteers to share their classmates' responses with the class.
- **Optional** Play a round of "Tic-Tac-Toe." Draw a grid on the board. Fill in the nine squares with the nine weather terms from Part A. Divide the class into two teams, X and O. Teams take turns reading the terms in the squares of their choice and using them in appropriate sentences to earn squares for their teams. For example: *It's cloudy today. It's usually hot in July.* The first team with three squares in a row wins.

This unit introduces vocabulary and expressions for talking about weather conditions, bodies of water and landforms, countries and nationalities, and numbers.

2 Language focus

This exercise presents and practices *What's the weather like?*

A 💿 CD2, Track 60

- Have students read the directions and study the photo. Ask: *What's Tommy doing?* (Chatting online.)
- Tell students that they will listen to a conversation between Tommy and his e-pal Josie about weather around the world.
- Play the recording. Students listen and read along.

> **Audio script**
> Same as the conversation in the Student's Book.

- Ask: *What kind of information does Tommy need?* (April weather around the world.) *Where does Josie live?* (In Santiago, Chile.)
- Ask: *What's the weather usually like in Santiago in April?* (Warm.) *What's the weather like today?* (Hot and sunny.) *Where is Josie going later?* (The park.)
- Play the recording again, or model the conversation. Students listen and repeat.
- **Optional** Have students practice in pairs.
- **Language Chart** Have students study the examples in the language chart. Tell students that the two question forms are slight variations of *What's the weather like?* Ask: *What words were added in the first question?* (In April.) *What word was added in the second question?* (Today.)
- Ask students what other types of words could be added to the question. (In Chile, in May, in the spring, etc.)
- Model the examples, pausing for students to repeat.

B 💿 CD2, Track 61

- Ask students to read the directions and the example. Tell students that they may refer back to Exercise 1A on page 100 to review the weather icons.
- Have students work individually to complete the questions and answers.
- Play the recording. Students listen and verify their answers.

> **Audio script**
> Same as the questions and answers in the Student's Book.

- Check answers with the class. Invite volunteers to read aloud one question and one answer each.
- Have students practice the conversations in pairs.

---

3 Speaking

This exercise practices asking about weather conditions.

- Ask students to read the directions aloud.
- Ask two volunteers to read the example conversation. Then ask two other volunteers to model the conversation, substituting a different month.
- Have students practice the conversation in pairs, asking and answering at least five questions.
- Ask students to share their results with the class. Ask random pairs to stand and act out their conversation. Students should not repeat any months. Continue until you have covered each of the twelve months. Ask the class if they agree with the answers.

- **Optional** Play a few rounds of a guessing game. Say: *It's (hot and sunny).* Students guess which month you have in mind by asking *What's the weather usually like in _____ ?* The first student who guesses correctly comes to the front and continues the activity.

> **Workbook**
> Assign the exercises on Workbook page 51. (Workbook answers begin on page T-190.)

> **Extra Grammar**
> Assign the exercises for the Extra Grammar, Lesson 29.

A It's Sunday afternoon. Tommy is in an
online chat room. Listen and practice.

> **What's the weather like?**
>
> **What's the weather like** in April?
> It's usually **rainy**.
> **What's the weather like** today?
> It's **warm** and **sunny** today.

● International Chat

Tommy: Hi, everyone! I'm doing my science
homework. I need information about April
weather around the world.
Josie: Hi, Tommy! I can help you.
Tommy: Great! Where do you live, Josie?
Josie: In Santiago, Chile.
Tommy: What's the weather like in Santiago in April?
Josie: It's usually warm. But it's not warm today.
Tommy: What's the weather like today?
Josie: It's hot and sunny. I want to go to the park later.
Tommy: That sounds fun! Thanks for your help! Sofia, can
you help me, too? Where do you live?

Now in
chat room:

● Tommy
● Sofia
● Lynn
● Garth
● Josie

B Complete more of Tommy's questions and answers
from the chat. Listen and check. Then practice.

1. **Tommy** What's the weather like in Chicago in April?

   Sofia _It's usually warm and rainy._

2. **Tommy** What's the weather like in New York in April?

   Lynn _It's usually cool_ and _cloudy_ .

3. **Tommy** What's the weather _like_ in New York today?

   Lynn _It's cool_ and _rainy_ today.

4. **Tommy** _What's the weather like_ in Winnipeg in April?

   Garth _It's usually cold_ and _snowy_ .

5. **Garth** _What's the weather like_ in Darwin in April?

   Tommy _It's usually hot_ and _sunny_ , but it's
   cool and cloudy now.

3 **Speaking**

Work with a classmate. Ask and answer questions about the weather in
your town or city in different months.

> What's the weather like in Rio in February?

> It's usually hot and sunny.

Natural wonders

1 Vocabulary

A Complete the sentences with the words in the box.
Then listen and practice.

> ☐ the Andes Mountains ☐ the Galápagos Islands ☑ Mammoth Hot Springs
> ☐ El Yunque Rain Forest ☐ the Jenolan Caves ☐ the Mississippi River

1. _Mammoth Hot Springs_ are in Yellowstone National Park in the United States.

2. Some people live on houseboats on _the Mississippi River_ .

3. _The Galápagos Islands_ are in the Pacific Ocean.

4. _The Jenolan Caves_ are in Australia.

5. _El Yunque Rain Forest_ is in Puerto Rico.

6. People ski in _the Andes Mountains_ .

B Kate loves the outdoors. Complete her sentences with the words in the box.

> ☐ cave ☐ hot spring ☐ island ☐ mountain ☐ rain forest ☑ river

1. I want to go canoeing on a _____ river _____ .

2. I want to climb a really big _____ mountain _____ .

3. I want to take a boat ride around an _____ island _____ in the sea.

4. I want to take pictures of birds and other animals in a _____ rain forest _____ .

5. I want to see the inside of a big, underground _____ cave _____ .

6. I want to sit and relax in a _____ hot spring _____ .

Natural wonders

This lesson presents and practices the names of bodies of water and landforms and can
(for possibility).

1 Vocabulary

This exercise presents and practices the names of some bodies of water and landforms.

A CD2, Track 62

• Focus students' attention on the words in red. Explain any words they are unsure of.

• Model the new words. Students listen and repeat.

• Ask students to look at the photos of the six scenic spots. Give students several minutes to study the photos and the incomplete sentences.

• Have students work individually to complete the sentences.

• Play the recording. Students listen and verify their answers.

Audio script

Same as the captions in the Student's Book.

• Check answers with the class. Invite volunteers to read the completed sentences.

• Play the recording again, or model the sentences. Students listen and repeat.

• **Optional** Call out the *Andes.* Students respond with *Mountains.* Continue until you have called out each word in the box. Continue the activity by reversing the order if desired.

Note: Explain to students that *the* is used with many names of geographical places. A few of the rules are as follows:

1. Use *the* with proper names of areas of water with the exception of lakes: *the Pacific Ocean, the Suez Canal, the Gulf of Mexico.*

2. Use *the* with countries whose names include words like *republic, states,* or *kingdom: the People's Republic of China, the United States, the United Kingdom.*

3. Use *the* with countries that have plural names: *the Philippines, the Netherlands.* Do not use *the* with countries that have singular names.

4. Use *the* with groups of islands and mountain ranges: *the Bahamas, the Himalayas.*

5. Do not use *the* with continents, cities, streets, or addresses.

B

• Ask students to read the directions. Then focus their attention on the words in the box and on the example sentence.

• Have students work individually to complete the sentences.

• Check answers with the class. Invite volunteers to come to the front to write their answers on the board.

• **Optional** Have students choose three of the activities in the sentences that they would like to do without telling anyone their choices. Have students work in pairs to guess what their partners would like to do, using the example below:

A: You want to go canoeing on a river.

B: No, I don't.

A: You want to sit and relax in a hot spring.

B: Yes, I do.

2 Language focus

This exercise presents and practices *can* (for possibility).

A 💿 CD2, Track 63

- Have students read the directions and look at the photo. Ask: *Where's Kate?* (Yellowstone National Park.) *What's she doing?* (Talking with a guide.)
- Explain *guide*. (A park worker who takes or directs tourists to places.)
- Play the recording. Students listen and read along.

> **Audio script**
> Same as the conversation in the Student's Book.

- Ask: *What three questions with* can *does Kate ask?* (What can you see on this trail? Can you see any animals? Can you buy any food around here?)
- Repeat the questions and ask random students to answer them. *What can you see on this trail?* (Mountains, hot springs, and rivers.) *Can you see any animals?* (Yes, you can.) *Can you buy any food around here?* (No, you can't.)
- Ask: *Who does* you *refer to in these questions?* (People in general.)
- Talk about the two uses of *can*. In the sentence *I can swim,* the <u>ability</u> to swim is expressed by *can*. In the sentence *You can swim in the river,* the fact that it is <u>possible</u> for people to swim in the river is expressed by *can*.
- Play the recording again, or model the conversation. Students listen and repeat.

- **Optional** Have students practice in pairs.
- **Language Chart** Focus students' attention on the first statement in the language chart. Ask: *How many* You can . . . *sentences are there in the conversation?* (Six.)
- Have students look at the two types of questions. Ask: *Which type takes a* Yes / No *answer, the first or the second?* (The second.) Have students find all the questions in the conversation that start with *Can you . . . ?* Focus students' attention on the short answers to those questions.
- Model the examples, pausing for students to repeat.

B 💿 CD2, Track 64

- Ask students to read the directions, look at the chart, and read the example.
- Have students work individually to complete the exercise.
- Play the recording. Students listen and verify their answers.

> **Audio script**
> Same as the sentences in the Student's Book.

- Check answers with the class. Invite volunteers to read aloud one answer each.

3 Listening

In this exercise, students listen for different activities.

💿 CD2, Track 65

- Ask students to read the directions and the activities in the chart.
- Tell students that they will listen to a conversation between Kate and a friend. Students should listen for the activities that exist near Kate's hometown.
- Play the recording. Students only listen.

> **Audio script**
> See page T-212.

- Play the recording again. Students listen and check the *Yes* or *No* box next to each activity.
- Play the recording once again. Students listen and verify their answers.
- Check answers with the class.

> **Workbook**
> Assign the exercises on Workbook page 52. (Workbook answers begin on page T-190.)

> **Extra Grammar**
> Assign the exercises for the Extra Grammar, Lesson 30.

2 Language focus

can (for possibility)

A Kate visits Yellowstone National Park. She's talking with a guide. Listen and practice.

Guide You can see a lot of amazing things in this park.

Kate So, what can you see on this trail?

Guide You can see some incredible mountains, hot springs, rivers . . .

Kate Can you see any animals?

Guide Yes, you can. You can see snakes and wolves. And sometimes you can see bears.

Kate I don't want to see any bears right now!

Guide And they don't want to see you!

Kate I'm hungry. Can you buy any food around here?

Guide No, you can't. You can buy food at hotels and at the souvenir shops. You were supposed to bring lunch!

Kate Oh, no! I forgot!

> **can (for possibility)**
>
> **You can** see a lot of amazing things.
> What **can you** see on this trail?
> **You can** see some incredible mountains.
> **Can you** buy any food around here?
> Yes, **you can**.
> No, **you can't**.

B What can you do at these parks? Look at the chart, and write sentences. Then listen and check.

Park Facilities and Activities	🚣	🎣	⛺	🐦	🏊
Kent Park	✓		✓	✓	
Ranch Park		✓	✓		
Thunder Park	✓			✓	✓

1. (Kent Park) _You can go canoeing. You can go camping. You can see birds._

2. (Ranch Park) _You can go horseback riding. You can go camping._

3. (Thunder Park) _You can go canoeing. You can see birds. You can go swimming._

3 Listening

Can people do these activities near Kate's hometown? Listen and check (✓) Yes or No.

	Yes	No
1. go canoeing	✓	☐
2. climb mountains	✓	☐
3. visit caves	✓	☐
4. go to hot springs	☐	✓
5. go dancing	✓	☐

Mini-review

1 Language check

A Look at the weather map for the United States and Canada.
Write questions and answers about the weather in the cities.

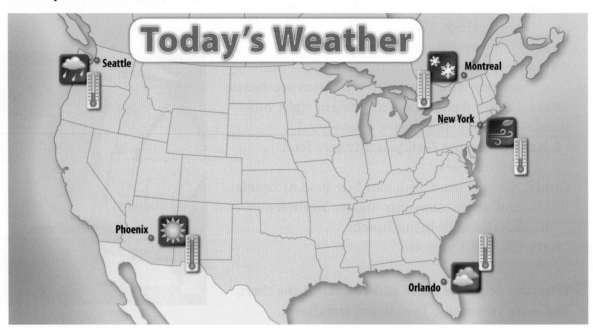

Today's Weather

Seattle
Montreal
New York
Phoenix
Orlando

1. (Montreal) _What's the weather like in Montreal?_
   It's cold and snowy.

2. (Orlando) _What's the weather like in Orlando?_
   It's warm and cloudy.

3. (New York) _What's the weather like in New York?_
   It's cool and windy.

4. (Seattle) _What's the weather like in Seattle?_
   It's cool and rainy.

5. (Phoenix) _What's the weather like in Phoenix?_
   It's hot and sunny.

B Match the words to complete the sentences.

1. You can sit and relax in that ___c___ .   a. caves
2. You can go canoeing on that ___e___ .   b. beach
3. You can climb that ___d___ .   c. hot spring
4. You can go underground in those ___a___ .   d. mountain
5. You can go dancing in ___f___ .   e. river
6. You can go swimming at the ___b___ .   f. town

This lesson reviews the language presented and practiced in Lessons 29 and 30.

1 Language check

This exercise reviews the structures presented so far in this unit.

A

- Focus students' attention on the weather map. Ask a few questions about the location of the cities on the map – for example, *Is Montreal in Canada or in the United States?* (It's in Canada.)

- Invite a volunteer to read the directions and the example question and answer.

- Students work individually to write the questions and answers.

- Check answers with the class. Invite pairs of students to read the questions and answers aloud.

- **Optional** Have students work in pairs to read all the questions and answers. Have each pair create one original question and answer about the weather in a city in their country.

B

- Invite a volunteer to read the directions and the example aloud.

- Have students work individually to complete the exercise.

- Check answers with the class. Invite volunteers to read aloud the two parts of each sentence.

C

- Have students read the directions, look at the pictures, and then read the conversation.
- Explain *vacation plans*. (Where people will go on vacation and what they will do there.)
- Say the sentences below. Ask students to say *True* if the sentences are correct and *False* if they are incorrect.
  1. Jesse *thinks the park sounds really interesting*. (False.)
  2. *You can see bats in the caves at the park.* (True.)
  3. *You can swim at the beach.* (True.)
  4. *You can't see an island.* (False.)
  5. Jesse *wants to go.* (True.)
- Have students work individually to complete the conversation.
- Check answers with the class.
- Have students practice the conversation in pairs.

---

2 Listening

In this exercise, students listen for the order of five places.

💿 **CD2, Track 66**

- Have students look at the photo and read the directions and the list of places.
- Explain to students that they will listen to a TV show that features a guide in Japan talking about her adventures during a tour. Students should listen for the order of the places the guide talks about.
- Play the recording. Students only listen.

Audio script
See page T-212.

- Play the recording again. Students listen and number the places in the order the guide talks about them.
- Play the recording once again. Students listen and verify their answers.
- Check answers with the class. Write the words on the board. Invite volunteers to come to the board to write their answers.

Workbook
Assign the exercises on Workbook page 53. (Workbook answers begin on page T-190.)

Game
Assign the game on Student's Book page 121.

C Jesse and his father talk about vacation plans. Complete their conversation with *you can*, *you can't*, *what can you*, and *can you*.

Jesse I don't know, Dad. The park sounds a little boring.

Mr. Willis Boring? The park sounds really interesting!

Jesse But _what can you_ do there?

Mr. Willis _You can_ do a lot of things. _You can_ hike and camp . . .

Jesse You can hike and camp here in our town!

Mr. Willis Yes, _you can_ . But _can you_ climb mountains in our town? _Can you_ see caves in our town?

Jesse No, _you can't_ . Maybe the park is OK. _Can you_ see bats in the caves?

Mr. Willis Yes, and _you can_ see them fly out of the caves at night. There's also a great beach.

Jesse _What can you_ do at the beach?

Mr. Willis _You can_ go swimming. Or _you can_ take a boat ride to an island.

Jesse OK. I want to go. Let's tell Mom we have a plan!

2 Listening

Jesse and his father watch *Adventure Vacations* on TV. This week's show is in northern Japan. Listen and number the places in the correct order.

_5_ cave

_3_ hot spring

_4_ island

_1_ mountain

_2_ river

Go to page 121 for the Game.

World of friends

1 Vocabulary

A Can you say "hello" in other languages? Match the languages to the correct greetings. Then listen and practice.

1. Arabic _c_	4. Italian _a_	a. Buon giorno!	d. Geia sou!
2. German _f_	5. Portuguese _b_	b. Olá!	e. Zdravstvuite!
3. Greek _d_	6. Russian _e_	c. Ahalan!	f. Guten Tag!

B Tommy meets a lot of friends online. Where are they from? Complete their sentences with the words in the box. Then listen and practice.

☐ Germany ☐ Greece ☐ Italy ☑ Morocco ☐ Portugal ☐ Russia

1. My name is Khalil. I live in ___Morocco___ . "Ahalan!"

2. I'm Karl. I live in ___Germany___ . "Guten Tag!"

3. "Buon giorno!" I'm Carlotta. I live in ___Italy___ .

4. "Geia sou!" I'm Christina. I live in ___Greece___ .

5. I'm Ivan. I live in ___Russia___ . "Zdravstvuite!"

6. I'm Emilia. I live in ___Portugal___ . "Olá!"

C Work with a classmate. Look at Part B. Ask and answer questions about where Tommy's friends are from and what languages they speak.

> Is Ivan from Russia?

> Does Emilia speak Italian?

> Yes, he is.

> No, she doesn't. She speaks Portuguese.

This lesson presents and practices the names of several countries and nationalities and Who + (verb) . . . ?

Review of Lesson 30

- Write the six vocabulary words from Lesson 30 on the board. Review with students.
- Write on the board: *I want to go to a / an _____.* Ask students to complete and write this sentence on a slip of paper. Then ask them to walk around the room, repeating this sentence until they find a classmate with the same sentence. Ask random students to share their results with the class: *_____ and I want to go to a / an _____.*
- Divide the class into two teams or into three or four smaller groups. Read the words below. Teams compete to unscramble the words into statements or questions. Each team elects a representative to write the answer on the board. The first team to do so correctly wins a point for the team.

Note: Before reading the words, tell students if it is a statement or a question.

Statement: *hike, rain, can, forest, in, a, you* (You can hike in a rain forest.)

Question: *do, island, can, an, you, on, what* (What can you do on an island?)

Question: *you, bears, a, can, see, cave, in* (Can you see bears in a cave?)

Question: *bats, can, night, you, at, see* (Can you see bats at night?)

1 Vocabulary

This exercise presents and practices the names of several countries and nationalities.

A 💿 CD2, Track 67

- Ask students to read the directions.
- Model the names of the languages for the students.
- Have students work individually to match the languages to the correct greetings. Tell them to leave blank any of those that they are unable to do.
- Play the recording. Students listen and verify their answers, matching any remaining items.

Audio script
Same as the words in the Student's Book.

- Check answers with the class. Ask pairs of students to stand and say the language and the greeting.
- Play the recording again, or model the languages. Students listen and repeat.

B 💿 CD2, Track 68

- Ask students to read the directions and the words in red in the box. Read the names of the countries. Ask students to call out the corresponding nationalities.
- Focus students' attention on the photos and the incomplete sentences.
- Have students work individually to complete the sentences with the words in the box.
- Play the recording. Students listen and verify their answers.

Audio script
Same as the sentences in the Student's Book.

- Check answers with the class.
- Play the recording again, or model the sentences. Students listen and repeat.
- **Optional** Ask random students to stand and read the sentences.

C

- Ask students to read the directions.
- Model the example conversation with a volunteer. Then ask two other volunteers to model the conversation, using questions of their own.
- Have students ask and answer questions in pairs.

2 Language focus

This exercise presents and practices *Who* + (verb) . . . ?

A 💿 CD2, Track 69

- Ask students to read the directions and look at the photo. Ask students if they or any of their friends have e-pals. Tell students they will listen to Claudia ask Tommy about his online friends.
- Play the recording. Students listen and read along.

> **Audio script**
> Same as the conversation in the Student's Book.

- Ask: *Who wants some new e-pals?* (Claudia.) *Who plays soccer?* (Karl and Emilia.) *Who lives in Germany?* (Karl.)
- Play the recording again, or model the conversation. Students listen and repeat.
- **Optional** Have students practice in pairs.
- **Language Chart** Have students study the examples in the language chart. Explain that if *Who* is followed by a verb, the verb will have an *-s* ending.
- Tell students to focus on the answers to the two questions. Ask: *Do we use* do *or* does *in the answer?* (It depends on the subject in the answer.) Review the usage of *do* and *does*. Call out the following pronouns: *you, he, we, she, it, they.* Students respond with *do* or *does*.
- Model the examples, pausing for students to repeat.

B 💿 CD2, Track 70

- Focus students' attention on the directions and the e-mail messages. Ask: *Who is the first e-mail from?* (Khalil.) *How about the second?* (Christina.)
- Tell students that they should read the e-mail messages again and complete the questions and answers.
- Have students work individually to complete the exercise.
- Play the recording. Students listen and verify their answers.

> **Audio script**
> Same as the questions and answers in the Student's Book.

- Check answers with the class.
- Have students practice the questions and answers in pairs.

3 Listening

In this exercise, students listen for the names of e-pals and their hobbies.

💿 CD2, Track 71

- Tell students that they will listen to Tommy and Rafael talk about Tommy's e-pals' hobbies. Students should listen for who does which hobby.
- Play the recording. Students only listen.

> **Audio script**
> See page T-212.

- Play the recording again. Students listen and check the correct name or names.
- Play the recording once again. Students listen and verify their answers.
- Check answers with the class.

> **Workbook**
> Assign the exercises on Workbook page 54. (Workbook answers begin on page T-190.)

> **Extra Grammar**
> Assign the exercises for the Extra Grammar, Lesson 31.

2 Language focus

A Claudia wants new e-pals. She asks Tommy about his online friends. Listen and practice.

Claudia Can you help me find some new e-pals?

Tommy Well, maybe you can write to my e-pals. Karl, Emilia, Ivan, and Carlotta are really interesting.

Claudia Do they like sports?

Tommy Sure. One of them plays tennis, two of them play soccer, and . . .

Claudia Who plays soccer?

Tommy Karl and Emilia do. Karl lives in Germany. The others live in Greece, Morocco, Italy . . .

Claudia Oh! Who lives in Italy?

Tommy Carlotta does.

Claudia Great! I'll write to Karl and Carlotta. I love soccer, and I want to learn German and Italian.

Who + (verb) . . . ?
Who lives in Italy?
Carlotta **does.**
Who plays soccer?
Karl and Emilia **do.**

B Read these messages from Tommy's newest e-pals. Write questions and answers. Listen and check. Then practice.

● From: Khalil ⊟☒

I like music, and I watch a lot of American movies. I go camping a lot. Do you like to go camping?

● From: Christina ⊟☒

I live near beautiful islands. You can swim and relax on the beach. I like music. I play the guitar and the piano.

1. Who lives near beautiful islands?   *Christina does.*
2. Who watches movies?   *Khalil does.*
3. Who plays the guitar?   *Christina does.*
4. *Who goes camping?*   Khalil does.
5. *Who likes music?*   Both Christina and Khalil do.

3 Listening

Tommy talks about his e-pals, Ivan, Emilia, and Christina. Who does these things? Listen and check (✓) the correct name or names.

	Ivan	Emilia	Christina
1. take photographs		✓	
2. speak four languages	✓		
3. swim every day			✓
4. play the guitar	✓		✓

1 Vocabulary

A **Listen and practice.**

100 one hundred	167 one hundred and sixty-seven
1,000 one thousand	2,412 two thousand, four hundred and twelve
10,000 ten thousand	85,000 eighty-five thousand
100,000 one hundred thousand	960,102 nine hundred sixty thousand, one hundred and two

B **Listen and practice.**

☐ 154 ☐ 17,000 ☐ 20,000 ☑ 25,000 ☐ 90,000 ☐ 100,000

C **This Sunday is International Day at school. Students are giving presentations. Listen and complete their sentences with the correct numbers from the box in Part B.**

1. Every year, _25,000_ people run from Sydney to Bondi Beach in the Fun Run.

2. There are _17,000_ kinds of birds in my country.

3. There are _100,000_ people in the city of Guaynabo.

4. _90,000_ people can watch a soccer game in Maracanã Stadium.

5. There are _154_ national forests in the United States.

6. There are _20,000_ "Mounties" – a special group of police officers – in Canada.

International Day

This lesson presents and practices numbers higher than 101 and What + (noun) . . . ?

Review of Lesson 31
- Call out the foreign language greetings from Lesson 31. Students respond with the name of the language. Then call out the languages one by one. Students respond with the appropriate country.
- On the board, write: *Karl lives in Germany. Christina plays the guitar. Carlotta speaks Italian. Khalil likes music.*
- Ask students to make questions using *Who* + (verb) . . . ? for the answers on the board without looking back at Lesson 31.
- Invite volunteers to write one answer each on the board.

1 Vocabulary

This exercise presents and practices numbers higher than 101.

A CD2, Track 72
- Focus students' attention on the numbers.
- Play the recording. Students listen.

> **Audio script**
> Same as the numbers in the Student's Book.

- Play the recording again. Students listen and repeat.
- Write the eight numbers on the board. Point to them randomly, one by one. Students respond chorally with the correct number. Conduct the activity individually for extra practice if desired.

Note: Explain to students that the numbers can be read with or without the word *and* inserted before the last one or two digits. If the first of the last two digits is zero, the *and* comes before the last digit – for example, *one hundred and two*. If it is not, the *and* comes before the last two digits; for example, *four hundred twelve* may also be read as *four hundred and twelve*.

B CD2, Track 73
- Focus students' attention on the numbers in red in the box.
- Play the recording. Students only listen.

> **Audio script**
> Same as the numbers in the Student's Book.

- Play the recording again. Students listen and repeat.
- Write the number 154 on the board.
- Have a volunteer read the number in two ways. (One hundred and fifty-four <u>and</u> one hundred fifty-four.)

C CD2, Track 74
- Ask students to read the directions. Explain *presentations*. (Oral reports.) Then focus students' attention on the photos.
- Tell students that they will listen to the presentations and should fill in the blanks with the correct numbers from the box in Part B.
- Play the recording. Students only listen.

> **Audio script**
> Same as the sentences in the Student's Book.

- Play the recording again. Students listen and write the numbers.
- Play the recording once again. Students listen and verify their answers.
- Check answers with the class. Ask random students to come to the board to write their answers.

2 Language focus

This exercise presents and practices *What + (noun)...?*

A 💿 CD2, Track 75

- Ask students to read the directions and look at the photo. Ask: *Who is talking in the conversation?* (Claudia and Mr. Baker.) *Who is Mr. Baker?* (Zach's father.)
- Play the recording. Students listen and read along.

> **Audio script**
> Same as the conversation in the Student's Book.

- Write four times on the board: *What __ do __ ?* Say: *Mr. Baker asked Claudia four of these kinds of questions. What were they?* (What school subjects do you like? What sports do you play? What sports does he like? What sports do they play?)
- Invite volunteers to come to the board to complete the questions.
- Ask: *What other* What . . . ? *questions do you know?* (What's your name? What are you doing? What color is it? What time is it?)
- Play the recording again, or model the conversation. Students listen and repeat.
- **Optional** Have students practice in pairs.
- **Language Chart** Have students study the three examples in the language chart. Ask: *What are the nouns in each question?* (Subjects, sports.) *How about the verbs?* (Like, play.)
- Ask: *Which pronouns take* do? (I, you, we, they.) *Which pronouns take* does? (He, she.) *Which pronouns do you see in the answers?* (I, he, they.)
- Model the examples, pausing for students to repeat.

B 💿 CD2, Track 76

- Have volunteers read the directions and the example aloud.
- Fill in the second blank together as a class.
- Have students work individually to complete the conversation.
- Play the recording. Students listen and verify their answers.

> **Audio script**
> Same as the conversation in the Student's Book.

- Check answers with the class.
- Have students practice the conversation in pairs.

....

3 Speaking

This exercise practices talking about personal preferences.

- Focus students' attention on the directions and the words in the box. Tell students they may use the words in the box or their own ideas.
- Ask students to give one example for each word in the box.
- Invite a volunteer to model the conversation with you, following the example.
- Have students work in pairs to ask and answer questions. Encourage them to ask about as many topics as possible.

> **Workbook**
> Assign the exercises on Workbook page 55. (Workbook answers begin on page T-190.)

> **Extra Grammar**
> Assign the exercises for the Extra Grammar, Lesson 32.

2 Language focus

What + (noun) . . . ?

What subjects do you like?
I like math and science.
What sports does he like?
He doesn't like sports.
What sports do they play?
They play all sports.

A Zach's father, Mr. Baker, asks Claudia some questions. Listen and practice.

Mr. Baker Great presentation, Claudia! Are there really 17,000 species of birds in the Colombian rain forest?

Claudia At least! Some scientists think there are 20,000. And there are 130,000 species of plants.

Mr. Baker You know a lot, Claudia! What school subjects do you like?

Claudia I like math and science.

Mr. Baker And Zach says you're athletic. What sports do you play?

Claudia Well, I play soccer, Ping-Pong, basketball, tennis . . .

Mr. Baker Wow! And your brother? What sports does he like?

Claudia He doesn't like sports.

Mr. Baker What about your parents? What sports do they play?

Claudia Well, they play tennis and golf. My father plays golf 365 days a year!

B Now Mr. Baker talks with Rafael. Complete their conversation. Listen and check. Then practice.

Mr. Baker <u>What sports</u> do you like, Rafael?

Rafael I like soccer, tennis, and basketball. How about you? <u>What sports do you like</u> , Mr. Baker?

Mr. Baker Oh, I like all sports, especially baseball.

Rafael I want to introduce you to my father, but his English isn't very good.

Mr. Baker <u>What language does he</u> speak? Portuguese?

Rafael Yes. <u>He speaks</u> Portuguese and some Spanish.

Mr. Baker Great! I speak a little Spanish, too. Let's find him!

3 Speaking

Ask your classmates questions. Use the words in the box or your own ideas.

colors   **music groups**   **subjects**   **video games**
foods   **sports**   **TV shows**

What sports do you like?   I like basketball.

Read

A Read the article quickly. Check (✓) the main idea.

☐ 1. The air is dirty and the oceans are rising.

☑ 2. Global warming is a big problem, but everyone can help.

☐ 3. It's hotter these days and many animals are dying.

Global Warming

Look around you. What's the weather like these days? In many places like Antarctica and Greenland it's usually cold, but now it's hotter. The ice in these cold places is **melting**, and the water in the oceans is **rising**. The air is **dirty**. Many species of plants and animals are **dying**. This is a serious problem and it has a name – *global warming*.

Can we stop global warming? Yes, we can. Scientists think there's still time to **save** our incredible planet. So, what can we do? Here are some ideas:

• Use less water, paper, and electricity.

• Walk, bike, or take the bus – don't drive.

• **Recycle** paper and **plastic** items.

• Ask your classmates, friends, and family for ideas.

And don't forget . . . our actions can save the world for many years to come. Let's start today.

Go to page 125 for the **Vocabulary Practice.**

B 🔊 Read the article slowly. Check your answer in Part A.

C Answer the questions.

1. What's the weather usually like in Greenland? *It's usually cold.*

2. What's the ice doing in cold places? *It's melting.*

3. What's the air like around the world? *It's dirty.*

4. Can we stop global warming? *Yes, we can.*

5. What can you do to help? Name one thing. *(Answers will vary.) Use less water, paper, and electricity. / Walk, bike, or take the bus – don't drive. / Recycle paper and plastic items.*

This lesson practices reading, listening, and writing skills.

Review of Lesson 32

- Write any 20 numbers between 100 and 999,999 in random order on the board. Ask three or four students to come to the board. Give each student a piece of chalk or a whiteboard marker. Call out one of the numbers. The first student to circle the correct number continues with the next group of students.

- Divide the class into four groups. Assign each group one of the following categories: *foods, sports, subjects, colors.* Write on the board: *What _____ do you like?* Have students use the model question to find a classmate who shares a common preference.

Read

This exercise practices reading for information about weather and the environment.

A

- Have students look at the photos. Ask: *What do you see in the photos?* (A place with a lot of ice and a person on a bicycle in a city.)

- Focus students' attention on the title of the article. Write the term *global warming* on the board. Ask: *Do you know what global warming means?* Elicit that it refers to the idea that Earth's atmosphere is getting warmer and that the weather is changing as a result.

Culture Note
Greenland is at the center of the problem of global warming. It is the fastest warming place on our planet. The average temperature in Greenland has risen 4 degrees in the last ten years. Compare this with a 1.4-degree increase in temperatures worldwide since 1880. If all of Greenland's ice melted, sea levels would rise by 20 feet. This means that as many as 100 million people around the world who live in coastal areas could lose their homes. More than a million different species of animals are in danger of extinction because of the changes to their habitat caused by global warming.

- Invite a volunteer to read the directions and the statements aloud. Remind students that they should read quickly to find the main idea and that they should not read every word carefully.

- Have students work individually to read the article quickly and check the main idea. Do not check answers at this point.

B 🔊 **CD2, Track 77**

- Invite a volunteer to read the directions aloud. Remind students that they should read slowly and carefully, and concentrate on getting the meaning of the entire text.

- List the new vocabulary words on the board: *melt, rise, dirty, die, save, recycle, plastic.* Explain their meaning. (Melt: to turn from a solid into a liquid [point to the picture for an example of ice melting and turning

into water]; rise: to move from a lower to a higher place; dirty: not clean; die: not to live anymore; save: to rescue from harm; recycle: to reuse [or use again] for a different purpose – for example, tires are recycled and made into shoes; plastic: an artificially made material that people can make into many different objects – for example, plates, utensils, raincoats, bottles, and toys are all made of plastic.)
As an alternative, have students use their dictionaries to find the meanings of the new vocabulary words.

- Have students read the article again.

- Have students check their answer in Part A in pairs. Elicit the answer from one pair.

- **Optional** Play the recording. Students listen and read along.

Audio script
Same as the article in the Student's Book.

Get Connected Vocabulary
Have students do the exercise on Student's Book page 125 in class or for homework. (Get Connected Vocabulary answers are on page T-125.)

C

- Invite a volunteer to read the directions and the first question aloud.

- Ask: *What's the weather usually like in Greenland?* Elicit the answer. (It's usually cold.)

- Have students work individually to answer the questions.

- Have students check their answers in pairs.

- Check answers with the class. Invite volunteers to read aloud one answer each.

- **Optional** Elicit several different answers for question 5 with different suggestions for controlling global warming. List the ideas on the board. Ask students: *Which of these things are you doing now?* Check the things that students are already doing.

Listen

In this exercise, students listen for information about projects for a science fair.

A 🔊 CD2, Track 78

- Focus students' attention on the photo. Ask: *Where are these students?* (Probably in a classroom.) *What are they doing?* (A project or homework.)
- Tell students they will listen to two friends, Isabel and Jeff, talk about their science projects.
- Have students read the first question and the example answer.
- Play the recording. Students only listen.

> ### Audio script
> See page T-213.

- Play the recording again. Students listen and answer the questions.

- Play the recording once again. Students listen and verify their answers.
- Check answers with the class. Invite volunteers to read aloud one question and answer each.

B

- Have students read the directions and all the questions.
- Read the first question with the class and elicit answers from several students. Remind students that there are no right or wrong answers for this exercise – they are giving their opinions.
- Have students work individually to answer the questions and give reasons for their answers.
- Have students work in pairs to compare answers, or elicit opinions from volunteers.

Write

In this exercise, students answer questions and write a paragraph about global warming and the things they can do to help our planet.

A

- Invite a volunteer to read the directions and the questions aloud.
- Tell students you will give them 30 seconds to think of one thing they can do to help our planet. Then have each student tell a student sitting nearby his or her idea.
- Have students work individually to answer the questions.
- **Optional** Have students ask and answer the questions in pairs.

> **Teaching Tip**
> When possible, give students very precise time limits for tasks and then keep track of the time. Stop them as soon as the time is up. This helps students focus on the task and get to work quickly. A class that moves at a brisk pace is more interesting and easier to control.

B

- Invite a volunteer to read the directions aloud. Tell students that they will use their answers in Part A to help them write about global warming and the things they can do to help our planet.
- Have students work individually to write their paragraph.
- Invite several volunteers to read their paragraphs to the class.
- **Optional** Have students work in groups of four and read each other's paragraphs. Write these questions on the board for students to answer: *How many different ideas does your group have for helping our planet? How many people in your group think we can save our planet?*

> ### Workbook
> Assign the exercises on Workbook page 56. (Workbook answers begin on page T-190).

That's a really serious problem.

Listen

A 💿 **Jeff and Isabel talk about their projects. Listen and answer the questions.**

1. What's Isabel making? _She's making a poster._
2. Who's doing a project for the science fair? _Isabel is._
3. Who can enter the recycling contest? _Everyone can enter._
4. What can the winners of the contest do? _They can go see the TV show Save the Planet._
5. Who wants to enter the contest? _Isabel does._

B **What do you think? Answer the questions. Give reasons.**
(Answers will vary.)

1. Do you think global warming is a serious problem? _____
2. Is recycling a good idea? _____
3. Do you think students can help save the planet? _____
4. Would you like to enter a recycling contest? _____
5. Do you think TV shows about our planet are interesting? _____

Your turn

Write

A **Think about some things you can do to help our planet. Answer the questions.**
(Answers will vary.)

1. What do you think about global warming? _____
2. What's one thing you can do to help? _____
3. What's one thing your family can do to help? _____
4. What can you and your classmates do to help? _____
5. Do you think there's still time to save our planet? _____

B **Write about your plans to help the planet. Use the answers in Part A to help you.**
(Answers will vary.)

⬤⬤⬤

I think global warming is _____

_____

_____

_____

◀▶

Language chart review

Who + (verb) . . . ?	What + (noun) . . . ?
Who goes camping a lot? I **do**. Pablo **does**. Sarah and Tim **do**.	**What colors** do you like? I like blue and yellow. **What languages** does he speak? He speaks French and Italian.

A Look at the pictures. Write questions and answers about the people.

Ken

Vicky

Sonya and Miguel

Marc

Kwan and Dave

Betsy

1. speak Italian
   Q: _Who speaks Italian?_   **A:** _Ken does._
2. have a pet parrot
   Q: _Who has a pet parrot?_   **A:** _Marc does._
3. eat a lot of ice cream
   Q: _Who eats a lot of ice cream?_   **A:** _Betsy does._
4. live on a houseboat
   Q: _Who lives on a houseboat?_   **A:** _Sonya and Miguel do._
5. like to play soccer
   Q: _Who likes to play soccer?_   **A:** _Vicky does._
6. collect comic books
   Q: _Who likes to collect comic books?_   **A:** _Kwan and Dave do._

Unit 8 Review

This lesson reviews the grammar and vocabulary introduced in Unit 8.

Language chart review

These charts summarize the main grammar presented and practiced in Unit 8.

- Books closed. Write on the board:

  Who + (verb) . . . ?   *What + (noun) . . . ?*

- Focus students' attention on the two types of questions on the board. Elicit several examples of nouns and verbs.

- Tell students you will say a series of questions with the first word missing. Have students listen and tell you whether to use *Who* or *What* to start each question. Then have them identify the verb or the noun that helped them decide which word to use and whether that word is a verb or a noun.

  _____ *collects T-shirts?* (Who <u>collects</u> T-shirts? verb)

  _____ *sports does he play?* (What <u>sports</u> does he play? noun)

  _____ *eats a lot of ice cream?* (Who <u>eats</u> a lot of ice cream? verb)

  _____ *foods do you like?* (What <u>foods</u> do you like? noun)

- Books open. Have students study the examples in the Language chart review.

- Invite volunteers to ask a classmate one of the two types of questions featured in the charts.

- Answer any questions students may have.

....

Exercises A through C (pages T-112 to T-113)

Note: Students can do these exercises for homework or in class. They should do these exercises with minimal teacher input or help. If you choose to do these exercises as homework, briefly review the exercise directions in class. Make sure that students understand what they should do. Check the answers with the class during the next class meeting. If you choose to do the exercises in class, follow the directions below.

Exercise A

- Have a student read the directions and look at the pictures and the captions.

- Have students work individually to write questions and answers about the people in the pictures.

- Check answers with the class. Invite volunteers to read aloud one question and answer each.

Exercise B

- Have a volunteer read the directions and the example question and answer.
- Explain that there are two parts to the task. First, students look again at Part A on page 112 and write *What . . . ?* questions with the words given. Then, they write answers to the questions.
- Have students work individually to write *What . . . ?* questions using the words given.
- Have students work individually to write answers to the questions.
- Check answers with the class.
- Have students ask and answer the questions in pairs.

Language chart review

These charts summarize further grammar presented and practiced in Unit 8.

- Have students study the examples in the charts.
- Remind students that to ask about the weather in a particular month in a particular place, they use *in . . . in . . .* (What's the weather like in <u>May</u> in <u>New York</u>?)
- Remind students also that both the question and answer in the *Can . . . ?* pattern use the pronoun *you* because *you* refers to both a person or to people in general.
- Answer any questions students may have.

Exercise C

- Have students read the directions.
- Tell students that they should look at the language charts to help them.
- Have students work individually to complete the conversation.
- Have students check their answers in pairs.
- Check answers with the class. Invite volunteers to read the conversation aloud.

> **Optional Unit Wrap-Up**
>
> - If students did the Review exercises for homework, check answers with the class.
>
> - Assign each student one phrase from Exercise A – for example: *speak Italian, have a pet parrot,* etc. Students make a *Yes / No* question with the phrase: *Do you speak Italian? Do you have a pet parrot?,* etc. They walk around the room and ask other students their question. Set a time limit for the activity. When the time is up, ask students questions with *Who.* (*Who has a pet parrot?*) Students answer with the classmates' names and *do* or *does.*
>
> - Have students work individually to write questions such as the ones in Exercise B, using their classmates' names. Students ask the questions and classmates answer.

Theme Project

- Assign the *At Home* section of the Unit 8 Theme Project on Student's Book page 133.

Workbook

- Assign the Unit 8 Check Yourself on Workbook page 57. (Workbook answers begin on page T-190.)

Extra Practice Worksheets

- Assign the Unit 8 Extra Practice worksheets starting on page T-155.

Extra Speaking Practice Worksheet

- Assign the Unit 8 Extra Speaking Practice worksheet on page T-172.

Arcade Activities

- Assign the Unit 8 Arcade activities found at: www.cambridge.org/connectarcade

Learning Log

- Assign the Unit 8 Learning Log. These can be downloaded from the Teacher Support Site at: www.cambridge.org/connect2e/teacher

Quiz

- Give the Unit 8 Quiz on page T-183.

Test

- Give the Unit 8 Test (Form A and / or Form B). These can be downloaded from the Teacher Support Site at: www.cambridge.org/connect2e/teacher

B Look again at Part A. Write *What* questions with the words.
Then answer the questions.

1. dessert / Betsy / like
   Q: _What dessert does Betsy like?_   A: _She likes ice cream._
2. instrument / Marc / play
   Q: _What instrument does Marc play?_   A: _He plays the guitar._
3. game / Sonya and Miguel / like
   Q: _What game do Sonya and Miguel like?_   A: _They like cards._
4. languages / Ken / speak
   Q: _What languages does Ken speak?_   A: _He speaks English and Italian._
5. sport / Vicky / play
   Q: _What sport does Vicky play?_   A: _She plays soccer._
6. color / Kwan and Dave / like
   Q: _What color do Kwan and Dave like?_   A: _They like orange._

Language chart review

What's the weather like?
What's the weather like? It's usually **sunny**.
What's the weather like? It's **cool** and **rainy**.

can (for possibility)
What **can you** do here? **You can** go hiking.
Can you see any animals? Yes, **you can**. / No, **you can't**.

C Betsy asks Sonya about life on a houseboat. Look again at the language charts. Then complete the conversation.

Betsy Do you like living on a houseboat in Florida, Sonya?
Sonya Well, yes, I do. It's a lot of fun.
Betsy What's it like? What _can you_ do on a houseboat?
Sonya A lot of things! _You can_ go swimming, and _you can_ go canoeing.
Betsy _What's_ the weather _like_ in Florida? Is it always warm?
Sonya Yes, it's usually warm. Actually, today it's very hot!
Betsy Wow! What _can you_ do in Florida?
Sonya Well, _you can_ visit Miami. It's a great city.
Betsy What _can you_ do there?
Sonya _You can_ go to the Miami Aquarium. It's an interesting place.
Betsy What _can you_ see there?
Sonya _You can_ see a lot of fish and learn about the ocean.
Betsy Wow! That's fascinating. I want to go to Florida.

Go to page 133 for the **Theme Project.**

Game What's wrong?

Work with a classmate. What's wrong with the picture? Write sentences with the words in the box. The pair that finishes first is the winner.

| ☐ bed | ☐ guitar | ☑ sandwich | ☐ sneakers |
| ☐ bicycle | ☐ pizza | ☐ skirt | ☐ soccer balls |

1. *There's a sandwich in the home store.*
2. *There's a bicycle in the clothing store.*
3. *There are shoes in the restaurant.*
4. *There's a pizza in the electronics store.*
5. *There are soccer balls in the music store.*
6. *There's a guitar in the sports store.*
7. *There's a skirt in the bookstore.*
8. *There's a bed in the shoe store.*

This game reviews *There is / There are* . . . .

- Have students study the picture. Ask them to read the directions, the words in the box, and the example sentence.

- Elicit how to play the game:

  – The eight objects in the box are in the wrong stores in the mall. Students work with a classmate to write a sentence about the location of each object. The pair that finishes first is the winner.

- Have students work in pairs to write the sentences.

- Check answers with the class. Invite volunteers to come to the board to write their answers.

- **Optional** Play a round of "Tic-Tac-Toe." On the board, fill in the nine squares of a tic-tac-toe grid with the following nine words: *pencils, cat, hamburger, bicycles, flower, computer, swimming pool, elephants, T-shirt.* Divide the class into two teams. One team is X, the other is O. Teams earn points by using the word of the chosen square in a true sentence beginning with *There is* or *There are.* (Examples: *There are pencils on my desk* or *There's no swimming pool in the library.*) If they do so correctly, the word is erased and an X or an O is written in the square. The first team to earn three squares in a row (across, down, or diagonally) wins.

- As an alternative for a more silly game, you may want to ask students to use the words to make "weird" sentences. (Examples: *There are pencils in Tommy's ears* or *There's a swimming pool in the library.*) The game is played in the same way.

Teaching Tip When playing games with the class, stop at the peak of enjoyment. In this way, you will avoid having an overly excited class and students will look forward to playing the next time. Always set rules and divide the class into teams of equal ability. Do not tolerate bad sportsmanship.

Unit 2 Game — Who is it?

This game reviews the names of leisure activities popular with teens.

- Focus students' attention on the picture. Ask students to read the characters' names and what they say.
- Call out *Watch DVDs*. The class responds with the names of the characters who watch DVDs. (Felix and Eric.) Continue with *Use the Internet, Take guitar lessons,* and *Listen to music*, but ask individual students to respond.
- Use the sample conversation to demonstrate the task with a student. You are Classmate 1, and the student is Classmate 2. Then invite two new volunteers to demonstrate the task once again.
- Have students play the game in pairs. Students should play at least four times.

Teaching Tip

When drilling with the class for pronunciation or grammar, always drill first as a group before moving on to individual drill. In this way, you will be able to correct any problems without singling out students. Students will feel more competent and confident using the language.

Game Who is it?

Read what these students do in their free time. Then play a game with a classmate.

Classmate 1 Choose a person in the picture. Don't tell your classmate. Answer Classmate 2's questions.

Classmate 2 Classmate 1 is thinking of a person in the picture. Ask Classmate 1 questions. Guess the person.

Classmate 2 Do you watch DVDs?
Classmate 1 Yes, I do.
Classmate 2 Are you Miyoko?
Classmate 1 No, I'm not.
Classmate 2 Do you take guitar lessons?
Classmate 1 Yes, I do.
Classmate 2 Are you Eric?
Classmate 1 Yes, I am.

I collect trading cards.
I listen to music.
I use the Internet.
I play video games.
I read magazines.

I watch DVDs.
I take guitar lessons.
I use the Internet.
I play soccer.
I hang out with my friends.

I watch DVDs.
I hang out at the mall.
I talk on the phone.
I read books.
I draw pictures.

I take guitar lessons.
I listen to music.
I in-line skate.
I play video games.
I draw pictures.

Bruno

Eric

Miyoko

Felix

I collect trading cards.
I talk on the phone.
I play video games.
I read books.
I hang out with my friends.

Janice

Lucia

I hang out at the mall.
I take guitar lessons.
I in-line skate.
I play soccer.
I read magazines.

 **Game Play ball!**

A Work with a classmate. Read the clues. Then write the correct words on the ball. The pair that finishes first is the winner.

a. A biker wears a on his or her head.

b. A lot of people do 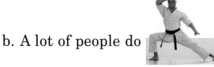 in Asia.

c. Skateboarders wear knee .

d. Tennis players wear on their feet.

e. People at the beach.

f. You can in a park.

g. A baseball player has a .

h. Each player wears a with a number.

i. is a fun sport.

j. teams play on a field.

k. People in a pool or at the beach.

l. People wear gloves on their .

B Write each numbered letter from the puzzle. Then write the answer.

Q: W   h   a   t   i   s   y   o   u   r
    1   2   3   4   5   6   7   8   9   10

    f   a   v   o   r   i   t   e   s   p   o   r   t ?
    11 12 13 14 15 16 17 18   19 20 21 22 23

A: (Answers will vary.)

Unit 3 Game Play ball!

This game reviews the names of sports and sports equipment.

A

- Focus students' attention on the crossword puzzle. Ask: *What's unusual about this crossword puzzle?* (It's in the shape of a soccer ball.)
- Elicit how to play the game:
  - The sentences and icons labeled *a* through *l* give clues for the words students should put in the spaces in the crossword puzzle.
- Have students work with a classmate to complete the puzzle.
- Check answers with the pair that finished first. If the puzzle is correct, that pair is the winner. If not, check the puzzle of the next pair.

B

- Have students read the directions. Elicit how to discover the question.
  - Students fill in the blanks with numbered letters from the crossword puzzle in Part A.
- Have students work individually to write the secret question and then answer it.
- Check answers with the class.

> **Teaching Tip** Try to follow up vocabulary, grammar points, or conversations with an activity or a game. An EFL (English as a Foreign Language) or ESL (English as a Second Language) classroom is an artificial environment, so games and activities not only enable students to have fun but also give them a reason to use the language. If students are able to use the language, they will remember it better.
>
> *Note:* For more games and activities, see page T-186.

This game reviews words for types of music and music preferences.

- Give students one or two minutes to read the directions and study the game board. While they are doing this, draw a simplified version of the Start row of the game. Draw two circles to represent the two sides of a coin. Label one *Heads = 1* and the other *Tails = 2*. Explain that students will flip a coin to decide how many spaces to move – one space for heads and two spaces for tails.

- Invite a volunteer to come to the board to demonstrate the game with you. Flip a coin, show the student whether it is heads or tails, and say the number – for example, *Tails – two*. Then move your marker two spaces. Complete the sentence: *A music CD costs ($14.99)*. (Any amount of money is correct.)

- Have the volunteer repeat the steps.

- Have students play the game in pairs.

- **Optional** Ask random students to share with the class a personal-information sentence from the game, such as *A rock band I like is _____ .*

Teaching Tip
When pairing students or dividing them into small groups, pay special attention to the abilities of the pair or group. Some students learn at a slower pace or are less attentive. Others are shy and reluctant to speak up. Make sure the pairs or groups are of mixed abilities and personality types that will work well together.

Unit 4 Game All about music

Play the game with a classmate. Use things in your bag as game markers.
Use a coin to find out how many spaces to move. Heads = 1, Tails = 2. *(Answers will vary.)*

- Take turns. Flip a coin and move your marker to the correct space.
- Complete the sentence or follow the directions.
- The person who gets to FINISH first, wins.

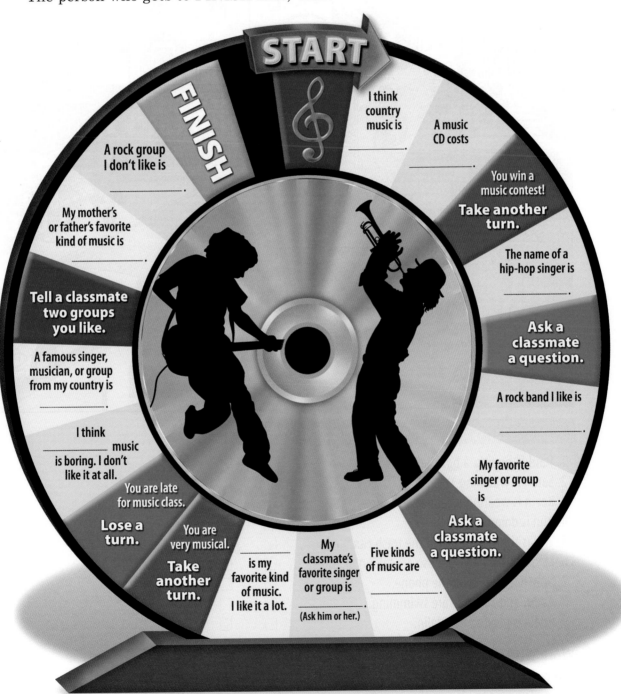

Game What are they doing?

A Look at the picture for one minute. Then cover the picture, and read the sentences. Check (✓) T (true) or F (false).

	T	F
1. Paul is buying a baseball glove.	☐	✓
2. Sarah is watching TV.	✓	☐
3. Kevin is wearing a helmet.	✓	☐
4. Ann is doing karate.	☐	✓
5. Will is throwing trash in the trash can.	✓	☐
6. Ms. Kean and Mr. Cardoso are taking pictures.	☐	✓
7. Dmitri is talking on the phone.	✓	☐
8. Adam and Suzanne are swimming.	✓	☐
9. Adela is playing the violin.	☐	✓

B Work with a classmate. Close your book. Your classmate's book is open. How many things can you remember from the picture? Tell your classmate. Your classmate says *Yes* or *No*. Then switch roles.

> John is reading a book.

> No, he isn't. He's listening to music.

This game reviews present continuous affirmative and negative statements.

A

- Explain "What are they doing?" Then ask students to read the directions. Explain *cover the picture*.

- Elicit how to play the game:
  - Students are allowed to look at the picture for one minute. Then they must cover the picture and check whether the statements are true or false from memory.

- Tell students to begin. When one minute is up, tell students to stop and cover their picture.

- Have students work individually to read the sentences and check T for true and F for false.

- Check answers with the class. Invite volunteers to come to the board to write their answers. Students may refer to their books.

B

- Ask volunteers to read the directions and the example aloud.

- Have students play the game in pairs. Encourage students to keep score of the number of correct statements. The student in each pair who makes more correct statements wins.

> **Teaching Tip**
> Use previously learned vocabulary and grammar patterns as much as possible in your lesson. A suggested activity to review language is to focus students' attention on any large scene in the Student's Book. Then ask individual students to say anything they can about the picture.

Unit 6 Game X and O

This game reviews *Where + (be) . . . going?*

A

- Ask students to read the directions and study the pictures. While they are doing this, draw a simplified version of the game on the board. (You may write numbers to represent the pictures in the Student's Book.)

- Invite a volunteer to come to the front of the room and demonstrate the game with you. Say: *I'm X and you're O.* Point to a picture – for example, picture 11. Ask: *Where is she going?* The student answers, using the picture in the book as a cue: *She's going to the bank.* (Prompt the student if necessary.) Have the student mark picture 11 on the board with an *O.* Explain that this is now his or her picture because the sentence was correct. Then have the student point to a picture and ask you the question using the pronoun in the book. Pretend to give an incorrect answer. Explain that you cannot mark the picture with an *X* because the answer was not correct. Make sure students understand that once a picture is marked *X* or *O,* it cannot be used again.

- Have students play the game in pairs using the game in their books and marking the pictures *X* or *O.* Explain that if they are not sure if an answer is correct, they should verify it with you. The student who has the most marked pictures wins the game.

- **Optional** Play the game again with the class divided into two teams, *X* and *O.* Use the game you drew on the board. Students from each team take turns coming to the board, pointing to a picture, and asking the question for the other team to answer.

B

- Ask students to read the directions. Ask: *How do you complete this exercise?* (Complete the sentences with the correct information based on the pictures.)

- Have students work individually to complete the exercise.

- Check answers with the class. Have volunteers write one sentence each on the board.

- **Optional** Have students make appropriate questions for the statements in Part B – for example, 1. *Where's Bill going?*

Teaching Tip Give students frequent opportunities to ask as well as answer questions. To help students develop their skills at forming questions, have them ask each other general questions about the pictures in the Student's Book. Use this activity as a warm-up or a wrap-up to any one of your lessons. If your class is a large one, select a few students each class meeting to participate. Choose students according to birth dates, alphabetical order of first or last names, or seating arrangements in the classroom.

Game X and O

A Play the game with a classmate. Take turns.

One person is *X* and one person is *O*. X starts.
Classmate X Point to a picture. Ask *Where's / Where are* _____ *going?*
Classmate O Answer the question.

▶ Is the answer correct? Mark the picture with an *O*.
▶ Not correct? Do not mark the picture.

Now Classmate O points to a picture and asks a question.
Classmate X answers. Continue playing until all the pictures
are marked *X* or *O*. The player with the most marks wins.

1 he

2 she

3 they

4 she

5 he

6 you

7 he

8 they

9 you

10 he

11 she

12 you

B These people are all on a bus. Where are they going? Complete the sentences.

1. Bill *is going to the circus* .

2. Jed and Mindy *are going to a restaurant* .

3. Henry *is going to the mall* .

4. Carl *is going to the soccer game* .

5. Pierre and Paulette *are going to the beach* .

Game Food puzzle

Work with a partner. Look at the photos. Guess the names of the items, and label the photos. Then write the names of the food items to complete the puzzle. The pair that finishes first is the winner.

ACROSS

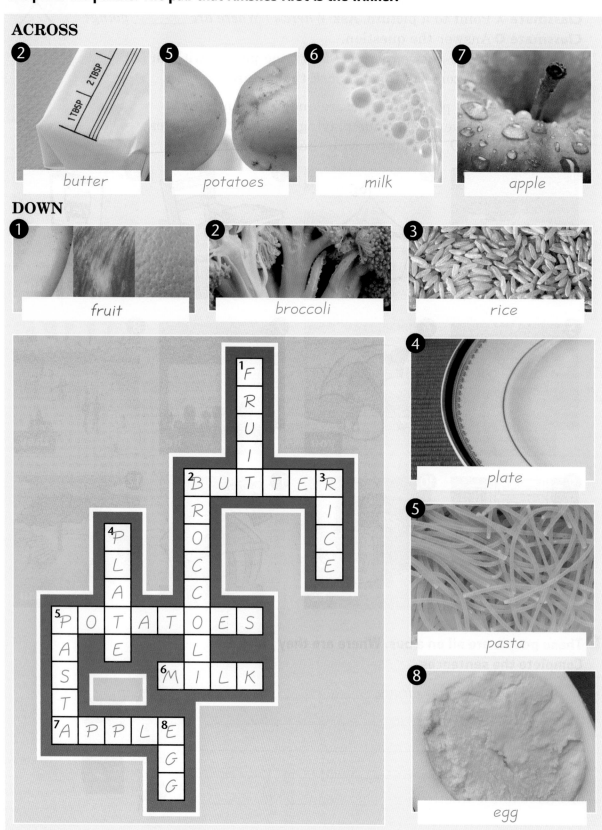

2 butter

5 potatoes

6 milk

7 apple

DOWN

1 fruit

2 broccoli

3 rice

4 plate

5 pasta

8 egg

This exercise reviews the names of common foods.

- Have students read the directions. Elicit how to play the game:
  - Students work with a classmate. They look at each photo and write the name of the item under it. Then they write the words in the crossword puzzle. The pair that finishes first is the winner.

- Ask students to look at the example. Then have them do 2 across. Ask: *What's the word?* (Butter.) Ask: *What letter does it share with* fruit? (T.)

- Have students work with a classmate to complete the crossword puzzle.

- Check answers with the class.

- **Optional** Ask students to choose one of the words in the puzzle and use it in a sentence.

- **Optional** Play a guessing game. Ask a volunteer to come to the front and choose a food or drink item that he or she likes. Have the volunteer write it on a scrap of paper. Students try to guess the item by asking *Do you like to eat (drink) _____ ?* The student who guesses correctly replaces the volunteer and continues the activity.

Teaching Tip   The Teacher's Edition offers a variety of games and activities. Your class will have its own particular favorites. If students have worked hard and time permits, let them choose an activity. Some ideas:

- Let the winners of pair competitions take your place and lead the next round of the game.

- Ask students to choose a popular English song and teach it to them.

- If time permits and if the equipment is available, let the class choose an age-appropriate video or DVD in English to watch as a special treat.

Unit 8 Game What's the weather like?

This exercise reviews common weather terms.

- Give students one or two minutes to read the directions and study the game board. While they are doing this, draw a simplified version of the Start row of the game. Explain that students will flip a coin to decide how many spaces to move – one space for heads and two spaces for tails.

- Ask students to choose something as a marker – for example, an eraser or a coin.

- Invite a volunteer to come to the board to demonstrate the game with you. Flip a coin and say the number – for example, *Tails – two*. Move your marker two spaces to the square marked September. The volunteer then asks the appropriate question: *What's the weather like in September?* You answer the question. The volunteer then flips the coin and repeats the steps.

- Have students play the game in pairs.

Game What's the weather like?

Play the game with a classmate. Use things in your bag as game markers.
Use a coin to find out how many spaces to move. Heads = 1, Tails = 2.

- Take turns. Flip a coin and move your marker to the correct space.

Classmate 1 Ask a question about the weather, using the words in the space.

Classmate 2 Answer the question.

June. What's the weather like in June?   It's usually warm and rainy.

- The person who gets to FINISH first, wins.

Get Connected Vocabulary Practice

Unit 1

Complete the sentences with the words in the box.

☐ backup (n.) ☐ Broadway ☐ drums (n.) ☑ lead (adj.) ☐ special (adj.) ☐ typical (adj.)
musical (n.)

1. My friend is the main singer in the band. She's the ____lead____ singer.
2. My cousin isn't the lead singer in the band. He sings ____backup____ .
3. Many people have dogs and cats. They're ____typical____ pets.
4. Brian plays the ____drums____ in our school band.
5. We like our English teacher a lot. She's a very kind and ____special____ person to us.
6. *Lion King* is a great ____Broadway musical____ . The actors sing, dance, and act.

Unit 2

The underlined words belong in other sentences. Write the words where they belong.

1. That company has a lot of good review (v.) ideas. ____marketing____
2. There's a quiz tomorrow. Can you help me marketing (n.)? ____review____
3. That's a great creator (n.). They make very good computer games. ____company____
4. Do you answer all of your e-mail company (n.) every day? ____messages____
5. This computer check out (v.) helps me study math. ____software____
6. That man is the messages (n.) of a really cool video game. ____creator____
7. Software (n.) this cool video game. Look! You can play it online. ____Check out____

Get Connected Vocabulary Practice

Unit 1

This exercise provides practice of the new vocabulary items in the Unit 1 Get Connected reading on Student's Book page 12.

- Tell students that this exercise will help them remember the new vocabulary items that appear in boldface in the article.
- Have students read the directions and the example sentence.
- Focus students' attention on the items in the box. Model each vocabulary item. Students listen and repeat.
- Invite volunteers to try to explain the meaning of each vocabulary item. If they cannot do this, have them turn to the article on Student's Book page 12. Have them read the sentences in which the vocabulary items appear, and try to guess the meanings again.

- Have students work individually to complete the other sentences.
- Have students work in pairs to check their answers.
- Check answers with the class. Invite volunteers to read the completed sentences aloud.
- **Optional** Assign the vocabulary practice exercise as homework.

Unit 2

This exercise provides practice of the new vocabulary items in the Unit 2 Get Connected reading on Student's Book page 26.

- Tell students that this exercise will help them remember the new vocabulary items that appear in boldface in the article.
- Have students read the directions and the example sentence.
- Focus students' attention on the underlined word or words in each sentence. Model each vocabulary item. Students listen and repeat.
- Invite volunteers to try to explain the meaning of each vocabulary item. If they cannot do this, have them turn to the article on Student's Book page 26. Have them read the sentences in which the vocabulary items appear, and try to guess the meanings again.

- Have students work individually to write the words in the sentences in which they belong.
- Have students work in pairs to check their answers.
- Check answers with the class. Invite volunteers to read the completed sentences aloud.
- **Optional** Assign the vocabulary practice exercise as homework.

Unit 3

This exercise provides practice of the new vocabulary items in the Unit 3 Get Connected reading on Student's Book page 40.

- Tell students that this exercise will help them remember the new vocabulary items that appear in boldface in the article.
- Have students read the directions and the example sentence.
- Focus students' attention on the items in the box. Model each vocabulary item. Students listen and repeat.
- Invite volunteers to try to explain the meaning of each vocabulary item. If they cannot do this, have them turn to the article on Student's Book page 40. Have them read the sentences in which the vocabulary items appear, and try to guess the meanings again.

- Have students work individually to complete the other sentences.
- Have students work in pairs to check their answers.
- Check answers with the class. Invite volunteers to read the completed sentences aloud.
- **Optional** Assign the vocabulary practice exercise as homework.

Unit 4

This exercise provides practice of the new vocabulary items in the Unit 4 Get Connected reading on Student's Book page 54.

- Tell students that this exercise will help them remember the new vocabulary items that appear in boldface in the article.
- Have students read the directions and the example sentence.
- Focus students' attention on the items in the box. Model each vocabulary item. Students listen and repeat.
- Invite volunteers to try to explain the meaning of each vocabulary item. If they cannot do this, have them turn to the article on Student's Book page 54. Have them read the sentences in which the vocabulary items appear, and try to guess the meanings again.
- Have students work individually to complete the other sentences in the advertisement.

- Have students work in pairs to check their answers.
- Check answers with the class. Invite volunteers to read the completed sentences aloud.
- **Optional** Assign the vocabulary practice exercise as homework.

Unit 3

Complete the sentences with the words in the box.

1. _Speed skaters_ skate fast, so they wear helmets.
2. You can win ___medals___ at our school's Sports Day.
3. Henry is my _half brother_. We have the same father.
4. He's a great ___author___. His books are really famous.
5. She's the 2008 _world champion_ skateboarder.

☐ author (n.)
☐ half brother (n.)
☐ medals (n.)
☑ speed skaters (n.)
☐ world champion (adj.)

Unit 4

Complete the advertisement with the words in the box.

☐ album (n.)   ☐ convenient (adj.)   ☐ million (n.)   ☐ sell (v.)
☐ audio books (n.)   ☑ download (v.)   ☐ rent (v.)

ROXY'S Rock, Pop, and More!

Visit the new Roxy's Rock, Pop, and More Web site! You can _download_ songs, and it's cheap! We have over one ___million___ new rock and pop hits. Buy a song or an ___album___. But wait, there's more! We ___rent___ TV shows and _audio books_, too. Or you can _download_ a movie for $2.99. So visit our Web site – it's easy and _convenient_!

Unit 5

Circle the correct words to complete the sentences.

1. My little sister has a lot of very cute (dolls / peaches).
2. We have tickets to walk around in that old (play / castle). It's very big.
3. I love this candy. It's (traditional / delicious)!
4. Buy two (tickets / dolls) at the movie theater.
5. Let's dance to this (delicious / traditional) Mexican song.
6. The actors in that (castle / play) are very good.
7. Apples, bananas, and (candy / peaches) are healthy foods.

Unit 6

Complete the sentences with the words in the box.

☐ butter (n.)   ☐ cows (n.)   ☐ farm (n.)   ☐ pounds (n.)   ☐ weighs (v.)   ☑ wire (n.)

1. That ___wire___ is for Ken's new radio-controlled airplane.
2. I want to buy two ___pounds___ of potatoes to make some potato salad.
3. ___Cows___ give us milk.
4. Do you like ___butter___ on your popcorn?
5. My mother isn't heavy. She only ___weighs___ 120 pounds.
6. My aunt and uncle live on a ___farm___ . They have lots of animals.

Unit 5

This exercise provides practice of the new vocabulary items in the Unit 5 Get Connected reading on Student's Book page 68.

- Tell students that this exercise will help them remember the new vocabulary items that appear in boldface in the letter.
- Have students read the directions and the example sentence.
- Focus students' attention on the items in parentheses in each sentence. Model each vocabulary item. Students listen and repeat.
- Invite volunteers to try to explain the meaning of each vocabulary item. If they cannot do this, have them turn to the letter on Student's Book page 68. Have them read the sentences in which the vocabulary items appear, and try to guess the meanings again.

- Have students work individually to complete the other sentences.
- Have students work in pairs to check their answers.
- Check answers with the class. Invite volunteers to read the completed sentences aloud.
- **Optional** Assign the vocabulary practice exercise as homework.

Unit 6

This exercise provides practice of the new vocabulary items in the Unit 6 Get Connected reading on Student's Book page 82.

- Tell students that this exercise will help them remember the new vocabulary items that appear in boldface in the article.
- Have students read the directions and the example sentence.
- Focus students' attention on the items in the box. Model each vocabulary item. Students listen and repeat.
- Invite volunteers to try to explain the meaning of each vocabulary item. If they cannot do this, have them turn to the article on Student's Book page 82. Have them read the sentences in which the vocabulary items appear, and try to guess the meanings again.
- Have students work individually to complete the other sentences.

- Have students work in pairs to check their answers.
- Check answers with the class. Invite volunteers to read the completed sentences aloud.
- **Optional** Assign the vocabulary practice exercise as homework.

Unit 7

This exercise provides practice of the new vocabulary items in the Unit 7 Get Connected reading on Student's Book page 96.

- Tell students that this exercise will help them remember the new vocabulary items that appear in boldface on the Web site.
- Have students read the directions and the example sentence.
- Focus students' attention on the items in the box. Model each vocabulary item. Students listen and repeat.
- Invite volunteers to try to explain the meaning of each vocabulary item. If they cannot do this, have them turn to the Web site on Student's Book page 96. Have them read the sentences in which the vocabulary items appear, and try to guess the meanings again.

- Have students work individually to complete the other sentences.
- Have students work in pairs to check their answers.
- Check answers with the class. Invite volunteers to read the completed sentences aloud.
- **Optional** Assign the vocabulary practice exercise as homework.

Unit 8

This exercise provides practice of the new vocabulary items in the Unit 8 Get Connected reading on Student's Book page 110.

- Tell students that this exercise will help them remember the new vocabulary items that appear in boldface in the article.
- Have students read the directions and the example sentence.
- Focus students' attention on the words in bold in each sentence on the right. Model each vocabulary item. Students listen and repeat.
- Invite volunteers to try to explain the meaning of each vocabulary item. If they cannot do this, have them turn to the article on Student's Book page 110. Have them read the sentences in which the vocabulary items appear, and try to guess the meanings again.

- Have students work individually to complete the other sentences.
- Have students work in pairs to check their answers.
- Check answers with the class. Invite volunteers to read the completed sentences aloud.
- **Optional** Assign the vocabulary practice exercise as homework.

Unit 7

Complete the sentences with the words in the box.

☐ column (n.) ☑ newspaper (n.) ☐ recipe (n.)
☐ cookbook (n.) ☐ nutrition (n.) ☐ sections (n.)

1. Some people think it's important to know world news. They read
   a _newspaper_ every day.
2. He's a great cook. His new _cookbook_ has a lot of great dishes in it.
3. There's a lot of sugar in candy and soda. They aren't very healthy.
   There isn't much _nutrition_ in them.
4. Our Sunday newspaper is big. There are ten _sections_ in it.
5. That cookbook has an amazing _recipe_ for chocolate cake.
   I want to make it.
6. She writes a _column_ for her high school newspaper. She
   writes about teen fashion.

Unit 8

What sentence is next? Match the sentences on the left with the sentences on the right.

1. Clean up your room. _f_

2. You have a lot of paper. _g_

3. It's hot today. Hurry up and eat your ice cream. _e_

4. There's more water in the oceans these days. _c_

5. The neighbor's pet snake is very sick. _d_

6. The soda is in the refrigerator. _a_

7. Give those plants water! _b_

a. It's in that **plastic** (adj.) bottle.

b. They're **dying** (v.)!

c. The water is **rising** (v.).

d. Can someone **save** (v.) it?

e. It's **melting** (v.).

f. It's really **dirty** (adj.).

g. **Recycle** (v.) it!

Theme Project: Make a poster about things you like and things you're good at.

Theme: Citizenship

Goal: To create stronger relationships in your classroom community

At Home

Read about Valeria.

Hi! I'm Valeria Dias, and I'm 14. I'm athletic. I'm pretty good at soccer and volleyball. I'm also good at dancing. I like sports very much. I like gym a lot, too.

Complete the chart. Use your dictionary, if necessary. *(Answers will vary.)*

Things I'm good at	Things I like
1.	1.
2.	2.
3.	3.

Draw pictures or bring photos of the things you are good at and the things you like to class.

In Class

Make a poster. Use the sample poster as a model.

Tell your group about the things you are good at and the things you like.

> I'm musical. I'm good at the piano and the violin. I'm pretty good at English, too. I like . . .

Display the posters in your classroom. Walk around and look at all of them. Who likes the same things you like? Who's good at the same things you're good at?

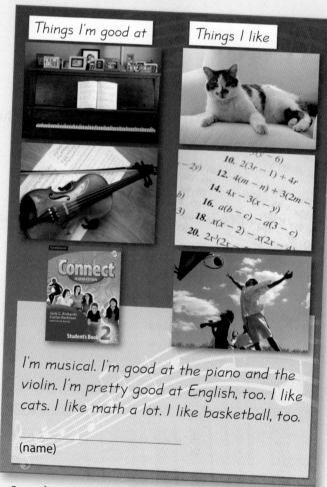

Sample poster

Project preparation

- The class before the project, have students read the *Theme Project*, *Theme*, and *Goal* information. Explain that this project will help them create stronger relationships in their classroom community.

- Focus students' attention on the sample poster in the book. Say: *Look at the sample poster. You will make a poster like this one about things you are good at and things you like.*

- Focus students' attention on the *At Home* section. Explain that they will do this section for homework.

- Have students read the directions and check that they understand what they should do. At home, students should read the text about Valeria and complete the chart about things they are good at and things they like. Remind students that they can use their dictionaries to find the meanings of words they do not know. They should then find photos of things they are good at and things they like to bring to the next class. Tell students that if they cannot find photos, they can draw pictures.

- To finish, invite volunteers to name things they are good at and things they like, and write the things on the board.

Day of the project

Materials needed
Poster board or large paper for each student, tape or glue or paste, markers

- Explain to students that they will work individually to make a poster about things they are good at and things they like, using the sample poster as a model.

- Distribute materials. Have each student make an individual poster. Make sure students do not write their names on their posters yet.

- Have students form groups and present their posters to their group, using the language in the speech balloon as a cue.

- Display the posters in your classroom. Have students walk around and look at all of them.

- To finish, ask students to name classmates who like the same things they do and classmates who are good at the same things they are.

Option

Have students use information from the posters to play a game. Write the name of one student on a slip of paper, but do not show it to the student's classmates. Have them ask *Yes / No* questions to guess the student. For example:

Q: Is it a boy?
A: Yes.
Q: Is he athletic?
A: No.
Q: Is he good at the piano?
A: Yes.
Q: Is it Rodrigo?
A: Yes.

Have the student who guesses correctly write the name of a different student on a slip of paper, and play the game again.

Future use of posters

Keep these posters to practice *Does he / she . . . ?* in Unit 2 and *Who + (verb) . . . ?* in Unit 8. For example:

A: Does Erica play the piano?
B: Yes, she does.

         OR

A: Who plays basketball?
B: John does.

> **Culture Note** ....
>   In the U.S., mothers and fathers who spend a lot of their free time driving their school-age children around to activities after school and on weekends are called Soccer Moms and Dads. Public transportation systems in most parts of the U.S. are not as good as in many other countries, and often the locations of various activities students attend are spread out. Some students are engaged in so many after-school and weekend activities (such as classes, sports, and lessons) that both mothers and fathers are constantly busy taking them from activity to activity.

Unit 2 Theme Project

Project preparation

- The class before the project, have students read the *Theme Project*, *Theme*, and *Goal* information. Explain that this project will help them learn more about the teachers in their school and become better acquainted with their school community.

- Focus students' attention on the sample booklet page in the book. Say: *Look at this sample booklet page. You and your group will make two pages like this one about two teachers in your school.*

- Focus students' attention on the *At Home* section. Explain that they will do this section for homework.

- Have students read the directions and check that they understand what they should do. At home, students should read the text about Mr. Ramos.

- Have students look at the *Before Class* section. Explain that they should interview a teacher about what he or she does in the morning, in the afternoon, in the evening, and in his or her free time to complete the chart. Remind students that they can use their dictionaries to find the meanings of words they do not know. They should then find or take a photo of the teacher to bring to the next class. Tell students that if they cannot find or take a photo, they can draw a suitable picture of the teacher.

- To finish, invite volunteers to give you sample questions they could ask teachers about morning, afternoon, evening, and free-time activities. Write their questions on the board.

Day of the project

Materials needed
Plain firm paper for each group, tape or glue or paste, markers, stapler

- Have students work in small groups. Remind students that each group will make two pages for a booklet about teachers in their school, using the sample booklet page as a model.

- Distribute materials. Have each group look at all the charts and photos or drawings and choose two teachers. Each group then makes a booklet page for each of the two teachers.

- Have each group choose a leader and then join another group. Have the group leader present the information in the group's two booklet pages to the other group, using the language in the speech balloon as a cue.

- Gather all the booklet pages and staple them together into one booklet. Have students pass around the booklet for all groups to look at.

- To finish, ask volunteers to name which teachers they would like to know more about.

Option

Make statements about the teachers in the booklet. For example: *She's from Tokyo.* Then invite volunteers to guess which teacher the statement is about. Invite other volunteers to make statements about teachers in the booklet and have students guess the teachers.

Future use of the booklet

Keep this booklet to practice the *What time / When . . . ?* questions in Unit 3. For example:

A: What time / When does Mr. Rojas go to school?
B: At 7:30.

Culture Note
In the U.S., many teachers coach sports or act as advisors for clubs after school. Teachers take on coaching and acting as advisors for many reasons. Some teachers enjoy being involved in a particular sport. Other teachers take on coaching or advising to earn some extra money. Sports teams usually meet every day during the sports season. Clubs and other activities like math league or chorus meet once or twice a week after school.

Unit 2

Theme Project: Make a booklet about teachers in your school.
Theme: Citizenship
Goal: To become better acquainted with your school community

At Home

Read about Mr. Ramos.

This is Mr. Ramos. He teaches science. He gets up at 6:30 a.m. He eats breakfast at home. Then he goes to school. He doesn't go home at 2:30 p.m. – he coaches soccer after school. He eats dinner with his family at 6:30 p.m. He plays with his son in the evening. He reads in his free time.

Mr. Ramos

Before Class

1 Talk to a teacher at your school. Ask questions and complete the chart. Use your dictionary, if necessary. *(Answers will vary.)*

	Name	Subject	Morning	Afternoon	Evening	Free time
Questions:			Do you eat breakfast at school?			
Answers:						

Draw a picture or bring a photo of the teacher to class.

In Class

2 Look at all the charts. Choose two teachers.

3 Make a page for each teacher. Use the sample page as a model.

4 5 Choose a group leader. Present your teachers to another group.

> This is Mrs. White. She teaches art class. She eats . . .

6 Give your group's pages to the teacher. The teacher staples together the pages.

7 Pass around the booklet. Which teacher do you want to know more about?

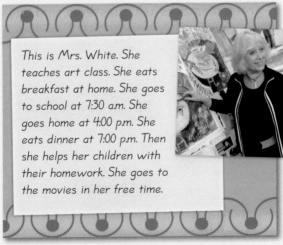

This is Mrs. White. She teaches art class. She eats breakfast at home. She goes to school at 7:30 a.m. She goes home at 4:00 p.m. She eats dinner at 7:00 p.m. Then she helps her children with their homework. She goes to the movies in her free time.

Sample booklet page

Theme Project: Make a sports card.
Theme: Cultural diversity
Goal: To learn about sports in different countries

At Home

Read about ice hockey in Canada.

Ice hockey is very popular in Canada. Canadians like it a lot. Ice hockey is exciting. Teams play on a skating rink. Players wear helmets and kneepads. They use hockey sticks and a puck.

Complete the chart. Use your dictionary and the Internet, if necessary. *(Answers will vary.)*

Country	Popular sport	Information

Draw pictures or bring photos of the sport to class.

In Class

Make a sports card. Use the sample sports card as a model.

Tell your group about your sport.

> Baseball is very popular in Japan. Teams play on a field. They use a . . .

Don't show your card to the group. Say the name of your country. The other group members ask questions, and guess the sport.

> Japan

> Do they wear uniforms?

> Yes, they do.

> Is it baseball?

> Yes, it is.

Display the sports cards in your classroom. Walk around and look at all of them. Vote on the most interesting sport.

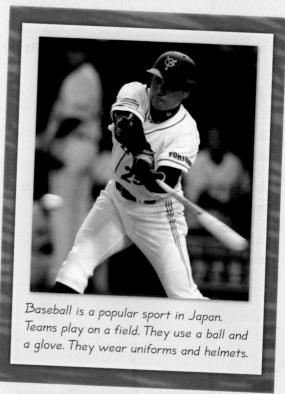

Baseball is a popular sport in Japan. Teams play on a field. They use a ball and a glove. They wear uniforms and helmets.

Sample sports card

Unit 3 Theme Project

Project preparation

- The class before the project, have students read the *Theme Project*, *Theme*, and *Goal* information. Explain that this project will help them learn more about sports in different countries.

- Focus students' attention on the sample sports card in the book. Say: *Look at the sample sports card. You will make a card like this one about a sport in another country.*

- Focus students' attention on the *At Home* section. Explain that they will do this section for homework.

- Have students read the directions and check that they understand what they should do. At home, students should read the text about ice hockey in Canada and complete the chart about a popular sport in a different country. Remind students that they can use their dictionaries to find the meanings of words they do not know. They should then find photos of the sport to bring to the next class. Tell students that if they cannot find photos, they can draw pictures.

- To finish, invite volunteers to name sports that are popular in different countries. For example: *American football is popular in the United States.*

Day of the project

Materials needed
Plain or colored paper for each student, tape or glue or paste, markers

- Explain to students that they will work individually to make a sports card, using the sample sports card as a model.

- Distribute materials. Have each student make an individual sports card.

- Have students form groups and present their sports cards to their group, using the language in the speech balloon as a cue.

- Have each group join another group. Have each student say the name of the country where his or her sport is popular. Remind students not to show their cards to the other group. The other group members ask questions to try to guess the sport, using the language in the speech balloons as cues.

- Display the sports cards in your classroom. Have students walk around and look at all of them.

- To finish, ask students to vote on the most interesting sport.

Option

Have students play another game with the sports cards. Shuffle the cards and give one to each student. Explain that students should not show other students their cards. Have one student stand up and say, *Please ask me questions.* Classmates should ask at least three questions, and then guess the sport on the student's card. For example:

Q: Do the players use balls?
A: Yes.
Q: Do the players use bats?
A: No.
Q: Do the players use rackets?
A: Yes.
Q: Is the sport tennis?
A: Yes.

Note: If your class is too large for every student to have a turn answering questions, play the game in small groups.

Future use of sports cards

Keep these sports cards to practice *What* + (noun) . . . ? questions in Unit 8. For example:

Q: What equipment do baseball players use?
A: They use balls, bats, and gloves.

> **Culture Note** In the U.S., different school sports are played in different seasons. Spring sports include track and field, baseball, golf, and tennis. Track and field and tennis are traditionally sports for both boys and girls, but schools often have girls' softball teams instead of baseball teams. The big fall sport in the U.S. is American football. It is traditionally a boys' sport. There is not a corresponding girls' sport, but some girls may join cheerleading squads during the American football season. Soccer is another fall sport that is played by both boys and girls. Winter sports include basketball and volleyball, which are played by both girls and boys. Other winter sports include wrestling for boys and bowling for boys and girls.

Project preparation

- The class before the project, have students read the *Theme Project*, *Theme*, and *Goal* information. Explain that this project will help them learn more about the price of common items in dollars and will help them share interests with their classmates.

- Focus students' attention on the sample advertisement in the book. Say: *Look at the sample advertisement. You will make an advertisement like this one for a store you choose.*

- Focus students' attention on the *At Home* section. Explain that they will do this section for homework.

- Have students read the directions and check that they understand what they should do. At home, students should read the advertisement and the text, choose an activity, and list four things they need for their activity and the prices of the four things. Tell them to use the Internet if necessary. Remind students that they can use their dictionaries to find the meanings of words they do not know. They should then find photos of the items to bring to the next class. Tell students that if they cannot find photos, they can draw pictures.

- To finish, invite volunteers to tell you some activities and the items they need in order to do them. Write the activities and the items on the board. Ask students how much they think the items cost, and let volunteers guess the prices. Write the guesses next to the items.

Day of the project

Materials needed

Plain or colored paper for each student, tape or glue or paste, markers, stapler

- Explain to students that they will work individually to make an advertisement for their store, using the sample advertisement as a model.

- Distribute materials. Have each student make an individual store advertisement.

- Have students form groups and present their advertisements to their group, using the language in the speech balloon as a cue.

- Gather all the advertisements and staple them together into a booklet of store advertisements. Have students pass around the booklet of advertisements for all groups to look at.

- Display the booklet in the classroom.

- To finish, ask volunteers which activities and equipment are the coolest, and why.

Option

Have students use information from the ads in the booklet to review *How much is / are _____ ?* from this unit. For example:

A: *How much are the brushes?*
B: *They're nine ninety-nine.*

Future use of the booklet

Keep the booklet to practice *I want / don't want* + to (verb) in Unit 6. For example:

A: *I don't want to buy a glove. I want to buy a bat.*

> **Culture Note**
>
> Many popular movies and TV shows made in the U.S. often feature product placement. Product placement helps companies advertise their products and get maximum exposure. These companies know that people, especially teens, like watching movies and TV. They also know that moviegoers will be more likely to buy the products they see movie characters using, driving, eating, or drinking in movies. For example, a snack food company might pay a fee to the producers of a movie to feature a particular kind of potato chip. When a teen moviegoer sees a movie character eating this kind of potato chip, he or she might be more inclined to buy the product because it is "cool" to eat the same kind of snack that a popular movie character eats.

Unit 4

Theme Project: Make a booklet of advertisements.

Theme: Consumer awareness; cultural diversity

Goal: To learn the price of common items in dollars; to share interests

At Home

Read the advertisement.

Hi! I'm Lydia. In my free time, I paint pictures. I need special things for painting. Look at this advertisement from my favorite art store.

Martin's Art Store

Art Supply Sale
Canvas $25.25
Brushes $9.99
Paints $18.70 (each tube)
Easel $129.99

Choose an activity. _My activity is (Answers will vary.)_____ .

What do you need for your activity? Write four items and their prices. Use your dictionary or the Internet, if necessary. (Answers will vary.)

1. _____ _____   3. _____
2. _____ _____   4. _____

Draw pictures or bring photos of the items above to class.

In Class

ℹ️ **Choose a name for your store. Make an advertisement for your store. Use the sample advertisement as a model.**

👥 **Tell your group about the items in your store.**

> I like skiing. Skis are $600.00. Boots are $350.00. A jacket is . . .

👥 **Give your group's pages to the teacher. The teacher staples together the pages.**

🔄 **Pass around the booklet. What equipment and activities are the coolest? Why?**

Sample advertisement

Theme Project: Make a city guide for tourists.
Theme: Citizenship
Goal: To create awareness of your city or town; to provide information for visitors

At Home

Read about Julie's favorite place in New York.

Today, I am with my friends at South Street Seaport. There are many things to do here. There are people taking a boat ride. Over there, some people are watching street performers. Right now, we're visiting a museum. It's really interesting.

What are two of your favorite places in your city? Write their names. Then write three things you do in each place. Use your dictionary, if necessary. *(Answers will vary.)*

Place 1:	Place 2:
1.	1.
2.	2.
3.	3.

Draw pictures or bring photos of the places and the activities to class.

In Class

👥 **Look at all the places. Choose two places.**

👥 **Make a page for each place. Use the sample page as a model.**

👥👥 **Choose a group leader. Present your places and activities to another group.**

> This is Central Park. These people are walking on a path. These people are . . .

👥 **Give your group's pages to the teacher. The teacher staples together the pages.**

🔄 **Pass around the guide. What are your favorite activities? Why?**

Central Park

Walk on a path!

Go biking!

Visit the zoo!

Sample city guide page

Project preparation

- The class before the project, have students read the *Theme Project*, *Theme*, and *Goal* information. Explain that this project will help them learn more about their city or town and provide information for visitors.

- Focus students' attention on the sample city guide page in the book. Say: *Look at the sample city guide page. You and your group will make two city guide pages like this one about your city or town.*

- Focus students' attention on the *At Home* section. Explain that they will do this section for homework.

- Have students read the directions and check that they understand what they should do. At home, students should read the text about Julie's favorite place in New York and complete the chart about two of their favorite places in their city or town. Tell students that they can use their dictionaries to find the meanings of words they do not know. They should then find photos of the two places and the things they can do in each place to bring to the next class. Tell students that if they cannot find photos, they can draw pictures.

- To finish, invite volunteers to name some interesting places in the city or town where they live. Write the places across the top of the board. Then have volunteers tell you things people can do in each place. List the activities under the places.

Day of the project

Materials needed

Plain firm paper for each group, tape or glue or paste, markers, stapler

- Have students work in small groups. Remind students that they will make two city guide pages, using the sample page as a model.

- Distribute materials. Have each group look at all the charts and the photos or pictures and choose two of their favorite places in their city or town to visit. Each group then makes a page for each of the two places.

- Have each group choose a leader and then join another group. Have the group leader present the information in the group's two city guide pages to the other group, using the language in the speech balloon as a cue.

- Gather all the pages and staple them together to make a city guide. Have students pass around the city guide for all groups to look at.

- To finish, ask volunteers which activities in the places are their favorites, and why.

Option

Have students use information from the city guide to review the present continuous. Practice questions and answers. For example:

A: What are you doing?
B: I'm visiting the zoo.

Future use of the city guide

Keep this city guide to practice *Where + (be) . . . going?* questions and answers in Unit 6. For example:

A: Where are you going?
B: I'm going to the library.

> **Culture Note**
> In the U.S., many activities for people of all ages are offered through public libraries. For example, in the summer, young children can enter a library program and win small prizes for reading a specific number of books. Children can also go to Story Hour at the library to listen to someone read a picture book. There are drama and writing workshops for teens at many libraries. For adults there are often free book clubs, lectures, concerts, computer training, movies, and other events. There are also usually many volunteer opportunities at public libraries.

Project preparation

- The class before the project, have students read the *Theme Project*, *Theme*, and *Goal* information. Explain that this project will help them create stronger relationships in their classroom community.

- Focus students' attention on the sample poster in the book. Say: *Look at the sample poster. You and your group will make a poster like this one about things you want to do this weekend.*

- Focus students' attention on the *At Home* section. Explain that they will do this section for homework.

- Have students read the directions and check that they understand what they should do. At home, students should read the text about Hyun's weekend activities and write a list of four things they would like to do this weekend. Remind students that they can use their dictionaries to find the meanings of words they do not know. They should then find photos of the activities to bring to the next class. Tell students that if they cannot find photos, they can draw pictures.

- To finish, invite volunteers to tell you some things they would like to do this weekend.

Day of the project

Materials needed
Poster board or large paper for each group, tape or glue or paste, markers

- Have students work in small groups. Remind students that they will make a poster of weekend activities, using the sample poster as a model.

- Distribute materials. Have each group look at all the lists and the photos or pictures, and choose one weekend activity for each member of the group. Each group then makes a poster.

- Have each group choose a leader and then join another group. Have the group leader present the information on the group's poster to the other group, using the language in the speech balloon as a cue.

- Display the posters in your classroom. Have students walk around and look at all of them.

- To finish, ask volunteers which activities from the posters do they want to do this weekend.

Option

Play a memory game with the posters. Turn the posters around or cover them so that the students cannot see them. Divide the class into two teams. Ask a volunteer to say the name of a classmate. A student from the other team should give a sentence about what the named student wants to do over the weekend. For example:

A: Claudia
B: She wants to see a horror movie.

If the sentence is accurate and correct, the team gets a point.

Future use of posters

Keep these posters to practice *would like* in Unit 7. For example:

A: Would you like to go to the movies?
B: No, thanks. I'd like to go to the baseball game.

Culture Note

Many school-age teens in the U.S. are allowed to stay out later on weekend nights than on school nights. These nights are often filled with social activities rather than with clubs, classes, and so on. Many teens have curfews – times by which they have to be in at night. In most cases, the weekend curfew is later than the school week curfew. For example, a student might have to be home by 9:30 or 10:00 during the week, but he or she can stay out until 11:00 or 12:00 on weekend nights. Teens are expected to call their parents if they will be later – and when they miss their curfews, they often are "grounded." This means that they are not allowed to go out or socialize with friends, or they lose a privilege, such as the use of a car, for a specific period of time.

Theme Project: Make a weekend activity poster.
Theme: Relationships; citizenship
Goal: To create stronger relationships in your classroom community

At Home

Read about Hyun's weekend activities.

I usually relax at home on weekends, but I like to do other things, too. This Saturday, I want to see the new horror movie. I love horror movies. On Sunday, I want to go to a concert with my friends. I want to eat at a restaurant before the concert. Weekends are great!

Write four activities you want to do this weekend. Use your dictionary, if necessary. (*Answers will vary.*)

1. _____   3. _____

2. _____   4. _____

Draw pictures or bring photos of the activities to class.

In Class

Look at all the activities. Choose one activity for each person.

Make a poster. Use the sample poster as a model.

Choose a group leader. Present your poster to another group.

> Keiko likes to go to concerts. This weekend, she wants to see the Taylor Swift concert. She's awesome!

Display the posters in your classroom. Walk around and look at all of them. What do you want to do this weekend?

Keiko
I want to see the Taylor Swift concert. She's awesome!

Cindy
I want to go to the city nature center. The birds there are beautiful.

Raul
I want to go to a Chicago Bulls basketball game. They're cool!

Sample poster

Theme Project: Make a group menu.
Theme: Healthy food
Goal: To share information about healthy foods

At Home

Read about Home Cooking Restaurant's menu.

Welcome to our restaurant! On today's menu, we have two healthy dishes for lunch. Try our vegetable soup or our chicken sandwich. There are carrots, peas, beans, and onions in the soup. There isn't any mayonnaise on the sandwich — there's only chicken, lettuce, and tomato on it. Both dishes are delicious!

Complete the chart. Use your dictionary, if necessary. *(Answers will vary.)*

Healthy dish	What's in it?
1.	1.
2.	2.

Draw pictures or bring photos of the foods to class.

In Class

Look at all the healthy dishes. Choose four dishes. Make a menu. Use the sample menu as a model.

Choose a group leader. Present your menu to another group.

> On our menu, we have pasta with sauce. There are tomatoes, onions, and meat in the sauce. We also have a salad. There are carrots, cheese, and lettuce in it. We also have . . .

Display the menus in your classroom. Walk around and look at all of them. Vote on the healthiest dish.

Menu

Pasta with sauce:
Pasta, tomatoes, onions, and meat

Salad:
Carrots, cheese, and lettuce

Fruit salad:
Bananas, apples, oranges, and grapes

Chicken and vegetable soup:
Chicken, carrots, beans, celery, and onions

Sample menu

Unit 7   Theme Project

Project preparation

- The class before the project, have students read the *Theme Project, Theme,* and *Goal* information. Explain that this project will help them share information about healthy foods.

- Focus students' attention on the sample menu in the book. Say: *Look at the sample menu. You and your group will make a healthy menu like this one.*

- Focus students' attention on the *At Home* section. Explain that they will do this section for homework.

- Have students read the directions and check that they understand what they should do. At home, students should read the "Home Cooking Restaurant" text and the menu in it and complete the chart with their own ideas for healthy dishes and the ingredients in them. Remind students that they can use their dictionaries to find the meanings of words they do not know. They should then find photos of two healthy dishes to bring to the next class. Tell students that if they cannot find photos, they can draw pictures.

- To finish, invite volunteers to tell you some of their favorite dishes. Have their classmates say whether the dish is healthy or unhealthy.

Day of the project

Materials needed
Plain or colored paper for each group, tape or glue or paste, markers

- Have students work in small groups. Remind students that they will make a menu, using the sample menu as a model.

- Distribute materials. Have each group look at all the healthy dishes in the charts and the photos or pictures, and choose four dishes. Each group then makes a menu.

- Have each group choose a leader and then join another group. Have the group leader present the group's menu to the other group, using the language in the speech balloon as a cue.

- Display the menus in your classroom. Have students walk around and look at all of them.

- To finish, have students vote on the healthiest dish.

Option

Have pairs write and then role-play short restaurant conversations. For example:

Server: Are you ready to order?
Customer: Yes, I'd like the pasta, please.
Server: Anything else?
Customer: Iced tea.
Server: OK. That's pasta and iced tea. Thank you.

Future use of menus

Keep these menus to review *What* + (noun) . . . ? in Unit 8. For example:

A: What desserts do you like?
B: I like ice cream and chocolate cake.

> **Culture Note**
> In the U.S., some very popular restaurants do not have menus. These are "all-you-can-eat" buffets. For one price, people can take many different foods from a cafeteria-style counter, and they can go back for more as many times as they like. Many buffets include salads, main dishes, and desserts. Because waste is such a problem at buffets, a lot of buffets have signs that say things like, "Take what you want, but eat all you take." And while most restaurants will give you a "doggie bag" – a container for you to take home the food you did not finish – you cannot usually take food home from a buffet.

Project preparation

- The class before the project, have students read the *Theme Project, Theme,* and *Goal* information. Explain that this project will help them learn more about different countries around the world.

- Focus students' attention on the sample poster in the book. Say: *Look at the sample poster. You will make a poster like this one about a different country.*

- Focus students' attention on the *At Home* section. Explain that they will do this section for homework.

- Have students read the directions and check that they understand what they should do. At home, students should read the text about Peru and complete the chart with information about a different country. Tell them to use the library or the Internet if necessary. Remind students that they can use their dictionaries to find the meanings of words they do not know. They should then find three photos of the things in their chart to bring to the next class. Tell students that if they cannot find photos, they can draw three pictures.

- To finish, have the class brainstorm as many country names as possible in English. Write the countries on the board. Have volunteers name important cities and famous places in the countries.

Day of the project

Materials needed
Poster board or large paper for each student, tape or glue or paste, markers

- Explain to students that they will work individually to make a poster about a country, using the sample poster as a model.

- Distribute materials. Have each student make an individual poster. Make sure students do not write the names of their countries on their posters yet.

- Have students form groups and present their posters to their group, using the language in the speech balloons as cues. The other group members try to guess the country on each poster.

- Have each group choose a leader and then join another group. Have the group leader present the information on the group's posters to the other group, using the language in the speech balloons as cues. Students from the other group try to guess the country on each poster. Students write the name of the country on the poster when it has been correctly identified.

- Display the posters in your classroom. Have students walk around and look at all of them.

- To finish, have students vote on the most interesting place.

Option

Use the posters to play a trivia memory game. Turn the posters around or cover them so that students can't see them. Divide the class into teams of four or five. Give the class three minutes to write as many facts as they can remember from the posters. At the end of five minutes, the group with the most facts wins.

Future use of posters

Keep these posters to practice *would like to* in Student's Book 4, Unit 1. For example:

A: *Are you going to go to Spain?*
B: *I'd like to, but I can't speak Spanish.*

Culture Note
Ecotourism and volunteer tourism are becoming increasingly popular with people in the U.S. An ecotourism vacation is one that respects the local environment and culture of the place people visit. Ecotourists try not to destroy plants and animals or disrupt the local way of living. They go to places where development is limited, and where there are environmentally friendly hostels and inns. Volunteer tourists spend their vacations going somewhere to help with something. For example, they might work at a place where injured wildlife is rehabilitated, or they might help count the number of birds or fish for a scientific organization.

Theme Project: Make an informational poster about a country.
Theme: Cultural diversity
Goal: To learn about different countries around the world

At Home

Read about Peru.

Machu Picchu

Visit Peru in South America. Go to Lima, an important city in Peru. It's sometimes sunny and cool there. You can go to Machu Picchu from Lima. It's a famous place in the mountains. It's very old and beautiful. You can also see the rain forest in Peru. So, check out Peru. It's a really fun place to visit.

Write the information. Use your dictionary, if necessary. *(Answers will vary.)*

Country: _____

Important city: _____

Famous place: _____

Things you can do: _____

Continent: _____

Weather in that city: _____

Draw three pictures or bring three photos of the things in your chart to class.

In Class

ⓘ **Make a poster. Use the sample poster as a model.**

👥 **Read the information on your poster. The other group members guess the country.**

> This country is in Central America. Cancun is . . .

> Is it Costa Rica?

👥👥 **Choose a group leader. Present your places to another group. Try to guess the country on each poster. Finally, write the correct countries on the posters.**

🌐 **Display the posters in your classroom. Walk around and look at all of them. Vote on the most interesting place.**

> This country is in Central America. Cancun is an important city there. It's hot and sunny there.
>
> You can visit Chichen-Itza.
>
> You can go to beautiful beaches.
>
> You can listen to mariachi music.
>
> _____
> (country)

Sample poster

Word List

This list includes the key words and phrases in *Connect Second Edition* Student's Book 2. The numbers next to each word are the page numbers on which the words first appear.

Key Vocabulary

Aa

action movie (78) _____
active (10) _____
activities (37) _____
actually (3) _____
admire (22) _____
adult (72) _____
adventure DVDs (46) _____
afternoon [in the . . .] (39) _____
again (37) _____
age (51) _____
air (110) _____
album (54) _____
all [at all] (11) _____
almost (47) _____
amazing (72) _____
animated movie (78) _____
answer (52) _____
anything (95) _____
appetizer (94) _____
apple (86) _____
Arabic (106) _____
artistic (8) _____
arts and crafts (38) _____
asleep (70) _____
At least! (109) _____
at night (37) _____
athlete (72) _____
athletic (8) _____
attention (61) _____
audio (54) _____
average (80) _____
awesome (72) _____

Bb

baby (64) _____
backup (12) _____
baked potato (94) _____
ball (65) _____
banana (86) _____
barbecue (74) _____
baseball bat (66) _____
baseball player (33) _____
basketball court (5) _____
bass (22) _____
bat [animal] (72) _____
bathing suit (65) _____
beans (94) _____
bear (103) _____
beautifully (76) _____

belt (66) _____
bike path (60) _____
biking (30) _____
bird (102) _____
black bean soup (94) _____
blanket (36) _____
blond (80) _____
boat (60) _____
boat ride (58) _____
body (type) (80) _____
bowling (53) _____
bracelet (66) _____
bread (88) _____
breakfast (16) _____
bring (36) _____
broccoli (86) _____
bug repellent (36) _____
busy (39) _____
butter (86) _____
butter cow (82) _____

Cc

cake (74) _____
camp (36) _____
campers (39) _____
campfire (38) _____
camping (50) _____
canoeing (38) _____
cards (74) _____
carrot cake (94) _____
castle (68) _____
cat (10) _____
catalog (47) _____
cave (102) _____
CD (28) _____
celebrate (74) _____
cents (46) _____
champion (40) _____
checklist (36) _____
check out (26) _____
cheese (86) _____
cheeseburger (94) _____
chicken (92) _____
chicken sandwich (94) _____
chocolate cake (94) _____
circus (72) _____
climb (102) _____
clothes (23) _____
clothing (23) _____
cloudy (100) _____

coat (66) _____
cold (100) _____
collect (18) _____
column (96) _____
come (52) _____
comedy (78) _____
comfortable (37) _____
company (26) _____
convenient (54) _____
cook [noun] (75) _____
cook [verb] (38) _____
cookbook (96) _____
cookie (87) _____
cool (100) _____
country (music) (44) _____
creator (26) _____
crossword puzzles (50) _____
cup (88) _____
curly (80) _____
cyclist (33) _____

Dd

dance lessons (18) _____
dancing (50) _____
dangerous (10) _____
delicious (68) _____
dessert (94) _____
die (110) _____
diner (94) _____
dinner (16) _____
dirty (110) _____
discover (46) _____
documentary (78) _____
dog (10) _____
doll (68) _____
dollars (46) _____
download (54) _____
drama (78) _____
dress (37) _____
drinks [noun] (88) _____
drums (12) _____
DVD (18) _____

Ee

each (46) _____
early (25) _____
easily (8) _____
eat (16) _____
eat out (24) _____
egg (86) _____

egg sandwich (87) _____
electric keyboard (22) _____
else (89) _____
end (81) _____
especially (109) _____
evening [in the . . .] (39) _____
everyone (101) _____
everything (67) _____
exhibit (72) _____
expensive (47) _____
eye (32) _____

Ff
farm (82) _____
fascinating (72) _____
fashion designer (23) _____
feet (32) _____
fence (40) _____
festival (72) _____
few [a few] (89) _____
find (107) _____
fish (94) _____
flashlight (36) _____
float (64) _____
fly (64) _____
follow (61) _____
foot (32) _____
for a change (87) _____
forget (103) _____
fork (88) _____
free time (18) _____
french fries (94) _____
Frisbee (64) _____
fruit (88) _____

Gg
German (106) _____
Germany (106) _____
get up (16) _____
glove(s) (32) _____
goggles (32) _____
golf (109) _____
Good! (93) _____
good (at something) (9) _____
go out (24) _____
grade (eighth grade) (21) _____
grades (52) _____
Greece (106) _____
Greek (106) _____
group (44) _____
guess (23) _____
guitar lesson (17) _____
guy (31) _____

Hh
hair (80) _____
hairstyle (80) _____
hand (32) _____
hang out (18) _____
hard [work hard] (23) _____
hardly ever (52) _____
hate (73) _____

head (32) _____
headphones (52) _____
healthy (87) _____
heavy (80) _____
height (80) _____
helmet (32) _____
help [noun] (101) _____
help [verb] (31) _____
high school [adjective] (22) _____
hike (38) _____
hiking boots (36) _____
hip-hop (music) (44) _____
horror movie (78) _____
horseback riding (38) _____
hotel (103) _____
hot spring (102) _____
houseboat (102) _____
how [How old is he?] (3) _____

Ii
ice cream (70) _____
iced tea (94) _____
idea (93) _____
incredible (72) _____
information (101) _____
in-line (skate) (18) _____
instrument (8) _____
interests (50) _____
island (102) _____
Italy (106) _____

Jj
jazz (44) _____
jazz band (22) _____
jazz club (22) _____
jelly (92) _____
jewelry (67) _____
jokes (8) _____
juice (88) _____
just a minute (37) _____

Kk
karate (30) _____
ketchup (92) _____
kind [what kind of] (45) _____
kite (64) _____
knee (32) _____
knee pad(s) (32) _____
knives [sing. knife] (88) _____

Ll
language (8) _____
lead (12) _____
learn (72) _____
leave (37) _____
lesson (17) _____
lettuce (92) _____
lifeguard chair (65) _____
light (60) _____
line [in line] (60) _____
listen (18) _____
lives (16) _____

long (80) _____
look (like) (81) _____

Mm
main dish (94) _____
make (8) _____
man (64) _____
many [how many] (89) _____
marketing (26) _____
maybe (31) _____
mayonnaise (92) _____
meat (86) _____
medium-length (80) _____
melt (110) _____
menu (94) _____
messages (26) _____
messy (10) _____
midnight (37) _____
milk (88) _____
milk shake (94) _____
million (54) _____
morning [in the . . .] (16) _____
Morocco (106) _____
mountain (102) _____
much [adjective] (45) _____
much [how much] (47) _____
much [very much] (11) _____
musical [adjective] (8) _____
musical [noun] (12) _____
musician (44) _____
mustard (92) _____

Nn
national forest (108) _____
Nature Center (73) _____
nature puzzles (46) _____
near (65) _____
necklace (66) _____
need (33) _____
never (52) _____
newspaper (96) _____
No kidding! (33) _____
nothing (87) _____
nutrition (96) _____

Oo
ocean (64) _____
off (to) (36) _____
one hundred thousand (108) _____
one thousand (108) _____
on time (52) _____
open (74) _____
or (17) _____
order (95) _____
outdoors (50) _____
over (11) _____
own [his own] (23) _____

Pp
paper airplanes (52) _____
parrot (10) _____
party game (74) _____

pasta (88) _____

pay (attention) (61) _____

pay for (66) _____

peach (68) _____

pepper (92) _____

person (50) _____

pet (10) _____

phone (18) _____

photograph (107) _____

piano (22) _____

piano lesson (19) _____

picnic area (60) _____

picture (8) _____

pie (94) _____

pillow (36) _____

plan [noun] (88) _____

plant [noun] (109) _____

plastic (110) _____

plate (88) _____

play [noun] (68) _____

poetry (50) _____

police officer (108) _____

pop (music) (44) _____

popcorn (25) _____

Portuguese (106) _____

potato (86) _____

pounds (82) _____

practice (22) _____

present [noun] (74) _____

presentation (109) _____

pretty (good at) (9) _____

Qq

question (21) _____

Rr

rabbit (10) _____

race car driver (36) _____

radio (36) _____

radio-controlled airplane (46) ____

raft (64) _____

raincoat (36) _____

rain forest (102) _____

rainy (100) _____

read (37) _____

recipe (96) _____

recycle (110) _____

refrigerator (87) _____

reggae (music) (44) _____

relax (74) _____

remember (36) _____

rent (54) _____

review (26) _____

rice (86) _____

ride (58) _____

ring (66) _____

rise (110) _____

river (102) _____

robot (72) _____

routine (16) _____

rules (61) _____

run (108) _____

Russia (106) _____

Russian (106) _____

Ss

sail (64) _____

salad (94) _____

salt (92) _____

sand (64) _____

save (110) _____

say (37) _____

scarf (66) _____

science kit (46) _____

scientist (109) _____

score (76) _____

sea (102) _____

seashells (64) _____

section (96) _____

sell (54) _____

shop for (66) _____

shopping (50) _____

side order (94) _____

sightseeing (58) _____

skate (18) _____

skateboarder (33) _____

skating [adjective] (23) _____

ski (30) _____

ski boot(s) (32) _____

skier (33) _____

sleep (24) _____

sleeping bag (36) _____

slim (80) _____

slow (75) _____

snack (92) _____

snake (10) _____

snowy (100) _____

soap (36) _____

soccer (2) _____

soccer practice (53) _____

soda (94) _____

software (26) _____

something (37) _____

song (49) _____

sound (101) _____

sound (like) (39) _____

souvenir (58) _____

souvenir shop (103) _____

special (12) _____

species (109) _____

spend (time) (50) _____

spider (10) _____

spoon (88) _____

sports equipment (32) _____

stadium (108) _____

stamps (18) _____

stand (60) _____

star map (46) _____

start (77) _____

stay (home) (24) _____

stay on (60) _____

stay up (24) _____

steak sandwich (94) _____

stop (37) _____

stories (38) _____

straight (80) _____

student (22) _____

study (47) _____

sunny (100) _____

sunscreen (36) _____

supplies (88) _____

supposed (to be) (37) _____

sure (79) _____

Sure! (33) _____

surf (30) _____

surfboard (66) _____

surprise (73) _____

survey (19) _____

swim (30) _____

swimmer (33) _____

swimming (51) _____

swimming lessons (38) _____

swim team (33) _____

Tt

take (18) _____

talented (23) _____

talk (18) _____

teach (22) _____

telescope (46) _____

temperature (100) _____

tennis (2) _____

tennis racket (66) _____

ten thousand (108) _____

theater (70) _____

then (16) _____

there [Hello there!] (2) _____

thrilling (72) _____

throw (52) _____

ticket (68) _____

today's [adjective] (94) _____

tonight (79) _____

too bad (47) _____

towel (36) _____

traditional (68) _____

trail (103) _____

trash (60) _____

trash can (60) _____

travel vest (46) _____

trip (59) _____

trolley (58) _____

trophy (40) _____

try on (66) _____

twenty-five thousand (108) _____

two thousand (108) _____

typical (12) _____

Uu

underground (102) _____

until (37) _____

us (81) _____

use (18) _____

Vv

vegetable soup (94) _____

video (18) _____

videotape [verb] (59) _____

violin (23) _____

Ww

wait (for) (60) _____

walk (58) _____

wall calendar (46) _____

want (79) _____

warm (100) _____

watch [verb] (16) _____

water (86) _____

water-ski (30) _____

wavy (80) _____

wear (32) _____

weather (100) _____

Web site (12) _____

week (23) _____

weekend (19) _____

weigh (82) _____

win (40) _____

windy (100) _____

wire (82) _____

wolves [*sing.* wolf] (103) _____

woman (81) _____

work (22) _____

would (95) _____

Introduction to Extra Practice

Included in this section is a photocopiable package. This package contains eight short Extra Practice worksheets, one for each unit in *Connect*. In addition, there are four 3-page Extra Practice review worksheets reviewing two units.

The Extra Practice worksheets give students additional practice in word work (spelling, vocabulary, grammar, or pronunciation) and in finding and correcting sentence mistakes.

The Extra Practice review worksheets give students additional opportunities to practice and personalize the new vocabulary, language, reading, and writing skills they learned in the preceding units.

Features of Extra Practice

- The content of the Extra Practice exercises is strictly limited to the language and skills presented and practiced in the lessons in each unit of the Student's Book.
- The focus of each Extra Practice worksheet is on the specific language and skills of the corresponding unit, but does assume knowledge of the previous units' content.
- Exercise types in Extra Practice are similar to those in the lessons.
- The focus of the Extra Practice reviews is on vocabulary, language skills (completing conversations), reading, and writing, using your own information.

Assigning Extra Practice worksheets

- These worksheets can be assigned as homework or done in class.
- Make a copy of the Extra Practice worksheet(s) for each student in your class.
- If you assign these worksheets as homework, be sure to check the answers in the next class.
- If you do these worksheets in class, have students work alone and then check answers in pairs.

List of Extra Practice Exercises

Unit 1	Page T-139	Unit 5	Page T-149
Unit 2	Page T-140	Unit 6	Page T-150
Units 1 & 2	Page T-141	Units 5 & 6	Page T-151
Unit 3	Page T-144	Unit 7	Page T-154
Unit 4	Page T-145	Unit 8	Page T-155
Units 3 & 4	Page T-146	Units 7 & 8	Page T-156
		Answer Key	Page T-159

Unit 1 All About You and Me

1 Word work

A Make lists of four words for each of the categories below. Write one word that does not belong in each list.

Example:

School subjects
math
soccer
science
art

Animals

Places in a neighborhood

Sports

Talents

B Exchange lists with a classmate. Circle the word that does not belong in each of your classmate's lists.

2 What's wrong?

Correct the sentences. There is one mistake in each sentence.

1. My name Jane Roberts.
   My name's Jane Roberts.

2. I'm student at Central School.
   _____

3. I from Canada.
   _____

4. I don't like snakes a lot.
   _____

5. I'm pretty good math.
   _____

6. I'm in Mr. Green math class.
   _____

Photocopiable

Unit 2 Our Lives and Routines

1 Word work

Circle the correct word to complete each verb phrase. Then match the verb phrases to the correct photos.

1. ((go)/ sleep / live) out _____d_____

2. (listen / watch / practice) DVDs _____

3. (talk / do / go) my homework _____

4. (live / teach / eat) dinner _____

5. (collect / go / practice) stamps _____

6. (go / practice / collect) the piano _____

2 What's wrong?

One sentence in each pair is correct. Check (✓) it.

1. ☐ I eat don't lunch at home.
   ☑ I don't eat lunch at home.

2. ☐ He teaches English at my school.
   ☐ He teach English at my school.

3. ☐ They don't hang out at the mall.
   ☐ They doesn't hang out at the mall.

4. ☐ I with my brother go to school.
   ☐ I go to school with my brother.

5. ☐ At 8:30, I watch TV.
   ☐ I at 8:30 watch TV.

6. ☐ She don't have an electric keyboard.
   ☐ She doesn't have an electric keyboard.

Units 1 & 2

1 Vocabulary

A Match. Write the letters.

1. watch _____   a. piano lessons
2. practice _____   b. home
3. collect _____   c. TV
4. take _____   d. homework
5. stay _____   e. stamps
6. do _____   f. the piano

B Read the clues. Write the words from the box.

> ☐ artistic   ☐ friendly   ☐ musical
> ☐ athletic   ☐ interesting

1. Can make friends easily _____
2. Is not boring _____
3. Can draw great pictures _____
4. Can play a lot of sports _____
5. Can play an instrument _____

C Write two words from the box in the correct column.

> ☐ breakfast   ☐ English   ☐ home   ☐ the guitar
> ☐ dinner   ☐ history   ☐ soccer ☐ to bed

Eat	Go	Play	Teach

2 Language focus

A Complete the conversation. Choose the correct words.

Luke _____ (Where's / Who's) she?

Peter She's _____ (my / your) sister.

Luke _____ (What's / Who's) her name?

Peter Her _____ (is / name's) Marie.

Luke She's very _____ (really / good) at basketball.

Peter Yes. She can play a lot of sports. She's very _____ (artistic / athletic).

Luke Is there a basketball _____ (park / court) in your neighborhood?

Peter Yes. Marie _____ (practices / eats) after school every day.

Luke _____ (Do / Are) you practice, too?

Peter Me? No! I'm _____ (very / not) good at sports at all!

B Look at the picture. The sentences below are incorrect. Write the sentences about the picture with the correct information.

1. She likes dogs a little.
   She doesn't like dogs a little. She likes dogs a lot.

2. She lives in an apartment.
   _____

3. She has three brothers.
   _____

4. There are five cats in the yard.
   _____

5. Her brother plays baseball.
   _____

C Complete the sentences. Circle the correct words.

1. (She / I) doesn't do her homework on Sunday night.
2. Do (he / you) go to bed at 10:00?
3. (I / She) eats breakfast at home.
4. (I / He) don't get up at 6:00 in the morning.
5. (I / My brother) have video games and a computer.

Photocopiable   © Cambridge University Press 2009

3 Reading

A Read about Manuel and his classmates.

Hello! My name is Manuel. I'm from Brazil. I like sports and music. I'm pretty good at soccer. I practice every day. I have two brothers and a sister. I have a dog, but I don't have a cat. I don't like cats very much.

Antonio and Martina are my friends. They're from Italy. Antonio is 13, and Martina is 12. We go to school together every day. Antonio is very smart, and he likes science very much. Martina doesn't like science at all. She can draw great pictures. She's very artistic. She takes art lessons on Saturday.

B Complete the sentences. Write *Manuel*, *Antonio*, or *Martina*.

1. _____ is athletic.

2. _____ is 12.

3. _____ has a dog.

4. _____ is very smart.

5. _____ takes art lessons on Saturday.

4 Writing

A Complete the information about yourself and a friend.

What's your name? _____   What's your friend's name? _____
How old are you? _____   How old is he or she? _____
Where are you from? _____   Where's he or she from? _____
What do you like? _____   What does he or she like? _____
What are you good at? _____   What's he or she good at? _____

B Now write about yourself and your friend. Use the information from Part A.

Hi! My name's _____ . _____

_____

_____

_____

_____

Unit 3 Sports and Activities

1 Word work

A Circle the eight words relating to camping in the lines below. Then write the words.

mastvsoaprhgeiflashlightproxzwcampfiremnbcaiopillowktwest

posiblanketadmtrvsunscreenwrenraincoatlamcuwtowelnesdeaq

1. _soap_   5. _____

2. _____   6. _____

3. _____   7. _____

4. _____   8. _____

B Circle the ten words relating to sports and sports equipment in the lines below. Then write the words.

hebtrxbaseballqrsvwhelmetjokerkarateniartoagogglestghilshskiboots

ragusswimmingniotnalglovesltbikingzcvnepaskateboardyzdxccanoeing

1. _baseball_   6. _____

2. _____   7. _____

3. _____   8. _____

4. _____   9. _____

5. _____   10. _____

2 What's wrong?

Correct the sentences. There is one mistake in each sentence.

1. Does he does karate at 8:30? _Does he do karate at 8:30?_

2. Don't gets up early. _____

3. When time do they do arts and crafts? _____

4. Skateboarders doesn't wear goggles. _____

5. When do Jenny go hiking? _____

6. Soccer players wear uniform. _____

Photocopiable

Unit 4 My Interests

1 Word work

Match the pieces of the price tags. Draw lines. Then write the price of each item.

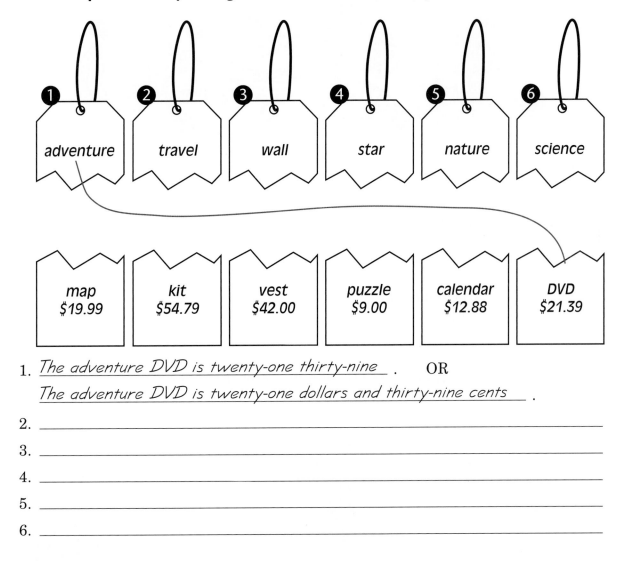

1. *The adventure DVD is twenty-one thirty-nine* .   OR

   The adventure DVD is twenty-one dollars and thirty-nine cents .

2. _____

3. _____

4. _____

5. _____

6. _____

2 What's wrong?

One sentence in each pair is correct. Check (✓) it.

1. ☐ I hardly never talk in class.
   ☑ I hardly ever talk in class.

2. ☐ The video sets are $24.99.
   ☐ The video sets is $24.99.

3. ☐ How much are the pop CD?
   ☐ How much are the pop CDs?

4. ☐ I don't like they at all.
   ☐ I don't like them at all.

5. ☐ I like to go shopping.
   ☐ I like to shopping.

6. ☐ He's great. I like he a lot.
   ☐ He's great. I like him a lot.

Units 3 & 4

1 Vocabulary

A Label the things at the Camp Coby Lost and Found.

1. _____
2. _____
3. _____

4. _____
5. _____
6. _____

7. _____
8. _____
9. _____

B Complete the phrases with the words in the box.

☐ cook   ☐ do   ☐ go   ☐ make   ☐ take   ☐ tell

1. _____ arts and crafts
2. _____ hot dogs
3. _____ canoeing

4. _____ stories
5. _____ swimming lessons
6. _____ a campfire

C What kind of music is it? Label the CDs with the words in the box.

☐ classical   ☐ country   ☐ jazz   ☐ pop   ☐ rock

1. _____
2. _____
3. _____

4. _____
5. _____

2 Language focus

A Complete the conversation with the words in the box.

☐ do	☐ don't	☐ hardly ever	☐ them	☐ we
☐ does	☐ every	☐ much	☐ they're	☐ when

Sandy How _____ are those hiking boots?

Scott _____ $49.99. They're for camp.

Sandy _____ you and your family like to go camping?

Scott Yes, _____ do.

Sandy _____ do you go camping?

Scott We go _____ summer.

Sandy _____ your sister go hiking?

Scott Yes. She always goes hiking, but she _____ _____ goes horseback riding.

Sandy Hiking and horseback riding are fun. I like _____ both a lot.

Scott You can come, too. _____ forget your sunscreen!

B Write complete sentences.

1. Soccer players / not / wear / helmets.

_____

2. Basketball players / not / wear / goggles.

_____

3. We / do arts and crafts / 10:15.

_____

4. Not / listen / radio.

_____

5. I / do karate / afternoon.

_____

6. Campers / tell stories / night.

_____

C Complete the sentences. Circle the correct words.

1. The Dixie Chicks are my favorite. I like (her / them) a lot.
2. How much (is / are) the video sets?
3. She hardly ever (writes / write) poetry.
4. The nature puzzles (are / is) twelve ninety-nine each.
5. He doesn't (like / like to) go dancing.
6. (Always he / He always) watches TV at night.

3 Reading

A **Read about Laurie and Ashley.**

    My sister, Ashley, and I are very busy teens. She likes to hang out with her friends at the mall. She usually goes on Saturday. I don't like to go to the mall. I like to skateboard and go biking in the park. She loves to talk on the phone and chat online, but that's boring. I usually read books, listen to music, or write poetry.

    But we always watch TV together on Sunday night. There's a show with a lot of pop groups and singers. It's really cool!

– Laurie Howe

B **Are these sentences true or false? Check (✓) T (true) or F (false).**

	T	F
1. Laurie and Ashley are good friends.	☐	☐
2. Ashley likes to go to the mall on Saturday.	☐	☐
3. Laurie likes to go to the mall, too.	☐	☐
4. Laurie likes to talk on the phone.	☐	☐
5. They always watch a TV show on Sunday night.	☐	☐

4 Writing

A **Are you and your best friend the same or are you different? Complete the chart. Check (✓) Yes or No.**

Do you like to . . . ?	You		Your friend	
	Yes	No	Yes	No
1. watch TV	☐	☐	☐	☐
2. listen to music	☐	☐	☐	☐
3. hang out with friends	☐	☐	☐	☐
4. talk on the phone	☐	☐	☐	☐
5. play sports	☐	☐	☐	☐
6. read books	☐	☐	☐	☐

B **Now write about yourself and your best friend. Use the information from Part A or your own ideas.**

_____ and I are busy teens. _____ likes to

_____ . _____

_____

_____

_____

        Photocopiable   © Cambridge University Press 2009

Unit 5 | Favorite Activities

1 Word work

Check (✓) the correct words to complete the sentences.

1. They take ☑ a boat ride.
   ☐ a museum.
   ☐ a show.

2. You throw ☐ the museum.
   ☐ the green light.
   ☐ a Frisbee.

3. I fly ☐ a trolley.
   ☐ a kite.
   ☐ a raft.

4. You try on ☐ a boat.
   ☐ a show.
   ☐ a jacket.

5. They wait for ☐ the green light.
   ☐ the seashells.
   ☐ trolley.

6. I float ☐ in the sand.
   ☐ on a raft.
   ☐ in the park.

7. You stand ☐ on a picnic.
   ☐ in line.
   ☐ on a video.

8. They sail ☐ a boat ride.
   ☐ a park.
   ☐ a boat.

2 What's wrong?

A Read Joy's postcard to her friend Lars. Underline the mistakes in her message. There are nine mistakes in the message.

Hello, Lars!

I'm <u>in</u> the beach! My sister are playing in the sand. She are happy. My brother is swimming. My dad is float on a raft. My mom and aunt is taking pictures. Uncle Tim is sail a boat. I'm collecting seashell. I'm don't swimming. We's having a great time!

See you soon!

Joy

Greetings!

B Write the correct word for each mistake in Part A.

1. _____at_____   4. _____   7. _____

2. _____   5. _____   8. _____

3. _____   6. _____   9. _____

Unit 6 Entertainment

1 Word work

Words like *map, swimmer,* and *spider* are <u>nouns</u>. Words like *cute, boring,* and *black* are <u>adjectives</u>. Words like *swim, go,* and *play* are <u>verbs</u>. Write *n* (noun), *adj* (adjective), or *v* (verb) next to the words below.

1. celebrate ___*v*___
2. awesome _____
3. musician _____
4. straight _____
5. sing _____

6. thrilling _____
7. blond _____
8. relax _____
9. team _____
10. documentary _____

2 What's wrong?

The underlined words are not correct. Match them to the correct sentences.

1. I don't want to see an <u>fascinating</u> movie. _____*action*_____
2. She has very long, <u>restaurant</u> hair. _____
3. Tonight, they're eating at a <u>relax</u>. _____
4. I'm going to the <u>blond</u>. _____
5. Monkeys are <u>action</u> animals. _____
6. We usually <u>movies</u> at home. _____

Photocopiable

Units 5 & 6

1 Vocabulary

A Look at the photos. Complete the phrases.

1. visit a _____

2. try on a _____

3. throw a _____

4. wait for a _____

5. take _____

6. collect _____

7. sail a _____

8. fly a _____

9. buy _____

10. float on a _____

B Read the clues. Write the words from the box.

☐ animals   ☐ movies   ☐ musicians   ☐ robots   ☐ teams

1. These aren't people, but they can walk and talk. You can see them at a science exhibit. _____

2. These people play instruments. They perform at concerts. _____

3. People go to theaters to see these for fun. _____

4. These are groups of people who play sports. _____

5. Some walk on two legs and some walk on four. Some fly. _____

C Circle the word that doesn't belong in each box.

amazing	comedy	belt	coat	eat cake
awesome	drama	bracelet	jacket	go shopping
boring	horror movie	necklace	racket	play party games
fascinating	incredible	ring	scarf	sing songs

Photocopiable

2 Language focus

A Rewrite the sentences in the present continuous.

1. They eat cake and open presents. _____

2. She doesn't throw trash in the trash can. _____

3. Do you play in the sand? _____

4. He goes to a concert in the park. _____

5. Does your father eat dinner in a restaurant? _____

B Look at the pictures. Then write the answers.

 1. What are they looking at?

_____

 2. Is she riding a trolley?

_____

 3. Are they sitting at the beach?

_____

 4. Are they relaxing at home?

_____

 5. What are you trying on?

_____

C Match the pictures to the sentences. Write the numbers.

1. She's average height and has curly, black hair.
2. He's average height. He has straight hair.
3. She's tall. She has medium-length hair.
4. He's slim. He has wavy hair.
5. She's short and thin. She has long, blond hair.

Photocopiable

3 Reading

A Read Jennifer's postcard from Honolulu.

Hi, Tim!
I'm relaxing at the beach in sunny Honolulu. We're
having a wonderful time. My dad is swimming in the
ocean. My mom is floating on a raft. Justin is
playing in the sand, and little Jan is collecting
seashells. My grandparents aren't here – they're
buying souvenirs at the hotel. I'm also taking a lot
of pictures to show you!
See you soon!
Jennifer

B Answer the questions in full sentences.

1. Where's Jennifer writing the postcard?

_____

2. Is her dad swimming in the ocean?

_____

3. What's Justin doing?

_____

4. What's Jan collecting?

_____

5. Where are Jennifer's grandparents buying souvenirs?

_____

4 Writing

Imagine you are on vacation with family or friends. Complete the postcard to a friend. Use the questions to help you.

Where are you?   What are your friends or family doing?
What are you doing?   Are you having fun?

Hi, _____ ! _____
I'm in _____ . _____
_____
_____
_____
_____
_____

Unit 7 | What We Eat

1 Word work

A Underline the uncountable nouns. There are 15 uncountable nouns.

apple	cup	iced tea	milk	rice
banana	egg	ketchup	pasta	salt
<u>bread</u>	fork	knife	pepper	soup
butter	fruit	lettuce	plate	spoon
cheese	hamburger	mayonnaise	potato	water

B Now write the countable nouns.

1. _____*apple*_____
2. _____
3. _____
4. _____
5. _____
6. _____
7. _____
8. _____
9. _____
10. _____

2 What's wrong?

Circle the correct word to complete each sentence.

1. There are three (hamburgers)/ cheese).

2. I don't like (butter / potato).

3. We have a little (cups / fruit).

4. There are a (lot of / little) forks.

5. How (many / much) lettuce is there?

6. There's (some / any) mustard in the cabinet.

Photocopiable

Unit 8 The Natural World

1 Word work

Read the clues. Write the words from the box.

□ cave	□ Germany	□ Italian	□ one hundred	□ warm
□ cold	□ island	□ mountain	□ one hundred thousand	□ windy

1. It's the opposite of *hot*. _____*cold*_____

2. It's a country. People speak German there. _____

3. Ten thousand + ninety thousand = this number. _____

4. It's dark inside this place. Bats live there. _____

5. This weather is when the wind blows. _____

6. If you can say "Buon giorno!" you can speak this language. _____

7. You need to wear hiking boots to climb this. _____

8. It's the opposite of *cool*. _____

9. 999,999 – 999,899 = this number. _____

10. There's water all around this place. Hawaii has many of these. _____

2 What's wrong?

Correct the sentences. There is one mistake in each sentence.

1. What's the weather usually likes in August in Australia?
   What's the weather usually like in August in Australia?

2. Who live in Greece?
   _____

3. What subjects does you like?
   _____

4. What the weather like in July?
   _____

5. You can going canoeing in summer.
   _____

6. It warm and sunny today.
   _____

Photocopiable

Units 7 & 8

1 Vocabulary

A Look at the photos. Write the shopping list.

1. _____
2. _____
3. _____
4. _____
5. _____

6. _____
7. _____
8. _____
9. _____
10. _____

B Complete the sentences with the words in the box.

☐ Arabic   ☐ German   ☐ Greece   ☐ Italy   ☐ Portugal   ☐ Russia

1. "Guten Tag!" means "hello" in _____ .

2. In Morocco, people speak _____ .

3. Portuguese is the official language in Brazil and in _____ .

4. _____ is a very big country.

5. People say "Buon giorno!" in _____ .

6. _____ has many beautiful islands.

C Circle the correct words.

1.   **637**   a. six hundred and thirty-seven
              b. sixty hundred and thirty-seven

2.   **2,851**   a. two hundred thousand, eight hundred and fifty-one
                b. two thousand eight hundred and fifty-one

3.   **90,004**   a. ninety hundred and four
                 b. ninety thousand and four

4.   **500,896**   a. fifty hundred thousand, eight hundred and ninety-six
                  b. five hundred thousand, eight hundred and ninety-six

2 Language focus

A Complete the conversation.

Jack Whew! It's hot today. _____ you like a drink?

Paul Yes, _____ . I'm really thirsty.

Jack What drinks do you like?

Paul Is _____ any juice or iced tea?

Jack There's juice, but there isn't _____ iced tea.

Paul Oh. How _____ juice do you have?

Jack There's a _____ juice. But there's a
_____ of soda. _____ you like a soda?

Paul No, _____ . I'd like _____ juice.

B Answer the questions with the sentences in the box.

> ☐ Hilda does.   ☐ It's cold and snowy.   ☐ They like basketball and soccer.
> ☐ I like math and art.   ☐ No, you can't.

1. What subjects do you like?

   _____

2. What's the weather like in New York in winter?

   _____

3. Who speaks German?

   _____

4. Can you go canoeing in a hot spring?

   _____

5. What sports do they like?

   _____

C Complete the lists with the words in the boxes.

> ☐ apples   ☐ cookies   ☐ mayonnaise   ☐ pepper   ☐ spoons   ☐ vegetable soup

How much . . . ?   _____   _____   _____
How many . . . ?   _____   _____   _____

> ☐ butter   ☐ knives   ☐ plates   ☐ water

There's a little . . .   _____   _____
There are a few . . .   _____   _____

3 Reading

A Read Tara's e-mail reply to Jake.

> **From: Tara**
>
> Hi, Jake!   July 28
> I'm so happy you're coming to Greece next week!
> Here are the answers to some of your questions.
> >>>>>> How's the weather in August?
> It's usually hot and sunny. But it's cloudy and warm today.
> >>>>>> Can you take a boat ride around the islands?
> Yes, you can. You can see some incredible things!
> >>>>>> Who speaks English in your family?
> My father, my sister, and I do. My mother doesn't speak any English.
> >>>>>> What sports do you play?
> I play soccer and tennis. My sister likes basketball and swimming.
> That's it. Bring your bathing suit and sunscreen!
> See you Sunday.
> Tara

Picture

B Are these sentences true or false? Check (✓) T (true) or F (false).

	T	F
1. The weather is usually cloudy and warm in Greece in August.	☐	☐
2. You can take a boat ride around the Greek islands.	☐	☐
3. Tara's mother speaks English.	☐	☐
4. Tara plays soccer, and her sister does, too.	☐	☐
5. Jake is going to Greece in August.	☐	☐

4 Writing

Imagine that an English-speaking friend wants to visit you. Complete the e-mail to your friend. Use the questions to help you.

> What can you do or see?   What's the weather usually like?
> What sports or fun things do you do?   Who speaks English in your family?

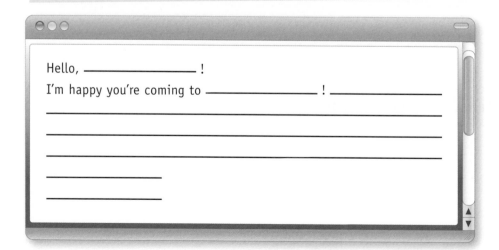

> Hello, _____ !
> I'm happy you're coming to _____ ! _____
> _____
> _____
> _____
> _____
> _____

Answer Key for Extra Practice

Note: *Multiple answers in a single sentence or by a single speaker are separated by a semicolon (;).*
Alternative answers are separated by a slash (/).

Unit 1 • All About You and Me

1 Word work

A Answers will vary.
Here are some examples:
Animals
cat
dog
parrot
rabbit
snake
spider
Places in a neighborhood
mall
bank
bookstore
candy store
gym
library
movie theater
music store
park
restaurant
school
store
tennis courts
video arcade
Sports
baseball
basketball
Ping-Pong
soccer
swimming
tennis
volleyball
Talents
dance
draw
play an instrument
play sports
speak languages
tell jokes

B Answers will vary.

2 What's wrong?

1. My <u>name's</u> Jane Roberts.
2. I'm <u>a</u> student at Central School.
3. <u>I'm</u> from Canada.
4. I don't like snakes <u>very much</u> / <u>at all</u>.
5. I'm pretty good <u>at</u> math.
6. I'm in Mr. <u>Green's</u> math class.

Unit 2 • Our Lives and Routines

1 Word work

1. <u>go</u> out; d
2. <u>watch</u> DVDs; f
3. <u>do</u> my homework; e
4. <u>eat</u> dinner; a
5. <u>collect</u> stamps; c
6. <u>practice</u> the piano; b

2 What's wrong?

1. I don't eat lunch at home.
2. He teaches English at my school.
3. They don't hang out at the mall.
4. I go to school with my brother.
5. At 8:30, I watch TV.
6. She doesn't have an electric keyboard.

Extra Practice • 1 & 2

1 Vocabulary

A 1. c
2. f
3. e
4. a
5. b
6. d

B 1. friendly
2. interesting
3. artistic
4. athletic
5. musical

C *eat* breakfast, dinner
   go home, to bed
   play soccer, the guitar
   teach English, history

2 Language focus

A Luke <u>Who's</u> she?
Peter She's <u>my</u> sister.
Luke <u>What's</u> her name?
Peter Her <u>name's</u> Marie.
Luke She's very <u>good</u> at basketball.
Peter She's very <u>athletic</u>.
Luke Is there a basketball <u>court</u> in your neighborhood?
Peter Marie <u>practices</u> after school every day.
Luke <u>Do</u> you practice, too?
Peter I'm <u>not</u> good at sports at all!

B 1. She doesn't like dogs a little. She likes dogs a lot.
2. She doesn't live in an apartment. She lives in a house.
3. She doesn't have three brothers. She has one brother.
4. There aren't five cats in the yard. There's one cat (in the yard).
5. Her brother doesn't play baseball. He plays soccer.

C 1. She
2. you
3. She
4. I
5. I

3 Reading

B 1. Manuel
2. Martina
3. Manuel
4. Antonio
5. Martina

4 Writing

A Answers will vary.

B Possible answer:
Hi! My name's Joe. I'm 12 years old. I'm from Canada. I like sports and music. I'm good at basketball. My friend's name is Paul. He's 13. He's from Canada, too. He likes video games and sports. He's good at math.

Unit 3 • Sports and Activities

1 Word work

A 1. soap
2. flashlight
3. campfire
4. pillow
5. blanket
6. sunscreen
7. raincoat
8. towel

B 1. baseball
2. helmet
3. karate
4. goggles
5. ski boots
6. swimming
7. gloves
8. biking
9. skateboard
10. canoeing

2 What's wrong?

1. Does he <u>do</u> karate at 8:30?
2. Don't <u>get</u> up early.
3. <u>What</u> time do they do arts and crafts?
4. Skateboarders <u>don't</u> wear goggles.
5. When <u>does</u> Jenny go hiking?
6. Soccer players wear <u>uniforms</u>.

Unit 4 • My Interests

1 Word work

1. The adventure DVD is twenty-one thirty-nine / twenty-one dollars and thirty-nine cents.
2. The travel vest is forty-two dollars.
3. The wall calendar is twelve eighty-eight / twelve dollars and eighty-eight cents.
4. The star map is nineteen ninety-nine / nineteen dollars and ninety-nine cents.
5. The nature puzzle is nine dollars.
6. The science kit is fifty-four seventy-nine / fifty-four dollars and seventy-nine cents.

2 What's wrong?

1. I hardly ever talk in class.
2. The video sets are $24.99.
3. How much are the pop CDs?
4. I don't like them at all.
5. I like to go shopping.
6. He's great. I like him a lot.

Extra Practice • 3 & 4

1 Vocabulary

A
1. hiking boots
2. blanket
3. raincoat
4. pillow
5. helmet
6. goggles
7. flashlight
8. towel
9. sleeping bag

B
1. do
2. cook
3. go
4. tell
5. take
6. make

C
1. country
2. jazz
3. classical
4. pop
5. rock

2 Language focus

A
Sandy	How <u>much</u> are those hiking boots?
Scott	<u>They're</u> $49.99.
Sandy	<u>Do</u> you and your family like to go camping?
Scott	Yes, <u>we</u> do.
Sandy	<u>When</u> do you go camping?
Scott	We go <u>every</u> summer.
Sandy	<u>Does</u> your sister go hiking?
Scott	She always goes hiking, but she <u>hardly ever</u> goes horseback riding.
Sandy	I like <u>them</u> both a lot.
Scott	<u>Don't</u> forget your sunscreen!

B
1. Soccer players don't wear helmets.
2. Basketball players don't wear goggles.
3. We do arts and crafts at 10:15.
4. Don't listen to the radio.
5. I do karate in the afternoon.
6. Campers tell stories at night.

C
1. them
2. are
3. writes
4. are
5. like to
6. He always

3 Reading

B
1. F		4. F	
2. T		5. T	
3. F			

4 Writing

A Answers will vary.

B Possible answer:
Julia and I are busy teens. Julia likes to watch TV. I watch TV a lot, too. We like to listen to music and hang out with friends. I like to talk on the phone, but Julia likes to send text messages to her friends. Julia likes to play sports, but I think sports are boring. I like to play the piano, but she doesn't play an instrument. We both love to read books.

Unit 5 • Favorite Activities

1 Word work
1. They take a boat ride.
2. You throw a Frisbee.
3. I fly a kite.
4. You try on a jacket.
5. They wait for the green light.
6. I float on a raft.
7. You stand in line.
8. They sail a boat.

2 What's wrong?

A Hello, Lars!
I'm <u>in</u> the beach! My sister <u>are</u> playing in the sand. She <u>are</u> happy. My brother is swimming. My dad is <u>float</u> on a raft. My mom and aunt <u>is</u> taking pictures. Uncle Tim is <u>sail</u> a boat, I'm collecting <u>seashell</u>. I'm <u>don't</u> swimming. <u>We's</u> having a great time!
See you soon!
Joy

B
1. at
2. is
3. is
4. floating
5. are
6. sailing
7. seashells
8. not
9. We're

Unit 6 • Entertainment

1 Word work
1. v
2. adj
3. n
4. adj

5. v
6. adj
7. adj
8. v
9. n
10. n

2 What's wrong?

1. action
2. blond
3. restaurant
4. movies
5. fascinating
6. relax

Extra Practice • 5 & 6

1 Vocabulary

A 1. visit a museum
2. try on a coat
3. throw a Frisbee
4. wait for a green light
5. take pictures
6. collect seashells
7. sail a boat
8. fly a kite
9. buy souvenirs
10. float on a raft

B 1. robots
2. musicians
3. movies
4. teams
5. animals

C boring; incredible; belt; racket; go shopping

2 Language focus

A 1. They're eating cake and opening presents.
2. She isn't throwing trash in the trash can.
3. Are you playing in the sand?
4. He's going to a concert in the park.
5. Is your father eating dinner in a restaurant?

B 1. They're looking at jewelry.
2. No, she isn't. She's taking a boat ride.
3. No, they aren't. They're at the movie theater / watching a movie.
4. Yes, they are. They're relaxing at home.
5. I'm trying on a scarf.

C 4
2
5
3
1

3 Reading

B 1. She's writing the postcard in Honolulu / at the beach.
2. Yes, he is.
3. Justin is / He's playing in the sand.
4. Jan is / He's collecting seashells.
5. Her grandparents are / They're buying souvenirs at the hotel.

4 Writing

Answers will vary. Possible answer:
Hi, Lynne!
I'm in Australia. I'm having a wonderful time. We're at the beach. My mom and dad are relaxing at the beach. My sister is swimming in the ocean, and my cousin is collecting seashells. My grandparents are floating on rafts. We're having fun!
See you soon!
Jeannie

Unit 7 • What We Eat

1 Word work

A 1. bread
2. butter
3. cheese
4. fruit
5. iced tea
6. ketchup
7. lettuce
8. mayonnaise
9. milk
10. pasta
11. pepper
12. rice
13. salt
14. soup
15. water

B 1. apple
2. banana
3. cup
4. egg
5. fork
6. hamburger
7. knife
8. plate
9. potato
10. spoon

2 What's wrong?

1. There are three <u>hamburgers</u>.
2. I don't like <u>butter</u>.
3. We have a little <u>fruit</u>.
4. There are <u>a lot of</u> forks.
5. How <u>much</u> lettuce is there?
6. There's <u>some</u> mustard in the cabinet.

Unit 8 • The Natural World

1 Word work

1. cold
2. Germany
3. one hundred thousand
4. cave
5. windy
6. Italian
7. mountain
8. warm
9. one hundred
10. island

2 What's wrong?

1. What's the weather usually <u>like</u> in August in Australia?
2. Who <u>lives</u> in Greece?
3. What subjects <u>do</u> you like?
4. <u>What's</u> the weather like in July?
5. You can <u>go</u> canoeing in summer.
6. <u>It's</u> warm and sunny today.

Extra Practice • 7 & 8

1 Vocabulary

A 1. ketchup
2. broccoli
3. carrot cake
4. jelly
5. potatoes
6. pasta
7. milk
8. eggs
9. bananas
10. cheese

B 1. German
2. Arabic
3. Portugal
4. Russia
5. Italy
6. Greece

C 1. a
2. b
3. b
4. b

2 Language focus

A Jack <u>Would</u> you like a drink?
Paul Yes, <u>please</u>.
Jack What drinks do you like?
Paul Is <u>there</u> any juice or iced tea?
Jack There's juice, but there isn't <u>any</u> iced tea.
Paul How <u>much</u> juice do you have?
Jack There's a <u>little</u> juice. But there's a <u>lot</u> of soda. <u>Would</u> you like a soda?
Paul No, <u>thanks</u>. I'd like <u>some</u> juice.

B 1. I like math and art.
2. It's cold and snowy.
3. Hilda does.
4. No, you can't.
5. They like basketball and soccer.

C *How much:* mayonnaise, pepper, vegetable soup
How many: apples, cookies, spoons
There's a little: butter, water
There are a few: knives, plates

3 Reading

B 1. F
2. T
3. F
4. F
5. T

4 Writing

Answers will vary. Possible answer:
Hello, Luke!
I'm happy you're coming to Brazil! The weather is usually hot and sunny in January. We can go swimming and go sightseeing. My mom and my brother speak English, but my father doesn't. I like to skateboard and play video games.
See you Sunday.
Paulo

Introduction to Extra Speaking Practice

Included in this section is a photocopiable package of Extra Speaking Practice. This package contains eight Extra Speaking Practice worksheets, one for each unit in *Connect*. These Extra Speaking Practice worksheets, most of which are interactive conversations, give students an additional opportunity to practice and personalize the new language and skills they learned in each unit.

Features of Extra Speaking Practice

- The content of Extra Speaking Practice is strictly limited to the language and skills presented and practiced in the lessons in each unit of the Student's Book.

- The focus of each Extra Speaking Practice exercise is on the specific language and skills of the corresponding unit, but does assume knowledge of previous units' content.

- Many exercise types in the Extra Speaking Practice, such as completing conversations, asking and answering questions, speaking with classmates, and playing guessing games, are similar to those in the lessons, while others extend the activity types by giving students multiple opportunities to practice interactive role plays.

- The Extra Speaking Practice worksheets provide students with an opportunity to practice the vocabulary and grammar in each unit in a natural context while fostering communication and community in the classroom.

Assigning Extra Speaking Practice worksheets

- These worksheets are intended to be done in class, usually in pairs.
- Make a copy of the Extra Speaking Practice worksheet(s) for each student in your class.
- Have students practice the conversations in pairs or in small groups.
- Walk around and help as needed.
- Check answers with the class.
- Invite volunteers to read their conversations to the class.

List of Extra Speaking Practice Exercises

Unit 1   All About You and Me

1 Practice

A Complete the questions. Ask a classmate all of the questions, and write his or her answers. Then complete the sentences.

1. **Q:** When's _____ birthday? **A:** _____
_____'s birthday is in _____ .

2. **Q:** How _____ are you? **A:** _____
He's / She's _____ .

3. **Q:** Are you good at _____ ? **A:** _____
He's / She's _____ .

4. **Q:** I like _____ . How about you? **A:** _____
He / She _____ .

5. **Q:** I don't like _____ . How about you? **A:** _____
He / She _____ .

B Now share something about your partner with two more classmates.

> Joe's birthday is in ...... He's ...

2 Practice

A Complete the chart with five things you like a lot. Then find five classmates who like the same things. Write their names.

> I like ......a lot. How about you?

> I like ......a little.

> I like it a lot, too.

> I don't like ......very much.

I like ... a lot.	Classmates
1.	
2.	
3.	
4.	
5.	

B Share one of the things that both you and a classmate like.

> ......and I both like ......a lot.

Photocopiable   **Extra Speaking Practice   T-165**

Unit 2 Our Lives and Routines

1 Practice

A Take a survey. Find a classmate for each activity in the chart. Write their names.

George, do you ...... every day?   Yes, I do.

Activity	Classmates
1. watch TV	
2. eat lunch at school	
3. do homework	
4. listen to music	
5. stay up late	

B Now write the results of your survey.

George watches TV every day.

1. _____

2. _____

3. _____

4. _____

5. _____

2 Practice

Work with a classmate. Read the questions and guess your partner's answers. Then ask your classmate the questions. Were your guesses correct?

Do you . . . ?	Your guesses		Classmate's answers	
	Yes	No	Yes	No
1. hang out with friends	☐	☐	☐	☐
2. stay home on Sunday	☐	☐	☐	☐
3. go out on Friday night	☐	☐	☐	☐
4. eat out with your family	☐	☐	☐	☐
5. go to the movies on the weekend	☐	☐	☐	☐
6. go to bed at 9:30 p.m.	☐	☐	☐	☐
7. talk on the phone every day	☐	☐	☐	☐
8. sleep late on the weekend	☐	☐	☐	☐

Number of correct guesses _____

Photocopiable   © Cambridge University Press 2009

Unit 3 Sports and Activities

Daily Schedule for Camp Busy Bee

Activity	Time
1. go hiking	8:30
2. go canoeing	9:15
3. take swimming lessons	
4. cook hot dogs	11:30
5. water-ski	
6. play baseball	1:30
7. go biking	
8. skateboard	4:45

Classmate 1: Work with a classmate. Take turns asking and answering questions to complete the daily schedule for Camp Busy Bee. Then compare your schedules. Are they the same?

Classmate 1 What time do they _go hiking_ ?
Classmate 2 They go hiking at _8:30_ .

Classmate 2: Work with a classmate. Take turns asking and answering questions to complete the daily schedule for Camp Busy Bee. Then compare your schedules. Are they the same?

Classmate 2 What time do they _go canoeing_ ?
Classmate 1 They go canoeing at _9:15_ .

Daily Schedule for Camp Busy Bee	
Activity	**Time**
1. go hiking	8:30
2. go canoeing	_9:15_
3. take swimming lessons	10:45
4. cook hot dogs	
5. water-ski	12:45
6. play baseball	
7. go biking	3:00
8. skateboard	

Photocopiable

Unit 4 My Interests

Classmate 1: Complete the survey for yourself. Then ask a classmate the questions. How many answers are the same? How many are different?

(Do you like to go dancing, Mike?) (No, I don't!)

Same as Classmate 2: _____   Different from Classmate 2: _____

	Your answers		Classmate 2's answers	
	Yes	No	Yes	No
1. Do you like to go dancing?	☐	☐	☐	☐
2. Do you sometimes sleep in class?	☐	☐	☐	☐
3. Do you like rock music a lot?	☐	☐	☐	☐
4. Do you always do your homework?	☐	☐	☐	☐
5. Do you like to write poetry?	☐	☐	☐	☐
6. Do you like to play video games?	☐	☐	☐	☐
7. Do you often come to class on time?	☐	☐	☐	☐
8. Do you like to cook?	☐	☐	☐	☐
9. Do you like to listen to jazz?	☐	☐	☐	☐
10. Do you like to spend time at the beach?	☐	☐	☐	☐

Classmate 2: Complete the survey for yourself. Then ask a classmate the questions. How many answers are the same? How many are different?

(Do you like to go shopping, Claire?) (Yes, I do!)

Same as Classmate 1: _____   Different from Classmate 1: _____

	Your answers		Classmate 1's answers	
	Yes	No	Yes	No
1. Do you like to go shopping?	☐	☐	☐	☐
2. Do you always listen to the teacher in class?	☐	☐	☐	☐
3. Do you like classical music a lot?	☐	☐	☐	☐
4. Do you usually come to class on time?	☐	☐	☐	☐
5. Do you like to write e-mails to friends?	☐	☐	☐	☐
6. Do you like to play tennis?	☐	☐	☐	☐
7. Do you like to do crossword puzzles?	☐	☐	☐	☐
8. Do you sometimes go bowling?	☐	☐	☐	☐
9. Do you often go to bed by 10:00 p.m.?	☐	☐	☐	☐
10. Do you like to spend time at video arcades?	☐	☐	☐	☐

Unit 5 Favorite Activities

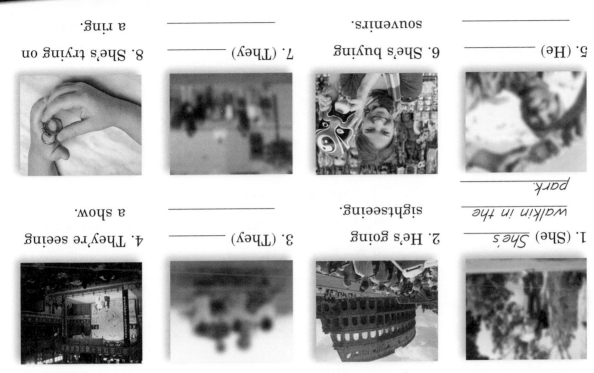

5. (He) _____

6. She's buying souvenirs.

7. (They) _____

8. She's trying on a ring.

1. (She) *She's walkin in the park.*

2. He's going sightseeing.

3. (They) _____

4. They're seeing a show.

Classmate 1: What are they doing? Ask a classmate questions, and write the answers.

Classmate 1 Number one. What's she doing?
Classmate 2 She's walking in the park.

Classmate 2: What are they doing? Ask a classmate questions, and write the answers.

Classmate 2 Number two. What's he doing?
Classmate 1 He's going sightseeing.

1. She's walking in the park.

2. (He) *He's going sightseeing.*

3. They're having a picnic.

4. (They) _____

5. He's taking a picture.

6. (She) _____

7. They're waiting for the green light.

8. (She) _____

Photocopiable

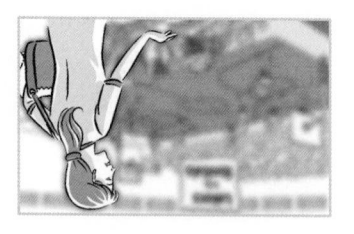

1. He's going to the science exhibit.

2. *They're going to the movie festival.*

3. She's going to the Nature Center.

4. _____

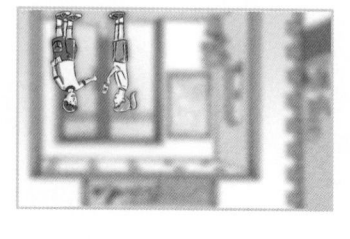

5. They're going to the concert.

6. _____

Classmate 2: Where are the people going? Ask a classmate. Write the answers.

Classmate 2 Number two. Where are they going?
Classmate 1 They're going to the movie festival.

Classmate 1: Where are the people going? Ask a classmate. Write the answers.

Classmate 1 Number one. Where's he going?
Classmate 2 He's going to the science exhibit.

1. *He's going to the science exhibit.*

2. They're going to the movie festival.

3. _____

4. She's going to the basketball game.

5. _____

6. He's going to the circus.

Unit 6 Entertainment

Unit 7 — What We Eat

1 Practice

A You're having a party! Ask five classmates what they would like to eat or drink at your party. Complete the chart.

> What would you like to eat or drink at my party?

> I'd like to . . .

Classmates	Food or drinks
1.	
2.	
3.	
4.	
5.	

B Use the results in Part A to make a shopping list. Add two things you would like to eat or drink. Share your list with a group of classmates. Who has the best list?

Shopping List for Party

Item   Classmates

1. _____ (for _____)
2. _____ (for _____)
3. _____ (for _____)
4. _____ (for _____)
5. _____ (for _____)

And I'd like _____ and _____ .

2 Practice

A Write the names of five different classmates and five food items in the chart. Then ask those classmates how much or how many of each food item is in their kitchen. Use *a little, a few, a lot, no,* or *some* in the answers.

> Kristen, how much pasta is in your kitchen?

> There's a little pasta in my kitchen.

Classmates	Food	Amount
1.		
2.		
3.		
4.		
5.		

B Share one of your results with the class.

> There's a little pasta in Kristen's kitchen.

Photocopiable

Unit 8 The Natural World

 Kate
 Tim
 Luke
 Keesha
 Bob

1. lives in Morocco
2. plays the piano
3. speaks Portuguese
4. likes history
5. collects stamps

Classmate 1 Who lives in Morocco?
Classmate 2 Luke lives in Morocco.

**Classmate 1: Who likes or does these things? Ask a classmate questions with Who . . . ?
Draw lines to match each activity to the correct person.**

**Classmate 2: Who likes or does these things? Ask a classmate questions with Who . . . ?
Draw lines to match each activity to the correct person.**

Classmate 2 Who likes science?
Classmate 1 Lisa likes science.

1. likes science 2. speaks Russian 3. lives in Portugal 4. collects T-shirts 5. plays the guitar

 Steve
 Jenna
 Lisa
 Tyler
 Jake

Answers for Classmate 1
1. Luke lives in Morocco.   4. Tim likes history.
2. Bob plays the piano.   5. Keesha collects stamps.
3. Kate speaks Portuguese.

Answer Key for Extra Speaking Practice

Note: *Multiple answers in a single sentence or by a single speaker are separated by a semicolon (;).*
Alternative answers are separated by a slash (/).

Unit 1 • All About You and Me

1 Practice

A Answers will vary.
Possible answers:
1. When's <u>your</u> birthday?
   <u>My birthday's in May.</u>
   <u>(Joe's)</u> birthday is in <u>May</u>.
2. How <u>old</u> are you?
   <u>I'm 13.</u>
   He's <u>13 / 13 years old</u>.
3. Are you good at <u>soccer</u>?
   <u>Yes, I am.</u>
   She's <u>good at soccer</u>.
4. I like <u>dogs</u>. How about you?
   <u>I like dogs very much.</u>
   He <u>likes dogs very much</u>.
5. I don't like <u>cats</u>. How about you?
   <u>I don't like cats at all.</u>
   She <u>doesn't like cats at all</u>.

B Answers will vary.

2 Practice

Answers will vary.

Unit 2 • Our Lives and Routines

1 Practice

A and B
Answers will vary.
Possible answers:
1. Jimmy watches TV every day.
2. Lisa eats lunch at school every day.
3. Paula does homework every day.
4. Nina listens to music every day.
5. Tommy stays up late every day.

2 Practice

Answers will vary.

Unit 3 • Sports and Activities

1. go hiking 8:30
2. go canoeing 9:15
3. take swimming lessons 10:45
4. cook hot dogs 11:30
5. water-ski 12:45
6. play baseball 1:30
7. go biking 3:00
8. skateboard 4:45

Unit 4 • My Interests

Answers will vary.

Unit 5 • Favorite Activities

1. What's she doing? She's walking in the park.
2. What's he doing? He's going sightseeing.
3. What are they doing? They're having a picnic.
4. What are they doing? They're seeing a show.
5. What's he doing? He's taking a picture.
6. What's she doing? She's buying souvenirs.
7. What are they doing? They're waiting for the green light.
8. What's she doing? She's trying on a ring.

Unit 6 • Entertainment

1. Where's he going? He's going to the science exhibit.
2. Where are they going? They're going to the movie festival.
3. Where's she going? She's going to the Nature Center.
4. Where's she going? She's going to the basketball game.
5. Where are they going? They're going to the concert.
6. Where's he going? He's going to the circus.

Unit 7 • What We Eat

1 Practice

Answers will vary.

2 Practice

A Answers will vary.
Possible answers:
1. a little milk
2. a few potatoes
3. a lot of fruit
4. no jelly
5. some ham

B Answers will vary.

Unit 8 • The Natural World

Classmate 1 answers:
1. Luke lives in Morocco.
2. Bob plays the piano.
3. Kate speaks Portuguese.
4. Tim likes history.
5. Keesha collects stamps.

Classmate 2 answers:
1. Lisa likes science.
2. Jake speaks Russian.
3. Steve lives in Portugal.
4. Jenna collects T-shirts.
5. Tyler plays the guitar.

Introduction to Quizzes

Included in this section is a photocopiable evaluation package. This package contains eight short Quizzes, one for each unit in *Connect*. These Quizzes give students an awareness of their own progress and teachers an awareness of the language points and skills in which their students need further practice.

Features of Quizzes

- The content of the Quizzes is strictly limited to the language and skills presented and practiced in the lessons in each unit of the Student's Book.
- The focus of each Quiz is on the specific language and skills of the corresponding unit, but does assume knowledge of previous units' content.
- Exercise types in the Quizzes are similar to those in the lessons.
- The focus of the Quizzes is both on vocabulary and on language skills.

Giving and scoring Quizzes

- The Quizzes are paper-and-pencil ones. Each unit Quiz is one page. Make a copy of the Quiz for each student in your class.
- Suggested scores are provided for each Quiz. Scores can help students see their own progress and what they need to study. Teachers are encouraged to adapt the use of the Quizzes to their own classroom needs.
- Teachers can also give marks for class participation since this also contributes to student learning.
- Students might retake tests to monitor their progress and build confidence. The goal is for students to do well on the Quizzes, as performance can be both a positive motivator and a confidence builder.

Unit 1 Quiz

Name: _____

Date: _____

A What's next? Check (✓) the correct responses.

1. Where are you from?
   ☐ It's in Colombia.
   ☐ I'm from Colombia.

2. Is there a swimming pool in your neighborhood?
   ☐ No, there isn't.
   ☐ No, there aren't.

3. She's not good at basketball.
   ☐ Yes. She's athletic.
   ☐ No. But she's artistic.

4. I don't like spiders at all.
   ☐ Yeah, they're not bad.
   ☐ Yeah, they're not very cute.

5. Who are they?
   ☐ He's my math teacher.
   ☐ My friends.

15 (3 points each)

B Match. Write the letters.

1. I'm not from _____   a. tennis courts.
2. There are no _____   b. parrots very much.
3. She's not _____   c. Puerto Rico.
4. He's pretty good _____ d. very friendly.
5. I don't like _____   e. at science.

15 (3 points each)

C Check (✓) the correct sentences.

1. ☐ I'm from Mr. Brown's math class.
   ☐ I'm in Mr. Brown's math class.

2. ☐ When's your birthday?
   ☐ What's your birthday?

3. ☐ There's isn't a big mall.
   ☐ There's no big mall.

4. ☐ He's much good at music.
   ☐ He's pretty good at music.

5. ☐ I like dogs and cats at all.
   ☐ I like dogs and cats a lot.

20 (4 points each)

Quiz Total: _____ out of 50

Photocopiable

Unit 2 Quiz

A Match. Write the letters.

1. practice _____   a. dance lessons
2. do _____   b. TV
3. eat _____   c. the piano
4. watch _____   d. dinner
5. collect _____   e. homework
6. listen to _____   f. stamps
7. take _____   g. home
8. stay _____   h. music

16 (2 points each)

B Complete the conversation. Circle the correct words.

Diane   You're good at the piano. (Are you / Do you) practice a lot?

Christine   Yes, I (don't / do). I (practice / practices) every day. I love music. (Do you / Does she) play the piano?

Diane   No, I (don't / doesn't). I (play / plays) the guitar a little. But I don't (take / takes) lessons.

14 (2 points each)

C Complete the sentences. Write the correct form of the verbs.

1. My best friend _____ (speak) three languages.

2. She _____ (live) in Brazil.

3. My mother _____ (go) to the movies every Friday.

4. My father _____ (watch) TV after dinner.

5. My brother _____ (play) on the school basketball team.

10 (2 points each)

D Complete the sentences. Circle the correct words.

1. (I / She) doesn't hang out at the mall.

2. (I / He) eats lunch at school.

3. She (doesn't / don't) like rock music.

4. I (doesn't / don't) play soccer.

5. (I / He) don't get up early on Saturday.

10 (2 points each)

Quiz Total: _____ out of 50

Name: _____

Date: _____

A Match each word in Column A to a word in Column B to make the name of an item. Then write the name of the item.

Column A

1. after _____
2. flash _____
3. sun _____
4. skate _____
5. rain _____
6. water- _____
7. hot _____
8. horse _____
9. base _____
10. camp _____

Column B

a. board _____
b. ball _____
c. fire _____
d. back _____
e. noon _____
f. dogs _____
g. light _____
h. ski _____
i. screen _____
j. coat _____

20 (2 points each)

B Match the questions to the correct answers.

1. Does she swim? _____
2. When does she swim? _____
3. Do they swim? _____
4. Does he swim? _____
5. What time do they swim? _____

a. No, he doesn't.
b. Yes, they do.
c. They swim at 4:00.
d. In the afternoon.
e. Yes, she does.

15 (3 points each)

C Complete the sentences. Circle the correct words.

1. Swimmers (doesn't / don't) wear helmets.
2. Does he (do / does) karate?
3. (Doesn't / Don't) bring your cell phone.
4. (What / When) time do you go hiking?
5. They do arts and crafts (in the / at) evening.

15 (3 points each)

Quiz Total: _____ out of 50

Photocopiable

Name: _____

Date: _____

A Circle the word that doesn't belong in each box.

Rock	Singer	Get good grades	Time	Money
country	musician	go shopping	always	cent
cook	band	do homework	much	dollar
jazz	DVD	listen to the teacher	never	hundred

10 (2 points each)

B Complete the conversation with the words in the box.

☐ him   ☐ how much are   ☐ how much is   ☐ it   ☐ it   ☐ it's   ☐ them   ☐ they're

Lou   This music store is really big. It has lots of CDs and DVDs.

Colin Oh, here are the rock CDs. I really like rock music. I listen to _____ all the time. Oh, here's the new CD by Bruce Springsteen. I like _____ a lot.

Lou   _____ it?

Colin _____ twenty-two fifty. That's not too expensive. I can get _____ .

Lou   Look at those posters of the rock group Coldplay. I like _____ a lot.

Colin _____ the posters?

Lou   Actually, _____ free when you buy the CD.

16 (2 points each)

C Complete the sentences. Circle the correct words.

1. I love to go shopping. I (always / never) go to the mall on Saturday.
2. Classical music is boring. I (always / hardly ever) listen to it.
3. I don't usually sleep late, but I (sometimes / never) sleep late on Saturday.
4. I like music, and I (like / like to) go dancing on Saturday night.
5. I like to (go camping / camping) in the summer.
6. My friends like (to spend / spend) time at the video arcade.
7. Alicia Keys is a great singer. I love (her / she)!
8. I have a lot of CDs. I listen to (it / them) a lot.
9. I (don't / doesn't) like to go camping.
10. I (usually / never) watch movies at home. I hardly ever go to the movie theater.
11. Cats are cute. I like (them / it) a lot.
12. How much (is / are) the boots?

24 (2 points each)

Quiz Total: ____ out of 50

A Circle the word that doesn't belong in each box.

museum	boat	bike path	baseball bat	belt
sand	Frisbee	green light	bracelet	scarf
seashells	kite	picnic area	tennis racket	trolley

B Complete the conversation with the present continuous.

Ryan Hello, Dave. It's Ryan. What _____ (you / do)?

Dave _____ (I / eat) lunch in the park. I'm with Jane. _____ (She / sit) right next to me. _____ (We / have) a picnic. What are you doing? Come and join us.

Ryan Thanks. _____ (I / not / do) anything special. Can I bring some food?

Dave No. We have lots of food. See you soon! Bye!

C Check (✓) the correct responses.

1. Is she collecting seashells?
   ☐ Yes, she does.
   ☐ Yes, she is.

2. What are you doing?
   ☐ They're walking in the park.
   ☐ We're walking in the park.

3. Are they standing in line?
   ☐ No, they aren't.
   ☐ No, they don't.

4. What's she trying on?
   ☐ A bracelet.
   ☐ A surfboard.

5. Are you waiting for the green light?
   ☐ Yes, you are.
   ☐ Yes, I am.

Unit 6 Quiz

Name: _____

Date: _____

A Complete the sentences with the words in the box.

☐ action movies   ☐ animated movies   ☐ comedies   ☐ dramas   ☐ horror movies

1. I really like funny movies. So I usually go to _____ .
2. _____ sometimes have cartoon characters like the Simpsons.
3. My friends like scary movies. We always see all the new _____ .
4. _____ are never boring. Something is happening all the time.
5. Kim likes serious movies. So she often goes to _____ .

10 (2 points each)

B Complete the chart with the words in the box.

☐ average height ☐ curly ☐ heavy ☐ long ☐ medium-length ☐ slim ☐ straight ☐ tall

Height	Body type	Hair length	Hairstyle

8 (1 point each)

C Complete the sentences with the simple present or the present continuous.

1. I usually _____ (hang out) with my friends after school. Today
   I _____ (do) my homework in the library.
2. Today my sister _____ (watch) TV, but she usually
   _____ (practice) the piano after school.
3. Tonight we _____ (eat) in a restaurant, but we usually
   _____ (eat) at home.
4. My uncles usually _____ (play) cards at family parties, but today
   they _____ (play) party games.
5. A Where _____ (you / go)?
   B _____ (we / go) to the movies.
   _____ (you / want to) come with us?

22 (2 points each)

D Complete the sentences. Circle the correct words.

1. Jeremy (has / is) average height.
2. Ella (wants / wants to) watch the game on TV.
3. My brothers (have / are) long hair.
4. A Do you want go to the concert?
   B Yes, I (come / do).
5. A Do you want to play cards?
   B No, I (don't / don't want).

10 (2 points each)

Quiz Total: _____ out of 50

Name: _____

Date: _____

A Circle the word that doesn't belong in each box.

forks	ketchup	iced tea	broccoli	bread
knives	mayonnaise	jelly	eggs	carrot cake
pasta	mustard	juice	lettuce	chocolate cake
spoons	plate	milk	potatoes	pie

10 (2 points each)

B Look at the picture. Complete the sentences. Circle the correct words.

1. We have (few / a lot of) cups.
2. There isn't (no / any) chicken on the plate.
3. (How much / How many) fruit do we have?
4. There is (a lot of / a little) fruit.
5. (How much / How many) eggs do we have?
6. There are (much / a lot of) eggs.
7. There is (a little / a few) jelly.
8. There (isn't any cookie / aren't any cookies).

24 (3 points each)

C Match. Write the letters.

1. Would you _____   a. milk is there?
2. How much _____   b. eggs do we have?
3. Is there _____   c. pasta?
4. What's your _____   d. any meat?
5. How many _____   e. any forks?
6. Are there _____   f. favorite appetizer?
7. What kind of _____   g. dessert would you like?
8. Do we have any _____   h. like dessert?

16 (2 points each)

Quiz Total: _____ out of 50

Photocopiable

Unit 8 Quiz

A Complete the chart with the words in the box.

☐ Arabic ☐ cold ☐ Greek ☐ Portuguese ☐ sunny
☐ cave ☐ cool ☐ hot ☐ river ☐ take a boat ride
☐ climb a mountain ☐ go camping ☐ hot spring ☐ Russian ☐ warm
☐ cloudy ☐ go canoeing ☐ island ☐ snowy ☐ windy

Weather	Temperature	Places	Outdoor activities	Languages

20 (1 point each)

B Complete the conversation. Circle the correct words.

Rafael Where are you going on your family vacation this year?

Paul We're going to a hot springs resort. I'd like to go to a ranch instead.

Rafael So, (who wants / who want) to go to the resort?

Paul My grandparents (do / go). They like to sit and relax in the spring water.

Rafael What else (can you do / you can do) at the resort? (Can you play / Can you plays) sports?

Paul Yes, (you can / you do). You (can play / do play) tennis and golf, and (you can / they can) swim in the swimming pool. But you (can't go / don't go) horseback riding.

Rafael Well, swimming is fun, right? (What's / What) the weather (like / likes) there?

Paul (It's / It) not very good. (We're / It's) usually very hot and sunny. I want to stay home. I don't want to go on the trip.

Rafael Can I go?

12 (1 point each)

C Write questions for the answers. Use *Who* + verb or *What* + noun and the words in parentheses in the correct form.

1. (have / a dog) **Q:** _____ **A:** Marilyn does.
2. (language / speak) **Q:** _____ **A:** He speaks French and English.
3. (play / tennis) **Q:** _____ **A:** We do.
4. (pets / have) **Q:** _____ **A:** We have a dog and a parrot.
5. (like / ice cream) **Q:** _____ **A:** I do!
6. (instrument / play) **Q:** _____ **A:** She plays the guitar and the piano.

18 (3 points each)

Quiz Total: ____ out of 50

Answer Key for Quizzes

Note: *Multiple answers in a single sentence or by a single speaker are separated by a semicolon (;).*

Quiz • Unit 1

A 1. I'm from Colombia.
2. No, there isn't.
3. No. But she's artistic.
4. Yeah, they're not very cute.
5. My friends.

B 1. c
2. a
3. d
4. e
5. b

C 1. I'm in Mr. Brown's math class.
2. When's your birthday?
3. There's no big mall.
4. He's pretty good at music.
5. I like dogs and cats a lot.

Quiz • Unit 2

A 1. c
2. e
3. d
4. b
5. f
6. h
7. a
8. g

B Diane   You're good at the piano. <u>Do you</u> practice a lot?

Christine   Yes, I <u>do</u>. I <u>practice</u> every day. I love music. <u>Do you</u> play the piano?

Diane   No, I <u>don't</u>. I <u>play</u> the guitar a little. But I don't <u>take</u> lessons.

C 1. speaks
2. lives
3. goes
4. watches
5. plays

D 1. She
2. He
3. doesn't
4. don't
5. I

Quiz • Unit 3

A 1. e; afternoon
2. g; flashlight
3. i; sunscreen
4. a; skateboard
5. j; raincoat
6. h; water-ski
7. f; hot dogs
8. d; horseback
9. b; baseball
10. c; campfire

B 1. e
2. d
3. b
4. a
5. c

C 1. don't
2. do
3. Don't
4. What
5. in the

Quiz • Unit 4

A cook; DVD; go shopping; much; hundred

B Lou   This music store is really big. It has lots of CDs and DVDs.

Colin   Oh, here are the rock CDs. I really like rock music. I listen to <u>it</u> all the time. Oh, here's the new CD by Bruce Springsteen. I like <u>him</u> a lot.

Lou   <u>How much is</u> it?

Colin   <u>It's</u> twenty-two fifty. That's not too expensive. I can get <u>it</u>.

Lou   Look at those posters of the rock group Coldplay. I like <u>them</u> a lot.

Colin   <u>How much are</u> the posters?

Lou   Actually, <u>they're</u> free when you buy the CD.

C 1. always
2. hardly ever
3. sometimes
4. like to
5. go camping
6. to spend
7. her

8. them
9. don't
10. usually
11. them
12. are

Quiz • Unit 5

A museum; boat; green light; bracelet; trolley

B **Ryan** Hello, Dave. It's Ryan. What <u>are you doing</u>?

Dave <u>I'm eating</u> lunch in the park. I'm with Jane. <u>She's sitting</u> right next to me. <u>We're having</u> a picnic. What are you doing? Come and join us.

Ryan Thanks. <u>I'm not doing</u> anything special. Can I bring some food?

Dave No. We have lots of food. See you soon! Bye!

C 1. Yes, she is.
2. We're walking in the park.
3. No, they aren't.
4. A bracelet.
5. Yes, I am.

Quiz • Unit 6

A 1. comedies
2. Animated movies
3. horror movies
4. Action movies
5. dramas

B *Height* average height, tall
Body type heavy, slim
Hair length long, medium-length
Hairstyle curly, straight

C 1. hang out; 'm doing
2. is watching; practices
3. 're eating; eat
4. play; 're playing
5. **A** are you going
    B We're going; Do you want to

D 1. is
2. wants to
3. have
4. do
5. I don't

Quiz • Unit 7

A pasta; plate; jelly; eggs; bread

B 1. a lot of
2. any
3. How much

4. a lot of
5. How many
6. a lot of
7. a little
8. aren't any cookies

C 1. h
2. a
3. d
4. f
5. b
6. e
7. g
8. c

Quiz • Unit 8

A *Weather* cloudy, snowy, sunny, windy
Temperature cold, cool, hot, warm
Places cave, hot spring, island, river
Outdoor activities climb a mountain, go camping, go canoeing, take a boat ride
Languages Arabic, Greek, Portuguese, Russian

B **Rafael** Where are you going on your family vacation this year?

Paul We're going to a hot springs resort. I'd like to go a ranch instead.

Rafael So, <u>who wants</u> to go to the resort?

Paul My grandparents <u>do</u>. They like to sit and relax in the spring water.

Rafael What else <u>can you do</u> at the resort? <u>Can you play</u> sports?

Paul Yes, <u>you can</u>. You <u>can play</u> tennis and golf, and <u>you can</u> swim in the swimming pool. But you <u>can't go</u> horseback riding.

Rafael Well, swimming is fun, right? <u>What's</u> the weather <u>like</u> there?

Paul <u>It's</u> not very good. <u>It's</u> usually very hot and sunny. I want to stay home. I don't want to go on the trip.

Rafael Can I go?

C 1. Who has a dog?
2. What languages does he speak?
3. Who plays tennis?
4. What pets do you have?
5. Who likes ice cream?
6. What instruments does she play?

Vocabulary Games & Activities

1 Memory game

This game reviews vocabulary.

- Choose the vocabulary words to be reviewed. There should be 15 or more words. Words do not have to be related and can be chosen randomly from the lessons in any one unit.

- Divide the class into four or five teams. Write the list of words on the board. Give students ten seconds to study the list. Then erase the list. Do not allow teams to take notes.

- Alternating turns, teams should tell you one of the words from the list. If they are able to do so, they earn a point for their team. If not, they are eliminated from the game. The team with the most points wins.

  Option For added difficulty, read the list of words two or three times instead of writing it on the board.

2 Brainstorm

This game reviews sets of related words.

- Divide the class into four or five teams. Each team should select a "secretary" to write the team's answers on the board.

- Divide the board into four or five sections (depending on the number of groups), one section per team. Tell teams which section on the board is theirs.

- Call out a category such as *clothing, school supplies, school subjects, sports, food, drinks*, etc. Give teams three minutes to write a list of words that fits the category. At the end of the time limit, say "OK! Go!"

The secretaries rush to the front to write their team's lists on the board. Give students two minutes to write their lists. Then say "Stop!" Students return to their seats.

- Go over the lists. For each appropriate word, the team earns a point. For any inappropriate or misspelled words, two points are deducted.

  Option Teams may call out additional words to their secretaries while they are at the board, but they run the risk of being overheard by the other teams.

3 That's wrong!

This game reviews spelling.

- Choose the vocabulary words to be reviewed. It should be a list of about 20 or 30 words. They can be chosen randomly from any lesson.

- Divide the class into four or five teams. Slowly write the list of words on the board, purposely misspelling random words. As soon as a team notices that a word has been misspelled, one member should stand and call out

"That's wrong!" If the word is wrong, the team must spell the word correctly. If team members are able to do so, they earn a point for their team. If not, another team is given the chance to spell the word and earn a point. The team with the most points wins. Appoint one student to be the "judge" to let you know which team called out first.

4 Last and first letters

This activity reviews previously learned vocabulary.

- Divide the class into four or five groups. Tell the first group a vocabulary word. The group must tell you another word that begins with the last letter of the word you told them.

- Their word is then passed on to the next group, who in turn, must think of a word that begins with the last letter of the first group's word. If a group is unable to think of a word, or does so incorrectly, the word is passed on to the next group. Make sure groups are given an equal number of turns.

Grammar Games & Activities

1 Standing answers

This game reviews questions and their corresponding answers.

- Write a list of *Yes / No* questions to be reviewed. For a more challenging activity, write the questions in different tenses. Then write the short answers to these questions on separate slips of paper. Make enough sets of answers so that four or five teams all have the same slips. (It would be best if there were the same number of short answers and team members.)

- Divide the class into four or five teams. Distribute the answer slips. Ask the teams to distribute the slips among team members.

- Read one of the questions out loud. Team members holding the appropriate answers to that question stand and call out their answer. If they do so correctly, they earn a point for their team. If members of different teams stand simultaneously, they may also earn points. If a team member stands inappropriately, a point is deducted.

- The team with the most points wins.

2 Everyday tic-tac-toe

This game reviews sentence patterns in the simple present and daily routines.

- Draw a tic-tac-toe grid on the board (a grid with nine squares, 3 x 3). Fill in the squares with nine verbs that describe daily routines, for example: *get up, eat, go, do, take, practice, play, listen, watch.*

- Divide the class into two teams. One team is X, and the other is O. Flip a coin to decide which team goes first. Invite a student from that team to choose a verb and make a sentence in the simple present. If the sentence is correct, erase the verb and put the letter of the student's

team (X or O) on the square. If it isn't correct, leave the verb there.

- Repeat these steps with the other team. The first team to get three Xs or Os in a row, either horizontally, vertically, or diagonally, wins the game.

- If you want students to focus on practicing the third person singular, you could tell them that each sentence has to begin with *He, She*, or a person's name. The game can also be used to practice other verb forms.

3 Q & A relay

This game reviews question-and-answer patterns.

- Write a list of four questions. Designate a strong student to be the "reader." Ask the reader to stand at the back of the room or just outside the classroom with the list of questions.

- Divide the class into four teams. Designate a fourth of the board to each team. Ask each team to choose four representatives to come to the front.

- Give the first representative of each team a piece of chalk or a whiteboard marker. Say "Go!"

- The students holding the chalk or whiteboard marker race to the reader, who reads the first question. They then race back to their designated portion of the board and write the appropriate answer.

- Upon completion of the first answer, the first students hand over the chalk or whiteboard marker to the second students, who race to the reader for the second question. Continue until all four answers have been written on the board. Keep track of which team was the quickest.

- Give a point for each correct answer and two points for speed. The team with the most points wins.

4 Right or wrong?

This game reviews sentence patterns and grammar points.

- Divide the class into four teams. Ask each team to write a list of four statements or questions. Tell them that one, some, or all of the sentences should contain a mistake.

- The first team reads one of their sentences to the second team. The second team must determine whether or not the sentence has a mistake. If they do so correctly, they

earn a point for their team. If not, the first team earns a point. If the second team thinks there is a mistake, they must identify the incorrect part and correct it. If they do so correctly, they earn another point.

- The second team then reads a sentence for the third team, and the activity is continued.

Listening Games & Activities

1 Name that unit.

This game reviews listening to the conversations.

- Divide the class into four or five teams. Tell students that they may look at their Student's Books.

- Choose any conversation from the Student's Book. Note the unit and the page number of the conversation. Choose random key phrases from the conversation and call them out to the class. Do not say complete sentences.

- As soon as a team is able to tell you the unit and the page number of the conversation, the team should call out, "I can name that unit!"

- A correct answer earns a point for that team.

2 Magic word

This activity helps keep students attentive during class.

- Choose a word or a phrase that is particularly helpful to students and write it on the corner of the board. The words or phrases can be language that you use as part of your classroom language. (A few suggestions of helpful words are *pay attention, repeat, take turns, continue, groups,* etc.)

- Tell students that at some point during the class meeting, you will say this word or phrase. If they hear you do so, they should stand and say "Magic word!" The student who does so should receive a point. At the end of two weeks or a month, the student with the most points should receive some special treat. Some reward ideas would be to choose a game for the next class meeting or bring in a pop song for students to listen to. Ask students to come up with their own ideas for rewards, which depend on your approval.

3 Finish it.

This game reviews listening to the conversations.

- Choose several conversations to be reviewed.

- Divide the class into four or five teams. Read the first two words of the first line of the conversation. Team members call out "I can finish it!" if they know the sentence. If a team can finish the sentence, they earn a point for their team. They also earn one point each for any other sentences in the conversation that they can remember. If none of the teams can complete the sentence, keep adding a word or two until they can.

4 Learning about others

This activity reviews listening to personal information.

- As a wrap-up to every lesson, ask a student to come to the front and talk a little (about five sentences) about himself or herself – likes or dislikes, daily schedules, family members, etc.

- Ask students to make a chart in their notebooks where they can write the classmate's name and one thing they remembered hearing about that classmate.

- At the beginning of the next class meeting, ask two or three random students what they learned about their classmate.

Speaking / Pronunciation Games & Activities

1 Show me.

This game reviews letter sounds.

- Choose three or four target letter sounds to be reviewed. Write the letters that represent those target sounds on large pieces of paper, one sound per paper. Make three sets of the sounds.
- Divide the class into three teams. Give one student from each team a set of the papers. Call out a word containing one of the target sounds.

- The students hold up the piece of paper with the appropriate letters. The student who does so first wins a point for his or her team. If students hold up the correct paper simultaneously, each student earns a point. Add an extra point if they are able to pronounce the sound correctly.

2 Rhyming words

This game reviews words that rhyme.

- If you have not done so already, explain to students what rhyming words are. Give examples such as *cat / hat, cake / make, see / me.*
- Divide the class into four or five teams. Write a word on the board such as *book, ten,* or *ball.*

- Give teams one minute to come up with a list of rhyming words. Ask them to choose a team member to write the list on the board.
- Teams receive a point for each correct rhyming word. The team with the most points wins.

3 Pass it up.

This game reviews letter sounds.

- Choose a few words containing the target letter sounds you would like to review.
- Write the letters that represent those target sounds on large pieces of paper. Place them on the chalk rail or attach them to the board.
- Divide the class into four or five teams. Ask teams to stand in line in the front. If teams have more than five or six members, ask a few members from each team up to the front. Conduct the activity twice to make sure everyone has a chance to participate.

- Whisper one of the words you have chosen to the last student in each line. Then say "Go!"
- The students in each team whisper the word to one another in chain fashion. The last student to hear the word runs to the board, grabs the piece of paper with the appropriate sound, and gives it to you. If the student has done so correctly, he or she earns a point for the team.

4 Up or down?

This game reviews intonation.

- Have a list of both *Yes / No* and *Wh-* questions ready to read to the class. For example:

Yes / No questions	Wh- questions
Do you play tennis?	When's your birthday?
Are dogs friendly?	Where's San Juan?

- Divide the class into four or five teams. Ask a member from each team to stand.

- Read one of the questions in a robotic tone of voice. If the question is an interrogative one, students should point their index fingers upward and shout "Up!" If it is a *Wh-* question, they should point their index fingers down and shout "Down!" The first student to do so correctly earns one point for identifying the correct intonation.

  Option After identifying the intonation, ask the student to tell you how the last word of the question should be intonated. That student may then earn another point for saying the word with the appropriate intonation.

Answer Key for Workbook

Note: *Multiple answers in a single sentence or by a single speaker are separated by a semicolon (;).*
Alternative answers are separated by a slash (/).

Unit 1 • All About You and Me

Lesson 1 • New friends

1 Note: Answers to some questions will vary.
1. Where
2. How
3. When's
4. Is
   No, it's not. It's in Brazil.
5. Are
6. Where's
   It's in Japan.
7. What's
8. Where's

2
1. Where's San Francisco?
   It's in California.
2. Who are they?
   They're my classmates.
3. How old is Angelo?
   He's 13.
4. Are you in Sabrina's class?
   Yes, I am.
5. What's your name?
   My name's Nina.
6. Who's she?
   She's my science teacher.

Lesson 2 • Neighborhoods

1 **Beth** Is there a
 Tasha there isn't; there is a
 Beth Are there any
 Tasha there are; There are no
 Tasha There's no; There aren't

2 Note: Answers to the questions will vary.
1. Are there any parks?
2. Is there a big library?
3. Is there a movie theater?
4. Are there any tennis courts?
5. Are there any shoe stores?
6. Is there a gym?
7. Are there any restaurants?
8. Is there a skating rink?

Lessons 1 & 2 • Mini-review

1
1. Who; b
2. Is; a
3. What's; h
4. When's; e
5. Are; d
6. Is; c
7. Where; f
8. How; g

2
1. Yes, there is.
2. He's 12. He's not 13.
3. It's in December. It's not in May.
4. No, there isn't.
5. No, I'm not. I'm in Mr. Valli's history class.
6. They're not my teachers. They're my parents.

Lesson 3 • Talents

1 3
   5
   4
   6
   1
   7
   2
   8

2
1. musical
2. friendly
3. artistic
4. funny
5. athletic
6. smart
7. languages
8. draw

3 Answers will vary.

Lesson 4 • Our pets

1
1. **A** a lot
   B at all
2. **A** very much
   B a lot
3. **A** at all
   B a little
4. **A** very much
   B a little

2
a. 4
b. 3
c. 2
d. 1

3 Answers will vary.

Get Connected

1 Nora can play the piano.

2 1. artistic
2. musical
3. typical
4. famous
5. smart

3 1. They're from Thailand.
2. Yes, they are.
3. You can see the pictures in special stores and on the Internet.
4. No, she's not. She's a music teacher.
5. Yes, there is.

Check Yourself

A 1. Where are you from?
2. What's your name?
3. She's 12.
4. Who are they?
5. It's in October.
6. Are you in Mrs. Cook's class?

B 1. Is there a
Yes, there is.
2. Are there any
No, there aren't.
3. Is there a
No, there isn't.
4. Are there any
Yes, there are.
5. Is there a
No, there isn't.
6. Is there a
Yes, there is.

C 1. I like dogs a little.
2. I like rabbits a lot.
3. I don't like cats at all.
4. I like / don't like spiders very much.
5. I don't like snakes at all.
6. I like parrots a lot.

Unit 2 • Our Lives and Routines

Lesson 5 • School days

1 1. get up
2. eat breakfast
3. go to school
4. do homework
5. eat dinner
6. go to bed

2 1. I get up at 7:00. I don't get up at 8:00.
2. I don't eat breakfast with my friends. I eat breakfast with my family.

3. I eat lunch in the cafeteria. I don't eat lunch at home.
4. I don't do my homework at school. I do my homework at home.
5. I watch TV with my friends. I don't watch TV with my teachers.
6. I go to bed at 10:30. I don't go to bed at 11:30.

Lesson 6 • Free time

1 1. **A** Do you collect
B Yes, I do.
2. **A** Do you play
B No, I don't.
3. **A** Do you hang out
B No, I don't.
4. **A** Do you listen
B Yes, I do.
5. **A** Do you take
B Yes, I do.
6. **A** Do you watch
B No, I don't.
7. **A** Do you write
B Yes, I do.
8. **A** Do you talk
B Yes, I do.

2 1. draw; h
2. use; e
3. play; a
4. hang out; b
5. listen to; d
6. take; g
7. collect; c
8. play with; f

Lessons 5 & 6 • Mini-review

1 1. use the Internet
2. videos
3. collect stamps
4. funny
5. dangerous
6. Internet
7. computer
8. morning

2 My name is Rosa. Every day, I get up at 5:30 a.m. At 6:30, I eat breakfast with my family. Then I go to school. I walk with my sister and brother. I eat lunch with my friend, Katie, in the cafeteria. At 4:30, I take dance lessons. I'm pretty good at dancing. At 6:30, I eat dinner in the dining room at home. Then I do my homework. I don't like homework very much. I like music a lot. I listen to music every night. Ilegales is my favorite band. I don't watch TV. TV is boring. Then I go to bed at 10:30.

3 Answers will vary.

Lesson 7 • People I admire

1
1. works
2. goes
3. watches
4. collects
5. guesses
6. does
7. lives
8. takes
9. teaches
10. has
11. makes
12. practices

2 This is my cousin, Mary Ann. She's 13. She <u>lives</u> in Texas. She <u>gets up</u> at 6:30 every day. Then she <u>goes</u> to school. Mary Ann <u>works</u> hard in school. Mrs. Haywood is Mary Ann's favorite teacher. Mrs. Haywood <u>teaches</u> music.

After school, Mary Ann <u>does</u> her homework and <u>listens</u> to music in her room. She <u>has</u> a computer in her room. At night, she <u>talks</u> on the phone or <u>writes</u> e-mail messages to her friends.

3 Answers will vary.

Lesson 8 • The weekend

1
1. She doesn't play the piano.
2. She doesn't eat out with her friends.
3. She doesn't go to the movies with her brother.
4. She doesn't like popcorn.
5. She doesn't get up early.
6. She doesn't in-line skate at school.

2
1. Adina doesn't watch TV in the dining room.
2. He doesn't go to the movies every Saturday.
3. Gregorio doesn't stay home on Sunday.
4. She doesn't sleep late on Monday.
5. Julio doesn't talk on the phone at school.
6. Gina doesn't go out on Friday night.
7. He doesn't hang out at the mall.
8. She doesn't collect stamps.

Get Connected

1 Abigail Breslin is the star of *Kit Kittredge: An American Girl.*

2
1. set
2. message
3. practice
4. actor
5. review

3
1. F; He doesn't go to the set at 5:00 a.m. He goes to the set at 6:00 a.m.
2. T
3. F; They study for three to five hours every day.
4. F; She loves animals.
5. T

Check Yourself

A
1. Jess in-line skates after school.
2. They watch TV at 8:00.
3. Kevin doesn't take dance lessons.
4. Bridget goes out on Friday night.
5. My father doesn't teach music.

B
1. Do you collect stamps?
   Yes, I do. *OR* No, I don't.
2. Do you listen to music?
   Yes, I do. *OR* No, I don't.
3. Do you play video games?
   Yes, I do. *OR* No, I don't.
4. Do you watch DVDs?
   Yes, I do. *OR* No, I don't.

C
1. F; I don't go to school with my mother. I go to school with my sister.
2. F; I don't do my homework at 10:00. I do my homework at 7:30. / I go to bed at 10:00.
3. T
4. F; I don't play the piano at 4:00. I play tennis at 4:00.
5. T

Unit 3 • Sports and Activities

Lesson 9 • Sports fun

1
1. Does he play soccer?
   No, he doesn't.
2. Does he dance?
   Yes, he does.
3. Does he do karate?
   No, he doesn't.
4. Does he play the piano?
   Yes, he does.
5. Does he ski?
   No, he doesn't.
6. Does he surf?
   Yes, he does.

2
1. Does Miss Alvarez do karate?
   Yes, she does.
2. Does he ski?
   No, he doesn't.
3. Does Hiro go biking?
   Yes, he does.
4. Does Sarah water-ski?
   No, she doesn't.
5. Does she surf?
   Yes, she does.
6. Does Raul skateboard?
   No, he doesn't.
7. Does Angela swim?
   Yes, she does.
8. Does Mr. Miller play baseball?
   Yes, he does.

Lesson 10 • Sports equipment

1 1. Do skiers wear gloves?
 Yes, they do. Skiers wear gloves.
 2. Do cyclists wear ski boots?
 No, they don't. Cyclists don't wear ski boots.
 3. Do skateboarders wear knee pads?
 Yes, they do. Skateboarders wear knee pads.
 4. Do basketball players wear hats?
 No, they don't. Basketball players don't wear hats.
 5. Do swimmers wear goggles?
 Yes, they do. Swimmers wear goggles.
 6. Do baseball players wear uniforms?
 Yes, they do. Baseball players wear uniforms.
 7. Do soccer players wear hats?
 No, they don't. Soccer players don't wear hats.
 8. Do cyclists wear helmets?
 Yes, they do. Cyclists wear helmets.

2 Andy Do they wear uniforms?
 Andy Do they wear helmets?
 Andy Do they wear goggles?
 Andy Do they use knee pads?
 Andy Do they play on a field?

Lessons 9 & 10 • Mini-review

1 1. piano
 2. stamps
 3. uniform
 4. use
 5. hat
 6. write
 7. helmet
 8. active

2 6
 3
 1
 7
 2
 8
 5
 4

3 1. **A** Do
 B Yes, they do.
 2. **A** Do
 B No, I don't.
 3. **A** Does
 B Yes, he / she does.
 4. **A** Does
 B No, he / she doesn't.

4 Note: Answers to the questions will vary.
 1. Do
 2. Does
 3. Does
 4. Do

Lesson 11 • Off to camp

1 1. pillow
 2. towel
 3. flashlight
 4. blanket
 5. raincoat

2 1. wear hiking boots; Don't wear sneakers.
 2. Don't bring an MP3 player.
 3. don't bring your cell phone.
 4. bring bug repellent
 5. Use sunscreen
 6. don't bring a sleeping bag

3 Note: Answers may vary.
 1. Don't use cell phones.
 2. Don't listen to MP3 players.
 3. Don't play video games.
 4. Use the Internet.
 5. Do homework.
 6. Don't read comic books.
 7. Don't play the guitar.
 8. Don't bring magazines.

Lesson 12 • At camp

1 1. He goes canoeing at 9:30. *OR* At 9:30.
 2. They make a campfire at 6:00. *OR* They make a campfire in the evening.
 3. He goes horseback riding at 12:30. *OR* At 12:30.
 4. They go hiking at 1:45. *OR* At 1:45.
 5. They tell stories at 8:00. *OR* They tell stories in the evening.
 6. He takes swimming lessons at 10:45. *OR* He takes swimming lessons in the morning.
 7. He cooks hot dogs at 6:30. *OR* At 6:30.
 8. They do arts and crafts at 3:15. *OR* They do arts and crafts in the afternoon.

2 1. in the evening
 2. at night
 3. in the morning
 4. in the morning
 5. in the afternoon
 6. at night

3 1. When do your parents get up?
 My parents get up in the morning. *OR* In the morning.
 2. When do your friends eat lunch?
 They / My friends eat lunch in the afternoon. *OR* In the afternoon.
 3. What time do your classmates go home?
 They / My classmates go home at 2:30. *OR* At 2:30.
 4. When does your teacher use his computer?
 My teacher uses his computer in the morning. *OR* In the morning.

5. What time does your sister go to bed?
   She / My sister goes to bed at 10:30.
   OR At 10:30.
6. When does your best friend do homework?
   My best friend does homework in the
   evening. *OR* In the evening.

Get Connected

1 Tara's nickname is "Captain Kirk."

2 1. medals
   2. win
   3. races
   4. champion
   5. trophies

3 1. No, she isn't. She's from Washington.
   2. No, they don't usually swim in the same races.
   3. No, she doesn't.
   4. Yes, she does.
   5. Yes, it is.

Check Yourself

A 1. Don't listen to
   2. Wear
   3. Get up
   4. Don't use
   5. Wear
   6. Don't eat
   7. Use
   8. Don't bring

B 1. Do
      do
   2. Does
      doesn't
   3. Does
      does
   4. Do
      don't
   5. Do
      do
   6. Does
      doesn't

C 1. What time does he go canoeing?
      He goes canoeing at 8:15. *OR* At 8:15.
   2. When does she do arts and crafts?
      She does arts and crafts in the afternoon. *OR* In the afternoon.
   3. What time do they go hiking?
      They go hiking at 10:00. *OR* At 10:00.
   4. When do they make a campfire?
      They make a campfire in the evening. *OR* In the evening.
   5. What time does she go horseback riding?
      She goes horseback riding at 3:15. *OR* At 3:15.
   6. When does he tell stories?
      He tells stories at night. *OR* At night.
   7. What time do you take swimming lessons?
      I take swimming lessons at 9:30. *OR* At 9:30.

Unit 4 • My Interests

Lesson 13 • I like music.

1 1. REGGAE
   2. ROCK
   3. POP
   4. COUNTRY
   5. HIP-HOP
   6. CLASSICAL
   Mystery word: GROUPS

2 1. d   4. c
   2. e   5. a
   3. f   6. b

3 1. her   4. them
   2. them   5. it
   3. it   6. him

4 Answers will vary.

Lesson 14 • Let's look online.

1 1. How much are the puzzles?
   2. How much is the camera?
   3. How much are the backpacks?
   4. How much are the DVDs?
   5. How much is the watch?
   6. How much are the calendars?
   7. How much is the radio-controlled airplane?
   8. How much is the experiment kit?

2 1. How much are the books?
      They're $18.69 each.
   2. How much is the skateboard?
      It's $97.39
   3. How much are the travel vests?
      They're $59.99 each.
   4. How much are the CDs?
      They're $13.99 each.
   5. How much is the telescope?
      It's $90.00.
   6. How much is the star map?
      It's $19.98.

Lessons 13 & 14 • Mini-review

1 1. Yes, I do. I like it a lot.
   2. No, I don't. I don't like them.
   3. Cee-Lo. I really like him.
   4. Well, I like her, but she's not my favorite singer.
   5. Reggae is great. I really like it.
   6. Yes, I do. He's my favorite.
   7. No, I don't. I don't really like her.
   8. The Backstreet Boys are cool. I like them.

2 1. How much is
   2. How much are
   3. How much is
   4. How much is

5. How much are
6. How much is

3 1. F; They're $8.69 each.
2. T
3. F; It's $16.88.
4. F; They're $22.49 each.
5. T
6. F; They're $13.95 each.

Lesson 15 • Our interests

1 1. I like to go camping. I don't like to go shopping.
2. I like to ski. I don't like to do crossword puzzles.
3. He likes to write poetry. He doesn't like to play tennis.
4. She likes to play video games. She doesn't like to practice the piano.
5. She likes to go dancing. She doesn't like to watch TV.
6. I like to go to the movies. I don't like to do my homework.
7. I like to in-line skate. I don't like to read magazines.
8. He likes to spend time at the beach. He doesn't like to hang out at the mall.

2   Al   like to do crossword puzzles
Eddie   like to go camping
Al   don't like to go camping
Al   like to listen to music
Al   don't like to go shopping

Lesson 16 • In and out of school

1 1. d
2. c
3. b
4. a
5. e
6. f

2 1. sometimes
2. always
3. hardly ever
4. usually
5. hardly ever
6. usually
7. Sometimes
8. never

3 Answers will vary.

Get Connected

1 They're from New York City.

2 1. a classical   4. sell
2. album   5. musician
3. download

3 1. F; There are 20 musicians in This Ambitious Orchestra.
2. T
3. F; They sometimes write their own music.
4. F; Parents and teens like to come to the concerts.
5. T

Check Yourself

A 1. Mario likes her.
2. We like them a lot.
3. Peter doesn't like it.
4. I don't really like it.
5. Eric listens to him all the time.
6. She doesn't like him at all.

B 1. How much is
It's $12.75.
2. How much are
They're $22.99 each.
3. How much is
It's $14.75.
4. How much are
They're $8.00 each.
5. How much is
It's $67.50.
6. How much are
They're $49.95 each.

C 1. don't like to go
2. like to spend
3. don't like to play
4. usually
5. never
6. hardly ever
7. like to write

Unit 5 • Favorite Activities

Lesson 17 • In San Francisco

1 1. ride a trolley
2. take pictures
3. see a show
4. take a boat ride
5. walk in the park
6. go sightseeing

2 1. You're walking.
2. They're buying.
3. We're taking.
4. I'm riding.
5. She's going.
6. I'm writing.
7. They're doing.
8. We're practicing.

3 1. They're taking a boat ride.
   2. He's buying souvenirs.
   3. We're going sightseeing.
   4. She's walking in the park.
   5. They're seeing a show.
   6. I'm taking pictures.
   7. You're visiting a museum.
   8. We're riding a trolley.

4 Answers will vary.

Lesson 18 • At the park

1 1. aren't eating in the picnic area
   2. isn't staying on the bike path
   3. isn't waiting for the green light
   4. not sitting down in the boat
   5. aren't standing in line
   6. isn't throwing trash in the trash can

2 1. He isn't paying attention. He's reading a
      comic book.
   2. We aren't following the rules. We're throwing
      paper airplanes.
   3. I'm not reading a magazine. I'm using the
      Internet.
   4. She isn't writing poetry. She's listening to music.
   5. They aren't standing in line. They're walking
      in the park.
   6. He isn't practicing the piano. He's playing
      video games.

Lessons 17 & 18 • Mini-review

1 *Across*   *Down*
   3. SOUVENIRS 1. BOAT
   5. SHOW   2. TRASH
   7. BIKE   4. VISITING
   9. STANDING   6. WAITING
  10. PICTURES   8. PICNIC

2 1. Pedro and José aren't in-line skating.
      They're skateboarding.
   2. Mia isn't standing in line. She's doing
      a crossword puzzle.
   3. Cesar isn't walking in the park.
      He's sleeping.
   4. Denise and Julia aren't eating in the
      picnic area. They're taking pictures.
   5. Raul isn't talking on a cell phone. He's
      listening to music.
   6. Sherri isn't throwing paper airplanes.
      She's throwing trash in the trash can.

Lesson 19 • At the beach

1 1. No, he isn't. He's swimming in the ocean.
   2. Yes, they are.
   3. No, they aren't. They're having a picnic.
   4. No, she isn't. She's sailing a boat.
   5. No, he isn't. He's throwing a Frisbee.
   6. Yes, they are.

2 1. Is Scott playing in the sand?
      No, he isn't.
   2. Is Linda floating on a raft?
      Yes, she is.
   3. Are Josh and Brian sailing a boat?
      No, they aren't.
   4. Is Sally collecting seashells?
      Yes, she is.
   5. Is Alberto swimming in the ocean?
      No, he isn't.
   6. Are Natalie and Sasha having a picnic?
      Yes, they are.

Lesson 20 • At the store

1 1. RING
   2. SURFBOARD
   3. SCARF
   4. NECKLACE
   5. BRACELET
   6. COAT
   Secret word: RACKET

2 1. What are you shopping for?
   2. What's she buying?
   3. What are they looking at?
   4. What's he trying on?
   5. What's she paying for?
   6. What are you buying?
   7. What are you looking at?

Get Connected

1 Yes, she is.

2 1. play
   2. sailing
   3. shopping
   4. castle
   5. traditional

3 1. No, they aren't. They're working.
   2. Yes, they are.
   3. No, she isn't. She's spending two weeks at
      the park.
   4. No, they aren't. They're sailing and surfing.
   5. Yes, she is.

Check Yourself

A 1. I'm taking pictures.
   2. They're visiting a museum.
   3. She's riding a trolley.
   4. He's throwing trash in the trash can.
   5. We're waiting for the green light.
   6. You're buying souvenirs.

B 1. We aren't staying on the bike path.
   2. They aren't standing in line.
   3. She isn't playing in the sand.
   4. He isn't going sightseeing.
   5. I'm not eating in the picnic area.
   6. You aren't visiting a museum.

C 1. Is she looking at jackets?
No, she isn't. She's looking at shoes.
2. Is he buying comic books?
No, he isn't. He's buying a scarf.
3. Are they collecting seashells?
Yes, they are.
4. Are they throwing a Frisbee?
No, they aren't. They're flying a kite.
5. Are you going sightseeing?
Yes, I am.

Unit 6 • Entertainment
Lesson 21 • Where are you going?

1 1. Where's she going?
2. Where are they going?
3. Where's he going?
4. Where are you going?
5. Where are you going?
6. Where's she going?

2 1. Where's Amy going?
She's going to the museum.
2. Where's Mr. Parker going?
He's going to a concert.
3. Where are Ava and Jenna going?
They're going to the mall.
4. Where are you and Roberto going?
We're going to the soccer game.

Lesson 22 • Birthday parties

1 1. We're eating at a restaurant now.
2. He's writing poetry now.
3. They're going to the movies now.
4. I'm listening to music now.
5. They're hanging out with friends now.
6. We're playing party games now.
7. They're doing karate now.
8. She's eating cake now.

2 1. Antonio usually sleeps late. He's playing cards now.
2. Tomas usually watches TV. He's swimming now.
3. Jack usually does his homework. He's reading a book now.
4. Marla usually talks on the phone. She's listening to music now.
5. Kelly usually relaxes at home. She's hanging out at the mall now.
6. Jane usually reads magazines. She's using the Internet now.

3 Answers will vary.

Lessons 21 & 22 • Mini-review

1 1. is talking
2. stays
3. watch
4. is celebrating
5. is eating
6. have

2 1. Where's Dena going?
She's going to the shoe store.
2. Where's Mrs. Park going?
She's going to the movie theater.
3. Where's Mr. Dodd going?
He's going to the library.
4. Where are Will and Fran going?
They're going to the park.

3 1. F; Erica usually watches TV. She's reading a book now.
2. T
3. F; Scott usually skateboards. He's playing video games now.
4. F; Edwin usually eats dinner at home. He's eating at a restaurant now.
5. T
6. F; Alysha usually goes to the library. She's going to the circus now.

Lesson 23 • Let's see a movie.

1 **A** I want to go to the movies.
B What do you want to see?
A I want to see *Amazing Elephants*.
B Is it a documentary?
A Yes, it is. Do you want to come?
B No, thanks. I want to see a comedy.

2 1. We want to see a documentary.
2. **A** Do you want to see a comedy?
3. I want to see an animated movie.
4. **A** Do you want to see a drama?
5. I don't want to see an action movie.
6. I don't want to see a horror movie.

Lesson 24 • In line at the movies

1 1. slim
2. long
3. curly
4. tall
5. brown

2 1. does; b
2. hair; a
3. color; d
4. are; e
5. look; c

3 1. What does Aleta look like?
2. What color are Don's eyes?
3. What color is Viviana's hair?

4. What's Allen's hair like?
5. What does Paco look like?
6. What's Sara's hair like?

4 Answers will vary.

Get Connected

1 There are more than 20 million bats.

2 1. fascinating
2. exhibit
3. million
4. pounds
5. hair

3 1. They're going to the nature center.
2. Bats usually sleep in the daytime.
3. No, they can't.
4. It's short and brown.
5. They eat bugs.

Check Yourself

A 1. Where are you going?
2. What does he look like?
3. What color is her / his / your hair?
4. Yes, I do.
5. She's going to the movie festival.
6. I want to see an action movie.

B 1. We usually eat hamburgers. We're eating pizza now.
2. We usually watch TV. We're going to a concert now.
3. Mr. Goldman usually reads a book. He's going hiking now.
4. Karla usually goes to a basketball game. She's in-line skating now.
5. He usually plays baseball. He's relaxing at home now.
6. They usually hang out at the mall. They're visiting a museum now.

Unit 7 • What We Eat

Lesson 25 • I'm hungry!

1 1. apples; C
2. cheese; U
3. broccoli; U
4. bananas; C
5. potatoes; C
6. butter; U
7. eggs; C
8. rice; U

2 1. water
2. meat
3. potatoes
4. hot dogs
5. butter
6. rice
7. sandwich
8. apples

3 Answers will vary.

Lesson 26 • Picnic plans

1 1. How many
2. a little
3. a lot
4. How much
5. a lot
6. How much
7. a few
8. How many

2 1. We have a lot of fruit.
2. We have (six / a lot) of forks.
3. We have a lot of pasta.
4. We have a little milk.
5. We have two cups.
6. We have (three / a few) spoons.

3 1. How many cups are there?
There are five cups.
2. How many knives are there?
There are eight knives.
3. How many forks are there?
There are six forks.
4. How much juice is there?
There's a little juice.
5. How much bread is there?
There's a lot of bread.
6. How much pasta is there?
There's a lot of pasta.

Lessons 25 & 26 • Mini-review

1 1. How much bread
She has a lot of bread.
2. How many hamburgers
They want a few hamburgers.
3. How much broccoli
He needs a little broccoli.
4. How much milk
They need a lot of milk.
5. How many potatoes
She wants a few potatoes.
6. How much cheese
He has a little cheese.

2 1. How much juice do you drink every day?
2. How many brothers do you have?
3. How much fruit do you eat every morning?
4. How many comic books do you read every month?
5. How many cookies do you eat after school?
6. How much water do you drink in the morning?

Lesson 27 • A snack

1
4
8
1
6
5
7
3
2

2 Note: The order of the answers may vary.
1. There aren't any sandwiches.
2. There are some potatoes.
3. There isn't any mustard.
4. There's some jelly.
5. There's some lettuce.
6. There aren't any bananas.

3 Answers will vary.

Lesson 28 • On the menu

1 *Appetizers:* black bean soup, salad, vegetable soup
Main dishes: cheeseburger, chicken sandwich, fish, steak sandwich
Side orders: baked potato, French fries
Desserts: carrot cake, chocolate cake, ice cream
Drinks: iced tea, milk shake, soda

2
1. Would you like an appetizer?
2. Would you like a drink?
3. Would you like some ice cream?
4. Yes, please. I'd like some fish.
5. No, thanks.

3
1. **A** Do you like
   A Would you like
2. **A** Would you like
3. **A** Do you like
4. **A** Do you like
5. **A** Would you like

Get Connected

1 No, it isn't.

2
1. ketchup
2. refrigerator
3. recipe
4. newspaper
5. fruit

3
1. all over the world
2. sleep and eat
3. There's no recipe
4. meat and cheese
5. is very big

Check Yourself

A
1. How many; e
2. How much; d
3. How many; f
4. How many; b
5. How many; c
6. How much; a

B
1. There isn't; any
2. There are; some
3. There are some; eggs
4. There's; some
5. There are some; potatoes

C Note: Answers to the questions will vary.
1. Would you like some dessert?
2. Would you like a drink?
3. Would you like a hamburger?
4. Would you like some soup?
5. Would you like an appetizer?
6. Would you like some pizza?

Unit 8 • The Natural World

Lesson 29 • World weather

1
1. hot   3. rainy
2. cloudy   4. windy

2
1. It's hot and sunny today.
2. It's warm and rainy today.
3. It's cold and snowy today.
4. It's warm and cloudy today.
5. It's cool and windy today.
6. It's cold and sunny today.

3
1. What's the weather like in Chicago in January?
2. What's the weather like in Miami in August?
3. It's usually warm and cloudy.
4. What's the weather like in New York City today?
5. It's usually cold and sunny.

Lesson 30 • Natural wonders

1
1. mountain
2. island
3. hot spring
4. cave
5. river

2
1. What can you see in a rain forest?
2. Can you see bats in a cave?
3. Can you buy food and souvenirs at hotels?
4. Can you collect seashells in the mountains?
5. What can you see on this island?
6. What can you do in this park?

3 1. No, you can't. You can see snakes and spiders.
2. Yes, you can. You can buy food at the hotel.
3. You can go canoeing.
4. No, you can't. You can go hiking.
5. You can sit and relax.
6. You can see an underground cave.

Lessons 29 & 30 • Mini-review

1 1. What's the weather like in Tokyo in April?
2. What's the weather like in Buenos Aires in January?
3. What's the weather like in Tokyo in August?
4. It's usually warm and cloudy.
5. It's usually cool and cloudy.

2 1. **Q:** What can you see in the park?
A: hot springs
2. **Q:** What can you do at the beach?
A: swim
3. **Q:** Can you see a lot of birds in the rain forest?
A: birds
4. **Q:** Can you go camping in the cave?
A: go camping

Lesson 31 • World of friends

1 1. d
2. e
3. a
4. f
5. c
6. b

2 1. Tammy does.
2. Tina and Jan do.
3. Rodrigo does.
4. I do.
5. You do.
6. We do.

3 1. Who speaks Arabic?
2. Who takes pictures?
3. Who plays soccer?
4. Ingrid and Pamela do.
5. Anton does.
6. Aldo does.

Lesson 32 • International Day

1 1. five hundred and eighty-nine
2. three thousand four hundred and six
3. eighty-two thousand, seven hundred and forty-two
4. nine hundred fifty-five thousand, six hundred and ninety-eight

5. one hundred and ninety-nine
6. seventy-five thousand
7. two hundred eight thousand, six hundred and thirty-eight
8. seven hundred and seventy-seven
9. six thousand and twenty
10. five thousand four hundred and sixteen

2 1. What sports do you like?
I like baseball and basketball.
2. What languages does your father speak?
He speaks English and German.
3. What instruments do they play?
They play piano and guitar.
4. What animals does your mother like?
She likes cats and dogs.
5. What desserts do you eat?
I eat ice cream, cake, and cookies.
6. What subjects do you like?
I like English, science, and math.

3 Answers will vary.

Get Connected

1 Yes, it is.

2 1. melting
2. warm
3. mountains
4. dying
5. forest

3 1. F; Some people say a glacier is like a river of ice.
2. F; There aren't many snakes.
3. F; It sometimes snows in August.
4. T
5. T

Check Yourself

A 1. What can you see in this park?
2. What's the weather like today?
3. What's the weather like in December?
4. Who hangs out at the mall after school?
5. What movies do you like?
6. Can you buy food at this hotel?

B 1. What movies does Eliot watch?
He watches action movies and comedies.
2. What sports do Liza and Eliot play?
They play soccer and tennis.
3. What languages do Liza and Eliot speak?
They speak English and German.
4. What kinds of pets does Liza have?
She has a dog and spiders.

Audio Script for Student's Book 2

Unit 1 • All About You and Me

Lesson 1 New Friends

Page 2 Exercise 1A
Same as the captions in the Student's Book.

Page 3 Exercise 2B
Same as the conversation in the Student's Book.

Lesson 2 Neighborhoods

Page 4 Exercise 1

Carson   My neighborhood is pretty, but it's not very interesting. There's a beautiful park. There are two tennis courts, but there are no basketball courts. There are no restaurants in my neighborhood.

Johnny   I love my neighborhood. There's no gym, but there are many stores. There's a big mall, and there's a movie theater. It's exciting at night. It's really fun.

Page 5 Exercise 2

Carson   Your neighborhood sounds fun, Johnny. Tell me more about it.

Johnny   Well, there's a mall, and in the mall there's a great music store. And there's a big video arcade, too.

Carson   Are there any parks in your neighborhood?

Johnny   No, there aren't.

Carson   Are there any basketball courts?

Johnny   No, there aren't.

Carson   Well, is there a swimming pool?

Johnny   No, there isn't. But there's a great library. I like it a lot.

Carson   That's cool. Are there any schools in your neighborhood?

Johnny   No, there aren't. I ride the subway to our school.

Carson   So, Johnny, what's your favorite place in your neighborhood?

Johnny   Oh, that's easy. There's a bookstore at the mall. I go there a lot. There are always new comic books.

Lessons 1 & 2 Mini-review

Page 7 Exercise 2

1. This is my new school. It's a great school. There's a big library with lots of books.
2. There's a swimming pool in the school. We can swim there all year.

3. There's a gym with a basketball court. There are exciting basketball games in the gym on weekends.
4. There aren't any tennis courts at the school. But that's OK. I can play tennis at the park.
5. And there's a music room, too. The band plays there after school.

Lesson 3 Talents

Page 8 Exercise 1
Same as the sentences in the Student's Book.

Page 8 Exercise 2A

1. **Girl 1**   Silvio's really athletic.
   Girl 2   Yeah. He can play a lot of sports.
2. **Girl 1**   Beth can play a lot of instruments.
   Boy 1   Really?
   Girl 1   Oh, yes. She likes music. She's really musical.
3. **Boy 1**   Tony can speak Portuguese, Greek, and English.
   Boy 2   He's really smart! Maybe he can help me with my English homework.
4. **Girl 1**   Wow! Look at that picture. It's Lina's.
   Girl 2   It's beautiful. She's really artistic.

Page 9 Exercise 3A
Same as the conversation in the Student's Book.

Page 9 Exercise 4
Same as the sentences in the Student's Book.

Lesson 4 Our pets

Page 10 Exercise 1A
Same as the sentences in the Student's Book.

Page 11 Exercise 2A
Same as the conversation in the Student's Book.

Page 11 Exercise 2B
Same as the sentences in the Student's Book.

Unit 1 Get Connected

Page 12 Read
Same as the article in the Student's Book.

Page 13 Listen

Alex   Oh, hey, Anna. Is that your science homework?

Anna   Um, uh, no . . . but it's important stuff, Alex.

Alex   Let me see. Important stuff? The Plain White T's?

Anna   Yeah, they're really cool, and I like them
        a lot. They're my favorite band.
Alex   Come on, Anna, that's not very important.
        Hurry up! I have a lot of homework.
Anna   Yes, it *is* important! Look. It says here –
        they're from Chicago, and Tom – he's
        my favorite – is the lead singer. His last
        name is Higgenson. He writes songs, too.
Alex   Really?
Anna   Yeah. His song "Hey There Delilah" is
        about an awesome girl he knows. It's not
        about his girlfriend and . . .
Alex   That's great, Anna. Now can you please
        hurry and . . .
Anna   Well, what about you and Mariah?
Alex   Huh? Me and Mariah?
Anna   Yeah, Mariah Carey. You listen to her
        music online all the time. And you know,
        Alex, there's a computer in Mom and Dad's
        room. Use that one.
Alex   OK, OK. Have fun with the Plain White T's!
        But do your science homework!

Unit 2 • Our Lives and Routines

Lesson 5 School days

Page 16 Exercise 1A
Same as the sentences in the Student's Book.

Page 17 Exercise 2A
Same as the texts in the Student's Book.

Page 17 Exercise 3
1. On school days, I get up at 7:00 a.m. After I get
    up, I eat breakfast. I eat breakfast in the kitchen
    with my family.
2. At nine o'clock, I go to school with my friends.
    I have a lot of friends.
3. My first class is math. I like math a lot. Then
    I have science class. And then it's time for lunch.
    There is a great cafeteria in my school. I eat
    lunch in the cafeteria with my friends.
4. My last class is English. It's at 2:30. I go home
    at 3:45.
5. I'm tired after school, so I don't do my homework
    in the afternoon. I watch TV with my brother.
    We both like the sports channel.

Lesson 6 Free time

Page 18 Exercise 1A
Kate   I hang out at the mall. I in-line skate.
        I talk on the phone.
Rafael I collect stamps. I play video games. I use
        the Internet.
Ana   I listen to music. I take dance lessons. I
        watch videos and DVDs.

Page 19 Exercise 2
Same as the conversation in the Student's Book.

Lessons 5 & 6 Mini-Review

Page 21 Exercise 2
1. Sylvia   Hi, I'm Sylvia. In my free time, I read
             comic books, and I in-line skate. I don't
             hang out at the mall. A lot of my friends
             go to the mall, but I think it's boring. Oh,
             and I don't take dance lessons. I'm really
             not good at dancing.
2. Kenji   Hello, I'm Kenji. In my free time, I
             play video games with my friends, and
             I collect stamps. Stamps are really
             interesting. I also collect trading cards.
             It's fun. I don't talk on the phone. It's
             boring.
3. Adam   I'm Adam. I take piano lessons, and I
             play soccer. I don't hang out at the mall.
             I don't have time. But I read books. I like
             books a lot. They're fun.
4. Cindy   Good afternoon. I'm Cindy. I use the
             Internet every day after school. It's fun. I
             don't watch DVDs. I have no time. I play
             tennis every morning. Oh, I don't talk on
             the phone. It's not exciting.

Lesson 7 People I admire

Page 22 Exercise 1
1. I live in an apartment.
2. I work at Bradley Music School. I teach music to
    high school students.
3. I play in a jazz band.
4. I practice the piano every day.
5. I go to concerts every Saturday.
6. I have a piano, a bass, and an electric keyboard.

Page 22 Exercise 2A
Same as the text in the Student's Book.

Page 23 Exercise 2B
Same as the text in the Student's Book.

Page 23 Exercise 3
1. Caroline Zhang is an ice-skating star. She's
    American, but her family is from China.
2. She has one sister.
3. She lives with her family in California.
4. Caroline is very busy. She practices skating seven
    days a week.
5. Caroline is musical. In her free time, she plays
    the piano and the violin.
6. Her favorite singer is Gwen Stefani.

Page 23 Exercise 4A
Same as the verbs in the Student's Book.

Page 23 Exercise 4B
Same as the verbs in the Student's Book.

Lesson 8 The weekend

Page 24 Exercise 1A
Same as the sentences in the Student's Book.

Page 24 Exercise 2A
Same as the text in the Student's Book.

Page 25 Exercise 2C
Same as the sentences in the Student's Book.

Unit 2 Get Connected

Page 26 Read
Same as the article in the Student's Book.

Page 27 Listen
Julia Hey, Ben! What's wrong?

Ben I'm really tired, Julia. It's crazy – I have a lot of quizzes this week.

Julia Yeah?

Ben Well, I have an English quiz on Wednesday and a Spanish quiz on Thursday. And there are over fifty words to learn for each quiz!

Julia Wow, that *is* a lot . . . Hey, I have a great idea. We can study together. I have some cool software that makes vocabulary review like a game.

Ben That *is* a great idea, Julia! Do you have free time tonight? Around 6:00 or 7:00? I don't have piano class tonight, so I'm free.

Julia Let me think . . . Tomorrow is Monday. I have soccer practice at 3:30, and then I eat out with my parents. We don't eat at home on Monday.

Ben Wow, you're really busy. How about Tuesday?

Julia Tuesday's good. I don't have any extra classes on Tuesday. And, Ben, there's one more thing . . .

Ben Sure, Julia, what is it?

Julia Um, after we review vocabulary, can you help me with my math homework? I don't like math at all!

Ben No problem!

Unit 3 • Sports and Activities
Lesson 9 Sports fun

Page 30 Exercise 1A
Claudia Well, I like a lot of sports. Let's see. I do karate after school. It's fun! There's a swimming pool next to my house. I swim on the weekend. Sometimes my mom goes to the pool, too. On Saturdays, I go biking for a few hours. There's a great bike path near my house.

Zach I like sports, too. I play baseball at school. In the summer, I play with my friends every day. It's a lot of fun. I surf and water-ski, especially in the summer. My aunt and uncle live near the beach. It's great. During winter vacation, I ski a lot. I go with my family. We have a good time. I skateboard, too. I skateboard to school on nice days.

Page 30 Exercise 1B
Claudia I'm Claudia. I do karate, I swim, and I go biking.

Zach I'm Zach. I play baseball, I surf, I water-ski, I ski, and I skateboard.

Page 31 Exercise 2A
Same as the conversation in the Student's Book.

Page 31 Exercise 2B
Same as the conversation in the Student's Book.

Page 31 Exercise 3
Same as the questions in the Student's Book.

Lesson 10 Sports equipment

Page 32 Exercise 1A
1. I wear a helmet on my head.
2. I wear goggles on my eyes.
3. I wear gloves on my hands.
4. I wear knee pads on my knees.
5. I wear ski boots on my feet.

Page 33 Exercise 2A
Same as the conversation in the Student's Book.

Page 33 Exercise 2B
Same as the questions and answers in the Student's Book.

Page 33 Exercise 3
1. **Claudia** Oscar, what about these athletes?

   Oscar Let me think . . . Do they wear gloves?

   Claudia No, they don't. And they don't wear knee pads or helmets, either.

   Oscar Do they wear ski boots?

   Claudia Ski boots! That's crazy, Oscar. No, they don't wear ski boots.

   Oscar Well, what *do* they wear, then?

   Claudia Well, they use goggles. These athletes don't use a lot of sports equipment.

2. **Claudia** OK, Oscar. What about these athletes?

   Oscar Do they have team uniforms?

   Claudia Yes, they do. And each player has a different number on his uniform.

   Oscar Oh, I see. Like your soccer uniform.

   Claudia Yes!

   Oscar Do they use gloves?

   Claudia Yes, they do. They're special gloves. They use gloves to catch the balls.

3. **Oscar** Now these athletes – do they wear helmets?

Claudia Yes, they do. And they wear knee pads, too. It's a dangerous sport, you know.

Oscar Do they wear boots?

Claudia No, Oscar, they don't. They wear sneakers.

Oscar So, . . . they wear helmets, knee pads, and sneakers.

4. **Claudia** OK, Oscar. What do you know about these athletes?

Oscar Hmm . . . Let's see. They wear helmets, right?

Claudia Yes, they do. Helmets protect their heads. They ride fast, so they need them.

Oscar Do they use goggles?

Claudia No, they don't. They don't need goggles. But they wear gloves on their hands.

Oscar OK. They wear helmets and gloves, but they don't use goggles. Hmm . . . Do they use knee pads?

Claudia No, they don't.

Lessons 9 & 10 Mini-review

Page 35 Exercise 2A

1. So, Angela, tell us about your sisters? Do they surf?
2. And your parents? Do they ski?
3. Now your sister Kim. She's an athlete, too. Does she play soccer?
4. And your sister Keri. She looks athletic. Does she do karate?
5. OK, now we know your father likes biking. How about water-skiing? Does he water-ski, like your mother?

Page 35 Exercise 2B

Interviewer So, Angela, tell us about your sisters. Do they surf?

Angela No, they don't. They don't like water sports.

Interviewer And your parents? Do they ski?

Angela Yes, they do. They love the mountains.

Interviewer Now your sister Kim. She's an athlete, too. Does she play soccer?

Angela Yes, she does. She's a great player.

Interviewer And your sister Keri. She looks athletic. Does she do karate?

Angela Yes, she does. She likes it very much.

Interviewer OK, now we know your father likes biking. How about water-skiing? Does he water-ski, like your mother?

Angela No, he doesn't. He doesn't like the water.

Lesson 11 Off to camp

Page 36 Exercise 1A
Same as the items in the Student's Book.

Page 37 Exercise 2A
Same as the conversation in the Student's Book.

Page 37 Exercise 2B
Same as the rules in the Student's Book.

Lesson 12 At camp

Page 38 Exercise 1A
Same as the sentences in the Student's Book.

Page 38 Exercise 1B

Man At Camp Coby, campers get up early – at 6:30. At 7:15, they eat breakfast. And then at 8:00, they go horseback riding. It's a lot of fun.

After horseback riding, at about 10:00, they take swimming lessons. Then it's free time until lunchtime.

After lunch, at 1:15, they go canoeing. There are a lot of lakes near Camp Coby.

The mountains here are beautiful. So at 3:30, campers go hiking. They hike for about an hour.

Campers are tired after the hike. So at about 4:45, they do arts and crafts. Campers make posters, photo albums, and things like that.

Then it's dinnertime. The food is good here. After dinner, at 8:15, they make a campfire.

They all cook hot dogs at 8:30. The hot dogs are really good! Most campers enjoy this.

At nine, campers tell stories around the campfire. Some campers tell scary stories. Oohhhh! And at 9:30, all campers are tired, and they go to bed.

Page 39 Exercise 2A
Same as the conversation in the Student's Book.

Page 39 Exercise 2B
Same as the questions and answers in the Student's Book.

Page 39 Exercise 3

1. **Man** Hello. This is Camp Oakley! How can I help you?

Boy Can you tell me a little about the activities at Camp Oakley?

Man Sure. You can go hiking, tell stories . . .

Boy Oh, that's great! I love to go hiking. When do campers hike?

Man At ten. On Thursdays, campers eat lunch in the woods.

Boy Great!

2. **Boy** And what other activities are there?

   Man Well, campers go horseback riding . . .

   Boy Horseback riding! Wow! What time do campers go horseback riding?

   Man At 2:30.

3. **Man** And they do arts and crafts, too. That's at 11:30, just before lunch.

4. **Boy** Is there any free time at Camp Oakley?

   Man Well, it's hot here, so at 6:00, campers can take swimming lessons or have free time.

5. **Boy** So when do campers tell stories?

   Man At bedtime, in bed. All campers go to bed at 10:30.

   Boy Sounds great! Can I sign up?

Unit 3 Get Connected

Page 40 Read
Same as the article in the Student's Book.

Page 41 Listen

Sam Hey, Amy. What's on TV?

Amy It's a tennis match, Sam. Look, it's Serena Williams. She's a great tennis player.

Sam Yeah, I know. Her sister Venus is awesome, too.

Amy That's right. You know, Serena doesn't only play tennis. She designs clothes, too.

Sam Really? Does she design clothes for famous companies?

Amy Oh, yes. She designs for Nike and Puma.

Sam Wow! Does she have a company?

Amy Yes, she does. The name of her company is Aneres. They have offices in Florida, California, and Italy!

Sam Wow. Tennis player *and* fashion designer – she's athletic and artistic!

Amy Yeah.

Sam You know, I know a guy like that – really good at two different things. He goes to our school.

Amy Really? Do I know him?

Sam Sure you do. It's me! I am good at eating and . . .

Amy Oh, Sam . . .

Sam Do you have anything to eat? I'm hungry . . .

Amy Ugh!

Unit 4 • My Interests
Lesson 13 I like music.

Page 44 Exercise 1A
Same as the words in the Student's Book.

Page 44 Exercise 1B
1. Kanye West is a hip-hop singer.
2. Joshua Bell is a classical musician.
3. Sean Paul is a reggae singer.
4. Pink is a pop singer.

5. Jon Bon Jovi is a rock singer.
6. The Dixie Chicks are a country group.
7. Wynton Marsalis is a jazz musician.

Page 45 Exercise 2A
Same as the conversation in the Student's Book.

Page 45 Exercise 2B
Same as the sentences in the Student's Book.

Lesson 14 Let's look online.

Page 46 Exercise 1A
1. There's a star map.
2. There's a telescope.
3. There's a radio-controlled airplane.
4. There's a travel vest.
5. There are nature puzzles.
6. There are adventure DVDs.
7. There's a science kit.
8. There are wall calendars.

Page 46 Exercise 1B
1. The star map is seventeen dollars and fifty cents. / The star map is seventeen fifty.
2. The telescope is forty-nine dollars and ninety-five cents. / The telescope is forty-nine ninety-five.
3. The radio-controlled airplane is ninety-six dollars and ninety-nine cents. / The radio-controlled airplane is ninety-six ninety-nine.
4. The travel vest is fifty-two dollars and six cents. / The travel vest is fifty-two-oh-six.
5. The nature puzzles are nine dollars and eighty-nine cents each. / The nature puzzles are nine eighty-nine each.
6. The adventure DVDs are thirty-four dollars and seventy-nine cents each. / The adventure DVDs are thirty-four seventy-nine each.
7. The science kit is sixty dollars.
8. The wall calendars are sixteen dollars each.

Page 47 Exercise 2A
Same as the conversation in the Student's Book.

Page 47 Exercise 2B
Same as the conversation in the Student's Book.

Page 47 Exercise 3

Tina Hey, Ben, look at this cool watch in my catalog. Can you find the same one in your online catalog?

Ben Let me see. Yes, here it is.

Tina How much is it, Ben?

Ben It's $39.99.

Tina Well, it's $29.99 in *my* catalog.

Ben Really?

Tina OK. Now T-shirts. How much are they in your catalog, Ben?

Ben Uhh . . . $19.89.

Tina In *this* catalog, there are some T-shirts for $10.50 each!

Ben Wow, Tina! That's really cheap. Now *this* is a nice camera. It's $89.99.

Tina That *is* nice. There's a camera in this catalog, too.

Ben How much is it?

Tina It's $99.99.

Ben And hey, Tina, there are hiking boots here for sixty-eight dollars.

Tina There are hiking boots in this catalog, too. They're also sixty-eight dollars. And they look like good boots.

Ben Is there a backpack in your catalog, Tina? There's one here online, but I don't like it.

Tina Well, Ben, let's see. Yes. It's forty dollars, but it's a very good one.

Ben Forty dollars?

Tina How much is the one online?

Ben It's only ten dollars.

Tina Wow! That's a really good price.

Lessons 13 & 14 Mini-review

Page 49 Exercise 2

Rick Happy birthday, Beverly.

Beverly Thank you, Rick . . . Oh, a CD! It's Miley Cyrus. She's my favorite singer. I like her a lot. Pop music is my favorite kind of music. What's your favorite kind of music, Rick?

Rick Well, I think country music is cool. Carrie Underwood is great. I really like her.

Beverly I do, too! Do you like classical music?

Rick No, I don't like it at all.

Beverly Really? What about Yo-Yo Ma? A lot of people like him.

Rick Well, he's OK, but I don't really listen to classical music.

Beverly I see . . . Where do you buy music?

Rick I buy music on the Internet. One song is only ninety-nine cents.

Beverly I know. I buy a lot of music online, too.

Lesson 15 Our interests

Page 50 Exercise 1A

Same as the captions in the Student's Book.

Page 51 Exercise 2A

Same as the form in the Student's Book.

Page 51 Exercise 3

1. **Marta** Hello?

   Eve Hi, Marta. This is Eve. How's the new exchange student?

   Marta Karen? Great! She's really fun. She likes to go dancing.

   Eve You like to go dancing, too, right?

   Marta Oh, yeah, I love to go dancing. You know that! Karen and I go together.

2. **Eve** What other things do you and Karen do together?

   Marta Well, we go to the mall. Karen likes to go shopping. She looks for presents for her family. I don't like to go shopping. But I like to spend time with Karen, so I go.

   Eve I love to go shopping. Next time, let's all go together.

   Marta OK.

3. **Eve** What else does Karen like to do?

   Marta Well, she likes to play tennis. I don't like playing tennis at all, but we sometimes play tennis together. She's really good.

4. **Eve** How about movies? Does Karen like to go to the movies?

   Marta Well, *I* love to go to the movies, but *Karen* doesn't. She likes to watch DVDs at home. Hey! Why don't you come to my house tonight? Let's watch DVDs together.

   Eve Great idea! See you after dinner!

   Marta See you. Bye!

Lesson 16 In and out of school

Page 52 Exercise 1B

1. I usually do my homework.
2. I always come to class on time.
3. I usually listen to the teacher.
4. I sometimes answer a lot of the teacher's questions.
5. I . . . um, hardly ever . . . no, I *never* listen to music on my headphones in class.
6. Um. I sometimes get good grades.
7. I hardly ever sleep in class.
8. I never, um, I mean, I *hardly ever* throw paper airplanes in class.

Page 53 Exercise 2A

1. **Charlie** So, do you like to go out on weekends, Ana?

   Ana Uh-huh. Sometimes I go dancing. I go to the Hot Spots club with my friends. Come with us next week, Charlie.

   Charlie Oh, thanks, but I never go dancing. I can't dance.

2. **Charlie** What other things do you do on weekends, Ana?

   Ana Well, I always go shopping. I like to look for new DVDs. Do you like to go shopping?

   Charlie No. I hardly ever go shopping on weekends. There are too many people in the stores.

3. **Ana** So how do you spend your Saturdays and Sundays, Charlie?

   Charlie Well, I stay up late and watch movies on TV. So, I usually sleep late on weekends.

Ana   Oh, not me. I like to get up early on weekends, so I hardly ever sleep late.

4.   Ana   You know, I really like to go out and do things on weekends.

Charlie   Not me! I like to stay home. On weekends, I always read a lot. I love books.

Ana   Not me. I never read on weekends. For me, weekends are for fun with my friends.

5.   Charlie   So, do you play sports on weekends, Ana?

Ana   Oh, yes. I sometimes go bowling with friends. How about you?

Charlie   Yeah, I like to go bowling, so I go sometimes, too.

Ana   So, let's go together sometime.

Charlie   Good idea!

Page 53 Exercise 2B

Same as the script for Part A above.

Unit 4 Get Connected

Page 54 Read

Same as the article in the Student's Book.

Page 55 Listen

Yuki   That's a really cool MP3 player, Carlos. Can I see it?

Carlos   Sure, Yuki. Here. It's the new iPod Touch. It's really cool.

Yuki   Yeah, it's great.

Carlos   I hardly ever go to a music store now. I buy all my music online.

Yuki   Wow! . . . I never buy music online. I don't have an MP3 player.

Carlos   Really? It's so convenient. You download the songs to the MP3 player – you don't need a computer. It's awesome. Look, here's a really great country song, "Landslide," by the Dixie Chicks. I like it a lot.

Yuki   Country music? You're kidding, right? I don't like it at all.

Carlos   What's wrong with country music? I always listen to it.

Yuki   OK, OK. Well, I like to go to music stores. I often go on the weekend. It's fun.

Carlos   Really?

Yuki   Yeah. You can walk around and look at albums. You can also listen to some of them in the store. You can listen to the whole song – not like online.

Carlos   Yeah. That's right. Sometimes you can only listen to part of a song online. Hey, can I go shopping with you this weekend?

Yuki   Sure!

Unit 5 • Favorite Activities

Lesson 17 In San Francisco

Page 58 Exercise 1A

Same as the activities in the Student's Book.

Page 59 Exercise 2A

Same as the text in the Student's Book.

Page 59 Exercise 2B

Same as the sentences in the Student's Book.

Lesson 18 At the park

Page 60 Exercise 1A

Same as the rules in the Student's Book.

Page 61 Exercise 2A

Same as the conversation in the Student's Book.

Page 61 Exercise 2B

Same as the sentences in the Student's Book.

Page 61 Exercise 3

1.   Nan   Let's eat lunch here.

Lisa   Well, OK. It's nice here.

Ms. Nolan   Nan and Lisa! You're eating in the boat. Remember the rule about food?

Nan   Oh, right.

Lisa   Sorry, Ms. Nolan.

2.   Mr. Brown   Hey, Jeff! You're not following the rules!

Jeff   But, Mr. Brown, I'm wearing my helmet.

Mr. Brown   Yes, very good. But you're riding on the grass!

Jeff   Uh-oh. Sorry.

3.   Ms. Nolan   Look at Dan and Fred. What a mess!

Mr. Brown   I know. Their lunch bags and papers are all over.

Ms. Nolan   Hey, guys! Come and clean up your trash!

4.   Mr. Brown   Where's Brad?

Girl   There he is, Mr. Brown. Over there.

Mr. Brown   Oh, dear. Brad!

Brad   Yes, Mr. Brown?

Mr. Brown   Don't stand. It's dangerous!

Brad   OK. Sorry! Aaah!

5.   Peter   Hey, Molly. You have to wait.

Molly   But I'm just buying a drink.

Ms. Nolan   Molly!

Molly   Yes, Ms. Nolan?

Ms. Nolan   Peter is right. Wait with the other people in line.

Molly   OK. Sorry, Peter. Sorry, Ms. Nolan.

Lessons 17 & 18 Mini-review

Page 63 Exercise 2

1. **Kate** One ticket, please.
   Boy 1 Hey! You're not standing in line.
   Kate Oh, sorry. There's a line?
   Boy 1 Yes, there is.
   Man Here's your ticket. The popcorn and soda are over there.
2. **Kate** Are you still eating your lunch?
   Girl 1 Uh-huh. Uh-oh. I have to go. I'm late for my English class!
   Kate Wait! You're not putting your trash in the trash can.
   Girl 1 Oops! Sorry about that. I'm in a hurry.
3. **Kate** What a great place!
   Boy 2 Yeah. I like riding my bike here, too.
   Kate Hey! You're not staying on the bike path!
   Boy 2 Oh! You're right! I forgot.
4. **Girl 2** This T-shirt is perfect for my father.
   Kate Yeah, it is. I really like this poster, too.
   Girl 2 And look at these postcards. The pictures are beautiful!
   Kate This stuff is nice. I'm buying all my presents here!

Lesson 19 At the beach

Page 64 Exercise 1A

Same as the sentences in the Student's Book.

Page 65 Exercise 2A

Same as the conversation in the Student's Book.

Page 65 Exercise 2B

Same as the conversation in the Student's Book.

Page 65 Exercise 3

1. **Hannah** Hello?
   Lee Hi, Hannah. It's Lee. I'm at the beach. Why don't you come?
   Hannah Who's there?
   Lee Naomi's here. She's swimming in the ocean.
2. **Lee** And remember Tom and Ken? They're here, too.
   Hannah Oh, yeah? What are they doing? Are they playing ball?
   Lee No, they aren't. They're throwing a Frisbee around.
   Hannah Oh.
3. **Hannah** How about Dave? Is he there?
   Lee Yes. He's sailing a boat.
   Hannah Of course! That's his favorite thing.
4. **Lee** Oh, and Megan's here! Guess what she's doing?
   Hannah Is she swimming, too?
   Lee No, she isn't. She's too tired to swim. She's just floating on a raft.

5. **Hannah** And what about you, Lee?
   Lee Me? I'm having a great time. I'm taking pictures of everyone.
   Hannah That sounds fun.
6. **Hannah** Listen, Lee. I'm doing my homework now. When I'm finished, I'm going to the beach! See you later! Thanks for calling.
   Lee Bye!

Lesson 20 At the store

Page 66 Exercise 1A

Same as the sentences in the Student's Book.

Page 66 Exercise 1B

Same as the items in the Student's Book.

Page 67 Exercise 2A

Same as the conversation in the Student's Book.

Page 67 Exercise 2B

Same as the conversation in the Student's Book.

Page 67 Exercise 3

Same as the questions in the Student's Book.

Unit 5 Get Connected

Page 68 Read

Same as the letter in the Student's Book.

Page 69 Listen

Luisa Hello?
Matt Hi, Luisa! It's me, Matt.
Luisa Hi, Matt! Hey, wait a minute! You're on a trip with your family, right?
Matt Yeah, we're in Miami. But I'm really bored. I'm not enjoying it at all.
Luisa Bored? In Miami? Are you kidding? What are you doing?
Matt Nothing much. I'm sitting here in the hotel talking to you. No one is here with me.
Luisa Well, where is everybody?
Matt My father and little brother are at the beach today. My dad's swimming in the ocean, and Timmy is collecting seashells.
Luisa Well, that sounds like a lot of fun. I love the beach!
Matt Well, I don't. It's too hot at the beach. My mother and sister are shopping. They're buying souvenirs and looking around. I don't like to shop!
Luisa Oh, I love shopping!
Matt And my grandparents are sightseeing and taking pictures. It's too crowded for sightseeing.
Luisa I love sightseeing, too! Hmm, maybe next time, you can stay home, and *I* can go on a trip with your family!

Unit 6 • Entertainment

Lesson 21 Where are you going?

Page 72 Exercise 1A
Same as the sentences in the Student's Book.

Page 73 Exercise 2A
Same as the conversation in the Student's Book.

Page 73 Exercise 2B
Same as the questions and answers in the Student's Book.

Page 73 Exercise 3
1. **Cynthia** Joanne, do you have our tickets?
   Joanne Yes. They're in my bag.
2. **Ruben** Hey, Jerome! Wait! Stop running!
   Jerome I can't! I'm late! My team is waiting for me!
3. **Joanne** Hey, Cynthia! Do you want to do our homework together? Let's go to the library.
   Cynthia Sorry, but I want to do my homework with Sarah today. I'm going to her house now.
4. **Ruben** I don't want to go, Dad.
   Man Well, we're going, Ruben. Your brother wants to see the jugglers and the animals.
   Ruben Then let's go to the park. There's a zoo in the park, and there are jugglers, too.
   Man No, I'm sorry, Ruben. We're on *this* bus, and *this* bus is going to the circus.

Lesson 22 Birthday parties

Page 74 Exercise 1A
Same as the sentences in the Student's Book.

Page 75 Exercise 2A
Same as the texts in the Student's Book.

Page 75 Exercise 2B
Same as the sentences in the Student's Book.

Page 75 Exercise 3
1. **Tommy** You always send great presents, Aunt Jean! Thanks again.
   Aunt Jean You're welcome. How's your brother?
   Tommy He's great. He plays the piano in a band. He really loves it.
2. **Aunt Jean** How's your little sister?
   Tommy She's great, too. She's opening my presents. Two-year-olds are very funny.
3. **Aunt Jean** How's your mother?
   Tommy She's fine. She's very busy. She takes art lessons and goes shopping, and she spends a lot of time with her friends.

4. **Aunt Jean** Is your father working?
   Tommy No, he's home. He's cooking hot dogs in the backyard.

Lessons 21 & 22 Mini-review

Page 77 Exercise 2
Mariah Today's my birthday, and I'm having a party at home. My family usually celebrates my birthday at a restaurant. We eat cake and ice cream at the restaurant. Then I usually relax at home and play cards with my brother. It's OK, but it's a little boring. This year I'm celebrating at home. We're having a barbecue in the yard. My dad's cooking the hot dogs right now. All my friends are here. Listen! They're singing songs now. We're all having a good time!

Lesson 23 Let's see a movie.

Page 78 Exercise 1A
Same as the sentences in the Student's Book.

Page 79 Exercise 2A
Same as the conversation in the Student's Book.

Page 79 Exercise 2B
Same as the conversation in the Student's Book.

Page 79 Exercise 3
Same as the sentences in the Student's Book.

Page 79 Exercise 4
1. **Joe** So, Ted, what kind of movie do you want to see?
   Ted Oh, I like funny movies. Let's see something funny.
   Joe How about an animated movie? There's a new one playing right now.
   Ted No, animated movies are for kids. How about *It's a Crazy World*?
2. **Maggie** Do you want to see a movie, Joe? *Late at Night* is at the Winston Theater.
   Joe I want to see a movie, but not a horror movie. How about *Bye-Bye, Bad Guys*? There's a lot of adventure!
3. **Ted** Hi, Maggie. I want to go to a movie tonight. Do you want to come with me?
   Maggie Sure. Can I choose the movie?
   Ted Well, . . . what do you want to see?
   Maggie I want to see *To the Top*. It's a true story about a man who climbs mountains.
4. **Maggie** What kind of movie do you want to see, Connie?
   Connie Well, . . . there's a new movie at the City Theater. It's about a man named Vic. His mother is in the hospital, and his father can't work because he's too

old. Vic works hard, but he doesn't have any money . . .

Maggie Oh, I know. It's *Hospital Days*. It sounds good. Let's see it.

Lesson 24 In line at the movies

Page 80 Exercise 1A

Same as the sentences in the Student's Book.

Page 81 Exercise 2A

Same as the conversation in the Student's Book.

Page 81 Exercise 2B

Same as the questions and answers in the Student's Book.

Unit 6 Get Connected

Page 82 Read

Same as the article in the Student's Book.

Page 83 Listen

Jean Hey, Chris. Where are you going?
Chris Hi, Jean. I'm going to the bookstore. I want to buy a new book. Where are you going?
Jean I'm going to the town fair.
Chris Really?
Jean Yeah. I go every year. I love to go.
Chris So, what's it like?
Jean Oh, it's a lot of fun. There are a lot of fun games, great things to eat, and free concerts.
Chris Concerts?
Jean Yes. They're cool. The bands aren't famous, but some of them are amazing musicians.
Chris That sounds like fun. And how about food? Are there a lot of good things to eat?
Jean The food is incredible! They have a big barbecue and . . . Hey! Do you want to go with me and my friends?
Chris Sure. Sounds great. Forget the bookstore! I want to go to the fair!
Jean Great! Come on! Let's go!

Unit 7 • What We Eat

Lesson 25 I'm hungry!

Page 86 Exercise 1A

Same as the words in the Student's Book.

Page 87 Exercise 2A

Same as the conversation in the Student's Book.

Page 87 Exercise 2B

Same as the chart in the Student's Book.

Lesson 26 Picnic plans

Page 88 Exercise 1A

1. Rafael There's milk.

2. Ana There are cups.
3. Rafael There's juice.
4. Ana There's bread.
5. Rafael There are plates.
6. Ana There's fruit.
7. Rafael There's pasta.
8. Ana There are spoons.
9. Rafael There are forks.
10. Ana There are knives.

Page 89 Exercise 2A

Same as the conversation in the Student's Book.

Page 89 Exercise 2B

Same as the questions and answers in the Student's Book.

Page 89 Exercise 3

1. Girl Are you ready to go shopping?
    Boy Yeah. I'm making a list of things we need.
    Girl Well, I know we need hot dogs.
    Boy How many hot dogs do we need?
    Girl Hmm, I think 25 is enough.
    Boy OK, 25 it is!
2. Boy What about fruit? Everyone eats fruit at picnics.
    Girl You're right. We need a lot of fruit.
3. Boy Um, we have cheese in the kitchen, right?
    Girl No, we don't. Let's get a little.
4. Boy And pasta?
    Girl Mmm, I love pasta! Let's get a lot.
5. Boy OK. Now, we have soda. Do we need cups?
    Girl Yeah, I think we need a few cups.
6. Boy Anything else? Oh! We need cookies, don't we?
    Girl We need 60 cookies.

Lessons 25 & 26 Mini-review

Page 91 Exercise 2

Minnie I'm so excited about our class party, Amanda!
Amanda I am, too, Minnie! So, what do we need?
Minnie Well, we have 30 cups and 30 plates.
Amanda That's a lot! We only have 20 students in our class. How many forks and spoons do we have?
Minnie Let's see. We have 25 spoons. But we only have eight forks.
Amanda OK, so we need forks. How about juice? How much juice is there?
Minnie There's a little juice.
Amanda Great. How much fruit is there?
Minnie Well, there's a little fruit. We need some bananas and apples.
Amanda OK. How many cookies do we have?
Minnie We have a lot of cookies. We also have a lot of ice cream!
Amanda Good! Ice cream is my favorite food.

Lesson 27 A snack

Page 92 Exercise 1A
Same as the sentences in the Student's Book.

Page 93 Exercise 2A
Same as the conversation in the Student's Book.

Page 93 Exercise 2B
Same as the sentences in the Student's Book.

Lesson 28 On the menu

Page 94 Exercise 1A
Woman Appetizers
salad
black bean soup
vegetable soup

Main dishes
hamburger
cheeseburger
steak sandwich
chicken sandwich
today's fish
rice and beans with meat

Side orders
French fries
baked potato

Desserts
ice cream
cookies
chocolate cake
carrot cake
pie

Drinks
soda
iced tea
milk
milk shake

Page 95 Exercise 2A
Same as the conversation in the Student's Book.

Page 95 Exercise 2B
Same as the conversation in the Student's Book.

Page 95 Exercise 3
Same as the questions in the Student's Book.

Page 95 Exercise 4
1. **Server** What would you like?
   Ana I'd like some vegetable soup, please.
   Server Vegetable soup. What else would you like?
   Ana Hmm, I'd like the rice and beans with meat.
   Server And would you like something to drink?

Ana Yes. I'd like a milk shake and some carrot cake for dessert.
2. **Server** Are you ready to order?
   Zach Yes, I am. I'd like some iced tea and some French fries.
   Server Uh, would you like something else with that?
   Zach Oh, right! I'd like a steak sandwich, please.
   Server Great. Would you like a dessert?
   Zach I'd like some ice cream.
3. **Kate** I'd like some vegetable soup, please. And I'd like rice and beans with meat.
   Server Anything else?
   Kate Yes. I'd like some milk and some chocolate cake for dessert.
4. **Rafael** I'd like a steak sandwich.
   Server OK. Would you like French fries with that?
   Rafael Yes.
   Server How about a soda?
   Rafael Um, no thanks. I'd like iced tea, please.
   Server Would you like anything else?
   Rafael Yes! I'd like some chocolate cake, please.

Unit 7 Get Connected

Page 96 Read
Same as the Web site in the Student's Book.

Page 97 Listen
Nick I'm really hungry, Rachel. Let's make some pasta.
Rachel OK, Nick. But I'm not a very good cook. We need a cookbook.
Nick You're kidding, right? This is easy – it's only pasta.
Rachel OK. OK. Let's see. There are some tomatoes.
Nick How many do you have?
Rachel Four big ones. Do you think that's enough?
Nick I think so. How about meat?
Rachel Well, there's a little meat.
Nick Good. Now how about cheese? How much cheese is there?
Rachel Oh, there's a lot of cheese.
Nick Oh, and pasta! We need that, too! How much pasta is there?
Rachel Oh, no, Nick. There isn't any pasta.
Nick What! There isn't any pasta!
Rachel No. But it's OK, Nick. There are a few cans of vegetable soup. We can have soup.
Nick Well, OK. And we don't need a cookbook for that!

Unit 8 • The Natural World

Lesson 29 World weather

Page 100 Exercise 1A
Same as the sentences in the Student's Book.

Page 100 Exercise 1B
Same as the sentences in the Student's Book.

Page 101 Exercise 2A
Same as the conversation in the Student's Book.

Page 101 Exercise 2B
Same as the questions and answers in the Student's Book.

Lesson 30 Natural wonders

Page 102 Exercise 1A
Same as the captions in the Student's Book.

Page 103 Exercise 2A
Same as the conversation in the Student's Book.

Page 103 Exercise 2B
Same as the sentences in the Student's Book.

Page 103 Exercise 3
1. **Boy**   Tell me about your town, Kate. What outdoor things can you do nearby? Can you go canoeing?

   Kate   Yes, you can. I love to go canoeing. I go every weekend in the summer.
2. **Boy**   Awesome! I love to go canoeing. I like to hike, too, and I like to climb mountains. Can you climb any mountains?

   Kate   Yes, you can. I climb them a lot with my friends.
3. **Boy**   Cool. Sometimes there are caves where there are mountains. Can you visit any caves?

   Kate   Yes, you can. You can visit some very famous caves.
4. **Boy**   Can you go to any hot springs?

   Kate   No, you can't. But there are hot springs in other parts of Canada.
5. **Boy**   What about activities in town? What can you do at night?

   Kate   Well, you can go dancing . . .

Lessons 29 & 30 Mini-review

Page 105 Exercise 2
1. We're almost at the top, and it's cold here! We're wearing jackets and gloves and warm boots. But look at this fantastic view! OK, here we are . . . That's the town there below us. Incredible! Now we're going to sit down, make our fire, and have lunch before we start back down.

2. This is our raft, and this is all of our equipment. I think we're ready now. This is going to be an amazing trip. We plan to stay on this raft for four days. What's for dinner tonight? Fish!
3. Ahhh! What relaxing water. Oh, this is nice. I want to stay here all day.
4. Isn't this great? I'm sitting here, on a beautiful beach, surrounded by water, birds singing, and no other people are here – it's so quiet . . . I love it here . . . Oh, no!
5. Oh, this is so scary . . . It's cool and dark down here. OK. Here's my flashlight. That's better! Oh, help! Bats! Let's get out! Let's get out!

Lesson 31 World of friends

Page 106 Exercise 1A
Same as the words in the Student's Book.

Page 106 Exercise 1B
Same as the sentences in the Student's Book.

Page 107 Exercise 2A
Same as the conversation in the Student's Book.

Page 107 Exercise 2B
Same as the questions and answers in the Student's Book.

Page 107 Exercise 3
1. **Rafael**   So, Tommy, tell me about your e-pals, Ivan, Emilia, and Christina.

   Tommy   Well, they have a lot of hobbies – music, swimming, taking photographs . . .

   Rafael   Really? Who takes photographs?

   Tommy   Emilia does. She has 40 albums of her photographs.

   Rafael   Wow! Incredible!
2. **Tommy**   And one of them speaks four languages.

   Rafael   *Four* languages! Who speaks four languages?

   Tommy   Ivan does. He likes to study. He wants to visit me next year.

   Rafael   Cool!
3. **Rafael**   And who swims?

   Tommy   Christina does. She lives in Greece near beautiful islands. She swims every day.

   Rafael   Great!
4. **Rafael**   And who likes music?

   Tommy   Ivan and Christina do. They both play the guitar in a band.

   Rafael   I play the guitar, too. I want to meet them! Can I e-mail them?

   Tommy   Sure. They all like to make new friends.

Lesson 32 International Day

Page 108 Exercise 1A
Same as the numbers in the Student's Book.

     Photocopiable

Page 108 Exercise 1B

Same as the numbers in the Student's Book.

Page 108 Exercise 1C

Same as the sentences in the Student's Book.

Page 109 Exercise 2A

Same as the conversation in the Student's Book.

Page 109 Exercise 2B

Same as the conversation in the Student's Book.

Unit 8 Get Connected

Page 110 Read

Same as the article in the Student's Book.

Page 111 Listen

Jeff Hi, Isabel! What are you doing?

Isabel Hi, Jeff. I'm making a poster. Our class is doing a project on global warming for the science fair.

Jeff Great! That's a really serious problem. Our science class is doing a recycling project right now.

Isabel Oh, yeah? What are you doing?

Jeff Well, a lot of things. We're talking to our family and friends about recycling. And then we're having a contest.

Isabel Sounds great. Who can enter?

Jeff Everyone can enter. All you need is a group to work with.

Isabel And what does each group do?

Jeff They collect paper and plastic. The groups that collect a lot get a prize.

Isabel Cool. What's the prize?

Jeff They can go to see the TV show *Save the Planet*. You know, it's on Sunday nights at 7:30.

Isabel Right! I love that show. I want to enter! Can I have your notebook, please?

Jeff What?

Isabel I want to start collecting paper now!